D0709439

THE LEGACIES OF *THE BASIN OF MEXICO*

THE LEGACIES OF
THE BASIN OF MEXICO

EDITED BY

Carlos E. Cordova and Christopher T. Morehart

UNIVERSITY PRESS OF COLORADO
Denver

Published by University Press of Colorado
1624 Market Street, Suite 226
PMB 39883
Denver, Colorado 80202

The University Press of Colorado is a proud member of the Association of University Presses.

The University Press of Colorado is a cooperative publishing enterprise supported, in part, by Adams State University, Colorado State University, Fort Lewis College, Metropolitan State University of Denver, University of Alaska Fairbanks, University of Colorado, University of Denver, University of Northern Colorado, University of Wyoming, Utah State University, and Western Colorado University.

∞ This paper meets the requirements of the ANSI / NISO Z39.48-1992 (Permanence of Paper).

ISBN: 978-1-64642-406-1 (hardcover)
ISBN: 978-1-64642-407-8 (ebook)
https://doi.org/10.5876/9781646424078

Library of Congress Cataloging-in-Publication Data

Names: Cordova, Carlos E., 1965– editor. | Morehart, Christopher T., editor.
Title: The legacies of the Basin of Mexico, the ecological processes in the evolution of a civilization / edited by Carlos E. Cordova (Oklahoma State University) and Christopher T. Morehart (Arizona State University).
Description: Louisville : University Press of Colorado, [2023] | Includes bibliographical references and index.
Identifiers: LCCN 2022061294 (print) | LCCN 2022061295 (ebook) | ISBN 9781646424061 (hardcover) | ISBN 9781646424078 (ebook)
Subjects: LCSH: Sanders, William T. Basin of Mexico. | Sanders, William T.—Influence. | Parsons, Jeffrey R.—Influence. | Santley, Robert S.—Influence. | Indians of Mexico—Mexico—Mexico, Valley of—Antiquities. | Land settlement patterns, Prehistoric—Mexico—Mexico, Valley of. | Human ecology—Mexico—Mexico, Valley of. | Mexico, Valley of (Mexico)—Antiquities.
Classification: LCC F1219.1.M53 L44 2023 (print) | LCC F1219.1.M53 (ebook) | DDC 972/.501—dc23/eng/20230125
LC record available at https://lccn.loc.gov/2022061294
LC ebook record available at https://lccn.loc.gov/2022061295

Cover illustration: "Baño de Nezahualcoyotl" by Jose Maria Velasco, 1878. Public domain image from Wikiart.org.

Jeff Parsons in State College PA, 1965 with his 1950 Hudson, "The Green Hornet." Photo courtesy of Mary Hrones Parsons and John Speth.

We dedicate this book to the memory of
Jeffrey R. Parsons
(1939–2021)

The tribe of Basin of Mexico archaeologists mourns the loss of one of our great heroes, Jeff Parsons. He fused innovative field methods with a keen understanding of cultural setting, and shared his findings quickly, his high-caliber reports often documenting sites that since have vanished. He inspired us all, and we are in his debt for offering such a good example of an ideal colleague, and more practically, for providing the basis for so much of our own work; we are the lucky inheritors of troves of information gathered by his projects. Jeff's taste for survey work and its application to archaeological problems developed when he was an undergraduate at Penn State University, where he learned field techniques from geology professor Rob Scholten while studying the importance of the Basin of Mexico in Mesoamerican archaeology with Bill Sanders. Big things were to come from the resulting surveys in Mexico: a narrative that told a huge cultural evolutionary story in words and maps. Always, Jeff was thoroughly decent to his colleagues, ready to discuss finds and ideas and generous with his support. He had a marvelous optimistic attitude and a great sense of humor, and his physical courage is evidenced by the many remote and challenging places where he worked.

Susan T. Evans

Contents

Figures

Tables

THE LEGACIES OF *THE BASIN OF MEXICO*

1

The Legacies of the Green Book

CARLOS E. CORDOVA AND CHRISTOPHER T. MOREHART

INTRODUCTION

Most archaeologists who have worked or are still working in the Basin of Mexico are not very site-specific. They tend to think of questions that are broad intellectually but also broad empirically, both chronologically and regionally. This outlook has very strong historical precedents. On the one hand, this regional trend developed in the early-to-mid-twentieth-century work of many cosmopolitan Mexican and Mexican-resident archaeologists, iconographers, ethnographers, ethnologists, and ethnohistorians whose research took them all over Mexico. They included individuals such as Manuel Gamio, Laurette Séjourné, Pedro Armillas, Ángel Palerm, Zelia Nuttall, Jorge Acosta, Wigberto Jiménez Moreno, Román Piña Chan, Doris Heyden, Alfonso Caso, Eulalia Guzmán, Pedro Carrasco, Ignacio Bernal, Miguel León Portilla, among many others. It is not difficult to observe their intellectual fingerprints across a range of sites, regions and periods, and across the intellectual currents that influenced and continue to influence subsequent scholars.

https://doi.org/10.5876/9781646424078.c001

On the other hand, from the 1950s to the 1970s, archaeologists interested in new topics that were of relevance to emerging paradigms in both archaeology and anthropology established a broad perspective shared by many contemporary archaeologists and their students. Despite the development of this new comparative approach, archaeology in most of Mesoamerica still retained a focus on the larger sites, the centers of ancient cities and the monumentality of "high-culture," leaving out a vast number of people who lived in this region. Consequently, a series of questions that were basic to any historical reconstruction simply could not be answered from an archaeological perspective. How many archaeological sites existed? When were they occupied? How large were they? What kinds of sites were they? How many people lived in these sites? What were their lives like? How many people lived in the broader region? How were these settlements distributed in relation to the environment, to each other, to major centers of political power? What was the landscape and environment like at the time of occupation?

Answering these essential questions required knowledge of basic demographic and environmental data that did not exist. Historical records and documents were the only source of data to answer them. Although rich in content and coverage, such sources nevertheless lack information on a wide range of issues. Moreover, such documentation is largely limited to records written after the arrival of Spaniards and the establishment of New Spain. Some indigenous documents, both codices and later annals authored by indigenous writers, go back farther in time, but they often intermix with quasi-mythological histories that exist at spatial and temporal scales that are difficult to approximate with other forms of data. Hence, the only way to reconstruct deep history is to use archaeology, with a broad-scale and comprehensive perspective on ancient settlements and their environment.

One of the first steps in this direction was the settlement and cultural ecology research that William Sanders (1957) developed in his path-breaking dissertation research, itself influenced by preeminent scholars like Pedro Armillas, Ángel Palerm, and Gordon Willey. Sanders would go on to develop some of the key methodologies for a broader survey in the Teotihuacan Valley (i.e., Sanders 1965) and to serve as the central pivot for all the subsequent surveys. As other contributions discuss in more detail (Kolb; Nichols, this volume), many of the approaches and issues were laid out in a National Science Foundation–sponsored conference in 1960, which was eventually published in 1976 (Wolf 1976a). The broader Basin of Mexico was divided into a number of survey zones, and each zone received a full-coverage pedestrian survey. These survey zones include work led by Sanders in the Teotihuacan, Cuautitlan, and Temascalapa valleys of the northeast and northwest Basin of Mexico (e.g., Gorenflo and Sanders 2007; Parsons 1966; Sanders 1965; Sanders and Gorenflo 2007); work led by Jeffrey Parsons in the Texcoco, Chalco-Xochimilco, and Zumpango regions (e.g., Parsons 1971;

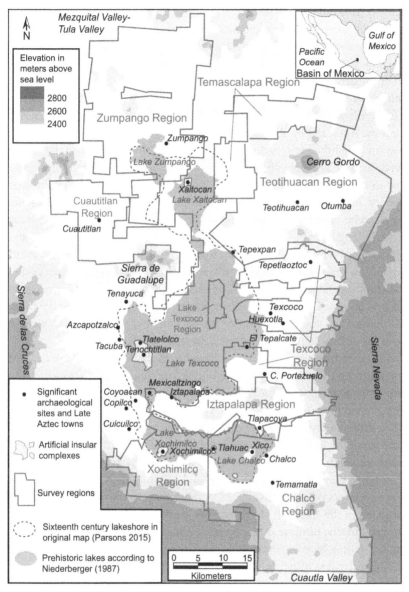

FIGURE 1.1. *Basin of Mexico survey regions. Based on Cordova (2022), Parsons (2015), and Niederberger (1987).*

Parsons and Morett 2004, 2005; Parsons et al. 1982; Parsons et al. 1983); and work led by Richard Blanton in the Ixtapalapa Peninsula (Blanton 1972) (see figure 1.1).

According to the original research formulation, these regional surveys would integrate with archaeological investigations at key cities, especially Teotihuacan but also at Tula, and would also incorporate findings from comparative ethnohistory (Wolf 1976b). These projects led to a large corpus of publications in both archaeology and ethnography and trained several cohorts of students, many of whom have already trained many of the archaeologists currently working in the Basin of Mexico and elsewhere.

This volume celebrates the continuing impact of the most notable contribution from this work, *The Basin of Mexico: Ecological Processes in the Evolution of a Civilization*. Authored by William T. Sanders, Jeffrey R. Parsons, and Robert S. Santley and published in 1979, the book synthesized the results of all the survey projects, as well as follow-up excavations at several sites. Theoretically, it was rooted in the prevailing ecological perspective that characterized archaeological theory at the time. It also outlined field and analytical methods, including the application of aerial photography, which were widely influential. The book proposed a long-term history of the Basin of Mexico by relating the growth and distribution of Prehispanic populations to environmental and political economic systems from the first agricultural villages during the Early Formative period to the complex states and empires that existed from the Classic period to the Postclassic period. This volume has been so useful that it has acquired the moniker, *La Biblia Verde*, the Green Bible or the Green Book, attesting to its essential place in the archaeological and historical literature of the area.

On the fortieth anniversary of the publication of the Green Book, we decided that it was time to recognize its impact on archaeological research, the formation of new archaeologists, and the interpretation of the complex societal and environmental processes that Sanders, Parsons, and Santley sought to explain. We thus invited a diverse number of researchers to discuss and contribute to a volume about the impact of the Green Book and related archaeological surveys in recent research in the Basin of Mexico and other parts of Central Mexico. The group of contributors represents several generations of archaeologists as well as specialists of other disciplines. Among them were those who directly participated in the Basin of Mexico survey, working side by side or under the supervision of one or more of the book's authors. This included a contribution of the late Jeffrey Parsons, the only living author of *The Basin of Mexico* at that time. The grave loss of Jeff in early 2021 was felt by the archaeological community not only in Mexico but around the world. Jeff was an extraordinary scholar, educator, and mentor. He was a perennially exciting voice of support, advice, and encouragement for several generations of anthropologists. For this reason, we dedicate this volume to Jeff's memory.

The goal of this introduction is not to provide a thorough history of the origins of the Green Book, as that is discussed in the contributions by Kolb, Nichols, Parsons and Gorenflo, and Gorenflo in this volume, as well as in previous publications (e.g., Fowler et al. 2015; Robertson and Gorenflo 2015). Jeff Parsons's

(2019) recently published memoirs provide a fascinating and invigorating biography of his personal experiences working in Mexico (and Peru). Instead, we focus here on some of the major contributions of the Green Book, the range of research that it synthesized, and, most importantly, the long legacy it established for understanding the deep history of this region and for the researchers and students that have followed in its path.

ESTABLISHING A LEGACY: A BROAD OVERVIEW OF THE GREEN BOOK

In addition to offering a broad background to the region, the Green Book (and its related reports) continues to serve as the primary explanatory text for one of the most informative archaeological records in Mexico. Methodologically, it offers direction on how to carry out full-coverage archaeological surveys, how to incorporate aerial photography into field methods, and how to record field data. Conceptually, it provides useful discussion on the range of approaches for analyzing survey data, including statistical sampling, ethnographic analogy, population and productivity estimations, and so on. It also offers an explicit framework for the essential decisions archaeologists must make in the field, lab, and office to classify, synthesize, and interpret survey data, including assigning sites to major time periods and ways to record multi-component sites. Moreover, the discussions of the sites, together with the several volumes of primary settlement data that have been published (i.e., Blanton 1972; Gorenflo and Sanders 2007; Parsons 1971, 2008; Parsons et al. 1982; Parsons et al. 1983; Sanders and Gorenflo 2007) or made available online, offer unparalleled sources of information for any archaeologist seeking to begin fieldwork in the Basin of Mexico, at the very least providing basic data on site location, site size, major time periods of occupation, and key ceramic types.

Most significant, however, was the demographic history the Green Book synthesized. The broad, full-coverage surveys permitted the reconstruction of long-term changes across a range of settlement types, from the Early Formative period (ca. 1500 BCE) to the end of the Late Postclassic period (ca. 1519 CE). The geographically distributed sampling zones allowed an assessment of the impact of regional environmental and political variation at different spatial scales on settlement change, demonstrating significant fluctuations in levels of cultural and sociopolitical integration across time. During the Early Formative period (ca. 1500–1100 BCE), considerable settlement was concentrated in the alluvial and lower piedmont zones in the southern Basin of Mexico (Sanders et al. 1979:94–95). Initially, most of these settlements were small villages and hamlets, with larger villages becoming more common. Although some degree of social ranking may have existed, little evidence was recorded of systemic inequality. This would change during the Middle and Late Formative (ca. 1100–300 BCE), which saw an increase in population, evidence of social and settlement hierarchies, and the development of centers of regional polities that may have integrated four or five clusters of sites, such as Cuicuilco (Sanders et al. 1979:97–98). Although most of the population growth occurred in the southern Basin, settlements also spread north, though population growth was not as dramatic in this area.

The increase in population and the development of regional sociopolitical hierarchies became pronounced during the Terminal Formative period (ca. 300 BCE–150 CE) (Sanders et al. 1979:98–103). Settlements during this time existed in most parts of the Basin of Mexico, including in the more arid northern region. Important settlement clusters were documented in the southern and eastern Basin of Mexico, each with several small centers perhaps controlled by fewer regional centers. Cuicuilco, for example, seems to have developed into a powerful urban center with a population of around twenty thousand people (Sanders et al. 1979:99). The Teotihuacan Valley experienced a noticeable change in population and organization during this time. The site of Teotihuacan became a regional center with a large resident population that enjoyed a regional influence similar to that of Cuicuilco and other Formative period centers in Central Mexico at the time (see also Plunket and Uruñela 2012).

Within a few centuries, substantial demographic and social change was recorded. Cuicuilco declined in importance, which possibly provided opportunities for Teotihuacan to take advantage of its favorable position in alternative economic networks, particularly obsidian exchange routes (Carballo and Pluckhahn 2007). This period also initially saw a dramatic reorganization of settlement distribution, with either negative or zero growth in some areas but a dramatic population increase and nucleation around Teotihuacan, where between 80 and 90 percent of the Basin of Mexico's population now resided (Sanders et al. 1979:107). One possibility for this regional population decline is the demographic pull exerted by Teotihuacan's urbanization (Parsons 1966).

By the Classic period (ca. 150–650 CE), Teotihuacan had developed to become the largest city in Mesoamerica and a likely empire that controlled the Basin of Mexico and influenced much of Central Mexico and areas as far away as the Maya Lowlands (Cowgill 2015; Sanders et al. 1979:127). In the Basin of Mexico, this period of time was marked by the highest population in the region's history with rural settlements and centers developing in multiple locations. Sanders and his colleagues (1979:114) speculated that the reorganization of the regional settlement system might have been a direct result of the development of the Teotihuacan state. New Classic period centers that formed outside of Teotihuacan during the Classic period seem to lack antecedents in the Formative period, suggesting colonization by Teotihuacan populations. The regional settlement system likely reflected systemic needs for a range of resources, including lacustrine resources and salt from the Basin's lakes, limestone for construction from the northern Basin and southern Mezquital Valley, obsidian resources from sources in Otumba and Pachuca, and agricultural products from a range ofs ecological zones (Sanders et al. 1979:126–27).

With Teotihuacan's decline in power and the collapse of its political economy by the seventh century CE, the demographic system in the Basin of Mexico also changed fundamentally. The following period, referred to as the Epiclassic period (ca. 650–900 CE), witnessed a period of regional population decline, the nucleation of population at a range of centers, and an apparent fragmentation and balkanization of the political landscape (Blanton 1976; Parsons 1971; Sanders et al. 1979). New forms and styles of material culture also became widespread, suggesting strong cultural changes in the absence of Teotihuacan's influence, perhaps due to both migration and local innovation. Outside the Basin of Mexico, many other political centers expanded in size and influence, and some have proposed that the heterogeneous landscape of much of Mesoamerica was integrated via particular beliefs and practices that integrated militarism and cosmology (López Austin and López Lujan 2000; Ringle et al. 1998). The fragmented and balkanized nature of politics is reflected in what several archaeologists have recognized as clusters or political economic provinces of related settlements in the north, east, west, and southern portions of the Basin (Sanders et al. 1979:130–37, see also Crider; Morehart, this volume). Many of these areas may have retained a degree of autonomy, but they were interrelated economically and culturally, not unlike a geopolitical system comprised of city-states (Charlton and Nichols 1997; Crider et al. 2007).

The regional population changed considerably in the Early Postclassic period (ca. 900–1200 CE). Settlements increased in number, size, and organization and spread out into areas not occupied during the Epiclassic period. Sanders and his colleagues (1979:138–39) refer to this transformation as a ruralization of the settlement system, a period when 70 percent of the population in the Basin of Mexico lived outside of provincial centers. Areas in the northern Basin of Mexico had a higher population density than the south, where fewer nucleated settlements existed (Sanders et al. 1979:148–49). Broadly speaking, they felt that the Basin of Mexico could be viewed as having a north-south dichotomy, with settlements in the north under the influence of the Tula state and settlements to the south maintaining relationships with Cholula. Another important indicator of this contrast can be observed in the distribution of key ceramic types. Key Red-on-Buff ceramics were widespread in the Basin of Mexico, but particularly in the north, where they had been interpreted as evidence of Tula's influence. In the southern Basin of Mexico, where Early Postclassic Red-on-Buff ceramics are not abundant, the Black-on-Orange ceramic tradition emerged, specifically Aztec I Black-on-Orange. As the name suggests, these ceramics have long been associated with the Aztecs, but Aztec I predates the appearance of the Aztec state by some centuries and exhibits strong stylistic affinities to decorated pottery types at Cholula (Sanders et al. 1979:152; see also Parsons et al. 1996).

By the end of the Early Postclassic period, the Tula state had collapsed. The following Middle Postclassic period (ca. 1200–1350 CE) appears to have experienced a dramatic population abandonment in the northern Basin of Mexico. Red-on-Buff pottery, which was considered a marker of Tula's influence, fell out of use. Different styles of Black-on-Orange pottery, referred to as Aztec II, became widely used throughout many parts of the Basin but apparently not in the northern Basin of Mexico, which Parsons and Gorenflo (this volume) view as evidence of a population decline. Many of the historical sagas that describe migration into the Basin likely began much earlier (Beekman and Christiansen 2003), but by the Middle Postclassic to early Late Postclassic periods, several ethnolinguistic groups existed in the region, most of which spoke Nahuatl but also Otomi. During this time, the city-state (*altepetl*) was the primary social unit that organized political relationships. Several city-states existed. Some became highly influential regional states, such as Azcapotzalco, Tenayuca, Texcoco, and Xaltocan, among others, and some would continue to be major centers of settlement well after this period.

The relationships between city-states in the Basin of Mexico would establish important organizational precedents that directly led to political centralization of the Basin of Mexico and much of Central Mexico during the Late Postclassic period (ca. 1350–1519 CE). During this time, what scholars have referred to as the Aztec empire formed from the confederation of polities, including the Mexica of Tenochtitlan, the Alcohua of Texcoco, and the Tepaneca of Tlacopan. The Aztec empire would conquer much of Central Mexico, frequently employing a system of indirect rule that left intact previously existing political structures in subject towns (Berdan et al. 1996; Hassig 1985). The transition between the Middle Postclassic and the Late Postclassic is often identified by the presence of Aztec III (and eventually IV) Black-on-Orange pottery as well as changes in other types, such as red ware. But as with any other chronological scheme, this neatness does not fully capture the reality of cultural and technological change. The widespread appearance of this pottery in the Basin of Mexico appears to reflect both the adoption of a regional style (likely centered at Tenochtitlan) and the way the Aztecs integrated previously autonomous provinces. The Aztec state apparently did not directly administer or control the market systems. But Aztec political centralization nonetheless facilitated market interaction between producers and consumers on a more regional level (see Hodge et al. 1993).

The regional population of the Basin of Mexico during the Late Postclassic was the highest in the area's entire history, with an estimated one million inhabitants—a demographic size the region would not experience again until several centuries after European conquest (Sanders et al. 1979:162). The settlement was characterized by the presence of local, nucleated centers and more dispersed settlements. Despite the existence of many rural settlements, over half of the population resided in centers, much of it in the Aztec capital of Tenochtitlan. City-states still remained one of the most important units of local social interaction as well as familial and community affiliation. Indeed, not only did the structure of the Aztec empire emerge from a city-state system, the hierarchical organization of city-states also facilitated economic production and labor organization critical to financing the political economy (Hicks 1982). The influence of city-state organization is also reflected in the settlement data. Most centers appear to have a core of monumental and administrative buildings surrounded by a periphery of increasingly more dispersed settlements that eventually merge with peripheral settlements tied into another city-state center (Sanders et al. 1979:163–64). The landscape of city-states was, moreover, organized into a series of provinces to organize tax collection for the empire (Berdan and Anawalt 1992). The introduction of tax or tribute goods into markets may also have contributed to a decline in craft production in many communities, as craftspeople turned to farming when they became unable to compete with essentially state-subsidized commodities (Brumfiel 1976).

In addition to a large and widely distributed settlement system, local communities and households in the Basin of Mexico also developed many different strategies to interact with the environmental landscape in order to produce the food and goods they needed for their households and for local and regional political obligations. Salt production sites became common along the shores of lakes Texcoco and Xaltocan (Millhauser 2012; Parsons 2006; Sanders et al. 1979:171–75). The well-known system of *chinampas* (raised fields) in the southern Basin of Mexico appears to have expanded during this time, where enough produce could be cultivated to support local populations as well as residents in larger cities like Tenochtitlan (Armillas 1971; Parsons 1976; Sanders et al. 1979:280). Many irrigation and terrace systems were constructed in both alluvial and foothill locations. Establishing the chronology of these systems is challenging, and some certainly pre-dated the Late Postclassic period (see discussions in Borejsza; McClung de Tapia and Acosta Ochoa, this volume). But the authors of the Green Book at least felt confident in the existence of strong evidence that many of these landscape investments, especially terracing, dated to the Late Postclassic period (Sanders et al. 1979:251).

This overview is largely schematic and drawn principally from the original survey publications. But one of the most important contributions of the Basin of Mexico survey projects was how they set the stage for several archaeologists who would go on to carry out more intensive archaeological projects in the areas and at the sites the surveyors identified. This can be seen perhaps most clearly in the case of research in the Teotihuacan Valley. This subregion of the Basin of Mexico witnessed a series of archaeological operations that directly built off of the surface survey's original work, methodologically demonstrating the importance of multi-phase research projects (see Kolb's contribution to this volume).

Several additional archaeological projects have built on the survey to develop intensive investigations (see Nichols, this volume). These include field projects in the Chalco and Xochimilco region (e.g., Frederick and Cordova 2019; Hodge 2008; Parsons et al. 1985), in the Texcoco region (Clayton 2013, 2016; Cordova 1997; Cowgill 2013; Crider 2013; Nichols et al. 2013), in the northern Basin of Mexico (Brumfiel 1991, 2005; De Lucia 2011; Farah 2019; Millhauser 2012; Morehart 2010; Overholtzer 2012; Rodríguez-Alegría 2008), as well as in the greater Teotihuacan Valley (Charlton et al. 1991; Evans 1988; Nichols and Charlton 1996; Stoner et al. 2015). A countless number of projects have been carried by archaeologists of the Instituto Nacional de Antropología e Historia (INAH) and the Universidad Nacional Autónoma de México (UNAM) throughout the Basin as well, and both Mexican and foreign archaeologists have directed many excavation projects within the urban districts of well-known ancient cities, such as Tenochtitlan, Teotihuacan, Tenayuca, and Cuicuilco, and Temamatla, among others (see Manzanilla 2014).

Finally, it is important to stress that the original Basin of Mexico surveys made important contributions to some of the most influential theoretical perspectives in anthropology at the time. Particular emphasis was put on a cultural ecological understanding of adaptation and social evolution (see Logan and Sanders 1976; Sanders 1957, 1962; Sanders and Price 1968; Sanders et al. 1979). Intellectually, their cultural ecological model integrates the ideas of several scholars, including some with somewhat opposing views, such as a Boserupian emphasis on technological innovation in agriculture, a Malthusian recognition of carrying capacities, Carneiro's ideas on circumscription, and Wittfogel's work on political complexity and irrigation. Population growth, sociopolitical complexity, and the nature of economic strategies were viewed as having close ties to the finite distributions of water, land, and a range of other important resources. This constellation of biological, social, and geophysical variables were systemically related to one another in a series of feedbacks of cause and effect that led to change (Sanders et al. 1979:395). Overall, this framing emphasized the ecologically adaptive nature of a range of institutions and practices. It offered archaeologists a model to explain and generalize about agricultural change, the development of inequality, and trade. Nonetheless, many scholars were critical of cultural ecology's emphasis on adaptation and the driving force of population growth and instead stressed more political and even exploitative aspects of change (e.g., Blanton 1976; Brumfiel 1976, 1992; Brumfiel and Earle 1987; Cowgill 1975; Morrison 1996; see also replies to Sanders and Nichols 1988).

Over time, a wider range of issues have become central to many archaeological projects, such as agency, power and exploitation, collective action, households, gender, materiality, and ethnicity, to name a few. Nevertheless, subsequent research programs in the Basin of Mexico that have pursued these topics were very much dependent on the original research that produced the Green Book. Furthermore, with growing evidence and concern for global climate change, ecological processes have once again become central to many of the questions archaeologists ask.

CONTINUING THE LEGACY: THIS BOOK

The final chapter in the Green Book, "Key Problems for Future Research," outlines areas the authors felt needed additional study (Sanders et al. 1979:413–18). They believed that their contribution provided solid empirical footing to refine and operationalize many persistent questions that stimulated archaeological research at the time and still do today, such as the roles of irrigation, population growth, technological change and innovation, economic exchange, warfare, social differentiation, and political integration. They also specifically noted a need to continue work on artifact and site chronology, the functional and demographic classifications of archaeological sites. They also recognized the need to integrate their research with similarly conducted regional surveys in other areas, particularly those directly adjacent to the Basin of Mexico surveys. They asserted that more synthesis between archaeology and ethnohistorical methods and data were needed, particularly for later periods of time. Given the emphasis on the relationship between human settlements and the environment that they pursued, they also recognized the need for a broad range of paleoenvironmental studies. Finally, they recognized the rapidly disappearing nature of the archaeological record in the expanding Mexico City Metropolitan Area and, consequently, the need to prioritize research in higher risk locations and to preserve a wide range of key sites, not just the ones with the largest architecture.

The thirteen chapters of this volume are all, in one way or another, heirs to the groundbreaking research of the Basin of Mexico surveys. They each also address different aspects of the key problems for future research that the Green Book recommended. To present the disparate contributions, we have organized the volume into five thematic parts. Part I centers on the history of research that led to the Green Book and beyond as well as testimonials about the survey work. The contributions in Part II address changing or refined perspectives on settlement and demography through recent research. Part III includes contributions on aspects of the landscape, environmental interaction, and resource procurement. Finally, Part IV presents new studies on the nature of the political economy of the Basin. In this final section, we briefly discuss each contribution and also emphasize the ways the chapters respond to the lacunae that Sanders, Parsons, and Santley recognized and contribute new methods, empirical data, and intellectual questions to the legacy the Green Book established.

The first two contributions in Part I are written by Deborah Nichols and Charles Kolb, respectively. These chapters offer in-depth descriptions of the history of archaeological research in the Basin of Mexico, including the specific projects that became the key sources of data for the Green Book. These chapters are especially compelling because both Nichols and Kolb were participants in the Basin of Mexico survey and excavation projects, particularly in the Teotihuacan Valley. Nichols provides an important overview of archaeology's history in the area, pointing out the social history of the field as well as the intellectual and methodological contexts that led to the Basin of Mexico survey projects. She describes how this work connected to emerging paradigms both in anthropology and in archaeology, particularly the rise in interest in social evolution and ecological adaptation that became key research problems. Nichols's chapter offers an excellent and thorough recognition of the long-term impact of these pioneering archaeologists, and also describes many important studies and projects carried out by contemporary researchers who are not contributors to the present volume. Kolb's chapter offers a chronology of research as well as a reflection on the organizational and logistical dimensions of the survey and excavation projects that led to the Green Book, especially, like Nichols, focusing on his experiences working in the Teotihuacan Valley. He examines some of the intellectual currents of the time and describes the challenges researchers faced, the productive contributions they made, and some of the areas that Kolb and his colleagues recognized needed development and refinement, including nomenclature, the definition of analytical units, and ceramic chronology.

The contributions in this volume's Part II draw attention to demographic issues and include new studies and data, reexaminations of empirical patterns, and reflections that range across the archaeological record. We are particularly honored to recognize the first chapter in this section, co-authored by Jeff Parsons, whose work, as we have discussed, established the legacy this book is meant to recognize. Another reason we are pleased that this volume is hosting this chapter is somewhat more prosaic among the community of Basin of Mexico archaeologists. Essentially, they ask, why Aztec II Black-on-Orange pottery, an important marker for the Middle Postclassic, is rare in the northern Basin compared to the southern and, especially, to the eastern Basin. Does this represent a Middle Postclassic population decline after the collapse of Tula? Or did Aztec II overlap in time with Aztec I into the Early Postclassic? Parsons and Gorenflo review a range of settlement data, including data on settlement continuity across phases, ceramic studies, and radiocarbon dates. They conclude that the absence of Aztec II materials in the northern Basin of Mexico does document a population decline in the wake of Tula's collapse.

Bioarchaeological research has expanded significantly since the research that led to the Green Book. The next chapter, by Meza-Peñaloza, Zertuche, and García

Chávez, employs the analysis of non-metric cranial traits, features that serve as useful proxies for genetic relationships within and between populations. They analyze several hundred cranial samples from several sites in the Basin of Mexico and the Toluca Valley that date from the Formative period to the Postclassic, including Teotihuacan, Xaltocan, Tlatilco, and Xico. Their analysis documents considerable population variation across space and time, with compelling patterns of biological continuity and discontinuity. Generally speaking, populations after the collapse of Teotihuacan (during the Epiclassic period) differ significantly from Classic-period Teotihuacan, calling into question the notion that inhabitants from Teotihuacan spread out into the Basin after the city's decline. Patterns of relationships at Teotihuacan, however, are also variable, reflecting varying degrees of interaction between inhabitants as well as varying degrees of biological affiliation with distant locations, such as the Gulf Coast. Of particular interest is their work at Xico in the Basin of Mexico, where long-term biological continuity apparently existed despite incredible demographic change.

Frederick's chapter takes up an important issue related to the use of settlement survey data to document the distribution of populations. He examines how the presented site tabulation and the distribution of survey data correspond, revealing that many of the "gaps" between sites are far from insignificant for understanding the settlement system (see also Cordova, this volume). The fact that the sites, as he observes, "are merely geographic subsets of larger artifact scatters suggests that settlement was more broadly dispersed in some places than the sites imply, and / or that post-depositional processes have dispersed the artifacts." Frederick offers three case examples in the southern Basin of Mexico to illustrate how the depositional environment of the Basin may have biased demographic reconstructions toward lower population estimates. In some depositional environments, such as alluvial areas, sites were often not recorded because intact components were buried and, hence, not visible to surveyors. On the one hand, including sites in alluvial areas might dramatically change our reconstruction of population history. On the other, the alluvial areas adjacent to recorded sites often have a much better and more intact record than the actual identified site loci. As other studies in this volume attest, Frederick's contribution points to the need for more geoarchaeological research, not only generally but also as a specific component of all archaeological research projects.

Gorenflo's chapter offers a much-needed perspective on the condition of archaeological resources in the Basin of Mexico. He examines the current state of preservation of some of the archaeological sites identified during the original surveys, documenting how demographic changes that have occurred in the region in the past forty or fifty years have affected some of the archaeological sites that the Green Book was written about. Morehart and Millhauser (2016) carried out a similar study, examining site locations in the Zumpango survey area with contemporary high-resolution satellite imagery. Gorenflo notes the incredible peri-urban explosion since the 1960s and 70s, a process of demographic expansion that has affected areas around Mexico City much more than the city itself. He also shows a long-term pattern in some areas of land use, particularly agriculture, which had persisted from the pre-Columbian period up to the mid- to late twentieth century, but has increasingly disappeared over the past forty years. These changes reflect national and global economic transformations that have led to a decrease in small farming and an increase in commercial and urban development as well as large-scale agriculture using heavy machinery. One of the take-home lessons from Gorenflo's chapter is that the incredible record that the archaeological surveys produced is of historic significance, especially because urban growth has caused many of the sites to disappear, while the future of those that remain untouched is uncertain.

The contributions to this volume's Part III are two studies of a larger body of research on environmental change. This corpus of research directly responds to the Green Book's assertion that more paleoecological research projects are needed. The chapter by Solleiro-Rebolledo and colleagues provides pedological and chemical analyses of the mosaic distribution of soils in the Teotihuacan Valley. By classifying the physical and chemical properties of soils, they assess the range of soil resources that were available to the inhabitants of the valley for intensive agriculture, pottery production, and house construction. They also consider how the use of soils for such activities may have affected the landscape that other groups subsequently inherited.

While soil and water was an important resource inland, so were resources in the lakes. Despite including the lakebeds of the southern Basin, however, large parts of the lakebeds were not surveyed (see figure 1.1). Parsons (2015) recognized this failure after reviewing the recent data of the center of Lake Texcoco and recent work in Xaltocan. In his contribution, Cordova uses examples of several *tlatel*-type settlements recorded by the Texcoco and Teotihuacan survey on the shores of former Lake Texcoco to explain how the dynamics of the lake influenced settlements in the lacustrine and peri-lacustrine areas. First, lake levels fluctuated dramatically from one period to the next, thus changing the location of resources and areas suitable for settlement. Second, the study of the stratigraphy and geomorphology around sites shows how diverse the lacustrine environment was, demonstrating that not all settlements in the lake were focused on salt production. Third, in agreement with Frederick's chapter, Cordova's chapter stresses the importance of off-site geoarchaeological research in the overall analysis of the population and economy of ancient settlements.

Part IV continues many of the themes of the previous section but focuses more specifically on resource exploitation and mosaic agricultural systems. Borejsza's chapter provides a long-term, regional reassessment of agricultural technological change, a developmental sequence that was a central component of the demographic reconstruction on which the Green Book was based. Borejsza deploys the concept of the "agricultural niche" to examine the historical evolution of agricultural strategies in Central Mexico, a perspective that can elucidate change not simply as a product of agricultural growth, as in Boserup's framing, but as a systemic historical process that is critically contingent on both physical and social precedent. Integrating a sizeable body of empirical data, Borejsza analyzes the distribution of progressively more intensive agricultural systems, from swidden to terracing to hydraulic systems such as canals and raised fields (*chinampas*). He finds empirical support for a degree of sequential developmental change across time, but his analysis demonstrates that this progression is far from a simple optimization strategy between the distribution of people and resources. Rather, this development was a historically material process in which established socioecological conditions shaped innovation and change.

McClung de Tapia and Acosta Ochoa's chapter provides a study of *chinampa* farming in the southern Basin of Mexico that aptly follows Borejsza's. *Chinampas* in this area have been extensively discussed yet have attracted surprisingly few archaeological field studies. This is significant because the role of the *chinampas* in this area is frequently discussed in reconstructions of the development of agricultural economies in the Basin of Mexico and, especially, of the connection between farming and the political economy of the Aztec state. Their project, at El Japón, Xochimilco, offers important data from the heart of the Basin of Mexico's *chinampa* zone. They present a range of archaeological, geological, and biological data to reconstruct the construction, maintenance, and use of *chinampas* and, hence, offer a solid methodological model for other researchers to follow. They recognize that dating *chinampas* is challenging for several reasons, but most of their chronological data converge to indicate that *chinampa* farming during the Aztec period, particularly the Late Postclassic, continued into the Colonial period.

The contributions in the final part of the book, Part V, examine politics and economy. Crider has taken on the broad regional dynamics of the Epiclassic period in the Basin of Mexico, offering important methodological advancements and interpretive steps for understanding the unique nature of the political economy in the wake of the collapse of Teotihuacan. Her analysis here and in previous papers has offered researchers significant comparative resources for synthetic understandings that integrate both macro-regional patterns and localized, subregional variation (both in historical and empirical terms and in classificatory terms). Her paper also directly addresses some of the chronological issues discussed in Parsons and Gorenflo's chapter, particularly the spatiotemporal nature of Early Postclassic ceramics and the cultural groups they represent. Finally, her regional ceramic study offers an incredible resource for reconstructing broad-scale patterns of production and exchange on par with other foundational projects that have helped to establish more comprehensive understandings of Prehispanic economic systems in the Basin of Mexico and surrounding regions.

Morehart, Huster, and Meza-Peñaloza's contribution suitably follows Crider's chapter. They explore the changes in the political landscape between the Epiclassic period to the Early Postclassic period in the northern Basin of Mexico and the southern Mezquital Valley. Examining a range of data on violence and conflict, they find some support for the long-held notion that this period of time was one of balkanization and political instability in the wake of Teotihuacan's collapse. Such instability, they suggest, may have resulted in competition and conflict between political actors occupying the region. Drawing on comparative perspectives on war, conflict, and state formation, they speculate that this geopolitical configuration likely sset up significant challenges for any effort to develop an integrated and centralized regional political economy and thus shaped the formation of the Tula state. The authors suggest that overcoming the power of competitors and establishing a more stable political and economic environment, a *Pax Tolteca*, would have been critical to any degree of longevity in state governance. They also find that the archaeological record provides some support for this possibility, though they recognize that substantiating the hypothesis further will require considerably more data and field research.

The final chapter, by Millhauser, captures an important aspect of historical change fundamental to any sense of the term "legacy." He provides a long-term consideration of the relationship between environmental interaction, political change, and inequality. Employing the concept of "slow violence," he examines how inequality is an intrinsically violent process that unfolds across time and in dialogue with both social and material precedent. He also incorporates considerable data on the Colonial period, a time that was not included in the original Basin of Mexico surveys, which is a lacuna that Sanders, Parsons, and Santley explicitly recognized (see above) and one that a handful of archaeologists in the area have worked tirelessly to correct (see, e.g., Charlton 1968, 1996; Charlton et al. 2005; Rodríguez-Alegría 2008).

CONCLUSION

As any reader familiar with the archaeology of this region will note, this volume is far from comprehensive in its coverage of archaeological research since the publication of the Green Book. In this limited introduction, it is difficult to recognize all the important research that has been done by both Mexican and non-Mexican archaeologists in the Basin of Mexico and at important sites in the area, such as the many existing and ongoing studies of Teotihuacan or the Templo Mayor, for example. We are grateful, therefore, for the comprehensive reviews that Kolb and Nichols provide. Moreover, we hope that this volume's contributions will convey not only the canonical importance of past work but, more importantly, the way it established a legacy of research that every contemporary archaeologist has inherited. The contributions in this volume stress the legacy of the Green Book, not as a static and unquestionable one, but as an evolving intellectual entity fed by several generations of archaeologists and other specialists. Over four decades after its publication, the Green Book remains the point of reference for most of the archaeological research in the Basin of Mexico and beyond.

Acknowledgments. We would like to thank the editorial staff of the University Press of Colorado who helped with this project and in particular to our editor, Allegra Martschenko, as well as the anonymous reviewers for their helpful comments and suggestions. Finally, we want to acknowledge those colleagues who participated in the discussions about the book, but were unable to contribute to this volume, Philip Arnold III, Sarah Clayon, Michelle Elliott, Kristin DeLucia, Wesley Stoner, Isabel Rodríguez López, Joaquín Arroyo-Cabrales, Eduardo Corona-Martínez, Felisa J. Aguilar-Arellano, Silvia Gonzalez, Samuel Rennie, David Huddart, Mari Carmen Serra Puche, Dan Healan, Patricia Fournier, and Cynthia Otis Charlton.

REFERENCES

Armillas, P. 1971. "Gardens on Swamps." *Science* 174:653–61.

Beekman, Christopher S., and Alexander F. Christensen. 2003. "Controlling for Doubt and Uncertainty through Multiple Lines of Evidence: A New Look at the Mesoamerican Nahua Migrations." *Journal of Archaeological Method and Theory* 19:111–64.

Berdan, Frances F., and Patricia R. Anawalt. 1992. *The Codex Mendoza*. 4 vols. University of California Press, Berkeley.

Berdan, Frances F., Richard E. Blanton, Elizabeth H. Boone, Mary G. Hodge, Michael E. Smith, and Emily Umberger. 1996. *Aztec Imperial Strategies*. Dumbarton Oaks, Washington, DC.

Blanton, Richard E. 1972. *Prehispanic Settlement Patterns of the Ixtapalapa Peninsula Region, Mexico*. Occasional Papers in Anthropology, no. 6. Department of Anthropology, The Pennsylvania State University, University Park.

Blanton, Richard E. 1976. "The Role of Symbiosis in Adaptation and Sociocultural Change in the Valley of Mexico." In *The Valley of Mexico: Studies of Pre-Hispanic Ecology and Society*, edited by Eric R. Wolf, 181–202. University of New Mexico Press, Albuquerque.

Blanton, Richard E. 1976. "The Role of Symbiosis in Adaptation and Sociocultural Change in the Valley of Mexico." In *The Valley of Mexico: Studies of Pre-Hispanic*

Ecology and Society, edited by Eric R. Wolf, 181–202. University of New Mexico Pres, Albuquerque.

Brumfiel, Elizabeth M. 1976. "Regional Growth in the Eastern Valley of Mexico: A Test of the 'Population Pressure' Hypothesis." In *The Early Mesoamerican Village*, edited by K. Flannery, 234–47. Academic Press, New York.

Brumfiel, Elizabeth M. 1991. "Tribute and Commerce in Imperial Cities: The Case of Xaltocan, Mexico." In *Early State Economies*, edited by H. J. M. Claessen and P. van de Velde, 177–98. Transaction Publishers, New Brunswick.

Brumfiel, Elizabeth M. 1992. "Breaking and Entering the Ecosystem: Gender, Class, and Fraction Steal the Show." *American Anthropologist* 89:676–86.

Brumfiel, Elizabeth, ed. 2005. *Production and Power at Postclassic Xaltocan/La producción local y el poder en el Xaltocan Posclásico*. Serie Aqueología de México, Instituto Nacional de Antropología e História and University of Pittsburgh, México, Mexico City and Pittsburgh.

Brumfiel, Elizabeth M., and Timothy K. Earle, eds. 1987. *Specialization, Exchange and Complex Societies*. Cambridge University Press, Cambridge.

Carballo, David M., and Thomas Pluckhahn. 2007. "Transportation Corridors and Political Evolution in Highland Mesoamerica: Settlement Analyses Incorporating GIS for Northern Tlaxcala, Mexico." *Journal of Anthropological Archaeology* 26:607–29.

Charlton, Thomas H. 1968. "Post-Conquest Aztec Ceramics: Implications for Archaeological Interpretation." *Florida Anthropologist* 21(1):96–101.

Charlton, Thomas H. 1996. "Early Colonial Period Ceramics: Decorated Red Ware and Orange Ware Types of the Rural Otumba Aztec Ceramic Complex." In *Arqueología mesoamericana: Homenaje a William T. Sanders*, edited by A. G. Mastache, J. R. Parsons, M. C. Serra Puche, and R. S. Santley, vol. 1, 461–79. Instituto Nacional de Antropología e Historia, Mexico City.

Charlton, Thomas H., and Deborah L. Nichols. 1997. "Diachronic Studies of City-States: Permutations on a Theme, Central Mexico from 1600 BC to AD 1600." In *The Archaeology of City-States: Cross-Cultural Approaches*, edited by Deborah L. Nichols and Thomas H. Charlton, 169–207. Smithsonian Institution Press, Washington, DC.

Charlton, Thomas H., Deborah L. Nichols, and Cynthia Otis-Charlton. 1991. "Aztec Craft Production and Specialization: Archaeological Evidence from the City-State of Otumba, Mexico." *World Archaeology* 23(1):98–114.

Charlton, Thomas H., Raúl García Chávez, Cynthia O. Charlton, Verónica Ortega, David O. Andrade O. D., and Teresa Palomares. 2005. "Salvamento arqueológico reciente en el valle de Teotihuacan: Sito TC-83, San Bartolomé el Alto." In *Arquitectura y urbanismo: Pasado y presente de los espacios en Teotihuacan*. Memoria de la Tercer Mesa Redonda de Teotihuacan, edited by María Elena Ruiz Gallut, and J. Jesús Torres Peralta, 343–72. Instituto Nacional de Antropología e Historia, Mexico City.

Clayton, Sarah C. 2013. "Measuring the Long Arm of the State: Teotihuacan's Relations in the Basin of Mexico." *Ancient Mesoamerica* 24(1):87–105.

Clayton, Sarah C. 2016. "After Teotihuacan: A View of Collapse and Reorganization from the Southern Basin of Mexico." *American Anthropologist* 118(1):104–20.

Cordova, Carlos E. 1997. "Landscape Transformation in Aztec and Spanish Colonial Texcoco." PhD dissertation, Department of Geography, University of Texas at Austin.

Cordova, Carlos E. 2022. *The Lakes of the Basin of Mexico: Dynamics of a Lacustrine System and the Evolution of a Civilization.* Springer, New York.

Cowgill, George L. 1975. "On Causes and Consequences of Ancient and Modern Population Changes." *American Anthropologist* 77:505–25.

Cowgill, George L. 2013. "Possible Migrations and Shifting Identities in the Central Mexican Epiclassic." *Ancient Mesoamerica* 24(1):131–49.

Cowgill, George L. 2015. *Ancient Teotihuacan: Early Urbanism in Central Mexico.* Cambridge University Press, Cambridge.

Crider, Destiny L. 2013. "Shifting Alliances: Epiclassic and Early Postclassic Interactions at Cerro Portezuelo." *Ancient Mesoamerica* 24(1):107–30.

Crider, Destiny L., Deborah L. Nichols, Hector Neff, and Michael D. Glascock. 2007. "In the Aftermath of Teotihuacan: Epiclassic Pottery Production and Distribution in the Teotihuacan Valley, Mexico." *Latin American Antiquity* 18(2):123–43.

De Lucia, Kristin. 2011. "Domestic Economies and Regional Transition: Household Production and Consumption in Early Postclassic Mexico." PhD dissertation, Northwestern University, Evanston, IL.

Evans, Susan T., ed. 1988. *Cihuatecpan: The Village in Its Ecological and Historical Context.* Vanderbilt University, Nashville, TN.

Farah, Kirby. 2019. "Constructing a Kingdom: Architectural Strategies and the Nature of Leadership at Postclassic Xaltocan, Mexico." *Journal of Social Archaeology* 19(1):92–115.

Fowler, William R., Ian G. Robertson, and L. J. Gorenflo. 2015. "Introduction: Taking Stock of Basin of Mexico Archaeology in the Early Twenty-First Century." *Ancient Mesoamerica* 26:127–34.

Frederick, C. D., and Carlos E. Cordova. 2019. "Prehispanic and Colonial Landscape Change and Fluvial Dynamics in the Chalco Region, Mexico." *Geomorphology* 331:107–26.

Gorenflo, L. J., and William T. Sanders. 2007. *Archaeological Settlement Pattern Data from the Cuautitlan, Temascalapa, and Teotihuacan Regions, Mexico.* Occasional Papers in Anthropology, no. 30. Department of Anthropology, The Pennsylvania State University, University Park.

Hassig, Ross. 1985. *Trade, Tribute, and Transportation: The Sixteenth-Century Political Economy of the Valley of Mexico.* University of Oklahoma Press, Norman.

Hicks, Frederic. 1982. "Tetzcoco in the Early Sixteenth Century: The State, the City and the Calpolli." *American Ethnologist* 9:230–49.

Hodge, Mary G., ed. 2008. *Place of Jade: Society and Economy in Ancient Chalco.* Serie Arqueología de México, University of Pittsburgh and Instituto Nacional de Antropología e Historia, Pittsburgh, Pennsylvania, and Mexico City.

Hodge, Mary G., Hector Neff, M. James Blackman, and Leah. D. Minc. 1993. "Black-on-Orange Ceramic Production in the Aztec Empire's Heartland." *Latin American Antiquity* 4:130–57.

Logan, Michael H., and William T. Sanders. 1976. "The Model." In *The Valley of Mexico: Studies in Pre-Hispanic Ecology and Society*, edited by Eric R. Wolf, 31–58. University of New Mexico Press, Albuquerque.

López Austin, Alfredo, and Leonardo López Luján. 2000. "The Myth and Reality of Zuyuá: The Feathered Serpent and Mesoamerican Transformations from the Classic to the Postclassic." In *Mesoamerican Classic Heritage: From Teotihuacan to the Aztecs*, edited by Davíd Carrasco, Lyndsay Jones, and Scott Sessions, 21–84. University Press of Colorado, Boulder.

Manzanilla, Linda R. 2014. "The Basin of Mexico." In *The Cambridge World Prehistory*, edited by C. Renfrew and P. G. Bahn, 976–94. Cambridge University Press, New York.

Millhauser, John K. 2012. "Saltmaking, Craft, and Community at Late Postclassic and Early Colonial San Bartolome Salinas, Mexico." PhD dissertation, Northwestern University, Evanston, IL.

Morehart, Christopher T. 2010. "The Archaeology of Farmscapes: Production, Power and Place at Postclassic Xaltocan, Mexico." PhD dissertation, Northwestern University, Evanston, IL.

Morehart, Christopher, and John Millhauser. 2016. "Monitoring Cultural Landscapes from Space: Evaluating Archaeological Sites in the Basin of Mexico Using Very High Resolution Satellite Imagery." *Journal of Archaeological Science: Reports* 10:363–76.

Morrison, Kathleen D. 1996. "Typological Schemes and Agricultural Change: Beyond Boserup in Pre-Colonial South India." *Current Anthropology* 37:583–608.

Nichols, Deborah L., and Thomas H. Charlton. 1996. "The Postclassic Occupation at Otumba: A Chronological Assessment." *Ancient Mesoamerica* 7:231–44.

Nichols, Deborah L., Hector Neff, and George L. Cowgill. 2013. "Cerro Portezuelo: An Overview." *Ancient Mesoamerica* 24:47–71.

Overholtzer, Lisa. 2012. "Empires and Everyday Material Practices: A Household Archaeology of Aztec and Spanish Imperialism at Xaltocan, Mexico." PhD dissertation, Northwestern University, Evanston, IL.

Parsons, Jeffrey R. 1966. "The Aztec Ceramic Sequence in the Teotihuacan Valley, Mexico." PhD dissertation, University of Michigan, Ann Arbor.

Parsons, Jeffrey R. 1971. *Prehispanic Settlement Patterns in the Texcoco Region, Mexico.* Memoirs of the Museum of Anthropology, no. 3. University of Michigan, Ann Arbor.

Parsons, Jeffrey R. 1976. "The Role of Chinampa Agriculture in the Food Supply of Aztec Tenochtitlan." In *Cultural Change and Continuity: Essays in Honor of James Bennett Griffin*, edited by Charles E. Cleland, 233–57. Academic Press, New York.

Parsons, Jeffrey R. 2006. *The Last Pescadores of Chimalhuacan, Mexico: An Archaeological Ethnography*. Anthropological Papers, no. 96. Museum of Anthropology, University of Michigan, Ann Arbor.

Parsons, Jeffrey R. 2008. *Prehispanic Settlement Patterns in the Northwestern Valley of Mexico: The Zumpango Region*. Memoirs of the Museum of Anthropology, no. 45. University of Michigan, Ann Arbor.

Parsons, Jeffrey R. 2015. "An Appraisal of Regional Surveys in the Basin of Mexico, 1960–1975." *Ancient Mesoamerica* 26:183–96.

Parsons, Jeffrey R. 2019. *Remembering Archaeological Fieldwork in Mexico and Peru, 1960–2003: A Photographic Essay*. Special Publication of the Museum of Anthropology, no. 3. University of Michigan, Ann Arbor.

Parsons, Jeffrey R., and Luis Morett. 2004. "Recursos acuáticos en la subsistencia azteca: Cazadores, pescadores y recolectores." *Arqueología mexicana* 12(68):38–43.

Parsons, Jeffrey R., and Luis Morett. 2005. "La economía acuática en el Valle de México: Perspectivas arqueológicas, históricas, y etnográficas." In *Etnoarqueología: El contexto dinámico de la cultura material a través del tiempo*, edited by E. Williams, 127–64. El Colegio de Michoacán, Zamora.

Parsons, Jeffrey R., Elizabeth Brumfiel, and Mary Hodge. 1996. "Developmental Implications of Earlier Dates for Early Aztec in the Basin of Mexico." *Ancient Mesoamerica* 7(2):217–30.

Parsons, Jeffrey R., Elizabeth M. Brumfiel, Mary H. Parsons, and David J. Wilson. 1982. *Prehispanic Settlement Patterns in the Southern Valley of Mexico: The Chalco-Xochimilco Region*. Memoirs of the Museum of Anthropology, no. 14. University of Michigan, Ann Arbor.

Parsons, Jeffrey R., Keith Kintigh, and Susan Gregg. 1983. *Archaeological Settlement Pattern Data from the Chalco, Xochimilco, Ixtapalapa, Texcoco, and Zumpango Regions, Mexico*. Technical Report, no. 14. Museum of Anthropology, University of Michigan, Ann Arbor.

Parsons, Jeffrey R., Mary Hrones Parsons, Virginia Popper, and Mary Taft. 1985. "Chinampa Agriculture and Aztec Urbanization in the Valley of Mexico." In *Prehistoric Intensive Agriculture in the Tropics*, edited by I. S. Farrington, 49–96. BAR International Series, no. 232. British Archaeological Reports, Oxford.

Plunket, Patricia, and Gabriela Uruñuela. 2012. "Where East Meets West: The Formative in Mexico's Central Highlands." *Journal of Archaeological Research* 20(1):1–51.

Ringle, William M., Tomás Gallareta Negrón, and George J. Bey. 1998. "The Return of Quetzalcoatl: Evidence for the Spread of a World Religion during the Epiclassic Period." *Ancient Mesoamerica* 9(2):183–232.

Roberston, Ian, and Larry J. Gorenflo. 2015. "Assessing the State of Basin of Mexico Archaeology in 2007." *Ancient Mesoamerica* 26:129–33.

Rodríguez-Alegría, Enrique. 2008. "Narratives of Conquest, Colonialism and Cutting-Edge Technology." *American Anthropologist* 110:33–43.

Sanders, William T. 1957. "Tierra y Agua, A Study of the Ecological Factors in the Development of Mesoamerican Civilizations." PhD dissertation, Harvard University, Cambridge, MA.

Sanders, William T. 1962. "Cultural Ecology of Nuclear Mesoamerica." *American Anthropologist* 64(1):34–44.

Sanders, William T. 1965. *The Cultural Ecology of the Teotihuacan Valley, Mexico*. Department of Sociology and Anthropology, The Pennsylvania State University, University Park.

Sanders, William T., and Deborah L. Nichols. 1988. "Ecological Theory and Cultural Evolution in the Valley of Oaxaca." *Current Anthropology* 29(1):33–80.

Sanders, William T., and Larry J. Gorenflo. 2007. *Prehispanic Settlement Patterns in the Cuautitlan Region, Mexico*. Occasional Papers in Anthropology, no. 29. Department of Anthropology, The Pennsylvania State University, University Park.

Sanders, William T., and Barbara J. Price. 1968. *Mesoamerica: The Evolution of a Civilization*. Random House, New York.

Sanders, William T., Jeffrey R. Parsons, and Robert S. Santley. 1979. *The Basin of Mexico: Ecological Processes in the Evolution of a Civilization*. Academic Press, New York.

Stoner, Wesley D., Deborah L. Nichols, Bridget Alex, and Destiny Crider. 2015. "The Emergence of Early-Middle Formative Exchange Patterns in Mesoamerica: A View from Altica in the Teotihuacan Valley." *Journal of Anthropological Archaeology* 39:19–35.

Wolf, Eric R., ed. 1976a. *The Valley of Mexico: Studies in Pre-Hispanic Ecology and Society*. University of New Mexico Press, Albuquerque.

Wolf, Eric R., ed. 1976b. "Introduction." In *The Valley of Mexico: Studies in Pre-Hispanic Ecology and Society*, edited by Eric R. Wolf, 1–10. University of New Mexico Press, Albuquerque.

PART I

The Basin of Mexico Survey and the Green Book Today

2

The Evolution of a Revolution

The Basin of Mexico: Ecological Processes in the Evolution of a Civilization

DEBORAH L. NICHOLS[1]

INTRODUCTION

The Basin of Mexico survey revolutionized how archaeologists in the Americas study urbanism, state formation, and environmental relations as regional phenomena. William T. Sanders, Jeffery R. Parsons, and Robert S. Santley published their synthesis of the survey, *The Basin of Mexico: Ecological Processes in the Evolution of a Civilization*, the "Green Book," in 1979 (Gándara 2011). The Basin of Mexico survey stands as one of the most important regional studies of modern archaeology (Ammerman 1981; Balkansky 2006; Blanton 2002, 2005; Blanton et al. 2005; Feinman 2015; Kowalewski 2008; Nichols 1996, 2006, 2018a; Parsons 2015; Serra Puche and Lazcano Arce 2009; Sugiura 2009; Sugiura and Nieto Hernández 2014). A historical perspective on this benchmark project illuminates

---

1 As many in the anthropology community are sadly aware, Professor Deborah Nichols passed away in July 2022. Deb was a long-term friend to many and mentor to countless more. She valued service and provided a meaningful model of leadership. We express our sympathy to her loved ones, colleagues, and students. Deb's commitment to archaeology helped to create the legacy that this volume seeks to celebrate.

https://doi.org/10.5876/9781646424078.c002

its underpinnings and lays the groundwork for the new directions presented in this volume.

POTSHERDS VICTORIOUS

Located in the central highlands of Mexico, urbanism in the Basin of Mexico began over 2,500 years ago. It was the geopolitical core of the largest and most influential Prehispanic cities and states in Mesoamerica and today is home to one the world's largest cities, Mexico City, the capital of the modern nation-state of Mexico. To Harvard economist Edward Glaeser (2011), the intensified flow of ideas and information among diverse people in urban agglomerations represents the "Triumph of the City."

Ancient urbanism in the Americas was largely unrecognized until the 1960s. V. Gordon Childe's (1950) "urban revolution" was a phenomenon of the "Old World" as the "cradle of civilization." The Triple Alliance and Inca empires continue to be omitted from many comparative studies today (Scheidel 2015). Although ancient archaeological sites abound in Mexico, they held little interest for Spanish colonizers except as a source of antiquities and curios. The Spanish leveled Tenochtitlan–Tlatelolco and used building stones from Mexica temples and palaces to create their own monumental edifices. By the fifteenth century, when the Triple Alliance formed, Teotihuacan's and Tula's great pyramids had already entered the realm of mythic time (Florescano 2002).

Mexico's independence from Spain began a turning point for archaeology. The Prehispanic past and its monuments again became important to state legitimization and historical validation, as they had been for the Mexica and the Toltecs (Bernal 1983; López Luján and De Anda Rogel 2019). Believed to have been built in a prior age of giants, Teotihuacan was the place where time began, where the gods sacrificed themselves to create the Fifth Sun of the Mexica cosmos and its laws and government. Mexica excavated at Teotihuacan and Tula for antiquities given as offerings at their own Great Temple to validate their place in history where "events were interpreted to fit patterns established in the past, and the past was conceived to accommodate present circumstances" (Umberger 1987:63, see also López Luján and De Anda Rogel 2019).

Foraging modern recognition of a glorious Prehispanic Indian past in Mexico began in the latter half of the seventeenth century with the first excavation at Teotihuacan (Bernal 1980). In 1905, Leopoldo Batres's project at the Sun Pyramid, the largest-scale excavations that had ever been undertaken in Mexico, established the Sun Pyramid as an icon of ancient Mexico and made Teotihuacan part of the historical consciousness of the modern state (Fash 2013) (see figure 2.1).

Less than a century ago, the Prehispanic culture history of the Basin of Mexico was mostly unknown. It was thought that there had only been two "great" Prehispanic cultures in Central Mexico: the Aztecs and the Toltecs (Bernal 1980).

FIGURE 2.1. *"Coming of Quetzalcoatl," panel of the mural, "The Epic of American Civilization," painted by José Clement Orozco. Commissioned by the Trustees of Dartmouth College. Reproduced with permission of the Hood Museum of Art, Dartmouth College.*

In the early 1930s, when José Clemente Orozco painted his famed mural, "The Epic of American Civilization," he assumed Teotihuacan was the Toltec capital that preceded the Aztecs (Coffey 2020). Recognizing greater time depth to Central Mexico's culture history began with Manuel Gamio's (1928) excavations at San Miguel Amantla / Azcapotzalco that produced the first Prehispanic cultural historical sequence. Harvard's Alfred Marston Tozzer (1921), who became Director of the International School, excavated a nearby mound called Coyotlatelco that identified the pottery complex that followed the collapse of Teotihuacan.

Gamio's (1922) excavations at Teotihuacan's Feathered Serpent pyramid were part of a more comprehensive study of the Teotihuacan Valley that launched the discipline of anthropology in Mexico. The Teotihuacan Valley was to have been the first place in Mexico where documenting local resources and archaeology would serve as a backdrop for the in-depth study of contemporary local people and improving life for villagers. Gamio's study later inspired Sanders, who praised "its level of method and synthesis, which in my [Sanders] view has never been approached in later anthropological studies in Meso-America" (Sanders 1957: xi). Sanders's dissertation also drew on the archival research, ethnography, and archaeology that shaped how he approached the Teotihuacan Valley survey. Gamio's excavations revealed the famous sculptures of the Feathered Serpent Pyramid that inspired subsequent investigations of Teotihuacan's governance, political ideology, and cosmology (Gazzola 2017; Gómez Chávez 2017; Sugiyama

2017). George Vaillant's (1930, 1931, 1935a, 1935b, 1938) excavations in the following decade at early village sites north of Mexico City established the Formative / Preclassic phases preceding Teotihuacan.

Stratigraphic excavation and ceramic seriation created the first relative archaeological chronology and culture history for the Basin of Mexico. Ignacio Bernal (1980) refers to the period from 1910 to 1950 in Mexican archaeology as "Potsherds Victorious." The dates assigned to the early archaeological chronologies, however, were too compressed because of the weight given to written texts that did not extend before twelfth and fourteenth centuries.

The Instituto Nacional de Antropología e Historia (INAH) was established in 1939 to take charge of Mexico's paleontological, archaeological, and historical patrimony (Robles García 2012). INAH's excavations of monumental architecture, such as those at Teotihuacan, generated public awareness of Mexico's ancient past (Robles García 2012). In Mexico, the past is seen as part of the living present (Bernal 1980), and the public's nationalist view of the past has sometimes been in tension with the mid-twentieth-century development of the processual, scientific archaeology that fostered the Basin of Mexico survey (Bernal 1983).

THE BATTLE OF THE PALACE VERSUS THE HUT

The first half of the twentieth century defined the culture history of ancient civilizations in Central Mexico, incorporated archaeology into anthropology, and established the INAH as the institutional context for archaeology and heritage management in Mexico. These developments conjoined with world events—the Great Depression, the Spanish Civil War, the Second World War and its aftermath, including the Cold War—to set the stage for a new generation of archaeologists who embraced a problem-oriented social science approach and a focus on structures of stratification, urbanism, and state formation. Although the Basin of Mexico survey had deep roots in Mexican archaeology, settlement pattern studies, tied with theories of cultural ecology, were part of what Bernal (1983:389–90) called "the battle of the *palace* versus the *hut*" that began in the mid-twentieth century (Flannery 1976).

An especially influential figure in the changing orientation of archaeology in the Basin of Mexico was Pedro Armillas, a charismatic archaeologist who fled Spain after its Civil War (Rojas Rabiela 1991). He studied at the new Escuela Nacional de Antropología, whose founding furthered ties between archaeology and anthropology. Armillas saw the applicability to archaeology in the Americas of both V. Gordon Childe's (1950) concept of the urban revolution and of a materialist approach to social evolution. His excavations at Teotihuacan apartment compounds furthered his interest in social evolution and suggested to him that Teotihuacan was a city, not a constellation of ceremonial precincts (Freeman 1986). Through Armillas, along with Sanders and Robert Adams (1965), Childe's "urban revolution" became part of anthropological archaeology's cannon (Smith 2009). Armillas strongly criticized archaeology's emphasis in Mexico on monumental architecture. Bernal (1980, 1983) credits Armillas with changing the orientation of archaeology in the Mexican highlands from an emphasis on arts and aesthetics to a more comparative social science and materialist approach. "Pedro Armillas was a pioneer in the truest sense of the word. Few of those who heard his discussions and presentations in the late forties and fifties will ever forget the impact of his statements on his listeners. To him, above all, is owed the reorientation of work in the Mexican highlands" (Wolf 1976:3) In parallel to Gordon Willey's (1953) 1945 path breaking study of settlement patterns in the Virú Valley of Peru, Armillas (1971) introduced the concept of landscape archaeology and advocated pedestrian archaeological survey. His thinking greatly influenced the post–Second World War generation of archaeologists.

The democratizing effect of the GI Bill of Rights of 1944 on US higher education brought a generation of students, mostly men, to universities with anthropology departments. Their interests in archaeology and anthropology lay in big questions of history from a middle and working-class perspective. Teotihuacan offered the opportunity to investigate Childe's (1950) concept of urban revolution. As graduate students, Sanders at Harvard and Eric R. Wolf and René Millon at Columbia were drawn to the Basin of Mexico by Wittfogel's (1938) hydraulic theory of the origins of early civilizations, along with Armillas's approach to archaeology and his view of Teotihuacan as a city.

When Gordon Willey (1988) moved to Harvard and shifted the focus of his research to the Maya region, Sanders became one of his students. Building on his work in the Virú Valley, Peru, Willey's (1983) Barton Ramie project in Belize included a settlement pattern survey that was one of the earliest archaeological projects to receive support from the National Science Foundation (Willey 1953). As part of the broad restructuring of scientific research in the US following the end of the Second World War and the onset of the Cold War, during an era of economic growth, the National Science Foundation (NSF) was launched in 1951; its social science division was added in 1954 (Patterson 1995). The NSF became the principal source of support for the Basin of Mexico survey and the Teotihuacan Mapping Project and many of the research projects derived from them.

These societal, institutional, and intellectual changes created the context for the Basin of Mexico survey. While still a graduate student of Willey's at Harvard, Sanders (1956) presented the conceptual framework drawn from his dissertation that would shape the Basin of Mexico survey. He defined a 25,000 sq. km area of Central Mexico, including the Basin of Mexico, Morelos, Tlaxcala, western Puebla and southern Hidalgo, as the Central Mexican Symbiotic Region, recognizing the environmental complementarity between the *tierra fria* of northern

Central Mexico and *tierra templada* of southern Central Mexico as a nuclear area for state formation and urbanism (see Borejsza, this volume).

Sanders attributed the early development of states and cities in Central Mexico to early agricultural intensification and specialized agricultural adaptations that could sustain large populations in a semi-arid climate with marked seasonal and annual variations. The micro-geographic diversity encouraged trade, specialization, and economic interdependences. Sanders adopted the term *symbiosis* to characterize those interdependencies. To test this neo-evolutionary, cultural ecological model required knowing the agricultural and population history. Documentary sources, however, did not even adequately cover rural areas in the early sixteenth century, much less earlier periods. Willey's settlement pattern survey offered a method for Sanders to test his ideas about doing "prehistoric cultural geography and offering a way to measure centralization of political power and internal differentiation on a regional scale over time from an explicitly materialist, cultural ecological framework" (Sanders 1999:13; Sanders et al. 1979:4).

Eric Wolf chaired a conference at the University of Chicago in 1960 that laid out objectives for long-term archaeological research in the Basin of Mexico, including urbanization and settlement patterns (Parsons 2015). This launched two complementary signal projects in the history of Americanist archaeology. Millon led the Teotihuacan Mapping Project to create the first comprehensive map of the ancient city and to determine "what kind of an urban center Teotihuacan was and the relations of Teotihuacanos with other great contemporary centers of Mesoamerica" (Millon 1973a:x). Sanders directed the Teotihuacan Valley Project, a systematic archaeological survey of 600 km2 that became the first stage of the Basin of Mexico survey (Sanders et al. 1979).

THE TEOTIHUACAN VALLEY PROJECT

The Basin of Mexico survey is one of the most influential regional archaeological projects ever undertaken (see figure 2.2). Demonstrating the importance of a regional perspective on ancient urbanism and state formation, it became a model for full-coverage surveys elsewhere in Mesoamerica, the Andes, the US Southwest, and other world regions (Adams 1965). The Project's underlying goal was to: (1) describe socioeconomic institutions in different periods from the establishment of sedentary villages ca. 1000 BCE to the defeat of the Triple Alliance in 1521 and the start of Spanish colonial rule; and (2) explain, in a materialist framework, "ecological processes of evolutionary change" and the centralization and differentiation of cultural systems as regional phenomena. Settlement patterns were seen as an indicator of how people "interact with their natural environment and with other human beings" (Sanders et al. 1979:15).

In 1960, however, there was no methodological precedent for a full-coverage survey in highland Mexico (Parsons, this volume). Earlier work, including a

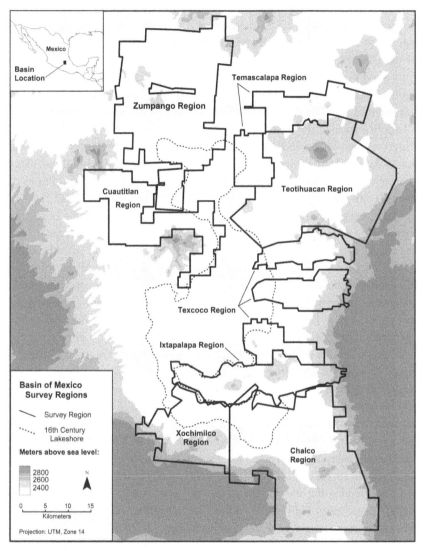

FIGURE 2.2. *Basin of Mexico survey regions. Prepared by L. J. Gorenflo.*

survey by Paul Tolstoy (1958) of the northern Basin of Mexico, showed that archaeological remains, artifact scatters, mounds, and rubble were visible on the ground surface in most areas. Sanders and his students still had to devise strategies to conduct a systematic pedestrian survey for the first time, as only a small number of archaeologists anywhere in the world were doing this kind of research (Parsons 2019). Willey employed aerial photographs to identify sites in the Virú Valley, but that approach appeared unfavorable for the Basin, where erosion, deposition, and plowing had reduced much Prehispanic architecture to mound remnants and artifact scatters. Nonetheless, Jeffrey Parsons drew on his experience with geological surveys to operationalize using aerial photographs for orienteering and mapping surface features and sites (Nichols 2006; Parsons 2019). Survey crews found an array of buildings, plans, and arrangements at sites in the Teotihuacan Valley. To improve the ceramic chronology and to better understand site architecture, Sanders excavated sites of different periods.

In anticipation of the 1968 Olympics in Mexico City, INAH launched a Special Project in 1962–64 at Teotihuacan, led by two of Mexico's most prominent archaeologists, Ignacio Bernal and Jorge Acosta. "Once again the Archaeology of State sought to enhance the ruin's value as potent symbol of the glories of Mexico's past, present, and future" Fash (2013:87). They excavated and restored facades along the Street of the Dead, along with the Temple of the Feathered Serpent, the final phase of the Moon Pyramid, and the Quetzalpapalotl palace. INAH's Special Project, the Teotihuacan Mapping Project, and the Basin of Mexico survey firmly established Teotihuacan as a city, and one of great influence and continuing historical legacy. At Teotihuacan, the 1960s saw a convergence of monumental archaeology and the "new" settlement archaeology, a necessary blend, in Bernal's (1983) view. These projects also began the careers of a generation of Mexican, Canadian, and US archaeologists (Fowler et al. 2015).

Sanders's Teotihuacan Valley Project was the first leg of the Basin of Mexico survey (Evans and Sanders 2000; Sanders 1986, 1987, 1994, 1995, 1996a, 1996b; Sanders and Evans 2001; Sanders et al. 1970, 1975) (see figure 2.2). Unlike the later surveys, the Teotihuacan Valley survey proceeded in stages, subsequently augmented by Thomas Charlton, Charles Kolb, Joseph Marino, and Jeffrey Parsons (Charlton and Nichols 2005; Kolb, this volume; Kolb and Sanders 1976). Parsons had been an undergraduate student at Penn State before working on the Teotihuacan Valley Project as a University of Michigan graduate student. In 1967, he extended the survey east to the Texcoco region (Parsons 1971). James Griffin, the doyen of University of Michigan archaeology, repeatedly challenged Parsons to excavate and be a "real" archaeologist. To Griffin, real archaeology meant digging. Parsons literally stood his ground, and countered, "To be a real archaeologist you have to do survey" (Nichols 2006). Today, regional settlement surveying is a fundamental part of archaeology, but in the 1960s it was pioneering.

Richard Blanton (1972), then a graduate student at the University of Michigan, surveyed the Ixtapalapa region in 1969. In 1969 and 1972 Parsons's team surveyed the southern Chalco-Xochimilco region and then moved north in 1973 to cover the Zumpango region (Parsons 2008; Parsons et al. 1982). After applying his survey methods in the Valley of Guatemala to look at Teotihuacan foreign relations, Sanders returned to survey the Cuauhtitlan and Temascalapa regions of the northern Basin in 1974 and 1975 (Gorenflo and Sanders 2007, 2008; Sanders and

Gorenflo 2007; Sanders and Murdy 1982a, b). Harold McBride (1974) had done a partial survey of the Cuauhtitlan region the year prior to Sanders's survey.

The origins of social complexity in the Formative period was a focus of much research in the 1970s, which moved away from diffusionism to explain interregional interactions. Some early villages first recorded by the surveys were excavated (Santley 1993; Serra Puche and Lazcano Arce 2009). Paul Tolstoy and colleagues (1977) resurveyed almost all of the Early and Middle Formative sites in the 1970s, including many found by Sanders and Parsons's surveys. The rapid growth of Mexico City and the concomitant destruction of many sites led to a hiatus in research on the Formative period for nearly four decades, until Wesley Stoner and I excavated at Altica, the earliest village Sanders had found during the Teotihuacan Valley survey (Stoner and Nichols 2019a). INAH salvage archaeologists recently made important discoveries at Zacatenco, first excavated by Vaillant (1930), where only remnants were still visible in 1974 when Sanders surveyed the Guadalupe Range (INAH 2016).

Just before Sanders began the northern Basin survey, Millon and colleagues (1973) presented the first comprehensive map of Teotihuacan. The Mapping Project revealed a much larger city in both area, ca. 20 km2, and population, which Millon estimated might have exceeded 100,000 people (cf. Cowgill 2015). Sanders's survey of the Teotihuacan Valley did not cover the area of the Teotihuacan Mapping Project. Consequently, pre-and post-Teotihuacan settlements within the Mapping Project area were not recorded by Sanders's survey.

The Basin of Mexico survey covered 3,100 km² and defined 3,900 sites (Gorenflo 2015). Parsons's (1971, 2015) site typology and method of population reconstruction built on estimation procedures developed during the Teotihuacan Valley project, and these have been adapted to other parts of Mesoamerica and the Andes (Balkansky 2006; Feinman 2015; Kowalewski 2008; Nichols 1996). It did not become clear until the Basin of Mexico survey was completed how radically the rapid growth of Teotihuacan in the first century CE restructured regional settlement patterns in one of the most dramatic changes of any period in Mesoamerica. Most settlements in the Basin of Mexico were abandoned, as 85 percent of the population became concentrated at Teotihuacan. Sanders, Parsons, and Santley (1979) concluded that coercion must have been involved in the hyper-nucleation at Teotihuacan, unaware when they wrote of the role of volcanic eruptions that caused people to flee there (Plunket and Uruñuela 2006).

Recognizing Teotihuacan, Tula, Tenochtitlan, Cholula, and Xochicalco as cities revolutionized understandings of ancient Mesoamerica. Publication of the Teotihuacan map made apparent "that our views of Teotihuacan were so warped for so long that our understanding of prehistoric Mesoamerica for the period (AD 200–700) when Teotihuacan played such a key role over so great an area had also become seriously twisted" (Parsons 1977:192–93). The Basin of

Mexico survey and the Teotihuacan Mapping Project also revolutionized how archaeologists investigate states and cities as spatial and regional phenomena. These projects developed in the context of theoretical shifts in anthropology and archaeology and social changes that encouraged a more "middle and working perspective" on archaeology, mostly by men, who often were first-and second-generation immigrants to Mexico and the US. They had grown up during the Great Depression and the rise of fascism, served in the military during the Second World War, and attended universities on the GI Bill, or, in the case of Armillas, had fought in the Spanish Civil War. Key institutional developments included the growth of the INAH and anthropology as the "national discipline of Mexico" (Bernal 1980) and the creation of the NSF in the US.

AFTER THE GREEN BOOK

Although survey has a long history in Mexican archaeology (Bernal 1983; Parsons 1971), the Basin of Mexico survey established the importance of the full-coverage survey (Blanton et al. 2005; Nichols 1996, 2004; Parsons 1972, 1989, 1990, 1997, 2015; Sanders 1965; Sanders et al. 1979). Other surveys in highland Mexico were modeled after the Basin of Mexico survey, including the Tula region (Cobean 1974; Crespo 1998; Healan and Stoutmire 1989; Mastache and Crespo 1974), Morelos (Hare 2001, 2004; Hare et al. n.d.; Hirth 1980, 2000; Montiel 2010), Toluca (Sugiura 2009), and Puebla-Tlaxcalla (Carballo and Pluckhahn 2007; García Cook 1976; Snow 1996). Long-term surveys took place also in Oaxaca (Balkansky et al. 2000; Blanton 1978; Blanton et al. 1982; Byland and Pohl 1994; Finsten 1996; Kowalewski et al. 1989; Markman 1981), the Gulf Coast (Santley and Arnold 1996; Stark 2006; Stoner 2012); the Pacific Coast (Lesure 2011); the Maya highlands (De Montmollin 1985; Sanders and Murdy 1982a, 1982b), and the Maya lowlands (e.g., Webster 1985). The Basin of Mexico survey also influenced surveys in other world regions, including the Andes (e.g., Covey 2014; Goldstein 2005; Stanish 1999; Wilson 1988), and, as discussed by Blanton and colleagues (2005:6), Eurasia (Cherry 2003; Fang et al. 2015); Africa (e.g., Wright 2007), and the US Southwest (Fish and Kowalewski 1990).

Sanders, Parsons, and Santley (1979) offered a materialist cultural evolutionary and ecological model of the origins and development of Prehispanic civilization in the Basin of Mexico. In addition to drawing on Steward, Wittfogel, and Armillas, with some modification, they also incorporated the ideas of agricultural economist Esther Boserup (1965) about population pressure as a driving force of agricultural intensification, as well as urbanism. Following Carneiro (1970), they understood that circumscription, competition, and differential access to strategic resources drove stratification, growth of commerce, and political centralization.

Even before *The Basin of Mexico* was published, criticism of prime mover models and population pressure in social change was intensifying (Blanton 1976).

Millon, unlike Sanders, did not embrace cultural evolutionism. Millon had first gone to Mexico to test Wittfogel's (1938) hydraulic theory, but his research at Teotihuacan led him to reject the hypothesis of a centralized irrigation authority at Teotihuacan for lack of evidence; he instead emphasized cooperative, rather than conflictive aspects of irrigation (Millon and Altschul 2015; Nichols 2018a). Millon's thinking presaged the current interest in collective action (e.g., Carballo and Feinman 2016; Nichols 2015, 2018b). Millon, along with Sanders, acknowledged Steward's important influence on his comparative perspective. The fact that Sanders's and Parsons's research focused on the hinterlands and Millon's focused on Teotihuacan also contributed to their differing views.

Armillas's (1971) important article on *chinampas* and landscape archaeology was published just as Parsons was surveying the *chinampa* zone of the southern Basin of Mexico. Theoretical framing of the politics of hydraulic agriculture has since shifted away from Wittfogel, along with new empirical evidence pointing to local community construction (Acosta Ochoa and McClung de Tapia, this volume; Frederick 2007; Morehart 2012). On the other hand, Luna Golya (2014) argues that *chinampa* expansion indeed depended on central, imperial management of water levels.

When the Basin of Mexico survey began, there was little recognition of the significance of lacustrine resources, lake transportation, and the cultivation of maguey (Parsons 2001, 2006; Serra Puche and Lazcano Arce 2009). Jeff Parsons and Luis Morett (2004, 2005) began the twenty-first century with a survey of the Texcoco lakebed. This was a full-coverage survey, but they applied a siteless approach and employed GPS technology to record site locations. The earlier Basin of Mexico survey had lacked good topographic maps to accurately record site locations. Gorenflo and Parsons revisited many sites to check their condition and confirm their location with GPS (Parsons 2015). The original survey crews had also photographed sites and their surroundings, photographs that can be used to confirm site locations (Bentley Historical Library 2020; Stoner and Nichols 2019a). The aerial photographs used to record sites during the survey now have become valuable documents of environmental history, as well as archaeology.

When the Green Book was published, archaeology was entering a new phase, variously called "processual-plus" and "post-processual" (Hegmon 2003; Nichols and Pool 2012). The 1980s ushered in critiques of processualism, neo-positivism, neo-evolutionism, and prime-mover models. Mexican archaeologist Manuel Gándara (2012) identifies this time with the growth of "thematic archaeologies" focusing on parts of the social spectrum, for example, gender or households, or on a technical approach, such as archaeometry and zooarchaeology. Theoretical diversification accompanied thematic archaeology; agency became in Gándara's (2012) words, "the buzzword," conceiving of people as social actors in contrast to structural explanations (Brumfiel 1992; Nichols and Pool 2012). To Parsons and

Sanders, social relations were as important as environmental relations in shaping settlement patterns, but they emphasized social structure (Sanders et al. 1979).

The intensified focus on social relations and agency developed as more women than ever began to direct archaeology projects in the Basin of Mexico and elsewhere. Although the Basin of Mexico survey was initiated by men, they trained and taught women, who went on to lead their own projects, including Elizabeth M. Brumfiel, Ana Crespo, Susan T. Evans, Mary Hrones Parsons, Mary Hodge, Linda Manzanilla, Guadalupe Mastache, Emily McClung de Tapia, Evelyn Rattray, Marí Carmen Serra Puche, and Yoko Sugiura. The current generation of archaeologists and students is even more diverse.

Because the Basin of Mexico survey was full coverage, it provided a "big picture" of the history of settlement, population, and land use (Blanton et al. 2005; Feinman 2015; Parsons 2015). The survey's archaeologists defined broad types of sites and changes in settlement, hierarchy, and regional sociopolitical relations and examined sites in relation to the biophysical landscape. The survey determined where sites were and, seemingly, where they were not. Sanders, however, was sufficiently concerned about the possibility of buried sites and irrigation features in alluvial settings to apply infrared-aerial photography (Nichols 1982, 1988). Many areas, however, were built over so quickly that they could not be inspected even a decade later. The technology was inferior to current multispectral imagery. Frederick's work (this volume) shows that the problem of buried sites is very real.

The survey data are robust in that they have been interpreted from different theoretical and conceptual frameworks and the artifact collections have been analyzed using methods and techniques that did not exist at the time of the survey (e.g., Smith 2017b) "Properly published," full-coverage surveys "can be used over and over again by different people for new and different purposes" (Sanders et al. 1979:20).

Full coverage surveys also facilitated early applications of geographic models to settlement pattern data (Brumfiel 1976; Earle 1976; Evans 1980; Evans and Gould 1982; García and Moragas-Segura 2017; Gorenflo 2006, 2015; Gorenflo and Gale 1990; Gorenflo and Garraty 2017; Smith 1979, 1980). Subsequently, GIS opened other new analytic and field approaches and Gorenflo (2015) constructed a GIS database with the Basin of Mexico survey for a closer examination of settlement ecology. Ortman and colleagues (2015) recently analyzed survey data to take up questions of urban scaling in a comparative framework.

Sanders, Parsons, and Santley used the survey data to generate the first regional archaeological population estimates for the Basin of Mexico for different time periods. Without a full-coverage survey approach, the magnitude of the population reorganization associated with the growth of Teotihuacan, and its later collapse, the change to the Postclassic city-states and the rapid increase in the

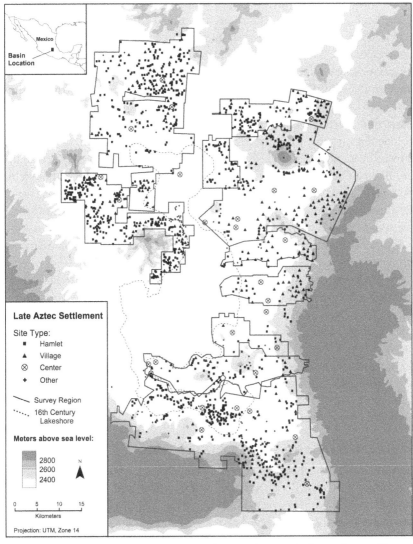

FIGURE 2.3. *Late Postclassic (1350/1400–1521 CE) Basin of Mexico Settlement Pattern Map. Sanders et al. (1979). Used with permission of Jeffrey R. Parsons.*

population during the fourteenth and fifteenth centuries would not have been known (Charlton and Nichols 1997; Paredes Gudiño 2005). The Late Postclassic population explosion, as Smith (2012:61) argues, "brought about a series of fundamental changes throughout Central Mexican society" (see figure 2.3).

Sanders (1976) took his demographic analyses a further step to compare estimates generated by archaeological data with documentary sources. In doing so,

Sanders had to wrestle with several problems. It was not possible to survey most of the large nucleated Late Postclassic towns and cities, such as Azcapotzalco (García Chávez et al. 1991), because they are overlain by Colonial period and modern construction. Sanders also had to address estimating rates of "the severest and most protracted human mortality ever to occur" that took place in the Americas following European expansion and reached Central Mexico in 1519–1521 (Cook and Lovell 1992:216). The earliest reliable census available for the Basin of Mexico puts the population between 404,000 to 407,000 in 1568 (Sanders 1976:130). No one disputes that a decline in population had already occurred by the mid-sixteenth century; the debate is over the magnitude. Sanders (1976) critiqued the "Berkeley School" estimates, showing why they were too high, although his estimate of 1.0 to 1.2 million for the population of the Basin of Mexico is generally considered conservative (Cook and Lovell 1992; Márquez Morfín and Storey 2017; Prem 1992; Whitmore 1991). The tragic population decline from disease and colonialism reshaped both ecology and society in the Basin of Mexico and throughout the Americas (Alchon 2003).

Historical archaeology that grew out of the Basin of Mexico survey has provided more nuanced understandings of the dynamics of change and persistence after 1521, especially in rural areas (Charlton et al. 2015; Fournier and Otis Charlton 2017). Until Thomas Charlton's work, most archaeologists were unaware that their collections of Aztec pottery included Colonial Red and Orange earthen wares and thus provide details about post-1521 settlement. Full-coverage archaeological survey is as valuable for understanding the Colonial and Republican periods as it is for the Prehispanic era, providing a complementary methodology to history and ethnohistory.

ENVIRONMENT AND SOCIETY POST-1979

Even before 1979, archaeologists were using data generated from the survey to critique the Green Book's cultural ecological and evolutionary framework (Brumfiel 1976; Earle 1976). Richard Blanton (1976) felt that a more robust theory than cultural ecology was needed to understand how change at the household and village level articulated with changes at larger spatial scales. He and his colleagues from the Valley of Oaxaca and Monte Albán survey looked to regional analysis and models from geography, as did Smith (1979, 1980) and Gorenflo (2006, 2015). Full-coverage survey made it possible to apply such models and debates ensued between the cultural ecological and political economy approaches. World systems theory and its modifications offered a framework at the inter-regional scales Sanders had sought with his concept of the "Central Mexican Symbiotic Region." These models heighten awareness that states are inter-dependent polities and both politics and environmental interactions are important. Full-coverage survey is a key method for analyzing those relations (Smith and Montiel 2001).

Debates between the cultural ecology and political economy approaches about urbanism prompted a series of projects in the 1980s at Postclassic sites that grew from the Basin of Mexico survey (Brumfiel 1980, 2005; Evans 1985, 1988a, 1988b; Charlton et al. 2000; Hodge 1997). Even by then, the rapid growth of Mexico City and surrounding towns and cities had already destroyed or covered many sites found during the Basin of Mexico survey. Nonetheless, these investigations revealed a diversity of Aztec urbanism and economy (Smith 2017a).

Restudy of the survey collections made possible new approaches for investigating Prehispanic economies at a regional scale and determining change over time. Mary Hodge and Leah Minc (1991) pioneered the analysis of ceramic commodity flows for the study of Middle and Late Postclassic markets, applying stylistic and chemical sourcing to Aztec pottery. Other archaeologists expanded this research to a greater variety of ceramics and other periods (Alex et al. 2012; Charlton et al. 2000, 2008; Clayton 2013; García Chávez 2004; Garraty 2006, 2013; Hodge and Minc 1991; Hodge et al. 1992, 1993; Ma 2003; Minc 2006, 2009; Minc et al. 1994; Neff and Hodge 2008; Neff et al. 1994, 2000; Nichols 2013, 2017b, 2020; Nichols et al. 2000, 2002, 2009, 2013; Rodríguez-Alegría et al. 2013; Stark 2017; Stoner et al. 2015; Stoner and Nichols 2019b; Stoner and Rodríguez-Alegría 2016; Crider this volume). This research has contributed to a major shift in the understanding of pre-modern state economies and the recognition of the role of commerce and household production in Prehispanic Mesoamerica (Feinman 2017; Nichols et al. 2017)

The growth of household archaeology complemented the settlement pattern surveys and furthered the shift from elite-centric approaches. Dominance and resistance narratives entered archaeology. James Scott's (1985) work on everyday practice and small acts of defiance gave archaeologists like Elizabeth Brumfiel "a beachhead from which to scout agency in the material record and to appreciate acts of resistance when they could not transcend structures of power—even if the oppressed do not realize revolution, they still create history" (Rosenzwig and Marston 2018:5).

The new ecology in anthropology, begun with Rappaport's (1968) *Pigs for the Ancestors*, emphasized ecosystems, population, and regulation, but also brought religion and ritual into environmental relations (Biersack 1999). Rappaport's work was one of the impulses for other new ecologies, including historical and political ecology. Historical ecology, resilience theory, and landscape ecology bring together conceptual tools—similar to Steward's (1955) cultural ecology—that facilitate the integration of historical data, including archaeological data, and provide new ways to construct arguments (McClung de Tapia and Martínez Yrizar 2017). Sanders never engaged the shift in cultural anthropology to a focus on culture as a symbolic system and the implications for settlement patterns. With echoes of Rappaport's ritual regulation, McClung de Tapia and Martínez

Yrizar (2017) argue that the complex ritual cycle in which *chinampa* farming was embedded mitigated cosmic and ecological, and, perhaps, political, instability as the Mexica expanded the system into their sacred lake waters. With the concepts of legacy and palimpsest, Mejia-Ramón and Johnson (2019), Millhauser and Morehart (2018), and Morehart (2016) examine the Basin of Mexico as a historical landscape and how land use is shaped by historical legacies. The land use data Sanders recorded for the northern Basin and Teotihuacan Valley could take this work another step and aid in better differentiating Prehispanic from later farming practices (Borejsza, this volume; Gorenflo and Sanders 2007, 2008).

The focus on relational frameworks in political ecology both grows out of the long-running concern of ecology with relationships and reinforces the move away from monolithic views of states and power (Blanton and Fargher 2008; Carballo and Feinman 2016; Millhauser and Morehart 2018). Blaikie and Brookfield (1987) recognized early in the development of political ecology that resource inequalities are both a cause and a consequence of stratification on small and large scales. Millhauser and Morehart (2018) show how, as state-sponsored infrastructure projects expanded in Aztec times, both wetlands and the people using them were differently impacted around Lake Xaltocan.

Ecologically oriented theories, such as those proposed by Sanders, Parsons, and Sanders (1979), attribute a generative role to the environment, along with the transformative power of people (Rosenzwig and Marston 2018:2). The reverse holds in some theories of collapse, where "the environment strikes back" and people are unable to overcome degradation, population overshoot, disaster, or novel infectious diseases. Paleoclimatologists (Lachiniet et al. 2012; Park et al. 2019; Stahle et al. 2011) have recently posited prolonged drought as a cause of or contributing factor in Teotihuacan's decline, although the mechanisms (reduced hinterland provisioning capacity, for example), are not spelled out (Gómez Chávez and Gazzola 2009; Moragas 2005; Nichols 2017a). With long-standing research about environmental relations, the Basin of Mexico should be a key region for collaboration between climate scientists and archaeologists.

CONCLUSIONS

Urbanism and human-environment relations represent two of archaeology's grand challenges. Sanders and Parsons recognized that these big questions required systematic regional data, a robust methodology, and a sustained commitment, through to the publication of the *The Basin of Mexico* book and multiple monographs. Big questions of archaeology drove the Basin of Mexico survey, resting on institutional and social developments in both Mexico and the United States. The data have proven robust, but they can be improved. Compared to early twenty-first-century remote-sensing capabilities, Sanders and Parsons and Millon's use of aerial photography, though pathbreaking in the 1960s, has now been surpassed. LiDAR, multispectral imaging, and geophysics offer important advances, but as complements to, *not* substitutes for, the full-coverage pedestrian survey. The aerial photographs employed during the survey in the 1960s and 1970s have themselves become important historical records of a landscape that no longer exists. Millhauser and Morehart's (2018) recent settlement map of the Lake Xaltocan area highlights the importance of updating the Basin of Mexico settlement pattern maps.

Mexican archaeologists have used the survey data and settlement pattern maps in salvage archaeology that has been especially important for understanding Teotihuacan's hinterlands (Charlton et al. 2005; Clayton 2013; Gamboa and Vélez Saldaña 2005; García Chávez 1991, 2004; García Chávez et al. 1991, 2005, 2015; Nichols 2020). As José Luis Lorenzo aptly put it, we cannot "defend, protect, and study something when we don't know where it is" (Lorenzo 1981:205). Therefore, integrating findings from salvage archaeology to improve the survey data and maps is a significant but important task.

The Basin of Mexico survey collections were "grab" samples of diagnostic pottery, figurines, and sometimes spindle whorls, collected primarily for dating. For logistical reasons, collections were not made at all small Late Postclassic sites. An inventory of Parsons's survey collections artifacts is underway. When the Basin of Mexico survey started, the revolution in technological studies of lithic artifacts was just beginning, and chipped stone artifacts were not routinely collected. Smith's survey of the Yautepec Valley of Morelos, which was modeled after the Basin of Mexico survey, employed a multi-stage approach to sampling surface artifacts that included lithics (Hare et al. n.d.; Montiel 2010). This improved dating multicomponent sites, information on site function, and sample comparability. The Basin of Mexico survey would have been better if it had used such systematic collection methods, and where still possible, supplementing the original collections remains worthwhile.

The Basin of Mexico and settlement pattern monographs amplified the impact of the Basin of Mexico survey on science and on Mexico's heritage. Sanders, Parsons, and Santley's (1979) book captured cultural ecology and neo-evolution at a moment when new theoretical frameworks were emerging in the social sciences. The Green Book made an enduring contribution by engaging big questions about the relationships of society and environment as regional and historical and by making the case for the full-coverage survey. I encourage new generations of archaeologists to build on and advance its legacy.

Acknowledgments. My introduction to archaeology in Mexico came though working on the final leg of the Basin of Mexico survey in Cuauhtitlan and the Ecatepec regions and then Temascalapa. That fieldwork shaped my career, and I am fortunate to have had the opportunity to work with both Bill Sanders and Jeff Parsons. None of this research would have been possible without the Consejo de Arqueología, Instituto Nacional de Antropología e Historia, Mexico. The Archaeology Program of the National Science Foundation provided the major funding for the Basin of Mexico survey with grants to William T. Sanders at The Pennsylvania State University and Jeffrey R. Parsons at the University of Michigan. Portions of this paper were worked on as part my 2018 Gordon R. Willey Lecture at the Peabody Museum, Harvard University, which was especially fitting as Bill Sanders talked of the Tozzer library as having been his intellectual home when he was a student there.

REFERENCES

Adams, Robert McCormick. 1965. *The Land behind Baghdad: A History of Settlement on the Diyala Plains*. University of Chicago Press.

Alchon, Suzanne Austin. 2003. *A Pest in the Land: New World Epidemics in a Global Perspective*. University of New Mexico Press, Albuquerque.

Alex, Bridget, Deborah L. Nichols, and Michael D. Glascock. 2012. "Complementary Compositional Analysis of Formative Period Ceramics from the Teotihuacan Valley." *Archaeometry* 54:821–34.

Ammerman, A. J. 1981. "Surveys and Archaeological Research." *Annual Review of Anthropology* 10:63–88.

Armillas, Pedro. 1971. "Gardens on Swamps." *Science* 174:654–61.

Balkansky, Andrew K. 2006. "Surveys and Mesoamerican Archaeology: The Emerging Macroregional Paradigm." *Journal of Archaeological Research* 14:53–95.

Balkansky, Andrew K., Stephen A. Kowalewski, Verónica Pérez Rodríguez, Thomas J. Pluckhahn, Charlotte A. Smith, Laura R. Stiver, Dmitri Beliaev, John F. Chalblee, Vernice Y Heredia Espinoza, and Roberto Santos Pérez. 2000. "Archaeological Survey in the Mixteca Alta of Oaxaca, Mexico." *Journal of Field Archaeology* 27:365–89.

Bentley Historical Library. 2020. Jeffrey R. Parsons Archaeological Sites Images. University of Michigan, Ann Arbor. Electronic document. https://quod.lib.umich.edu/b/bhl3ic, accessed August 1, 2020.

Bernal, Ignacio. 1980. *A History of Mexican Archaeology: The Vanished Civilizations of Middle America*. Thames & Hudson, New York.

Bernal, Ignacio. 1983. "The Effect of Settlement Pattern Studies on the Archaeology of Central Mexico." In *Prehistoric Settlement Patterns: Essays in Honor of Gordon R. Willey*, edited by Evon Z. Vogt and Richard M. Leventhal, 389–99. University of New Press and Harvard University Press, Albuquerque and Cambridge, MA.

Biersack, Aletta. 1999. "From the 'New Ecology' to the New Ecologies." *American Anthropologist* 101:5–18.

Blaike, Piers, and Harold Brookfield. 1987. *Land Degradation and Society*. Metheun, London.

Blanton, Richard E. 1972. *Prehepatic Settlement Patterns in the Ixtapalapa Peninsula Region, Mexico.* Occasional Papers in Anthropology, no. 6. Department of Anthropology, The Pennsylvania State University, University Park.

Blanton, Richard E. 1976. "The Role of Symbiosis in Adaptation and Sociocultural Change in the Valley of Mexico." In *The Valley of Mexico: Studies of Pre-Hispanic Ecology and Society,* edited by Eric R. Wolf, 181–202. University of New Mexico Press, Albuquerque.

Blanton, Richard E. 1978. *Monte Albán: Settlement Patterns at the Ancient Zapotec Capital.* Academic Press, New York.

Blanton, Richard E. 2002. "Archaeologist at Work." In *Archaeology: Original Readings in Method and Practice,* edited by Peter N. Peregrine, Carol R. Ember, and Melvin Ember, 398–408. Prentice Hall, Upper Saddle River, NJ.

Blanton, Richard E. 2005. "The Achievements of and Prospects of Survey Archaeology." In *Settlement, Subsistence, and Social Complexity,* edited by Richard E. Blanton, 295–301. Cotsen Institute of Archaeology, University of California, Los Angeles.

Blanton, Richard E., and Lane F. Fargher. 2008. *Collective Action in the Formation of Pre-Modern States.* Springer, New York.

Blanton, Richard E., Mary Hrones Parsons, Luis Morett Alatorre, and Carla M. Sinopoli. 2005. "Introduction." In *Settlement, Subsistence, and Social Complexity: Essays Honoring the Legacy of Jeffrey R. Parsons,* 1–18. Cotsen Institute of Archaeology, University of California, Los Angeles.

Blanton, Richard E., Stephen A. Kowalewski, Gary M. Feinman, and Jill Appel. 1982. *Monte Albán's Hinterland,* pt. 1: *The Prehispanic Settlement Patterns of the Central and Southern Parts of the Valley of Oaxaca, Mexico.* Memoirs of the Museum of Anthropology, no. 15. University of Michigan, Ann Arbor.

Boserup, Ester. 1965. *The Conditions of Agricultural Growth: The Economics of Agrarian Change under Population Pressure.* Aldine, Chicago.

Brumfiel, Elizabeth M. 1976. "Regional Growth in the Eastern Valley of Mexico: A Test of the 'Population Pressure' Hypothesis." In *The Early Mesoamerican Village,* edited by K. Flannery, 234–47. Academic Press, New York.

Brumfiel, Elizabeth M. 1980. "Specialization, Market Exchange, and the Aztec State: A View from Huexotla, Mexico." *Current Anthropology* 21:459–78.

Brumfiel, Elizabeth M. 1992. "Breaking and Entering the Ecosystem: Gender, Class, and Fraction Steal the Show." *American Anthropologist* 89:676–86.

Brumfiel, Elizabeth, ed. 2005. *Production and Power at Postclassic Xaltocan / La producción local y el poder en el Xaltocan Posclásico.* Serie Aqueología de México, Instituto Nacional de Antropología e História and University of Pittsburgh, México, Mexico City & Pittsburgh.

Byland, Bruce, and John M. D. Pohl. 1994. *In the Realm of 8 Deer: The Archaeology of Mixtec Codexes.* University of Oklahoma Press, Norman.

Carballo, David M., and Gary M. Feinman. 2016. "Cooperation, Collective Action, and the Archaeology of Large-scale Societies." *Evolutionary Anthropology* 25:288–96.

Carballo, David M., and Timothy Pluckhahn. 2007. "Transportation Corridors and Political Evolution in Highland Mesoamerica: Settlement Analyses Incorporating GIS for Northern Tlaxcala, Mexico." *Journal of Anthropological Archaeology* 26:607–29.

Carneiro, Robert L. 1970. "Theory of the Origin of the State." *Science* 169:733–38.

Charlton, Thomas H., and Deborah L. Nichols. 1997. "Diachronic Studies of City-States: Permutations on a Theme, Central Mexico from 1600 BC to AD 1600." In *The Archaeology of City-States: Cross-Cultural Approaches*, edited by Deborah L. Nichols and Thomas H. Charlton, 169–207. Smithsonian Institution Press, Washington, DC.

Charlton, Thomas H., and Deborah L. Nichols. 2005. "Settlement Pattern Archaeology in the Teotihuacan Valley and the Northeastern Basin of Mexico A. P. (After Parsons)." In *Settlement and Subsistence in Early Civilizations: Essays Reflecting the Contributions of Jeffrey R. Parsons*, edited by Richard E. Blanton, 43–62. Cotsen Institute of Archaeology, University of California, Los Angeles.

Charlton, Thomas H., Deborah L. Nichols, and Cynthia Otis Charlton. 2000. "Otumba and Its Neighbors: Ex Oriente Lux." *Ancient Mesoamerica* 11:247–66.

Charlton, Thomas H., Raúl García Chávez, Cynthia O. Charlton, Verónica Ortega, David O. Andrade O. D., and Teresa Palomares. 2005. "Salvamento arqueológico reciente en el valle de Teotihuacan: Sito TC-83, San Bartolomé el Alto." In *Arquitectura y urbanismo: Pasado y presente de los espacios en Teotihuacan*. Memoria de la Tercer Mesa Redonda de Teotihuacan, edited by María Elena Ruiz Gallut, and Jesús Torres Peralta, J., 343–72. Instituto Nacional de Antropología e Historia, Mexico City.

Charlton, Thomas H., Cynthia L. Otis Charlton, Deborah L. Nichols, and Hector Neff. 2008. "Aztec Otumba, AD 1200–1600: Patterns of the Production, Distribution, and Consumption of Ceramic Products." In *Pottery Economics in Mesoamerica*, edited by Christopher A. Pool and George J. Bey III, 237–66. University of Arizona Press, Tucson.

Charlton, Thomas H., Patricia Fournier, and Cynthia Otis Charlton. 2015. "Historical Archaeology in the Basin of Mexico and the Central Mexican Symbiotic Region: Development, Present Status, Future Prospects." *Ancient Mesoamerica* 27:459–70.

Cherry, John F. 2003. "Archaeology beyond the Site: Regional Survey and Its Theory and Practice." In *Theory and Practice in Mediterranean Archaeology: Old World and New World Perspectives*, edited by J. K. Papadapolous and Richard M. Levanthal, 137–59. Cotsen Institute of Archaeology, University of California, Los Angeles.

Childe, V. Gordon. 1950. "The Urban Revolution." *Town Planning Review* 21:3–17.

Clayton, Sarah. 2013. "Measuring the Long Arm of the State: Teotihuacan's Relations in the Basin of Mexico." *Ancient Mesoamerica* 24:87–105.

Cobean, Robert H. 1974. "Archaeological Survey of the Tula Region." In *Studies of Ancient Tollan: A Report of the University of Missouri Tula Archaeological Project*, edited by Richard Diehl, 6–10. University of Missouri Monographs in Anthropology 1. University of Missouri, Columbia.

Coffey, Mary K. 2020. *Orozco's American Epic: Myth, History, and the Melancholy of Race.* Duke University Press, Durham, NC.

Cook, Noble David, and W. George Lovell. 1992. "Unraveling the Web of Disease." In *"Secret Judgments of God": Old World Disease in Colonial Spanish America*, edited by Noble David Cook and W. George Lovell, 213–42. University of Oklahoma Press, Norman.

Covey, R. Alan. 2014. *Regional Archaeology in the Inca Heartland: Hanan Cuzco Surveys.* Memoirs of the Museum of Anthropology, no. 55. University of Michigan, Ann Arbor.

Cowgill, George L. 2015. *Ancient Teotihuacan: Early Urbanism in Central Mexico.* Cambridge University Press, Cambridge.

Crespo, Ana M. 1998. "La expansion de la frontera norte (y la cronología oficial para Teotihuacan)." In *Los ritmos de cambio en Teotihuacan: Reflexiones y discusiones de su cronología*, edited by Rosa Brambila and Rubén Cabrera, 323–34. Instituto Nacional de Antropología e Historia, Mexico City.

De Montmollin, Olivier. 1985. *Settlement Pattern Survey in the Rosario Valley, Chiapas, Mexico.* Centre of Latin American Studies Working Papers, no. 41. Centre of Latin American Studies, University of Cambridge, Cambridge.

Earle, Timothy. 1976. "A Nearest-Neighbor Analysis of Two Formative Settlement Systems." In *The Early Mesoamerican Village*, edited by K. Flannery, 195–224. Academic Press, New York.

Evans, Susan T. 1980. "Spatial Analysis of Basin of Mexico Settlement: Problems with the Use of the Central Place Model." *American Antiquity* 45:866–75.

Evans, Susan T. 1985. "The Cerro Gordo Site: A Rural Settlement of the Aztec Period in the Basin of Mexico." *Journal of Field Archaeology* 12:1–18.

Evans, Susan T., ed. 1988a. *Cihuatecpan: The Village in Its Ecological and Historical Context.* Vanderbilt University, Nashville, TN.

Evans, Susan T., ed. 1988b. *Excavations at Cihuatecpan, an Aztec Village in the Teotihuacan Valley.* Publications in Anthropology, no. 36. Vanderbilt University, Nashville, TN.

Evans, Susan T., and Peter Gould. 1982. "Settlement Models in Archaeology." *Journal of Anthropological Archaeology* 1:275–304.

Evans, Susan T., and William T. Sanders, eds. 2000. "The Aztec Period Occupation of the Valley," pt. 1: "Natural Environment, Twentieth-Century Occupation, Survey Methodology and Site Descriptions." In *The Teotihuacan Valley Project Final Report*, vol. 5. Occasional Papers in Anthropology, no. 25. Department of Anthropology, The Pennsylvania State University, University Park.

Fang, Hui, Gary M. Feinman, and Linda M. Nicholas. 2015. "Imperial Expansion, Public Investment, and the Long Path of History: China's Initial Political Unification and Its Aftermath." *Proceedings of the National Academy of Sciences* 112:9224–27.

Fash, William L. 2013. "A Millennial Legacy: The Teotihuacan Sun Pyramid as the Central Place in the Centennial of Mexican Independence, and the Archaeology of the State in Mexico." In *Constructing, Deconstructing, and Reconstructing Social Identity: 2,000 Years of Monumentality in Teotihuacan and Cholula, Mexico*, edited by Saburo Sugiyama, Tomoko Taiguchi, and Shigeru Kabata, 83–94. Journal of the Cultural Symbiosis Research Institute Aichi Prefectural University, Japan.

Feinman, Gary M. 2015. "Settlement and Landscape Archaeology." *International Encyclopedia of the Social and Behavioral Sciences*, edited by Neil J. Smelser and Paul B. Bates, 654–58. Elsevier, New York.

Feinman, Gary M. 2017. "Aztec Political Economy: A New Conceptual Frame." *Antiquity* 91:1663–66.

Finsten, Laura M. 1996. "Periphery and Frontier in Southern Mexico: The Mixtec Sierra in Southern Mexico." In *Pre-Columbian World Systems*, edited by Peter N. Peregrine and Gary M. Feinman, 77–96. Prehistory Press, Madison, WI.

Fish, Suzanne K., and Stephen A. Kowalewski. 1990. *The Archaeology of Regions: A Case for Full-Coverage Survey*. Smithsonian Institution Press, Washington, DC.

Flannery, Kent V. 1976. *The Early Mesoamerican Village*. Academic Press, New York.

Florescano, Enrique. 2002. "Los paradigmas mesoamericanos que unificaron la reconstrucción del pasado: El mito de la creación del cosmos; la fundación del reino maravilloso (Tollán), y Quetzalcóatl, el creador de estados y dinastías." *Historia Mexicana* 52:309–59.

Fournier, Patricia G., and Cynthia L. Otis Charlton. 2017. "Post-Conquest Rural Aztec Archaeology." In *Oxford Handbook of the Aztecs*, edited by Deborah L. Nichols and Enrique Rodríguez-Alegría, 643–61. Oxford University Press, New York.

Fowler, William R., Ian G. Robertson, and L. J. Gorenflo. 2015. "Introduction: Taking Stock of Basin of Mexico Archaeology in the Early Twenty-First Century." *Ancient Mesoamerica* 26:127–34.

Frederick, Charles D. 2007. "Chinampa Cultivation in the Basin of Mexico: Observations on the Evolution of Form and Function." In *Seeking a Richer Harvest: The Archaeology of Subsistence Intensification, Innovation, and Change*, edited by Tina L. Thurston and Christopher T. Fisher, 107–24. Springer, New York.

Freeman, Leslie G. 1986. "Pedro Armillas García (1914–1984)." *American Anthropologist* 88:687–92.

Gamboa Cabezas, Luis M., and Nadia Vélez Saldaña. 2005. "Un sitio teotihuacano de la fase Tlamimilolpa al sureste de la Cuenca de México: Huixtoco (San Buenaventura)." In *Arquitectura y urbanismo: Pasado y presente de los espacios en Teotihuacan; Memoria de la Tercera Mesa Redonda de Teotihuacan*, edited by María Elena Ruiz Gallut and Jesús Torres Peralta, 325–42. Instituto Nacional de Antropología e Historia, Mexico City.

Gamio, Manuel. 1922. *La población del Valle de Teotihuacán*. 3 vols. Dirección de Antropología, Secretaría de Agricultura y Fomento, Mexico City.

Gamio, Manuel. 1928. "Las excavaciones del Pedregal de San Angel y la cultura arcaica del Valle de México." *Annals of the XX International Congress of Americanists* 2:127–43.

Gándara, Manuel. 2011. *El analisis teorico en ciencias sociales: Aplicacion a una teoria del origen del estado en Mesoamerica.* El Colegio de Michoacán, Zamora.

Gándara, Manuel. 2012. "A Short History of Theory in Mesoamerican Archaeology." In *Oxford Handbook of Mesoamerican Archaeology*, edited by Deborah L. Nichols and Christopher A. Pool, 31–47. Oxford University Press, New York.

García Cook, Angel, ed. 1976. *El proyecto arqueológico Puebla-Tlaxcala*, vol. 1: Suplemento, *Communicaciones.* Fundación Alemana para la Investigación Científica, Puebla.

García Chávez, Raúl. 1991. "Desarrollo cultural de Atzcapotzalco y el area suroccidental de la Cuenca de México, desde el Preclásico Medio hasta el Epiclásico." Tesis de Licenciado, Escuela Nacional de Antropología e História, Instituto Nacional de Antropología e História, Mexico City.

García Chávez, Raúl. 2004. "De Tula a Azcapotzalco: Caracterización arqueológica de los altepetl de la Cuenca de México del Posclásico Temprano y Medio, a través del estudio cerámico regional." Tesis de doctorado, Universidad Nacional Autónoma de México, Mexico City.

García Chávez, Raúl, and Natalia Moragas-Segura. 2017. "Historia y arqueología de la formación del altepetl en la Cuenca de México durante el Posclásico Medio." *Revista española de antropología americana* 47:219–38.

García Chávez, Raúl, Michael D. Glascock, J. Michael Elam, and Harry B. Iceland. 1991. "The INAH Salvage Archaeology Excavations at Azcapotzaclo, Mexico: Analysis of the Lithic Assemblage." *Ancient Mesoamerica* 1:225–32.

García Chávez, Raúl, Luis M. C. Gamboa, and Nadia Vélez Saldaña. 2005. "Excavaciones recientes en un sitio de fase Tlamimilolpa en Cuautitlán Izcalli, Estado de México." In *Arquitectura y urbanismo: Pasado y presente de los espacios en Teotihuacan*. Memoria de la Tercer Mesa Redonda de Teotihuacan, edited by María Elena Ruiz Gallut, and Jesus Torres Peralta, J., 487–508. Instituto Nacional de Antropología e Historia, Mexico City.

García Chávez, Raúl, Luis M. Gamboa, and Nadia Vélez Saldaña. 2015. "Los sitios rurales y la estrategia expansionista del estado Teotihuacano par la captacion de recursos de la Cuenca de México." *Ancient Mesoamerica* 26:423–42.

Garraty, Christopher P. 2006. "The Politics of Commerce: Aztec Pottery Production and Exchange in the Basin of Mexico, A.D. 1200–1650." PhD dissertation, School of Human Evolution and Social Change, Arizona State University, Tempe.

Garraty, Christopher P. 2013. "Market Development and Expansion under Aztec and Spanish Rule in Cerro Portezuelo." *Ancient Mesoamerica* 24:151–76.

Gazzola. Julie. 2017. "Reappraising Architectural Processes at the Ciudadela through Recent Evidence." In *Teotihuacan: City of Fire*, edited by Matthew H. Robb, 38–37.

Fine Arts Museums of San Francisco, de Young and University of California Press, San Francisco and Los Angeles.

Glaeser, Edward. 2011. *Triumph of the City*. Penguin, New York.

Goldstein, Paul S. 2005. *Andean Diaspora: The Tiwanaku Colonies and the Origins of South American Empire*. University of Florida Press, Gainesville.

Gómez Chávez, Sergio. 2017. "The Underworld at Teotihuacan: The Sacred Cave under the Feathered Serpent Pyramid." In *Teotihuacan: City of Fire*, edited by Matthew H. Robb, 48–55. Fine Arts Museums of San Francisco, de Young and University of California Press, San Francisco and Los Angeles.

Gómez Chávez, Sergio, and Julie Gazzola. 2009. "Una propuesta sobre el proceso, factores y condiciones del colapso de Teotihuacan." *Dimensión antropológica* 31:7–57.

Gorenflo, L. J. 2006. "The Evolution of Regional Demography and Settlement in the Prehispanic Basin of Mexico." In *Population and Preindustrial Cities: A Cross-Cultural Perspective*, edited by G. Storey, 295–314. University of Alabama Press, Tuscaloosa.

Gorenflo, L. J. 2015. "Compilation and Analysis of Pre-Columbian Settlement Data in the Basin of Mexico." *Ancient Mesoamerica* 26:197–212.

Gorenflo, L. J., and Christopher P. Garraty. 2017. "Aztec Regional Settlement History and Chronology." In *Oxford Handbook of the Aztecs*, edited by Deborah L. Nichols and Enrique Rodríguez-Alegría, 77–91. Oxford University Press, New York.

Gorenflo, L., and N. Gale. 1990. "Mapping Regional Settlement in Information Space." *Journal of Anthropological Archaeology* 9:240–74.

Gorenflo, L., and W. Sanders. 2007. *Archaeological Settlement Pattern Data from the Cuautitlan, Temascalapa, and Teotihuacan Regions, Mexico*. Occasional Papers in Anthropology, no. 30. Department of Anthropology, The Pennsylvania State University, University Park.

Gorenflo, L., and W. Sanders. 2008. *Prehispanic Settlement Patterns in the Temascalapa Region, Mexico*. Occasional Papers in Anthropology, no. 31. Department of Anthropology, The Pennsylvania State University, University Park.

Hare, Timothy S. 2001. "Political Economy, Spatial Analysis, and Postclassic States in the Yautepec Valley, Mexico." PhD dissertation, Department of Anthropology, State University of New York, Albany.

Hare, Timothy S. 2004. "Using Measures of Cost Distance in the Estimation of Polity Boundaries in the Postclassic Yautepec Valley, Mexico." *Journal of Archaeological Science* 31:799–814.

Hare, Timothy S., Lisa Montiel, and Michael E. Smith. n.d. *Prehispanic Settlement Patterns in the Yautepec Valley, Morelos, Mexico*. Manuscript in preparation.

Healan, Dan M., and James W. Stoutamire. 1989. "Surface Survey of the Tula Urban Zone." In *Tula of the Toltecs: Excavations and Survey*, edited by Dan M. Healan, 203–38. University of Iowa Press, Iowa City.

Hegmon, Michelle. 2003. "Setting Theoretical Egos Aside: Issues and Theory in North American Archaeology." *American Antiquity* 68:213–43.

Hirth, Kenneth G. 1980. *Eastern Morelos and Teotihuacan: A Settlement Survey*. Publications in Anthropology, no. 25. Vanderbilt University, Nashville, TN.

Hirth, Kenneth G., ed. 2000. *The Xochicalco Mapping Project: Archaeological Research at Xochicalco*. 2 vols. University of Utah Press, Salt Lake City.

Hodge, Mary G. 1997. *Place of Jade: Society and Economy in Ancient Chalco*. Memoirs in Latin American Archaeology, University of Pittsburgh, Pittsburgh, PA.

Hodge, Mary G., and Leah Minc. 1991. "Aztec-Period Ceramic Distribution and Exchange Systems." Report submitted to the National Science Foundation., Washington, DC.

Hodge, Mary G., Hector Neff, M. James Blackman, and Leah D. Minc. 1992. "A Compositional Perspective on Ceramic Production in the Aztec Empire." In *Chemical Characterization of Ceramic Pastes in Archaeology*, edited by Hector Neff, 203–31. Monographs in World Archaeology, no. 7. Prehistory Press, Madison, WI.

Hodge, Mary G., Hector Neff, M. James Blackman, and Leah. D. Minc. 1993. "Black-on-Orange Ceramic Production in the Aztec Empire's Heartland." *Latin American Antiquity* 4:130–57.

INAH (Instituto Nacional de Antropología e Historia). 2016. "Recuperon los restos de más 140 antiguos habitantes de Zacatanco al norte de la CDMX." Electronic document, https://www.inah.gob.mx/boletines/5699-recuperan-los-restos-de-mas-de-140-antiguos-habitantes-de-zacatenco-al-norte-de-la-cdmx, accessed August 3, 2020.

Kintigh et al. 2014.

Kolb, Charles C., and William T. Sanders. 1976. "The Surface Survey." In "The Teotihuacan Period Occupation of the Valley," pt. 3: "The Surface Survey," edited by William T. Sanders, 484–678. In *The Teotihuacan Valley Project Final Report*, vol. 3. Occasional Papers in Anthropology, no. 21. Department of Anthropology, The Pennsylvania State University, University Park.

Kowalewski, Stephen A. 2008. "Regional Settlement Pattern Studies." *Journal of Archaeological Research* 16:225–85.

Kowalewski, Stephen A., Gary Feinman, Laura Finsten, Richard E. Blanton, and Linda Nicholas. 1989. *Monte Albán's Hinterland*, pt. 2: *Prehispanic Settlement Patterns in Tlacolula, Etla, and Ocotlán, the Valley of Oaxaca, Mexico*. Memoirs of the Museum of Anthropology, no. 23. University of Michigan, Ann Arbor.

Lachiniet, Matthew S., Juan Pablo Bernal, Ymane Asmeron, Victor Polyak, and Dolores Piperno. 2012. "A 2400 Yr Mesoamerican Rainfall Reconstruction Links Climate and Cultural Change." *Geology* 40(3):259–62. https://doi/10.1130/G32471.1.

Lesure, Richard. 2011. *Early Mesoamerican Social Transformations: Archaic and Early Formative Social Transformations in the Soconusco Region*. University of California Press, Berkeley.

López Luján, Leonardo, and Michelle De Anda Rogel. 2019. "Teotihuacan in Mexico-Tenochtitlan: Recent Discoveries, New Insights." *The PARI Journal* 19:1–26.

Lorenzo, José Luis. 1981. "Archaeology South of the Río Grande." *World Archaeology* 13:190–208.

Luna Goyla, Gregory. 2014. "Modeling the Aztec Agricultural Waterscape of Lake Xochimilco: A GIS Analysis of Lakebed Chinampas and Settlement." PhD dissertation, Department of Anthropology, The Pennsylvania State University, University Park.

Ma, Marina K. S. 2003. "Examining Prehispanic Ceramic Exchange in the Basin of Mexico: A Chemical Source Analysis from Azcapotzalco." Senior Honors Thesis in Anthropology, Dartmouth College, Hanover, NH.

Markman, Charles W. 1981. *Prehispanic Settlement Dynamics in Central Oaxaca, Mexico: A View from the Miahuatlan Valley*. Publications in Anthropology, no. 26. Vanderbilt University, Nashville, TN.

Márquez Morfín, Lourdes, and Rebecca Storey. 2017. "Population History in Precolumbian and Colonial Times." In *Oxford Handbook of the Aztecs*, edited by Deborah L. Nichols and Enrique Rodríguez-Alegría, 189–200. Oxford University Press, New York.

Mastache, Alba Guadalupe, and Ana María Crespo. 1974. "La ocupacíon prehispánica en el área de Tula, Hidalgo." In *Proyecto Tula*, edited by Eduardo Matos Moctezuma, pt. 1, 71–103. Colección Científica, 15. Instituto Nacional de Antropología e Historia, Mexico City.

McBride, Harold. 1974. "Formative Ceramics and Prehistoric Settlement Patterns in the Cuauhtitlan Region, Mexico." PhD dissertation, Department of Anthropology, University of California, Los Angeles.

McClung de Tapia, Emily, and Dina Martínez Yrizar. 2017. "Aztec Agricultural Production in a Historical Ecological Perspective." In *Oxford Handbook of the Aztecs*, edited by Deborah L. Nichols and Enrique Rodríguez-Alegría, 175–88. Oxford University Press, New York.

Mejía-Ramón, Andrés, and Nadia E. Johnson. 2019. "Sociopolitical Organization, Landscape Change, and Engineering in the Teotihuacan Valley Mexico, 1250 B.C.–A.D. 1810." *WIRES Water*, 6(2):e1335. https://doi.org/10.1002/wat2.1335.

Millhauser, John K., and Christopher T. Morehart. 2018. "Sustainability as a Relative Process; In Uneven Terrain: Archaeologies of Political Ecology," edited by John K. Millhauser, Christopher T. Morehart and Santiago Juarez. *Archaeological Papers of the American Anthropological Association*, 29(1):134–56.

Millon, R., B. Drewett, and G. Cowgill. 1973. *Urbanization at Teotihuacan, Mexico*, vol. 1: *The Teotihuacan Map*. University of Texas Press, Austin.

Millon, René and Jeffrey H. Altschul. 2015. "The Making of the Map: The Origin and Lessons of the Teotihuacan Mapping Project." *Ancient Mesoamerica* 26:135–51.

Millon, René. 1973. *Urbanization at Teotihuacan, Mexico*, vol. 1: *The Teotihuacán Map*, pt. 1: *Text*. University of Texas Press, Austin.

Minc, Leah. 2006. "Monitoring Regional Market Systems in Prehistory: Models, Methods, and Metrics." *Journal of Anthropological Archaeology* 25:82–116.

Minc, Leah. 2009. "Style and Substance: Evidence for Regionalism within the Aztec Market System." *Latin American Antiquity* 2:343–74.

Minc, Leah D., Mary G. Hodge, and M. J. Blackman. 1994. "Stylistic and Spatial Variability in Early Aztec Ceramics: Insights into Pre-Imperial Exchange Systems." In *Economies and Polities in the Aztec Realm*, edited by Mary G. Hodge and Michael E. Smith, 134–73. Institute for Mesoamerican Studies, University at Albany, State University of New York, Albany.

Montiel, Lisa. 2010. "Teotihuacan Imperialism in the Yautepec Valley, Morelos." PhD dissertation, Department of Anthropology. SUNY-Albany, Albany, New York.

Moragas Segura, Natalia. 2005. "Sobreviviendo al colapso: Teotihuacanos y coyotlatelcos en Teotihuacan." *Revista española de antropología americana* 35:33–50.

Morehart, Christopher. 2012. "Mapping Ancient Chinampa Landscapes in the Basin of Mexico: A Remote Sensing and GIS Approach." *Journal of Archaeological Science* 39:2541–51.

Morehart, Christopher. 2016. "Let the Earth Forever Remain! Landscape Legacies and the Materiality of History in the Northern Basin of Mexico." *Journal of the Royal Anthropological Institute* 22:939–61.

Neff, Hector, and Mary G. Hodge. 2008. "Serving Vessel Production at Chalco: Evidence from Neutron Activation Analysis." In *Place of Jade: Society and Economy in Ancient Chalco*, edited by Mary G. Hodge, 185–224. Latin American Archaeology Report. Instituto Nacional de Antropología e Historia, Mexico City; University of Pittsburgh, Pittsburgh.

Neff, Hector, et al. 1994. "Neutron Activation Analysis of Late Postclassic Polychrome Pottery from Central Mexico." In *Mixteca-Puebla: Discoveries and Research in Mesoamerican Art and Archaeology*, edited by H. B. Nicholson and Eloise Quiñones Keber, 117–41. Labyrinthos, Culver City, CA.

Neff, Hector, Michael D. Glascock, Thomas H. Charlton, Cynthia Otis Charlton, and Deborah L. Nichols. 2000. "Provenience Investigation of Ceramics and Obsidian from Otumba." *Ancient Mesoamerica* 11:207–322.

Nichols, Deborah L. 1982. "A Middle Formative Irrigation System near Santa Clara Coatitlán in the Basin of Mexico." *American Antiquity* 47(1):133–44.

Nichols, Deborah L. 1988. "Infrared Aerial Photography and Prehispanic Irrigation at Teotihuacan: The Tlajinga Canals." *Journal of Field Archaeology* 15:17–27.

Nichols, Deborah L. 1996. "An Overview of Regional Settlement Pattern Studies in Mesoamerica: 1960–1995." *Arqueología mesoamericana: Homenaje a William T. Sanders.* 2 vols. Edited by A. Guadalupe Mastache, Jeffrey R. Parsons, Mari Carmen Serra Puche, and Robert S. Santley, 1:59–96. Instituto Nacional de Antropología e Historia, Mexico City.

Nichols, Deborah L. 2004. "The Rural and Urban Landscape of the Aztec State." In *Mesoamerican Archaeology: Theory and Practice*, edited by Julia A. Hendon and Rosemary A. Joyce, 265–95. Blackwell, Malden, MA.

Nichols, Deborah L. 2006. "Archaeology on Foot: Jeffrey Parsons and Anthropology at the University of Michigan." In *Retrospectives: Works and Lives of Michigan Anthropologists*, edited by Derek Brereton, 106–35. Michigan Discussions in Anthropology, vol. 16. University of Michigan, Ann Arbor.

Nichols, Deborah L. 2013. "Merchants and Markets: The Archaeology of Aztec Commerce at Otumba Mexico." In *Merchants, Trade and Exchange in the Pre-Columbian World*, edited by Kenneth G. Hirth and Joanne Pillsbury, 49–83. Dumbarton Oaks Research Library and Collections, Washington, DC.

Nichols, Deborah L. 2015. "Intensive Agriculture and Early Complex Societies of the Basin of Mexico: The Formative Period." *Ancient Mesoamerica* 26:407–21.

Nichols, Deborah L. 2017a. "Teotihuacan." *Journal of Archaeological Research* 24:1–74.

Nichols, Deborah L. 2017b. "Farm to Market in the Aztec Empire." In *Rethinking the Aztec Economy*, edited by Deborah L. Nichols, Frances F. Berdan, and Michael E. Smit, 19–43. University of Arizona Press, Tucson.

Nichols, Deborah L. 2018a. "René Millon: 1921–2016." *Biographical Memoirs of the National Academy of Sciences*. www.nasonline.org/memoirs.

Nichols, Deborah L. 2018b. "Agricultural Practices and Environmental Impacts in Aztec and Pre-Aztec Central Mexico." In *Oxford Research Encyclopedia of Environmental Science*, edited by Peter Boguckli. Oxford University Press, New York. https://doi.org/10.1093/acrefore/9780199389414.013.175.

Nichols, Deborah L. 2020. "City, State, and Hinterlands: Teotihuacan and Central Mexico." In *Teotihuacan: The World beyond the City*, edited by Kenneth G. Hirth, David M. Carballo, and Bárbara Arroyo. Dumbarton Oaks Research Library and Collections, Washington, DC.

Nichols, Deborah L., and Christopher A. Pool. 2012. "Mesoamerican Archaeology: Recent Trends." In *Oxford Handbook of Mesoamerican Archaeology*, edited by Deborah L. Nichols and Christopher A. Pool, 1–30. Oxford University Press, New York.

Nichols, Deborah L., Mary J. McLaughlin, and Maura Benton. 2000. "Production Intensification and Regional Specialization: Maguey Fibers and Textiles in the Aztec City-State of Otumba." Ancient Mesoamerica 11:267–92.

Nichols, Deborah L., Elizabeth M. Brumfiel, Hector Neff, Thomas H. Charlton, Michael D. Glascock, and Mary Hodge. 2002. "Neutrons, Markets, Cities, and Empires: A Thousand-Year Perspective on Ceramic Production and Distribution in the Postclassic Basin of Mexico at Cerro Portezuelo, Chalco, and Xaltocan." *Journal of Anthropological Archaeology* 21:25–82.

Nichols, Deborah L. Christina Elson, Leslie G. Cecil, Nina Neivens de Estrada, Michael D. Glascock, and Paula Mikkelsen. 2009. "Chiconautla Mexico: A Crossroads of Aztec Trade and Politics." *Latin American Antiquity* 20:443–72.

Nichols, Deborah L., Hector Neff, and George L. Cowgill. 2013. "Cerro Portezuelo: An Overview." *Ancient Mesoamerica* 24:47–71.

Nichols, Deborah L. Frances F. Berdan, and Michael E. Smith, eds. 2017. *Rethinking the Aztec Economy*. University of Arizona Press, Tucson.

Ortman, Scott G., Andrew H. F. Cabaniss, Jennie O. Storm, and Luis M. A. Bettencourt. 2015. "Settlement Scaling and Increasing Returns in an Ancient Society." *Science Advances* 1:e1400066.

Paredes Gudiño, Blanca. 2005. "Análisis de flujos migratorios y composición multiétnica de la población de Tula, Hgo." In *Reacomodos demográficos del Clásico al Posclásico en el centro de México*, edited by Linda Manzanilla, 203–26. Universidad Nacional Autónoma de México Instituto de Investigaciones Antropológicas, Mexico City.

Park, Junjae, Roger Byrne, and Harold Böhnel. 2019. "Late Holocene Climate Change in Central Mexico and the Decline of Teotihuacan." *Annals of the Association of American Geographers* 109:104–20.

Parsons, Jeffrey R. 1971. *Prehistoric Settlement Patterns in the Texcoco Region, Mexico*. Memoirs of the Museum of Anthropology, no. 3. University of Michigan, Ann Arbor.

Parsons, Jeffrey R. 1972. "Archaeological Settlement Patterns." *Annual Review of Anthropology* 1:127–50.

Parsons, Jeffrey R. 1977. "Archaeological Research 1: Teotihuacán." *Latin American Research Review* 12:192–202.

Parsons, Jeffrey R. 1989. "Arqueología regional en la Cuenca de México: Una estrategía para la investigación futura." *Anales* 26:157–257.

Parsons, Jeffrey R. 1990. "Critical Reflections on a Decade of Full-coverage Survey in the Valley of Mexico." In *The Archaeology of Regions: A Case for Full Coverage Survey*, edited by S. Fish and S. Kowalewski, 7–31. Smithsonian Institution Press, Washington, DC.

Parsons, Jeffrey R. 1997. "Reflexiones sobre la conservación de colecciones arqueológicas. Arqueología." *segunda época*, 17:21–34.

Parsons, Jeffrey R. 2001. *The Last Saltmakers of Nexquipayac, Mexico: An Archaeological Ethnography*. Anthropological Papers, no. 92. Museum of Anthropology, University of Michigan, Ann Arbor.

Parsons, Jeffrey R. 2006. *The Last Pescadores of Chimalhuacan, Mexico: An Archaeological Ethnography*. Anthropological Papers, no. 96. Museum of Anthropology, University of Michigan, Ann Arbor.

Parsons, Jeffrey R. 2008. *Prehispanic Settlement Patterns in the Northwestern Valley of Mexico: The Zumpango Region*. Memoirs of the Museum of Anthropology, no. 45. University of Michigan, Ann Arbor.

Parsons, Jeffrey R. 2015. "An Appraisal of Regional Surveys in the Basin of Mexico, 1960–1975." *Ancient Mesoamerica* 26:183–96.

Parsons, Jeffrey R. 2019. *Remembering Archaeological Fieldwork in Mexico and Peru 1961–2003*. Special Publication, no. 3. Museum of Anthropology, University of Michigan, Ann Arbor.

Parsons, Jeffrey, and Luis Morett. 2004. "Recursos acuáticos en la subsistencia Azteca: Cazadores, pescadores, y recolectores." *Arqueología mexicana* 12(68):38–43.

Parsons, Jeffrey, and Luis Morett. 2005. "La economía acuática en el Valle de México: Perspectivas arqueológicas, históricas, y etnográficas." In *Etnoarqueología: El contexto dinámico de la cultura material a través del tiempo*, edited by E. Williams, 127–64. El Colegio de Michoacán, Zamora.

Parsons, Jeffrey R., Elizabeth M. Brumfiel, Mary Hrones Parsons, and David Wilson. 1982. *Prehispanic Settlement Patterns in the Southern Valley of Mexico: The Chalco-Xochimilco Region*. Memoirs of the Museum of Anthropology, no. 14. University of Michigan, Ann Arbor.

Patterson, Thomas C. 1995. *Toward a Social History of Archaeology*. Harcourt Brace & Company, Fort Worth, TX.

Plunket, Patricia, and Gabriela Uruñuela. 2006. "Social and Cultural Consequences of a Late Holocene Eruption of Popcatépetl in Central Mexico." *Quarternary International* 151:19–28.

Prem, Hanns J. 1992. "Disease Outbreaks in Central Mexico during the Sixteenth Century." In *"Secret Judgments of God": Old World Disease in Colonial Spanish America*, edited by Noble David Cook and W. George Lovell, 20–48. University of Oklahoma Press, Norman.

Rappaport, Roy A. 1968. *Pigs for the Ancestors: Ritual in the Ecology of New Guinea People*. Yale University Press, New Haven, CT.

Robles-García, Nelly M. 2012. "Mexico's National Archaeology Program." In *Oxford Handbook of Mesoamerican Archaeology*, edited by Deborah L. Nichols and Christopher A. Pool, 47–54. Oxford University Press, New York.

Rodríguez-Alegría, Enrique, John J. Millhauser, and Wesley D. Stoner. 2013. "Trade, Tribute, and Neutron Activation: The Colonial Political Economy of Xaltocan, Mexico." *Journal of Anthropological Archaeology* 32:397–414.

Rojas Rabiela, Teresa. 1991. *Pedro Armillas: Vida y obra*. 2 vols. Instituto Nacional de Antropología e Historia, Mexico City.

Rosenzweig, Melissa S., and John M. Marston. 2018. "Archaeologies of Empire and Environment." *Journal of Anthropological Archaeology* 52:87–102.

Sanders, William T. 1956. "The Central Mexican Symbiotic Region: A Study in Pre-Historic Settlement Patterns." In *Prehistoric Settlement Patterns in the New World*, edited by G. Willey, 115–27. Wenner-Gren Foundation for Anthropological Research, New York.

Sanders, William T. 1957. "Tierra y Agua: A Study of the Ecological Factors in the Development of Mesoamerican Civilizations." PhD dissertation, Department of Anthropology, Harvard University, Cambridge, MA.

Sanders, William T. 1965. "The Cultural Ecology of the Teotihuacan Valley, Mexico." Department of Sociology and Anthropology, The Pennsylvania State University, University Park.

Sanders, William T. 1976. "The Population of the Central Mexican Symbiotic region, the Basin of Mexico and the Teotihuacan Valley in the Sixteenth Century." In *The Native Population of the Americas in 1492*, edited by William M. Denevan, 85–150. University of Wisconsin Press, Madison.

Sanders, William T. 1999. "Three Valleys: Twenty-Five Years of Settlement Archaeology in Mesoamerica." In *Settlement Pattern Studies in the Americas: Fifty Years Since Virú*, edited by Brian R. Billman and Gary M. Feinman, 12–21. Smithsonian Institution Press, Washington, DC.

Sanders, William T., and Carson N. Murdy. 1982a. "Cultural Evolution and Ecological Succession in the Valley of Guatemala: 1500 BC–AD 1524." In *Maya Subsistence: Studies in Memory of Dennis E. Puleston*, edited by Kent V. Flannery, 19–64. Academic Press, New York.

Sanders, William T., and Carson N. Murdy. 1982b. "Population and Agricultural Adaptation in the Humid Highlands of Guatemala." In *The Historical Demography of Highland Guatemala*, edited by Robert M. Carmack, John Early, and Christopher Lutz, 23–34. Institute for Mesoamerican Studies Publication, no. 6. State University of New York at Albany.

Sanders, William T., and L. J. Gorenflo. 2007. *Prehispanic Settlement Patterns in the Cuautitlan Region, Mexico*. Occasional Papers in Anthropology, no. 29. Department of Anthropology, The Pennsylvania State University, University Park.

Sanders, William T., and Susan T. Evans, eds. 2000. "The Aztec Period Occupation of the Valley," pt. 2: "Excavations at T.A. 40 and Related Projects." In *The Teotihuacan Valley Project Final Report*, vol. 5. Occasional Papers in Anthropology, no. 26. Department of Anthropology, The Pennsylvania State University, University Park.

Sanders, William T., and Susan T. Evans, eds. 2001. "The Aztec Period Occupation of the Valley," pt. 3: "Syntheses and General Bibliography." In *The Teotihuacan Valley Project Final Report*, vol. 5. Occasional Papers in Anthropology, no. 27. Department of Anthropology, The Pennsylvania State University, University Park.

Sanders, William T., Anton. Kovar, Thomas H. Charlton, and Richard Diehl. 1970. "The Natural Environment, Contemporary Occupation and Sixteenth-Century Population of the Valley." In *The Teotihuacan Valley Project Final Report*, vol. 1. Occasional Papers in Anthropology, no. 3. Department of Anthropology, The Pennsylvania State University, University Park.

Sanders, William T., ed. 1986. "The Toltec Period Occupation of the Valley," pt. 1: "Excavations and Ceramics." In *The Teotihuacan Valley Project Final Report*, vol. 4. Occasional Papers in Anthropology, no. 13. Department of Anthropology, The Pennsylvania State University, University Park.

Sanders, William T., ed. 1987. "The Toltec Period Occupation of the Valley," pt. 2: "Surface Survey and Special Studies." *The Teotihuacan Valley Project Final Report*, vol. 4. Occasional Papers in Anthropology, no. 15. Department of Anthropology, The Pennsylvania State University, University Park.

Sanders, William T., ed. 1994. "The Teotihuacan Period Occupation of the Valley," pt. 1: "The Excavations." In *The Teotihuacan Valley Project Final Report*, vol. 3. Occasional Papers in Anthropology, no. 19. Department of Anthropology, The Pennsylvania State University, University Park.

Sanders, William T., ed. 1995. "The Teotihuacan Period Occupation of the Valley," pt. 2: "Artifact Analyses." In *The Teotihuacan Valley Project Final Report*, vol. 3. Occasional Papers in Anthropology, no. 20. Department of Anthropology, The Pennsylvania State University, University Park.

Sanders, William T., ed. 1996a. "The Teotihuacan Period Occupation of the Valley," pt. 3: "The Surface Survey." In *The Teotihuacan Valley Project Final Report*, vol. 3. Occasional Papers in Anthropology, no. 21. Department of Anthropology, The Pennsylvania State University, University Park.

Sanders, William T., ed. 1996b. "The Teotihuacan Period Occupation of the Valley," pt. 4: "Special Analyses, Miscellaneous Appendixes, and Volume Bibliography." In *The Teotihuacan Valley Project Final Report*, vol. 3. Occasional Papers in Anthropology, no. 24. Department of Anthropology, The Pennsylvania State University, University Park.

Sanders, William T., Jeffrey R. Parsons, and Robert S. Santley. 1979. *The Basin of Mexico: Ecological Processes in the Evolution of a Civilization*. Academic Press, New York.

Sanders, William T., Jeffrey R. Parsons, and Robert S. Santley. 1993. "Late Formative Period Society at Loma Torremote: A Consideration of the Redistribution vs. Great Provider Models as a Basis for the Emergence of Complexity in the Basin of Mexico." In *Prehispanic Domestic Units in Western Mesoamerica: Studies of Household, Compound, and Residence*, edited by Robert S. Santley and Kenneth G. Hirth, 67–86. CRC Press, Boca Raton.

Sanders, William T., Michael West, Charles Fletcher, and Joseph Marino. 1975. *The Formative Period Occupation of the Valley*, pts. 1 and 2. Occasional Papers in Anthropology, no. 10. Department of Anthropology, The Pennsylvania State University, University Park.

Santley, Robert S. 1993. "Late Formative Period Society at Loma Torremote: A Consideration of the Redistribution vs. the Great Provider Models as a Basis for the Emergence of Complexity in the Basin of Mexico." In *Prehispanic Domestic Units in Western Mesoamerica*, edited by Robert S. Santley and Kenneth G. Hirth, 67–86. CRC Press, Boca Raton, FL.

Santley, Robert S., and Philip J. Arnold III. 1996. "Prehispanic Settlement Patterns in the Tuxtla Mountains, Southern Veracruz Mexico." *Journal of Field Archaeology* 23:225–50.

Scheidel, Walter. 2015. "Rome, Tenochtitlan, and Beyond: Comparing Empires across Time and Space." *Princeton/Stanford Working Papers in Classics*. Classics Department, Princeton University, Princeton and Classics Department Stanford University, Stanford.

Scott, James. 1985. *Weapons of the Weak: Everyday Forms of Peasant Resistance*. Yale University Press, New Haven, CT.

Serra Puche, Marí Carmen, and J. Carlos Lazcano Arce. 2009. "Arqueología en el sur de la Cuenca de México: Diagnóstico y futura; In memoriam W. T. Sanders." *Cuicuilco* 16:19–38. http://www.scielo.org.mx/scielo.php?script=sci_arttext&pid=S0185-16592009000300002&lng=es&nrm=iso, accessed August 1, 2020.

Smith, Michael E. 1979. "The Aztec Marketing System and Settlement Pattern in the Valley of Mexico: A Central Place Analysis." *American Antiquity* 44:110–25.

Smith, Michael E. 1980. "The Role of the Marketing System in Aztec Society and Economy: Reply to Evans." *American Antiquity* 45(4):876–83.

Smith, Michael E. 2009. "V. Gordon Childe and the Urban Revolution: A Historical Perspective on a Revolution in Urban Studies." *The Town Planning Review* 80:3–29.

Smith, Michael E. 2012. *The Aztecs*. Willey Blackwell, Malden, MA.

Smith, Michael E. 2017a. "Aztec Urbanism: Cities and Towns." In *Oxford Handbook of the Aztecs*, edited by Deborah L. Nichols and Enrique Rodríguez-Alegría, 201–18. Oxford University Press, New York.

Smith, Michael E. 2017b. "From Teotihuacan to Tenochtitlan: Two Trajectories of Social Change." *Revista española de antropología americana* 47:239–54.

Smith, Michael E., and Lisa Montiel. 2001. "The Archaeological Study of Empires and Imperialism in Pre-Hispanic Mexico." *Journal of Anthropological Archaeology* 20:245–84.

Snow, Dean R. 1996. "Influencias clasicas en la region norte-centro de Tlaxcala." In *Antología de Tlaxcala*, edited by Angel García Cook and B. L. Merino Carrión, 230–36. Serie Arqueología Instituto Nacional de Antropología e Historia, Mexico City.

Stahle, D. W., Villanueva, J., Burnette, D. J., Cerano, J., Heim Jr., R. R., Fye, F. K., Acuña, R., Therrell, M. D., Cleaveland, M. K., and Stahle, D. K. 2011. "Major Mesoamerican Droughts of the Past Millennium." *Geophysical Research Letters* 38, L05703.

Stanish, Charles. 2003. *Ancient Titicaca: The Evolution of Complex Society in Southern Peru and Northern Bolivia*. University of California Press, Berkeley.

Stark, Barbara. 2006. "Systematic Regional Survey in the Gulf Lowlands in Comparative Perspective." In *Managing Archaeological Data: Essays in Honor of Sylvia W. Gaines*, edited by Jeffrey Hantman and Rachel Most, 155–67. Anthropological Research Paper, no. 57. Arizona State University, Tempe.

Stark, Barbara. 2017. "Aztec Imperialism and Gulf Ceramic Emulation: Comparison with Teotihuacan." In *Objects and Economy in the Aztec Empire*, edited by Deborah L. Nichols, Frances F. Berdan, and Michael E. Smith, 248–77. University of Arizona Press, Tucson.

Steward, Julian, ed. 1955. *Irrigation Civilizations: A Comparative Study.* Pan American Union, Washington, DC.

Stoner, Wesley D. 2012. "Modeling and Testing Political Boundaries in the Classic Tuxtla Mountains, Southern Veracruz, Mexico." *Journal of Anthropological Archaeology* 31:381–402.

Stoner, Wesley D., and Deborah L. Nichols. 2019a. "The Altica Project: Reframing the Formative Basin of Mexico." *Ancient Mesoamerica* 30:247–65.

Stoner, Wesley D., and Deborah L. Nichols. 2019b. "Early Ceramics, Compositional Variation, and Trade in Formative Period Central Mexico." *Ancient Mesoamerica* 30:311–37.

Stoner, Wesley D., and Enrique Rodríguez-Alegría. 2016. "The Trade in Cooking Pots under the Aztec and Spanish." *Ancient Mesoamerica* 27:97–107.

Stoner, Wesley D., Deborah L. Nichols, Bridget Alex, and Destiny Crider. 2015. "The Emergence of Early-Middle Formative Exchange Patterns in Mesoamerica: A View from Altica in the Teotihuacan Valley." *Journal of Anthropological Archaeology* 39:19–35.

Sugiura, Yoko Yamamoto. 2009. "Camiando el valle de Toluca arqueología regional, el legado William T. Sanders." *Cuicuilco* 47:88–111.

Sugiura, Yoko Yamamoto, and Rubén Nieto Hernández. 2014. "Una reflexión sobre la preservación del patrimonio arqueológico: El caso de los sitios de escala menor en el estado de México." *Anales de antropología* 48:75–95.

Sugiyama, Saburo. 2017. "The Feathered Serpent Pyramid at Teotihucan: Vestiges of Worship and Veneration." In *Teotihuacan: City of Fire*, edited by Matthew H. Robb, 56–61. Fine Arts Museums of San Francisco, de Young and University of California Press, San Francisco and Los Angeles.

Tolstoy, Paul, Suzanne Fish, Martin Boksenbaum, Kathryn Blair Vaughn, and Carol Smith. 1977. "Early Sedentary Communities of the Basin of Mexico." *Journal of Field Archaeology* 4:91–106.

Tolstoy, Paul. 1958. "Surface Survey in the Northern Valley of Mexico: The Classic and Postclassic Periods." *Transactions of the American Philosophical Society* 48(5):1–101.

Tozzer, Alfred M. 1921. "Excavation of a Site at Santiago Ahuitzotla, D. F., Mexico." *Bureau of American Ethnology Bulletin*, vol. 74. Smithsonian Institution, Washington, DC.

Umberger, Emily. 1987. "Antiques, Revivals, and References to the Past in Aztec Art." *Res: Anthropology and Aesthetics* 13:63–106.

Vaillant, George C. 1930. "Excavations at Zacatenco." *Anthropological Papers*, vol. 32, pt.1 American Museum of Natural History, New York.

Vaillant, George C. 1931. "Excavations at Ticoman." *Anthropological Papers*, vol. 32, pt. 2 American Museum of Natural History, New York.

Vaillant, George C. 1935a. "Excavations at El Arbolillo." *Anthropological Papers*, vol. 35, pt. 2. American Museum of Natural History, New York.

Vaillant, George C. 1935b. "Early Cultures of the Valley of Mexico: Results of the Stratigraphical Project of the American Museum of Natural History in the Valley of Mexico, 1928–1933." *Anthropological Papers*, vol. 35, pt. 3. American Museum of Natural History, New York.

Vaillant, George C. 1938. "A Correlation of Archaeological and Historical Sequences in the Valley of Mexico." *American Anthropologist* 40:535–73.

Webster, David. 1985. "Recent Settlement Surveys in the Copán Valley Honduras." *Journal of New World Archaeology* 7:39–51.

Whitmore, Thomas M. 1991. "A Simulation of the Sixteenth-Century Population Collapse in the Basin of Mexico." *Annals of the Association of American Geographers* 81:464–87.

Willey, Gordon R. 1953. "Prehistoric Settlement Patterns in the Virú Valley, Peru." *Bureau of American Archaeology Bulletin* 155:1–453.

Willey, Gordon R. 1983. "Settlement Patterns and Archaeology: Some Comments." In *Prehistoric Settlement Patterns: Essays in Honor of Gordon R. Willey*, edited by Evon Z. Vogt and Richard Levanthal, 445–62. University of New Mexico Press and Peabody Museum of Archaeology and Ethnology, Albuquerque and Cambridge, MA.

Willey, G. R., 1988. "The Southeast Classic Maya Zone: A Summary." In *The Southeast Classic Maya Zone: A Symposium at Dumbarton Oaks, 6th and 7th October, 1984*, edited by Elizabeth H. Boone and Gordon R. Willey, 395–408. Dumbarton Oaks Research Library and Collection, Washington, DC.

Wilson, David J. 1988. *Prehispanic Settlement Patterns in the Lower Santa Valley, Peru*. Smithsonian Press, Washington, DC.

Wittfogel, Karl A. 1938. "Die Theorie der orientalischen Gesellschaft." *Zeitschrift für Sozialforschung* 7(1/2):90–122.

Wolf, Eric R. 1976. "Introduction." In *The Valley of Mexico: Studies in Pre-Hispanic Ecology and Society*, edited by Eric R. Wolf, 1–10. University of New Mexico Press, Albuquerque.

Wright, Henry T. 2007. *Early State Formation in Central Madagascar: An Archaeological Survey of Western Avaradrano*. Memoirs of the Museum of Anthropology, no. 43. University of Michigan, Ann Arbor.

3

The Teotihuacan Valley Project and the Teotihuacan Mapping Project

Reflections on the Rural and Urban Classic Teotihuacan Period Research in the Teotihuacan Valley, 1962–1964

CHARLES C. KOLB

INTRODUCTION

In June 1960, Eric Wolf organized a National Science Federation–sponsored conference of eleven international archaeologists at the University of Chicago to evaluate the status of previous anthropological studies focusing on the Basin of Mexico and to coordinate future research. Although this was not the first conference of its kind, the 1960 meeting led to two analogous long-range plans, beginning in 1962. One was René Millon's Teotihuacan Mapping Project (TMP), based at the University of Rochester, which was centered on the Classic period ceremonial center at Teotihuacan, currently dated 1–550 CE (Hirth et al. 2020, revising Cowgill 2015) and its surrounding urban area (ca. 20 km²). The other was William Sanders's Teotihuacan Valley Project (TVP) (Kolb 2019a), based at The Pennsylvania State University, which concentrated on identifying and mapping rural settlements (505 km²) from all cultural periods (Paleo-Indian through Colonial); this pilot project transformed into the larger Basin of Mexico Project.

The TMP and TVP focused initially on two issues: (1) precisely defining chronological periods and phases using ceramic analyses, and (2) a field-by-field

https://doi.org/10.5876/9781646424078.c003

ground survey using aerial photographs to plot the extent of urban and rural settlement areas. Initially (1961–1964), the fieldwork involved test pitting (TMP) and small and large-scale excavations (TVP). In the summer of 1962, personnel from the TMP, TVP, and Instituto Nacional de Antropología e Historia (INAH) met weekly to discuss and refine ceramic types and define chronological periods. As a Penn State student, I worked on the TVP for my dissertation on Classic-period Teotihuacan, particularly focusing on settlement types, chronological phases, ceramics, and demographic models. With Sanders's approval, I was also a contractor (perhaps a "spy"?) hired by Millon to conduct surveys and assist in elaborating the Classic-period settlement types and ceramic phase chronologies and typologies in the urban center.

THE CHICLÍN CONFERENCE, 1946

Alfred Kroeber's (1925) archaeological surveys and ceramic analysis in coastal Peru influenced studies in 1941–1942 undertaken by the Institute of Andean Research, which in 1945 conceived the Virú Valley Project in north-central Peru. The planners established the Virú Committee at the Institute of Andean Research, augmented by colleagues, to undertake the research (Strong and Evans 1952:3–5; Willey 1953:xvii). A planning meeting was held on August 7–8, 1946 at the Chiclín Museum in Trujillo, Peru. This conference led to the formulation of eight projects for the period 1947–1948, particularly focused on stratigraphically defining chronologies through ceramic analysis (Ford and Willey 1949:18). The eighth was a "Study of Prehistoric Settlement Patterns" by Gordon R. Willey, who was mentored by Strong at Columbia University, graduating in 1942. From 1943 to 1950, he worked under the direction of Julian Steward on the first six volumes of the *Handbook of South American Indians*, notably on volume 5, *The Comparative Ethnology of South American Indians* (Steward 1949).

James Bennyhoff (1952) wrote a strong critique of the Virú cultural sequence, which would later net him a position with René Millon's TVP. Steward convinced Willey to "withdraw from the 'stratigraphic race' being run by others and to undertake a 'settlement pattern survey'" (Vogt 2004:403). Willey did not appreciate the potential of the settlement pattern survey either as a new viewpoint for archaeologists or as an integrating force for the various other studies being conducted in the valley. After the 1946 field season (Willey 1946), Willey later stated (1974:154): "As I walked over the stony and seemingly endless remains of Virú's prehistoric settlements, I felt I had been misled by Steward and dealt a marginal hand by my colleagues. The latter were getting tangible pottery sequences to delight the heart of any self-respecting archaeologist while I was chasing some kind of wraith called 'settlement patterns' that had been dreamed up by a social anthropologist"—meaning Steward.

THE VIRÚ VALLEY MODEL

Ford and Willey (1949) initially prepared *Surface Survey of the Virú Valley, Peru* as a two-part report: Part 1: *Virú Valley: Background and Problems* and Part 2: *Cultural Dating of Prehistoric Sites in Virú Valley, Peru*. Collier (1955) wrote the traditional *Cultural Chronology and Change as Reflected in the Ceramics of the Virú Valley, Peru*. Willey's final report on the settlement pattern study, *Prehistoric Settlement Patterns in the Virú Valley, Peru*, had four objectives (1953:1):

1. To describe a series of prehistoric sites with reference to geographic and chronologic position.
2. To outline a developmental reconstruction of these prehistoric settlements with relation to function as well as sequence.
3. To reconstruct cultural institutions insofar as these may be reflected in settlement configurations.
4. To compare the settlement history of Virú with the other regions of Peru.

Willey noted that the project was "an experimental work" (1953:1). Aerial photographs of the valley were used to create maps of probable site locations, and three Jeeps had the photos mounted on plywood and fastened to the vehicles' hoods. The 315 sites recorded represented about one-fourth of the prehistoric sites that could be observed on the surface; 1,200 were ultimately recorded. Thus, "some of the following inequalities in the nature of our sample should be mentioned: (1) We surveyed more large than small sites. (2) We surveyed more sites in the upper sections of the valley than the lower, as these were usually constructed of rock and presented better preserved remains of houses. (3) Midden sites on the beach and mound or refuse sites in the cultivated lower sections of the valley were slighted" (Ford and Willey 1949:19–20).

In addition to the methodological influences of the Virú project, Steward's seminal *Theory of Culture Change: The Methodology of Multilinear Evolution* (1955), popular with many anthropologists of the time, was also influential on research paradigms developed by William Sanders and others who conducted archaeological investigations in the Basin of Mexico in the 1960s.

THE CHICAGO CONFERENCE 1960

At the beginning of the 1960s, Eric Wolf (1960, 1961) applied for and received a modest grant from the National Science Foundation (NSF) to hold a conference entitled Coordinated Anthropological Research in the Valley of Mexico. The conference brought together a select group of international specialists on Mesoamerica to focus on two general objectives: (1) to assess the present state of knowledge of anthropological studies in the Basin of Mexico, and (2) to develop a plan for future research. The project's twelve specific concerns (Sanders 1965:8) bore strong similarities to the Virú Valley project objectives but were more interested in environment and ecology and sociocultural and diachronic economic change:

1. Changes in the natural and man-made environment in the Valley of Mexico over time and the possible correlation of these changes with cultural factors.
2. The characteristics of settlement in the Valley and changes in the settlement patterns over time and related population problems.
3. The nature of the relationships between hamlets, villages, towns, cities, and similar units at various periods, including a discussion of relations between specific sites.
4. Problems of urbanization.
5. The characteristics of symbiotic regions in the Valley in various periods of time and their social consequences.
6. The relevance of environment to agriculture and settlement patterns to problems of social controls at various levels.
7. Patterns of ceremonial control at various time levels.
8. Patterns of political control at various time levels.
9. Patterns of warfare in the Prehispanic Period.
10. Effects of the Spanish conquests and colonization on social and cultural groups in the Valley of Mexico.
11. Cultural persistence or change in major patterns throughout all known time periods within the Valley.
12. Causal or functional relationships between various cultural patterns at different time levels.

The conference took place at the University of Chicago June 6–9, 1960, with Wolf as the convener (Wolf 1961). The conferees had previously undertaken studies in the Basin of Mexico, particularly in the Teotihuacan Valley area (see list in table 3.1). Among them was William J. Mayer-Oakes, who had conducted and published (1959) stratigraphic excavations with Classic-era ceramics at the site of El Risco, located west of the Teotihuacan Valley.

All but four (Adams, Bopp, Coe, and Deevey) went on to conduct anthropological fieldwork in the Basin of Mexico. The attendee list (see table 3.1) raises a couple of unanswered questions: Why was Willey or someone else involved in the Virú Valley Project not invited to the Chicago conference? And why were several major scholars of the Basin of Mexico not invited? These would include Paul Tolstoy of Queens College CUNY and later the Université de Montréal, author of a publication on survey in the Teotihuacan Valley (Tolstoy 1958), and Muriel Noé Porter Weaver, excavator at Chupícuaro and Tlatilco, the latter the basis of her 1951 Columbia University doctoral dissertation, and author of three editions of *The Aztecs, Maya, and Their Predecessors: Archaeology of Mesoamerica* (Porter Weaver 1993).

TABLE 3.1. Attendees to the University of Chicago Conference "Coordinated Anthropological Research in the Valley of Mexico," June 6–9, 1960

Attendees	Birth-death dates
Robert McCormick Adams	1926–2018
Pedro Armillas García	1914–1984
Pedro Carrasco Pizana	1921–2012
Michael D. Coe	1929–2019
Edward S. Deevey Jr.	1914–1988
William J. Mayer-Oakes	1923–2005
René F. Millon	1921–2016
Ángel Palerm Ibiza	1917–1980
Román Piña Chan	1920–2001
William T. Sanders	1926–2008
Monica Bopp[a]	1942–2018
Eric R. Wolf (convener)	1923–1999

a. Wolf lists her as an attendee (1976:5).

The conference's long-range research program necessitated a division of the Basin of Mexico into six geographic areas and an additional six areas outside of the Basin (Sanders 1965:8–9). The conferees recommended that future research concentrate on the northeastern part of the Valley of Mexico, specifically the Valley of Teotihuacan and the vicinity of Texcoco. In his report to the NSF on the results of the conference, Wolf summarized arguments favoring the selection of the focus region. He further commented that an agreement to study the Teotihuacan Valley had been reached with a division of labor between Sanders and Millon, whereby Millon would undertake a comprehensive survey and mapping of urban Teotihuacan while Sanders would focus on the rural areas of the Valley (Millon et al. 1973:x; Sanders 1965:7–8; Vaillant 1937, 1938; Wolf 1976:5).

Wolf offered the following rationale for the focus on the selected region: "The Valley of Teotihuacán, containing the largest prehistoric site in Middle America, is the ideal region in which to study the origin and early development of urban civilization. The region of Texcoco offering a unique combination of archaeological sites, native annals and conquest-period written resources, is the ideal region in which to study the later development of pre-Hispanic civilization, and the cultural processes transforming that civilization into the patterns of colonial and modern Mexico. While we advocate that future effort be concentrated in this part of the Valley, we do of course recognize that research calculated to illuminate the rise and fall of Teotihuacán or Texcoco be carried out at other sites in the Valley of Mexico as well" (Wolf 1976:5).

THE TEOTIHUACAN VALLEY PROJECT

Sanders directed the Teotihuacan Valley Project that undertook a "full-coverage" archaeological survey of 505 km². This became the first stage of the larger Basin of Mexico survey (Sanders, Parsons, and Santley 1979). Four specific objectives of the Teotihuacan Valley Project (Sanders 1965:9) were to

1. Trace the history of the development of agriculture in the Valley with a special focus on irrigation, terracing, and other patterns of land use.

TABLE 3.2. Teotihuacan Valley Project personnel (1964)

Senior Staff	Affiliation	Period	Survey Team Focus
Dr. William T. Sanders	Penn State	May–September	All periods
Dr. Anton J. Kovar	Penn State	May–July	Paleobotany
Graduate Students			
Joe Marino	Penn State	January–March and June–September	Toltec and Classic periods
Dick Diehl	Penn State	May–September	Preclassic and Toltec periods
Charlie Kolb	Penn State	September–November	Classic period
Charlie Fletcher	Penn State	May–September	Preclassic period
Bill Mather III	Penn State	May–September	Photography
Warren Barbour	Penn State	May–September	Unspecified
Dan Shaffer	Penn State	May–September (?)	Contemporary potters
Jeff Parsons	Michigan	May–September	Aztec period
Tom Charlton	Tulane	May–September	Aztec and Colonial periods

2. Define and trace the history of rural and urban community types.
3. Construct, on the basis of data on settlements, at least a relative profile of population history.
4. Finally, and on a higher level of abstraction, to explore the functional relationships among such phenomena as settlement patterns, agricultural techniques, and demography, and, by analyzing the interaction between these patterns, to throw light on the urban development of the area.

Fieldwork began in June 1960 and was completed by September 1964. The analysis of the data and artifacts collected, and publication of the results, would span more than four decades. Sanders (see Kolb 2019b), Parsons, Marino, Diehl, Kolb, Charlton (see Kolb 2010), McCullough, Fletcher, and West, among others were engaged in twenty-one mostly small-scale excavations in 1961–62, while the systematic survey of the Valley, starting with a field-by-field survey, was abandoned for a general survey in 1962, followed by an attempted field-by-field survey in 1963–1966. Sanders and Kolb (1994) reported on excavations at the Classic period site of Maquixco Bajo (TC-8:1–2, 3, 4, and Pyramid) undertaken in 1961–62 (Kolb 2018). TVP personnel used a cumbersome fourteen-page "Site Survey Schedule"; additional sheets were added to pages 9–14; hence, some site file folders had thirty-five or more sheets (Kolb 1979a:365–66). More about the fieldwork and the personnel have been chronicled by Jeff Parsons (2019). Participants of the 1964 Teotihuacan Project and affiliations, and their foci appear in table 3.2.

Ultimately, 134 Classic period sites with combined total of 570 discrete chronological phases or components were delineated. Site TC-46 (Tlatenco) was excavated by Tom Charlton (1994). Kolb and Sanders (1996a, 1996b) published reports on the Classic period settlement patterns and a reconstruction of the rural and urban settlements (Kolb 1979a). Studies not part of my dissertation included a critique of chronologies (Kolb 1979b), and essays on *candeleros* (Kolb 1988a) and clay figurines (Kolb 1995). Calculations of demographic estimates and formulae derived from archaeological contexts were published in a *Current Anthropology* article (Kolb et al. 1985) and a monograph focusing on marine shell trade at Classic Teotihuacán examined natural and skeuomorphic representations of shells from urban and rural sites in the Teotihuacan Valley (Kolb 1987, 1996). Ceramic analyses were reported on Thin Orange Ware (Kolb 1973, 1984, 1986), Copoid ware (Kolb 1988b), and Granular ware (Kolb 1988c), in addition to a petrographic analysis of all Classic wares and types (Kolb 1997).

TEOTIHUACAN MAPPING PROJECT

Millon began archaeological research in Mexico in 1950. His initial study of urban Teotihuacan confirmed that the Pyramid of the Sun and probably also the Pyramid of the Moon were built during the earliest phase of the urban center. In 1962, he received a three-year NSF grant to map Teotihuacan, and led "a team of young, relatively unknown archaeologists, a cadre of graduate students, and a loyal crew of local residents of the Teotihuacan Valley on a venture whose intensity and complexity none had imagined" (Millon and Altschul 2015). Nichols (2017) details Millon's move from Berkeley to Rochester and aspects of his early field work. Bennyhoff, who specialized in California prehistory, received his doctorate at Berkeley in 1961; Millon persuaded him to join the TMP in 1962. Bruce Drewitt joined the project at its inception and would direct most of the field survey from 1964 to 1966, graduating from Berkeley in 1967 (Drewitt 1967). The field survey began with nine months of fieldwork in June 1962 with Millon, Bennyhoff, and Drewitt, focusing on the northwestern section called the Old City (also known as Oztoyahualco), to determine the outer limits of the city (see figure 3.1: Map of Urban Teotihuacan; Millon et al. 1973).

Initially, Sanders and Millon had agreed that the urban-rural demarcation was defined by a strip 100 meters or more in width that had no structural remains or other signs of occupation dating to Teotihuacan times (Millon et al. 1973:8, Cowgill et al. 2003:6). An initial rapid surface survey of the city's perimeter was completed by December 1962. The area encompassed 53 km². By 1963, however, the width of the strip was increased to 300 meters. Cowgill and colleagues (2003:15) note that "the area of early Teotihuacan occupation extends to the northwest, well beyond the published map. In the course of bounding the city in 1962 Millon located a northwestern extension that was occupied only early in the city's history, during or before the Tzacualli phase. It covered an area of about 4 km²." Unfortunately, the NSF denied funds for mapping this extension

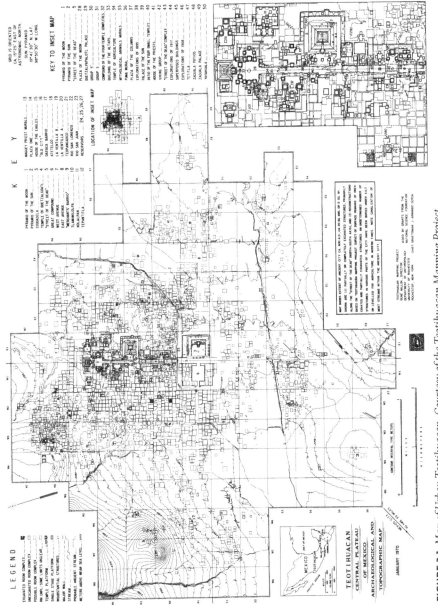

FIGURE 3.1. Map of Urban Teotihuacan. Courtesy of the Teotihuacan Mapping Project.

in detail, and it was never adequately surveyed (Millon et al. 1973:8). The TMP used the term "site" rather loosely, "to refer to any spatially distinct occurrence of evidence of a Teotihuacan period occupation, with or without associated architectural evidence" (Cowgill et al. 2003:5). This initial work was followed by more than three continuous years of fieldwork from June 1963 to October 1966, at which point approximately 90 percent of the city had been mapped. A total of 715 sites were designated numerically in a single ascending sequence for the entire 1962 survey (Millon 1964:14, Cowgill et al. 2003:6). An example of an original site record is presented below:

Site Number: 556
Survey Date: 11/19 and 11/22/1962
Surveyed by: JB [James Bennyhoff]
Maps: 74, 55, 54 San Lorenzo

Very extensive sherd area in a series of milpas, maguey, and alfalfa field on the flat crown of San Lorenzo hill (at the southeast edge of San Lorenzo). Main road (Federal Highway) crosses western quarter of the site and access roads cross the center. Alfalfa fields are considerably altered. Moderate rock. No structural features despite multiple exposures. Tepetate at 50 cm below surface in road. No mounding.

Moderate sherds: Miccaotli: wedge rim; [Teo.] IV: 4 buff rims, 6 SMO, 3 TO, 1 R/Y Rim; Coyo: 2 R/Y, 1 R; Mazapan: nw quarter; Aztec: 1 Chalco poly[chrome]

Comments added by Kolb (1979a):

TMP Site 556 was recorded as TVP Site TC-13 (San Lorenzo Tlamimilolpa) with three mounds TC-13:A, B, and C; nearby TC-14 TMP Sites 251 and 536 are within TMP Site TC-14 (Patlachique Barranca / Hacienda Tlajinga) and has thirteen mounds (TC-14:A through TC-14:N). TC-14:D is Site 536 and TC14:L is Site 251.

A revised TMP "Teotihuacan Site Survey Record" form was condensed onto a single page with thirty-six elements. The record form was adapted, likely by Bennyhoff, from the site survey form of the "California Archaeological Survey, Berkeley" (Heizer and Graham 1967:20, 22).

Field checking and test excavations, primarily to discern chronologies from the ceramics, required extensive field seasons that continued until the end of summer 1970. Laboratory analysis began in 1963, concentrating first on material collected from the surface and then on material recovered from test excavations. Managing the copious amount of information led to computerization of the data beginning in 1965 shortly after George Cowgill joined the project in the late summer of 1964. The collection of artifacts from surface survey and the

TABLE 3.3. Teotihuacan Mapping Project personnel (1964)

Senior Staff	Affiliation	Period
Dr. James A. Bennyhoff	Rochester[a]	January–December
Dr. René Millon	Rochester[a]	Two Spring visits; July–September
Dr. Clara Hall Millon	Rochester	July–September
Robert Bruce Drewitt	Toronto[a]	July–August
Dr. George L. Cowgill	Brandeis	August–September
Graduate Students		
Charlie Kolb	Penn State	January–September
Joe Marino	Penn State	May (returned to TVP in June)
Mike Spence	S. Illinois	June–September
Darlena Blucher	Brandeis	July–September
Jim Dow	Brandeis	July–September
Dan Hungerford	Rochester	July–September
Jane Quisenberry	Bennington	July–September
Karen and Dan Bruhns	California	July–August
Mexican support staff		
Pedro Baños	Teotihuacan	January–December
Zeférino Ortega	Teotihuacan	April–December?

a. formerly at UC–Berkeley

materials from twenty-eight test excavations, plus paper records, increased at a dramatic rate; the laboratory would ultimately house over 900,000 artifacts, as well as the archives (Huster et al. 2018).

THE 1964 TEOTIHUACAN MAPPING PROJECT FIELD SEASON

The 1964 TMP field season included a number of graduate students (see table 3.3). In January 1964, Bennyhoff and Kolb, along with technician Pedro Baños (Pedro's brother-in-law Zeferino Ortega would join in late summer) were tasked by Millon to survey major sections of the urban center west of the Ciudadela, particularly in the area south of the Eastern Avenue. We initially adhered to this guideline from January into February, but two significant, developing situations necessitated the alteration of the original plan. In late February through early April 1964, alfalfa fields in and near farmland (owned by Julian Villa Lobos) at La Ventilla, an ancient barrio southwest of the Ciudadela and within the Zona Arqueología at Teotihuacan, were being "excavated" by Villa Lobos himself using a John Deere tractor with a front-end loader for artifact recovery! INAH sent Juan Vidarte to excavate the residential compounds and the rich subfloor burials at La Ventilla A and B = 1:S1W2 and 2:S1W2 on the Millon site plan

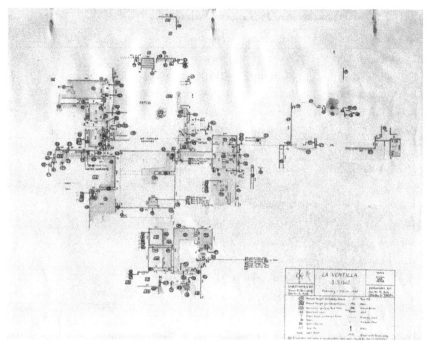

FIGURE 3.2. *La Ventilla 3:S1W2 February–March 1964. Drawn by C. C. Kolb.*

(Vidarte de Linares 1964). See the copy of my original 1963 to-scale site plan of La Ventilla drafted for the TMP in figure 3.2.

As time was of the essence, given the "pothunting" and the site being to create additional alfalfa fields, Bennyhoff and Kolb (1964), assisted by Baños, helped Vidarte by trenching along walls and exposing features in La Ventilla C = 3:S1W2. We exposed most of the interior and exterior walls to discern room patterns and sizes and architectural layouts; both sites had roughly similar but slightly different chronologies based on ceramics. In April, Villa Lobos backfilled 3:S1W2; INAH paid a *mordida* (bribe) to enable Vidarte de Linares (1964) to continue working at La Ventilla B on the incredibly rich subfloor burials for a couple of months after that.

Bennyhoff and I analyzed the 3:S1W2 ceramics, which helped refine the relative chronologies of the Tlamimilolpa and Xolalpan phases. There was no formal write-up of the 3:S1W2 work—just raw field notes. A copy of my original to-scale site plan drafted for the TMP is seen in figure 3.2. All of my field notes went into the TMP archive (I also had a separate, personal set of field notes and daily diary). Jim Bennyhoff and I spent nearly six weeks on this excavation and artifact analysis and, as a result, Millon was especially angry at Jim for spending so much time on this activity rather than surface survey. We later surveyed the area in and around the Great Compound, Rancho Las Palmas, and toward San Juan, including the field where Walmart would ultimately build their box store and parking area. I was privy to the scathing and "hostile" written messages and telephone calls from Millon to Bennyhoff and am convinced that these were the beginning of the split between René and Jim and the latter's eventual return to California (Hughes 1994) after the "new guy" arrived in mid-summer—that fellow was, of course, George Cowgill.

Secondly, contractors working for the Mexican Federal government began the construction of a major four-lane highway (*super-carretera*) from Ciudad México to the Zona Arqueología at Teotihuacan and a beltway, or *Periférico*, around the ceremonial center of the site as part of a decree by Presidente López Mateos to enhance tourism. The anticipated completion date was November 1964. Working their way toward Teotihuacan from the west, the builders were using heavy equipment to displace unsurveyed and unexcavated archaeological mounds along both sides of the Western Avenue as "fill" to build a compacted elevated base for the new highway. Bennyhoff and I had an opportunity to conduct some salvage work—drawing mound configurations for the TMP survey maps and making some artifact collections. The heavy equipment used by the contractors included bulldozers and LeTourneau scrapers followed by 12-ton soil compactors. Fortunately, I had been travelling to Mexico City on weekends in May and June and returning to San Juan on the second-class Flecha Roja bus on

TABLE 3.4. Teotihuacan Mapping Project survey crew chiefs and number of surveys (Cowgill et al. 2003:35)

Crew chief	Survey Cases: 1962–1969
Matthew Wallrath	1,050
Bruce Drewitt	752
Michael Spence	596
James Bennyhoff	565
René Millon	254
Joseph Marino	251
Charles Kolb (9 months 1964)	226
George Cowgill	150
Total	3,593
Pedro Baños	3,326
Grand Total	6,919

Mondays at 5:00 am traveling with many construction workers, engineers, and heavy equipment drivers who were coming to work. They were extremely sympathetic to the archaeological work we undertook and would inform me of their weekly work plans and attempted to let us finish the archaeological survey and artifact collecting. Over a two-week period, we were only somewhat successful.

However, by mid-summer, Cowgill, Millon, Drewitt, and the graduate students had begun to arrive and field teams were reconstituted to consist of a crew chief, a student assistant, and a workman, although sometimes there were two workmen and sometimes no student assistant (Cowgill et al. 2003:8–9), which was quite different from the Jim, Charlie, and Pedro team (see table 3.4).

Douglas W. Schwartz, director of the School of American Research in Santa Fe, New Mexico, hosted the seminar "The Valley of Mexico: Studies in Pre-Hispanic Ecology," convened by Eric Wolf on April 3–8, 1972 (the School of American Research would become the School for Advanced Research in 2007). Wolf noted that Millon and Sanders had carried out their tasks and that other researchers working in conjunction with them "have greatly added to our knowledge of development in the Valley" (Wolf 1976:5). The eleven presentations were organized into three topical parts: Part 1, "Chronology," featured papers by Barbara Price and René Millon. Part 2, "The Valley as an Ecological System," had papers by Michael Logan and William Sanders; one by Jeffrey Parsons; two other contributions authored by solely by Sanders; a paper coauthored by Sanders, Parsons, and Logan (with a commentary by Richard Blanton); and a paper by Blanton. Part 3, "Urban Society," had presentations by René Millon, Richard Diehl, and Edward Calnek. (Four of the presenters were Sanders's students.) Wolf edited the conference proceedings, which were published as *The Valley of Mexico: Studies in Pre-Hispanic Ecology and Society* (1976).

I had the opportunity to learn about Wolf's life and his vision on Mesoamerican archaeological research from different sources (Ghani and Wolf 1987; Kottak 2012; Silverman 1995). As a "neutral" ethnologist, who had just written *Sons of the Shaking Earth* (1959), Wolf was selected as coordinator (1960) and convener and editor (1976) based on his knowledge of the region. Actually, he was only peripherally interested in the planning and the actual archaeological research, which he found to be both exciting and significant.

CHRONOLOGY

Kolb (1979b:14–21) summarized the Obsidian Hydration Dating chronometric research conducted by Joseph Michels and colleagues (including Kolb) on obsidian excavated at Teotihuacan, especially from the Santa María Maquixco Bajo site (TC-8:1, 2, 3, 4) located west of the urban center. One reason for the skewed dates was the "accidental" mixing of obsidian samples from Preclassic (Cuanalan and Tezoyuca), Classic (TC-8), and Postclassic (Xometla) site excavations during the washing, drying, labeling, and cataloging of ceramic and lithic specimens at Hacienda Metepec during the summer of 1962. Sanders's three (mostly) preschool daughters would play games with the obsidian blades, moving them from one bag to another, before these were numbered or cataloged. I do not trust the Obsidian Hydration Dating results for the Maquixco excavations.

Much of the Basin of Mexico chronological research is based on relative chronology of artifacts, notably archaeological ceramics. During the 1960s, we were dependent on what little had been published in the path-breaking, monumental three-volume report, *La población del Valle de Teotihuacan*, volume 1(1):

TABLE 3.5. Classic phases covered by members of the TVP and TMP in the Teotihuacan Conference on Ceramics in Summer 1963

Phase	Presenter	Project	Fieldwork (excavation and survey)
Cuanalan	Mike West	TVP	Cuanalan and Tezoyuca excavations
Tezoyuca	Mike West	TVP	Cuanalan and Tezoyuca excavations
Tzacualli	Joe Marino	TVP	Preclassic and Classic site surveys
Teotihuacan	Joe Marino and Charlie Kolb	TVP	Classic site survey and excavations
Oxtotipac	John McCullough	TVP	Postclassic excavation
Xometla	John McCullough	TVP	Xometla
Mazapan	John McCullough	TVP	Postclassic survey
Aztec	W. T. Sanders	TVP	All excavations and surveys
Classic Phases: Miccaotli Tlamimilolpa Atoyac Xolalpan Metepec	J. A. Bennyhoff	TMP	Classic surveys and test pits

La población prehispánica, directed and edited by Manuel Gamio (1922), with an illustrated ten-page report on archaeological on excavated ceramics authored by Carlos Betancourt, as well as a *sobrito* issued in 1920 and as a chapter in volume 1(1) (1922:200–09). Gamio's contributions to stratigraphic excavations and settlement patterns are underrated; he passed away in 1960, just before the start of the TVP and TMP (León-Portilla 1962). The Swedish archaeologist Sigvald Linné (1899–1986) documented pottery excavated in residential areas of Teotihuacan, later published as *Archaeological Researches at Teotihuacan, Mexico* (Linné 1934) and *Mexican Highland Cultures: Archaeological Researches at Teotihuacan, Calpulalpan, and Chalchicomula in 1934–35* (Linné 1942; see also Wagner and Brunius 1988). French archaeologist Laurette Séjourné excavated in elite urban residential compounds and published a monograph on the pottery entitled *Arqueología de Teotihuacan: La cerámica* (Séjourné 1966), which contained monochrome line drawings generally lacking measurements and a few color illustrations. Better ceramic chronologies were obviously needed.

In the summer of 1963, a 12-session informal seminar-workshop on Teotihuacan Valley ceramics was held in San Juan Teotihuacan with attendees primarily from the staff of the TVP and the TMP (see table 3.5). A few staff from the Instituto Nacional de Antropología e Historia's (INAH) Proyecto Teotihuacan 1960–1964 (Ignacio Bernal, overall director) who were working in the urban ceremonial complex along the Avenue of the Dead (Miccaotli) attended the Classic period discussions. The sessions were held in the TMP facility, the Teotihuacan Archaeological Research Center at Calle Aldama 6, in the town of San Juan, where the organizer of the meetings, James Bennyhoff, utilized the growing pottery collections of the TMP. Collections from the TVP at Calzada Purificación 8 (and elsewhere in San Juan) were also brought to supplement the sessions. The sessions followed a chronological order from Preclassic through Postclassic with Jim Bennyhoff from the TMP survey team who had conducted been conducting excavations during the 1961 and 1962 field seasons and were engaged in the surface survey of 1963–1965 (Kolb 1979a).

Based on the notes by archaeologist Florencia Müller, the Instituto Nacional de Antropología e Historia published *Secuencia cerámica de Teotihuacan* (Gómez-Chavez 2008; Müller 1965, 1978). Bennyhoff wrote one book chapter (Bennyhoff 1966), but his extensive research on the ceramic chronology as part of the TMP was never published (Cowgill 2015:20–21). By 1981, Evelyn Rattray had completed a manuscript titled "The Teotihuacan Ceramic Chronology: Early Tzacualli to Metepec Phases," which was to be a volume in the Urbanization at Teotihuacan series, edited by Millon, but was never published. Numerous other versions of the Teotihuacan ceramic chronology were drafted during the 1980s and 1990s. Cowgill (2006) began a study to update the ceramics, but it, too, remained unpublished.

PUBLICATIONS

Teotihuacan Mapping Project Volumes: 1973–2012

The TMP Urbanization at Teotihuacan publications included four volumes. The initial volume was published in two parts by the University of Texas Press (Millon et al. 1973); the second volume, on mortuary practices, was published by the University of Utah Press (Sempowski and Spence 1994); the third volume, on ceramics and chronology, was copublished by the University of Pittsburgh and Universidad Nacional Autónoma de México (Rattray 2001); and the fourth volume, with digital files, was published electronically by Arizona State University (Cowgill et al. 2003).

I served as a manuscript reviewer for the University of Texas Press for several versions of the ceramics volume and for the University of Utah Press for the successfully published third volume and still another version of the ceramics volume in 1994 (Sempowski and Spence 1994), which remains the most comprehensive synthesis available on the ceramic assemblages. Cowgill (2006) also began work on a revised ceramics volume, but it was never published.

Teotihuacan Valley Project Volumes: 1965–2007

The TVP issued thirteen published monographs, beginning with an initial report in 1965 that synthesized information from 1961 through 1965 (Sanders 1965). A dozen other volumes were published beginning in 1975 by the Penn State Department of Anthropology and edited or coordinated by Sanders with, at times, Barbara Price or Susan Toby Evans as behind-the-scenes editors. The last volume was published in 2007 and are all available online at https://journals.psu.edu/opa/issue/archive. See also Sanders and colleagues (1994) and Sanders (1996) for other publications.

Combined Project Publications

Primary research syntheses based on both TVP and TMP research include William T. Sanders, Jeffrey R. Parsons, and Robert S. Santley's (1979) *The Basin of Mexico: Ecological Processes in the Evolution of a Civilization* and George L. Cowgill's (2015) *Ancient Teotihuacan: Early Urbanism in Central Mexico*. Two issues of *Ancient Mesoamerica* in 2015 were devoted to the status of studies in the Basin of Mexico (Fowler et al. 2015a, 2015b). Nichols (2017) and Manzanilla Naim (2017) have also written new summaries about Classic period Teotihuacan that utilize TVP and TMP data.

RESULTS OF THE TEOTIHUACAN PROJECTS

Positive

The TMP, TVP, and INAH cooperated in efforts to document the ceramic chronologies, types, and distribution of wares and fabrics. Thus, the TVP and TMP included Mexican archaeologists in the planning and execution of the projects. At least two generations of students were trained in field methods, laboratory processing of artifacts and publication, and proposal writing and review. The seminar-workshop model implemented along with these projects was very successful and helped level the ceramic analysis playing field, and the results, particularly of the TVP, were published quickly.

As it progressed, the TVP became more aware of urban influences at rural sites of the historic/Colonial period archaeology in the Basin (Charlton 2000). Consequently, the TMP, TVP, and INAH cooperatively produced data on more than 3,900 sites in the Basin and 2,500 "sites" in the urban center.

Negative

Surface surveys along the Southern and Northwestern sectors of the "Urban-Suburban-Rural Divide" (also called "No Sherd Land" or C/N, *casi nada*, areas). Sanders and Millon had originally agreed that a rural-urban boundary would be delineated when there was a 100 meter "*casi nada*" space between rural and urban architecture or artifact concentrations. Later, the TMP increased that figure to a 300-meter separation engulfing "suburban" sites—some already surveyed by TVP personnel—as Millon's urban center grew (Millon 1961, 1964, 1967). The urban-rural issue at Teotihuacan has been detailed by Gorenflo and Sanders (2017) and Gorenflo (2015), among others.

The TVP was troubled by the definition of a "site." Did artifact concentrations and architectural evidence both constitute sites? The TMP definition is likewise vague. Additionally, the site survey forms had some problems; the 1963

TVP site survey form (14 pages, 13 basic questions) was much too long; the 1963 TMP site survey form (1 page, 36 questions) did not allow for lengthy responses.

The initially slow pace of the TMP's urban surveys was due primarily to the complexity and volume of archaeological evidence. This issue was met by the fact that both the TVP and TMP survey teams were too small and needed more training both before going into the field and while in the field. Logistical problems were troublesome. The TMP was vexed by, among other issues, an inability to locate landowners or otherwise unable to secure permissions to survey, especially in the northwest quadrant of the urban center.

In addition to these problems, the TVP's field-by-field survey strategy necessitated a more general survey, though it proved to be too general, leading to a return to the field-by-field strategy that had initially been tried. Essentially, the TVP was an initial attempt at large-area surveying and a prelude to the Basin of Mexico field project (Parsons 2015, 2019).

The TVP and TMP both lacked a multidisciplinary approach, including any evidence for hydrology (irrigation, water sources, drainage systems, etc.). The TVP and TMP were also both plagued by the problem of "insubstantial" residential structures (Robertson 2008).

A series of problems also affected the artifacts. First, the TVP and TMP both lacked a firm ceramic chronology that accounted for the Early Postclassic Coyotlatelco and Mazapan Toltec phases; the term Epiclassic had not yet entered our vocabulary.

The TMP's difficulties reaching exact counts of certain specific categories of artifacts were caused by poorly documented removal of some "special" objects (such as sherds) from assemblages; there was little effect on totals, but some were misplaced or damaged during analysis. Finally, the TVP's Classic period excavation and survey assemblages were transported to the Penn State Anthropology Lab and studied by one person, myself, who was responsible for cataloging and documenting the corpus from 1962 to 1969.

CONCLUSIONS: LESSONS LEARNED AND LEGACIES

The definition of what constituted an archaeological "site" was initially a perplexing issue for TVP personnel, while the identification of "insubstantial" residential structures vexed both projects, as did the resolution of what constituted boundaries between urban, suburban, and rural sites. Project directors and field supervisors understood that thorough field-by-field surveys were more efficient and yielded more finite results, but also that no strategy could yield 100 percent coverage, especially where contemporary residents now live. Site modification by modern chisel plowing and destruction through the use of heavy construction and excavation equipment has proceeded unabated since the 1960s; witness the loss of structures along the Western Avenue in 1963, used as fill for the bed of the *super-carretera*. The rapid expansion and encroachment of modern Mexico City over the past six decades has continued throughout the Basin of Mexico with an incalculable loss of archaeological sites and irrigation systems. No Classic-period sites currently exist in the Lower and Middle Teotihuacan Valley up to the Teotihuacan Archaeological Zone.

Fortunately, the fieldwork conducted by both projects served to refine chronologies and document ancient sites dating from the Paleo-Indian era to the Colonial period. When the two projects began in the early 1960s, the technologies and equipment available predated the Internet, laptop computers, cellphones, and Xerox® copying machines. Thermo-Fax® machines made by 3M could create non-archival dark brown images on heat sensitive sheets that curled, faded, and became brittle and unreadable within a few years; the TMP had one in the lab. Back at the universities, IBM Selectric® typewriters were just being introduced, replacing manual machines and paper survey forms were being reproduced by black ink Gestetner Cyclograph® duplicating machines and Mimeograph stencil duplicators rather than blue ink Ditto® spirit duplicators.

The TVP had a skimpy budget and was dependent on Second World War surplus equipment (sleeping cots, storage shelving, clothing, etc.; two trucks and a van together cost less than $100!). In the field, "ancient" but reliable measuring equipment included an alidade, a theodolite, a tripod, a plane table, and a surveyor's rod. Jeff Parsons showed us how to master those tools. Since Aztec sites very often occurred on top of Classic-period structures, Jeff and I frequently worked together in the Lower and Middle Teotihuacan Valley recording sites up to Santa María Maquixco Bajo (TC-8) and rejoined on the eastern side of the Archaeological Zone.

Much was accomplished by enthusiastic project directors, notably Bill Sanders, who transferred that fervor to his students. The students were sidetracked only by the "Great Infectious Hepatitis Epidemic" of the late summer of 1963. Kolb and McCullough spent a month in the ABC (American British Cowdray) Hospital in Mexico City, while Parsons was hospitalized in Ann Arbor. The greatest legacy of the TVP, which morphed into the Basin of Mexico Project, was the training of students—now into a fourth generation—who themselves became advocates of settlement pattern studies.

The current tasks of the TMP and TVP/Basin of Mexico Project personnel in this newer era of cultural heritage preservation are to conserve archaeological collections, paper and digital site records, and other documentation, including photographs, slides, maps, and plans; we have little control over site conservancy. All of us owe this conservation to future researchers and educators. Tom Charlton and Jeff Parsons deserve our stewardship of the legacies they helped to create (Kolb 2021; Parsons 2019). Personally, I owe a debt to Jim Bennyhoff and Fred Matson, who showed me what information can be derived from ceramic analyses.

Acknowledgments. Thanks to the "Three Cs," Carlos Cordova, Chris Morehart, and Charles Frederick, for coming up with the idea for this volume. I also acknowledge a nearly six-decade friendship with my colleagues, Dick Diehl and the late Jeff Parsons. Any errors of fact are from my field notes and daily diaries—*mea culpa.*

REFERENCES

Bennyhoff, James A. 1952. "The Virú Valley Sequence: A Critical Review." *American Antiquity* 17(3):231–49.

Bennyhoff, James A. 1966. "Chronology and Periodization: Continuity and Change in the Teotihuacan Ceramic Tradition." *Teotihuacan: Onceava Mesa Redonda*, 19–29. Sociedad Mexicana de Antropología, Mexico City.

Bennyhoff, James A., and Charles C. Kolb. 1964. "La Ventilla Excavation 3:S1W2: Field Notes." Ms. on file. Department of Anthropology, University of Rochester, Rochester, New York.

Charlton, Thomas H. 1994. "TC-46 (Tlaltenco)." In *The Teotihuacan Valley Project Final Report*, vol. 3: *The Teotihuacan Period Occupation of the Valley*, pt. 1: *The Excavations*, edited by William T. Sanders, 42–49 + 14 unnumbered. Occasional Papers in Anthropology, no. 19. Matson Museum of Anthropology, Department of Anthropology, The Pennsylvania State University, University Park.

Charlton, Thomas H. 2000. "Urban Influences at Rural Sites: Teotihuacán and Its Near Hinterlands." Foundation for the Advancement of Mesoamerican Studies Inc. Electronic document. http://www.famsi.org/reports/97025/97025Charlton01.pdf, accessed October 20, 2022.

Collier, Donald. 1955. "Cultural Chronology and Change as Reflected in the Ceramics of the Virú Valley, Peru." *Fieldiana: Anthropology*, no. 43. Chicago Natural History Museum, Chicago.

Cowgill, George L. 2006. "An Outline of the Ceramics of Teotihuacan, Mexico." Electronic document. https://docs.google.com/viewer?a=v&pid=sites&srcid =YXNiLmVkdXxnZW9yZ2VfY 293Z2lsbHxneDo2NjcyZmIwMzJmM2RlZTI5, accessed October 16, 2022.

Cowgill, George L. 2015. *Ancient Teotihuacan: Early Urbanism in Central Mexico*. Cambridge University Press, Cambridge.

Cowgill, George L., Ian G. Robertson, and Rebecca S. Sload. 2003. *Electronic Files from the Teotihuacan Mapping Project*. Updated by Cowgill through February 14, 2012. Department of Anthropology, Arizona State University, Tempe. Electronic document. https://doi.org/10.6067/XCV81C1WM3, accessed October 16, 2022.

Drewitt, Robert Bruce. 1967. "Irrigation and Agriculture in the Valley of Teotihuacan." PhD dissertation, Department of Anthropology, University of California, Berkeley.

Ford, James A., and Gordon R. Willey. 1949. "Virú Valley: Background and Problems." In *Surface Survey of the Virú Valley, Peru*, by James A. Ford, 29–89. Anthropological Papers, vol. 43, no. 1. American Museum of Natural History, New York.

Fowler, William R., L. J. Gorenflo, and Ian G. Robertson, eds. 2015a. "Special Section: Taking Stock of Basin of Mexico Archaeology in the Early Twenty-First Century," pt. 1. Special section, *Ancient Mesoamerica* 26(1):127–212.

Fowler, William R., L. J. Gorenflo, and Ian G. Robertson, eds. 2015b. "Special Section: Taking Stock of Basin of Mexico Archaeology in the Early Twenty-First Century," pt. 2. Special section, *Ancient Mesoamerica* 26(2):371–470.

Gamio, Manuel, ed. and dir. 1922. *La población del Valle de Teotihuacan*, vol. 1, pt. 1: *La población prehispánica*. Dirección de Talleres Graficos, Mexico City.

Ghani, Mohammad Ashraf and Eric Wolf. 1987. "A Conversation with Eric Wolf." *American Ethnologist* 14(2):346–66.

Gómez-Chavez, Sergio. 2008. "Florencia Emilia Jacobs Müller: Contribuciones a la arqueología y conocimiento de Teotihuacan." *Arqueología* 38:206–19.

Gorenflo, Larry J. 2015. "Compilation and Analysis of Pre-Columbian Settlement Data in the Basin of Mexico." *Ancient Mesoamerica* 26(1):197–212.

Gorenflo, Larry J., and William T. Sanders. 2017. *Archaeological Settlement Pattern Data from the Cuautitlan, Temascalapa, and Teotihuacan Regions, Mexico*. Occasional Papers in Anthropology, no. 30. Department of Anthropology, The Pennsylvania State University, University Park.

Heizer, Robert F., and John A. Graham. 1967. *A Guide to Field Methods in Archaeology*. National Press, Palo Alto, CA.

Hirth, Kenneth G., David M. Carballo, and Barbara Arroyo. 2020 *Teotihuacan: The World Beyond the City*. Dumbarton Oaks Research Library & Collection, Washington, DC.

Hughes, Richard E. 1994. "Memorial to James Allan Bennyhoff (January 3, 1926–August 4, 1993)." *Journal of California and Great Basin Archaeology* 16(1):2–12.

Huster, Angela C., Oralia Cabrera-Cortés, Marion Forest, Francis P. McManamon, Ian G. Robertson, and Michael E. Smith. 2018. "Documenting, Disseminating and Archiving Data from the Teotihuacan Mapping Project." *Antiquity* 92(363):e9 1–6.

Kolb, Charles C. 1973. "Thin Orange Pottery at Teotihuacan." In *Miscellaneous Papers in Anthropology*, edited by William T. Sanders, 309–77. Department of Anthropology, The Pennsylvania State University, University Park.

Kolb, Charles C. 1979a. "Classic Teotihuacan Period Settlement Patterns in the Teotihuacan Valley, Mexico." 2 vols. PhD dissertation, Department of Anthropology, The Pennsylvania State University, University Park.

Kolb, Charles C. 1979b. "The Classic Teotihuacán Period Chronology: Some Reflections." *Katunob: Newsletter-Bulletin on Mesoamerican Archaeology* 11(2):1–51.

Kolb, Charles C. 1984. "Technological and Cultural Aspects of Teotihuacan Period: Thin Orange Ware." In *Pots and Potters: Current Approaches in Ceramic Archaeology*, edited by Prudence M. Rice, 209–26. Institute of Archaeology Papers. University of California, Los Angeles.

Kolb, Charles C. 1986. "Commercial Aspects of Classic Teotihuacan Period 'Thin Orange' Wares." In *Economic Aspects of Prehispanic Highland Mexico*, edited by Barry L. Isaac, 155–205. JAI Press, Greenwich, CT.

Kolb, Charles C. 1987. *Marine Shell Trade and Classic Teotihuacán, Mexico*. BAR International Series, no. 364. British Archaeological Reports, Oxford.

Kolb, Charles C. 1988a. "Classic Teotihuacan *Candeleros*: A Preliminary Analysis." In *Ceramic Ecology Revisited, 1987: The Technology and Socioeconomics of Pottery*, edited by Charles C. Kolb, 449–646. BAR International Series, no. 436 (ii). British Archaeological Reports, Oxford.

Kolb, Charles C. 1988b. "Classic Teotihuacan Copoid Wares: Ceramic Ecological Interpretations." In *Ceramic Ecology Revisited, 1987: The Technology and Socioeconomics of Pottery*, edited by Charles C. Kolb, 345–448. BAR International Series, no. 436 (ii), British Archaeological Reports, Oxford.

Kolb, Charles C. 1988c. "Classic Teotihuacan Granular Wares: Ceramic Ecological Interpretations." In *Ceramic Ecology Revisited, 1987: The Technology and Socioeconomics of Pottery*, edited by Charles C. Kolb, 227–344. BAR International Series, no. 436 (ii). British Archaeological Reports, Oxford.

Kolb, Charles C. 1995. "Teotihuacan Period Figurines: A Typological Classification, and Their Spatial and Temporal Distribution in the Teotihuacan Valley." In *The Teotihuacan Valley Project Final Report*, vol. 3: *The Teotihuacan Period Occupation of the Valley*, pt. 2: *Artifact Analyses*, edited by William T. Sanders, 275–465. Occasional Papers in Anthropology, no. 20. Matson Museum of Anthropology, Department of Anthropology, The Pennsylvania State University, University Park.

Kolb, Charles C. 1996. "Marine and Fresh Water Molluscs from Rural Teotihuacán Sites." In *The Teotihuacan Valley Project Final Report*, vol. 3: *The Teotihuacan Period Occupation of the Valley*, pt. 4: *Special Analyses, Miscellaneous Appendices, and Volume Bibliography*, edited by William T. Sanders, 920–23. Occasional Papers in Anthropology, no. 24. Matson Museum of Anthropology, Department of Anthropology, The Pennsylvania State University, University Park.

Kolb, Charles C. 1997. "Analyses of Archaeological Ceramics from Classic Period Teotihuacán Mexico, A.D. 150–750." In *Materials Issues in Art and Archaeology*, edited by Pamela B. Vandiver, James R. Druzik, John F. Merkel, and John Stewart, vol. 5, 247–62. Symposium Proceedings 463, Materials Research Society, Pittsburgh, PA.

Kolb, Charles C. 2010. "In Memoriam: Tom—We Hardly Knew Ye: Thomas H. Charlton, 1938–2010." *Ancient Mesoamerica* 21(2):207–10.

Kolb, Charles C. 2018. "Mesoamerica in the Classical Period. *Encyclopedia of Global Archaeology*, 2nd ed., edited by Claire Smith." Living reference work entry, first online:

August 20, 2018. Springer, Cham, Switzerland. Electronic document. https://link
.springer.com/content/pdf/10.1007/978-3-319-51726-1_2899-1.

Kolb, Charles C. 2019a. "William T. Sanders." *Encyclopedia of Global Archaeology*, 2nd ed.,
edited by Claire Smith. Living reference work entry, first online: November 20, 2019.
Springer, Cham, Switzerland. Electronic document. https://link.springer.com
/content/pdf/10.1007%2F978-3-319-51726-1_3472-1, accessed October 20, 2022.

Kolb, Charles C. 2019b. "Frederick R. Matson." *Encyclopedia of Global Archaeology*, 2nd
ed., edited by Claire Smith. Living reference work entry, first online: January 25, 2019.
Springer, Cham, Switzerland. Electronic document. https://link.springer.com
/referenceworkentry/10.1007%2F978-3-319-51726-1_3427-1, accessed October 20, 2022.

Kolb, Charles C. 2021. "In Memoriam: Jeffrey R. Parsons (October 9, 1939–March 19,
2021)." *The SAA Archaeological Record* 21(4):39.

Kolb, Charles C., Thomas H. Charlton, Warren DeBoer, Roland Fletcher, Paul F. Healy,
Robert R. Janes, Raoul Naroll, and Daniel Shea. 1985. "Demographic Estimates in
Archaeology: Contributions from Ethnoarchaeology on Mesoamerican Peasants
[and comments and reply]." *Current Anthropology* 26(5):581–99.

Kolb, Charles C., and William T. Sanders. 1996a. "The Surface Survey: Classic Period
Settlement Patterns in the Teotihuacán Valley." In *The Teotihuacan Valley Project Final
Report*, vol. 3: *The Teotihuacan Period Occupation of the Valley*, pt. 3: *The Surface Survey*,
edited by William T. Sanders, 484–653. Occasional Papers in Anthropology, no. 21.
Matson Museum of Anthropology, Department of Anthropology, The Pennsylvania
State University, University Park.

Kolb, Charles C., and William T. Sanders. 1996b. "Urban and Rural Settlement in the
Teotihuacán Valley: A Reconstruction." In *The Teotihuacan Valley Project Final Report*,
vol. 3: *The Teotihuacan Period Occupation of the Valley*, pt. 3: *The Surface Survey*, edited
by William T. Sanders, 654–717. Occasional Papers in Anthropology, no. 21. Matson
Museum of Anthropology, Department of Anthropology, The Pennsylvania State
University, University Park.

Kottak, Conrad Phillip. 2012. *Eric Robert Wolf 1923–1999: A Biographical Memoir*. National
Academy of Sciences, Washington, DC.

Kroeber, Alfred L. 1925. "The Uhle Pottery Collection from Peru." *University of California Publications in American Archaeology and Ethnology* 21:191–264.

Leon-Portilla, Miguel. 1962. "Manuel Gamio, 1883–1960." *American Anthropologist*
64(1):356–55.

Linné, Sigvald. 1934. *Archaeological Researches at Teotihuacan, Mexico*. New Series Publication, no. 1. The Ethnographical Museum of Sweden / Etnografiska Museet,
Riksmuseets etnografiska avdelning. Stockholm. Republished 2003 with an introduction by George L. Cowgill. University of Alabama Press, Tuscaloosa.

Linné, Sigvald. 1942. *Mexican Highland Cultures: Archaeological Researches at Teotihuacan, Calpulalpan, and Chalchicomula in 1934–35*. New Series Publication, no. 7. The

Ethnographical Museum of Sweden, Stockholm / Etnografiska Museet, Riksmuseets etnografiska avdelning, Stockholm. Republished 2003 with an introduction by George L. Cowgill. University of Alabama Press, Tuscaloosa.

Manzanilla Naim, Linda Rosa. 2017. *Teotihuacan, ciudad exceptional de Mesoamérica.* Opúsculos. El Colegio Nacional, Mexico City.

Mayer-Oakes, William J. 1959. "A Stratigraphic Excavation at El Risco, Mexico." *Proceedings of the American Philosophical Society* 103(3):332–73.

Millon René, and Jeffrey H. Altschul. 2015. "The Making of the Map: The Origin and Lessons of the Teotihuacan Mapping Project." *Ancient Mesoamerica* 26:135–51.

Millon, René. 1961. "The Northwestern Boundary of Teotihuacán: A Major Urban Zone." In *Homenaje a Pablo Martínez del Río, en el vigésimoquinto aniversario de la primera edición de los orígenes americanos,* edited by Ignacio Bernal et al., 311–18. Instituto Nacional de Antropología e Historia, Mexico City.

Millon, René. 1964. "The Teotihuacán Mapping Project." *American Antiquity* 29:345–52.

Millon, René. 1967. "Extensión y población de la ciudad de Teotihuacan en sus diferentes períodos: Un cálculo provisional." In *Teotihuacan: Onceava Mesa Redonda,* 57–78. Sociedad Mexicana de Antropología, Mexico City.

Millon, René, R. Bruce Drewitt, and George Cowgill. 1973. *Urbanization at Teotihuacan, Mexico,* vol. 1: *The Teotihuacan Map,* pt. 2: *Maps.* University of Texas Press, Austin.

Müller, Florencia. 1965. "Secuencia cerámica de Teotihuacan." *Katunob: Newsletter-Bulletin on Mesoamerican Archaeology* 5(4):16–25.

Müller, Florencia. 1978. *La cerámica del centro ceremonial de Teotihuacan.* Publica, Instituto Nacional de Antropología e Historia, Mexico City.

Nichols, Deborah L. 2017. "Teotihuacan." *Journal of Archaeological Research* 24(1):1–74.

Parsons, Jeffrey R. 2015. "An Appraisal of Regional Surveys in the Basin of Mexico, 1960–1975." *Ancient Mesoamerica* 26(1):183–96.

Parsons, Jeffrey R. 2019. *Remembering Archaeological Fieldwork in Mexico and Peru, 1960–2003: A Photographic Essay.* Special Publication, no. 3. Museum of Anthropology, University of Michigan, Ann Arbor.

Porter Weaver, Muriel Noé. 1993. *The Aztecs, Maya, and Their Predecessors: Archaeology of Mesoamerica,* 3 eds. Seminar, New York and London, 1972; Academic, New York, 1981; Academic, San Diego, 1993.

Rattray, Evelyn Childs. 2001. *Teotihuacan: Ceramics, Chronology, and Cultural Trends / Teotihuacan: Cerámica, cronología y tendencias culturales.* Bilingual and co-published: Latin American Archaeology Publications, University of Pittsburgh, and Investigaciones Antropológicas, Universidad Nacional Autónoma de México, Mexico City.

Robertson, Ian G. 2008. *"Insubstantial" Residential Structures at Teotihuacán, Mexico.* Foundation for the Advancement of Mesoamerican Studies. Electronic document. http://www.famsi.org/reports/06103/06103Robertson01.pdf, accessed October 20, 2022.

Sanders, William T. 1965. *The Cultural Ecology of the Teotihuacán Valley: A Preliminary Report of the Results of the Teotihuacán Valley Project*. University Park: The Pennsylvania State University, Department of Sociology and Anthropology.

Sanders, William T., ed. 1996. *The Teotihuacan Valley Project Final Report*, vol. 3: *The Teotihuacan Period Occupation of the Valley*, pt. 3: *The Surface Survey*. Occasional Papers in Anthropology, no. 21. Matson Museum of Anthropology, Department of Anthropology, The Pennsylvania State University, University Park.

Sanders, William T., and Charles C. Kolb. 1994. "TC-8 (Maquixco Bajo)." In *The Teotihuacan Valley Project Final Report*, vol. 3: *The Teotihuacan Period Occupation of the Valley*, pt. 1: *The Excavations*, edited by William T. Sanders, 1–41. Occasional Papers in Anthropology, no. 19. Matson Museum of Anthropology, The Pennsylvania State University, University Park.

Sanders, William T., Jeffrey R. Parsons, and Robert S. Santley. 1979. *The Basin of Mexico: Ecological Processes in the Evolution of a Civilization*. Studies in Archaeology. Academic, New York.

Sanders, William T., and Charles C. Kolb. 1996. "Urban and Rural Settlement in the Teotihuacán Valley: A Reconstruction." In *The Teotihuacan Valley Project Final Report*, vol. 3: *The Teotihuacan Period Occupation of the Valley*, pt. 1: *The Excavations*, edited by William T. Sanders, 654–717. Occasional Papers in Anthropology, no. 21. Matson Museum of Anthropology, Department of Anthropology, The Pennsylvania State University, University Park.

Sanders, William T., Charles C. Kolb, and Larry J. Gorenflo. 1994. *The Teotihuacan Valley Project Final Report*, vol. 3: *The Teotihuacan Period Occupation of the Valley*, pt. 1: *The Excavations*, edited by William T. Sanders. Occasional Papers in Anthropology, no. 19. Matson Museum of Anthropology, Department of Anthropology, The Pennsylvania State University, University Park.

Séjourné, Laurette. 1966. *Arqueología de Teotihuacan: La cerámica*. Fondo de Cultura Económica, Mexico City.

Sempowski, Martha L., and Michael W. Spence. 1994. *Urbanization at Teotihuacan, Mexico*, vol. 3: *Mortuary Practices and Skeletal Remains at Teotihuacan*, edited by René Millon. University of Utah Press, Salt Lake City.

Silverman, Sydel Finfer [wife of Eric Wolf]. 1995. Personal communication. Tarrytown, New York. February 23–24, 1995.

Steward, Julian H., ed. 1949. *Handbook of South American Indians*, vol. 5: *The Comparative Ethnology of South American Indians*. Smithsonian Institution, Bureau of Ethnology Bulletin, no. 143. US Government Printing Office, Washington; reprinted 1963, Cooper Square, New York.

Steward, Julian H. 1955. *Theory of Culture Change: The Methodology of Multilinear Evolution*. University of Illinois Press, Urbana [7 printings, paperback ed. 1973, print on demand 2008].

Strong, William Duncan, and Clifford Evans Jr. 1952. *Cultural Stratigraphy in the Virú Valley Northern Peru: The Formative and Florescent Epochs*. Columbia University Press, New York.

Tolstoy, Paul. 1958. "Surface Survey of the Northern Valley of Mexico: The Classic and Post Classic Periods." *Transactions of the American Philosophical Society* 48(5):1–101.

Vaillant, George C. 1937. "History and Stratigraphy in the Valley of Mexico." *Scientific Monthly* 44(4):307–24.

Vaillant, George C. 1938. "A Correlation of Archaeological and Historical Sequences in the Valley of Mexico." *American Anthropologist* 40(4):535–73.

Vidarte de Linares, Juan. 1964. *Exploraciones arqueológicas en el Rancho La Ventilla: Informe al Departamento de Monumentos Prehispanicas*. Instituto Nacional de Antropología e Historia, Mexico City.

Vogt, Evan Z., Jr. 2004. *Gordon Randolph Willey: March 7, 1913–April 28, 2001: Biographical Memoir*. National Academy of Science, Washington, DC.

Wagner, Ulla, and Stajfan Brunius. 1988. "In Memoriam: Sigvald Linné 1899–1986." *Ethnos: Journal of Anthropology* 53(1–2):124–25.

Willey, Gordon R. 1946. "The Virú Valley Program in Northern Peru." *Acta Americana* 4(4):224–38.

Willey, Gordon R. 1953. *Prehistoric Settlement Patterns in the Virú Valley, Peru*. Smithsonian Institution, Bureau of American Ethnology, Bulletin no. 155. US Government Printing Office, Washington, DC.

Willey, Gordon R. 1974. "The Virú Valley Settlement Pattern Study." In *Archaeological Researches in Retrospect*, edited by Gordon R. Willey, 149–78. Winthrop, Cambridge, MA.

Wolf, Eric R. 1959. *Sons of the Shaking Earth: The People of Mexico and Guatemala; Their Land, History, and Culture*. University of Chicago Press.

Wolf, Eric R. 1960. "Report of a Conference to Plan Anthropological Research in the Valley of Mexico." Ms. On file. Department of Anthropology, The Pennsylvania State University, University Park.

Wolf, Eric R. 1961. "Conferences: Coordinated Anthropological Research in the Valley of Mexico." *Current Anthropology* 2(1):68.

Wolf, Eric R., ed. 1976. *The Valley of Mexico: Studies in Pre-Hispanic Ecology and Society*. School of American Research, Albuquerque, New Mexico.

PART II

New Approaches to the Green Book's Contribution to Settlement and Demography

4

Why Is Aztec II Black-on-Orange Pottery So Scarce in the Zumpango Region?

A Regional Perspective from the Basin of Mexico on Tula's Collapse and Its Aftermath

JEFFREY R. PARSONS AND L. J. GORENFLO

INTRODUCTION

In this chapter, we consider how Early and Middle Postclassic settlement patterning and ceramic distributions in the Basin of Mexico illuminate Tula's collapse in the twelfth century CE and the impact of that collapse on subsequent developments within and around the Basin. Specifically, we focus on the absence of Aztec II Black-on-Orange (B/O) pottery in the far northwestern Basin (the Zumpango region), an area where both Tollan-phase Red-on-Buff and Aztec III B/O ceramics were abundant in the preceding Early Postclassic and subsequent Late Postclassic periods, respectively (see figure 4.1). These questions emerged from the seminal 1979 volume (Sanders et al. 1979) but remain inadequately studied, despite their implications for the sociocultural evolution of the Basin and surrounding regions in highland Mesoamerica.

BACKGROUND

Sanders, Parsons, and Santley (1979) reported that their regional surveys had detected large-scale depopulation during the Middle Postclassic (Early Aztec)

https://doi.org/10.5876/9781646424078.c004

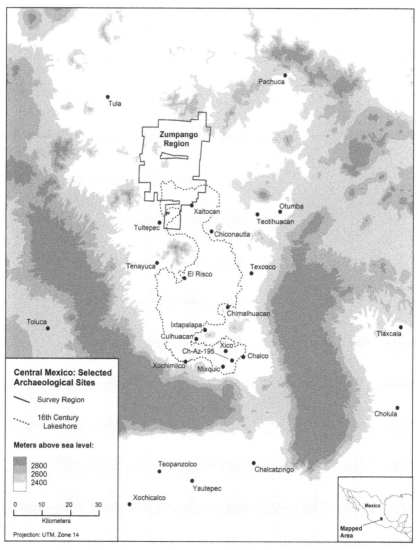

FIGURE 4.1. *Map of Central Mexico, showing principal localities and places mentioned in the text.*

in the Zumpango region (see table 4.1, figure 4.2a). They concluded that this massive loss of population was linked to the turmoil that accompanied the collapse of Tula in the twelfth century. Nevertheless, Parsons (2008) remained uncomfortable with the idea that there could have been such a massive demographic decline in a region that had apparently been so densely inhabited during both the preceding Early Postclassic (see figure 4.2b) and the subsequent Late Postclassic (see figure 4.2c).

Parsons's skepticism concerns the definition of the Late Toltec and Early Aztec phases, which depend heavily on the occurrence of three diagnostic ceramic types with imprecise distributions in space and time throughout the Basin of Mexico: Mazapan Red/ Buff (Early Postclassic/Late Toltec, similar to Tollan phase Red/ Buff defined at Tula), and Aztec I B/O and Aztec II B/O (lumped together in the Basin surveys to define Middle Postclassic/Early Aztec). Archaeologists defined these ceramic categories in the

TABLE 4.1. Basin of Mexico Epiclassic and Postclassic chronology

600

Years CE	Major Period	Phase
1520	Late Postclassic/ Late Aztec	Aztec III (Late Aztec)
1400	Middle Postclassic/ Early Aztec	Aztec II-III (?) Aztec II Aztec I (?)
1200	Early Postclassic/ Late Toltec	Aztec I (Early Aztec) Mazapan-Tollan (Late Toltec)
900		Coyotlatelco
600	Epiclassic/Early Toltec	

southern and central Basin during the early and mid-twentieth century (Boas and Gamio 1921; Brenner 1931; Franco 1945, 1949; Franco and Peterson 1957; Griffin and Espejo 1947, 1950; Noguera 1935; Vaillant 1938) and at Tula (Acosta 1940, 1941, 1944, 1945).

Some of these early investigators felt there was some degree of chronological overlap and spatial separation between Mazapan and Aztec I, but their views remained suggestive rather than definitive. Based on his work at Tula, Acosta (1952) felt that the chronological relationships between Culhuacan (Aztec I) B/O and Tenayuca (Aztec II) B/O (as defined by Griffin and Espejo 1947, 1950) were unclear. Vaillant (1938) conducted a definitive study of the relationships between these ceramic types based on his excavations at Chiconautla (see figure 4.1) and other Postclassic sites, but never published results of this study.

Studies during subsequent decades (e.g., Mayer-Oakes 1959; Müller 1952; O'Neill 1962; Parsons 1966, 1971; Parsons, Brumfiel, Parsons, and Wilson 1982; Sanders 1965, 1986; Séjourné 1970, 1983; Tolstoy 1958) refined our understanding of these ceramics within the Basin of Mexico and at nearby Tula (Cobean 1978, 1990). Mayer-Oakes's (1959) pioneering stratigraphic excavations at El Risco in the west-central Basin were especially important for determining chronological relationships between Mazapan Red/Buff, Aztec I B/O, and Aztec II B/O. At El Risco, Mayer-Oakes found Mazapan Red/Buff and Aztec I B/O ceramics co-occurring in levels stratigraphically below those with Aztec II B/O pottery. Tolstoy's (1958) seriation of surface collections from the northern Basin suggested a partial chronological overlap between Aztec I and Aztec II B/O. O'Neill's (1962) deep stratigraphic excavations at Chalco, and Séjourné's (1970) at Culhuacan, also indicated partial chronological overlap between Aztec II B/O

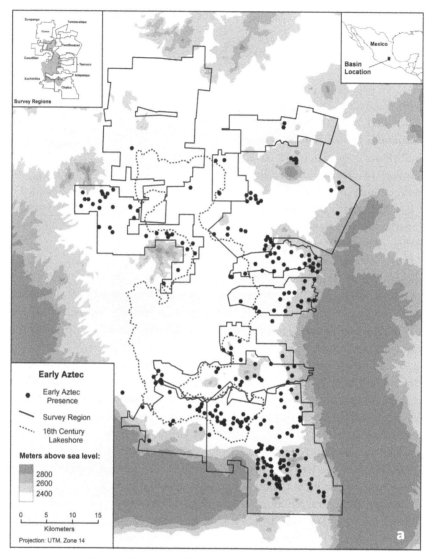

FIGURE 4.2. *Late Toltec and Early, Middle, and Late Postclassic occupation in the Basin of Mexico: (a) Middle Postclassic (Early Aztec) occupation in the Basin of Mexico; (b) Early Postclassic (Late Toltec/Mazapan) occupation in the Basin of Mexico; (c) Late Postclassic (Late Aztec) occupation in the Basin of Mexico; and (d) Late Toltec sites with Early Aztec occupation.*

and later stages of the Aztec I B/O sequence at those sites, a relationship later confirmed by Brumfiel (2005b) at Xaltocan.

The decision by Sanders, Parsons, and Santley (1979) to lump Aztec I B/O and Aztec II B/O together as archaeological indicators of the Middle Postclassic

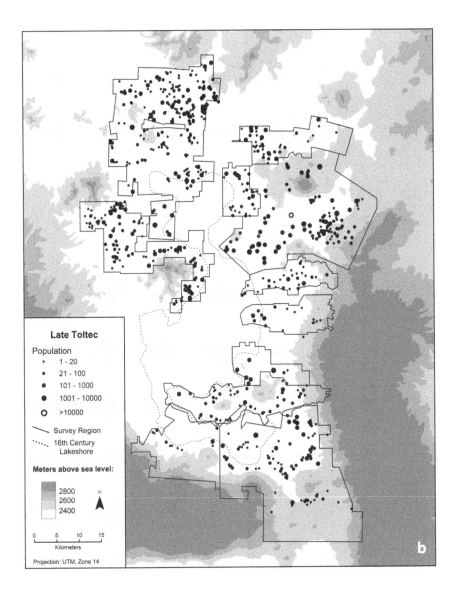

Late Toltec

Population
- ·   1 - 20
- •   21 - 100
- ●   101 - 1000
- ⬤   1001 - 10000
- ○   >10000

—   Survey Region
·····   16th Century Lakeshore

Meters above sea level:

2800
2600
2400

N

0   5   10   15
Kilometers

Projection: UTM, Zone 14

b

(Early Aztec) overlooked the potential temporal overlap between Aztec I B/O (and possibly even Aztec II B/O) and Mazapan-Tollan Red/Buff, as well as the possibility that Aztec I B/O and Aztec II B/O differed significantly in terms of their absolute chronology. However, apart from the major exception of Xaltocan, Aztec I B/O was never encountered in any quantity until the surveys had extended into the southern Basin. Archaeologists had simply overlooked this potential difficulty until having to confront the virtual absence of *both* Aztec I B/O and Aztec II B/O in the Zumpango region (Parsons 2008).

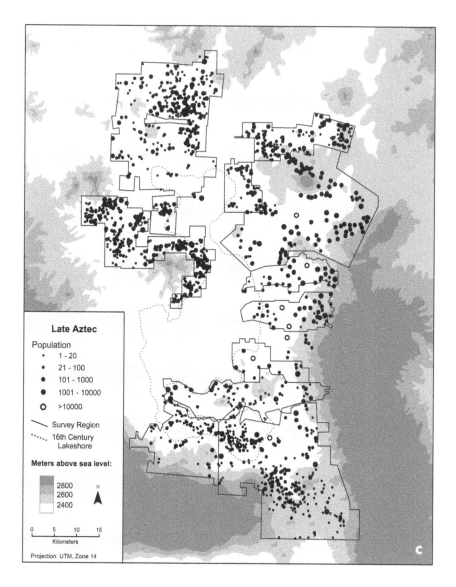

Based on the above observations, in the following pages we explore three interrelated questions:

1. Did part of the Early Postclassic (Late Toltec) ceramic assemblage presently defined in the Zumpango region extend chronologically into the Middle Postclassic? If so, our Late Toltec assemblage in that part of the Basin needs refinement to separate Early Postclassic and Middle Postclassic components. This uncertainty was reinforced by the difficulty of defining immediate post-Tollan ceramics outside of Tula itself, where Aztec II B/O occurs in deposits

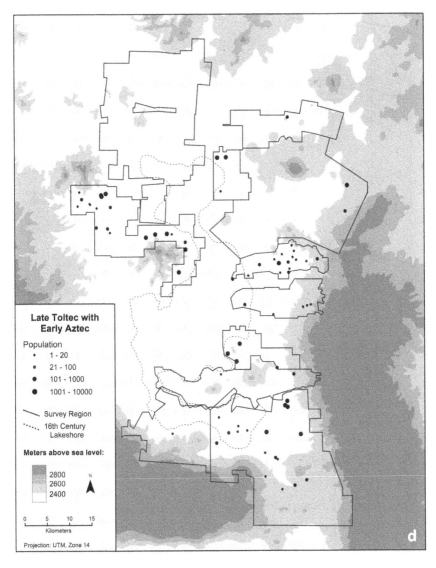

associated with the era of that center's destruction in the twelfth century (Mastache et al. 2002:42).

2. Was one distinctive variant of B/O pottery,[1] which had been lumped into the Late Aztec (Aztec III B/O) category during the Zumpango survey, chronologically equivalent to Aztec II B/O in this part of the Basin? This variant, which

---

[1] This variant has sometimes been referred to informally as Aztec II-III B/O, but it should not be confused with Franco's (1949, 1957) much differently defined Aztec II-III B/O, which falls clearly into our Aztec III B/O category.

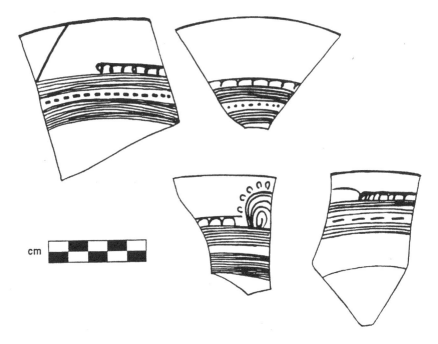

FIGURE 4.3. *Typical Variant D Black/Orange decoration. Adapted from Hodge and Minc (1991:131, figure 3.5).*

looks stylistically intermediate between typical Aztec II and III types, had been distinguished as Variant D of B/O decoration on certain vessel forms by Parsons (1966:plate 32) and by Hodge and Minc (1991:131) (see figure 4.3). Vaillant (1938:541) long ago distinguished at Chiconautla a *late* variant of his Aztec II B/O category (designated as IIc), which appears to be very similar to Variant D.

3. Were Mazapan-Tollan Red/Buff, Aztec I B/O, and Aztec II B/O ceramics in use over different ranges of absolute time in different parts of the Basin of Mexico? If so, then the periods of absolute time defined by their presence would be different in different parts of the Basin.

If any or all of these questions could be answered in the affirmative, the hypothesized Middle Postclassic population loss in the Zumpango region might need to be reconsidered. If, on the other hand, none could be answered in the affirmative, the hypothesized Middle Postclassic population decline would stand on a firmer foundation. Resolving the question of depopulation in the northern third of the Basin of Mexico during the immediate aftermath of Tula's demise in the twelfth century has obvious implications for understanding the nature of that demise.

THE CHRONOLOGY AND DISTRIBUTION
OF MAZAPAN-TOLLAN RED/BUFF, AZTEC I
B/O, AND AZTEC II B/O CERAMICS

By the late 1980s, there was general consensus on the following. This chronology, with some adjustments in absolute dating, continues to be generally accepted (e.g., Cowgill 1996):

1. Mazapan-phase Red/Buff pottery (or similar variants) occurred throughout the Basin of Mexico, closely related to Tollan-phase material at nearby Tula, and dating to ca. 900–1150 CE;

2. Aztec I B/O that occurred in quantity only in the southern third of the Basin of Mexico and at Xaltocan in the northern Basin was closely related to ceramic types found further south in Morelos (Norr 1987; Smith 1983), as well as to the east and southeast at Cholula and throughout southwestern Puebla (Müller 1978; Noguera 1954; Plunket 1990), probably at least partially contemporary with Mazapan-Tollan and dating to ca. 1000–1250 CE; and

3. Aztec II B/O occurring throughout the Basin of Mexico and at Tula, probably dated to ca. 1200–1350 CE, after which it was everywhere superseded by Aztec III B/O, with the Aztec II B/O generally presumed to be characteristic of Middle Postclassic occupation throughout the Basin.

Reexamination of Late Toltec Collections from the Zumpango Region

Several years ago, Parsons and Robert Cobean reexamined most of the original surface collections from surveyed Late Toltec sites in the Zumpango region. They found that this material is identical to Cobean's Tollan phase at Tula: it includes not only diagnostic Red/Buff pottery, but also most other characteristic ceramic types (Cobean 1978, 1990). Consequently, we assume that the Late Toltec occupation in the Zumpango region is coeval with the duration of the Tollan phase at Tula. If the Tollan phase defined at Tula does not extend into the Middle Postclassic, then neither would the Late Toltec occupation in the Zumpango region. Given Tula's proximity to the Zumpango region (see figures 4.1 and 4.2), this assumption appears reasonable.

The Chronological Status of Aztec II–III (Var. D) B/O

The chronological placement of Aztec II-III (Var. D) B/O remains unclear, but should probably continue to be lumped into the general Aztec III B/O category. It occurs in surface collections throughout the Zumpango region and elsewhere in the Basin of Mexico, but never in clear Aztec II contexts and always closely associated with typical Aztec III B/O and other types of Late Postclassic (Late Aztec) pottery. To be certain how Aztec II-III (Var. D) B/O is distributed in time and space, we would need a full-scale reanalysis of the surface collections from all Basin surveys, as well as new stratigraphic excavations at key sites. However, at present we have no reason to think that Aztec II-III (Var. D) B/O is coeval with typical Aztec II B/O. Thus, we continue to assume that (Var. D) B/O is Late Aztec in date, although it may well occur early within that phase, and perhaps even begins in the late Middle Postclassic (as Vaillant originally thought).

Early-to-Middle Postclassic Settlement Continuity and Discontinuity in the Basin of Mexico

High occupational continuity might indicate comparative social stability, whereas non-continuity might signal major disruptive forces during the periods when Mazapan-Tollan Red/Buff, Aztec I B/O, and Aztec II B/O ceramics were in use. For example, serious social instability in Middle Postclassic times might have disrupted networks for exchanging ceramics defining Early and Middle Postclassic occupation in the Basin of Mexico.

Settlement survey data indicate varying degrees of occupational continuity at Early-to-Middle Postclassic and Middle-to-Late Postclassic sites in different parts of the Basin. These data indicate a much higher degree of settlement continuity in the southeastern (Chalco region), eastern (Texcoco region), and northwest-central Basin (Cuauhtitlan region) relative to the northern (Zumpango, Teotihuacan, and Temascalapa regions), southwestern (Xochimilco region), and south-central (Ixtapalapa region) parts of the surveyed Basin (see table 4.2). Focusing on Aztec I and II in the Chalco-Xochimilco region, of the 121 sites with an Early Aztec presence, 27.2 percent (33 sites) have only Aztec I B/O, 14.9 percent (18 sites) have only Aztec II B/O, and 16.5 percent (20 sites) have both (see figure 4.4). This co-occurrence had been known for some time at particular sites, such as Culhuacan at the western end of the Ixtapalapa peninsula (Blanton 1972; Boas and Gamio 1921; Brenner 1931; Parsons, Brumfiel, Parsons, and Wilson 1982; Séjourné 1970). Regarding the Mazapan-Aztec I transition in the Chalco-Xochimilco region, 10.9 percent of the Mazapan sites (11 of the 101 sites) have Aztec I B/O, while 10.7 percent (13 sites) of the Early Aztec sites have Mazapan Red/Buff pottery (see figure 4.4). At dozens of sites throughout that region, a distinctive Mazapan-related Early Postclassic (Late Toltec) ceramic assemblage often occurs in surficial association with Aztec I B/O or Aztec II B/O occupations (Parsons, Brumfiel, Parsons, and Wilson 1982). O'Neill's (1962) and Hodge's (2008) excavations at Chalco encountered Mazapan-related Red/Buff ceramics only in trace quantities (see also Parsons et al. 1996). At nearby Xico, however, Mazapan-related Red/Buff, Aztec I B/O, and Aztec II B/O all occur, although most of the Late Toltec (Mazapan-related) occupation is concentrated at the northern end of Xico Island, while the main Early Aztec (mixed Aztec I B/O and Aztec II B/O) settlement occurred less than 200 meters away on an offshore artificial island in the lakebed to the east. At Xico, the Early Aztec settlement

TABLE 4.2. Early and Middle Postclassic settlement continuity and discontinuity at surveyed sites in the Basin of Mexico. Aztec I and II are combined as Early Aztec (EA). Late Aztec (LA) sites areas are defined by the presence of Aztec III B/O pottery. Table entries include sites with no estimated resident population (e.g., ceremonial sites, which are not shown in figs. 4.2b, 4.2c, and 4.2d).

Survey Area[a]	LA Sites (no.)	EA Sites (no.)	LA Sites with EA (%)	Late Toltec Sites (no.)	EA Sites with Late Toltec (%)	Late Toltec Sites with EA (%)
Chalco	287	103	35.9	90	16.5	20.0
Xochimilco	91	18	19.8	11	5.6	9.1
Ixtapalapa	75	19	25.3	48	15.8	6.3
Texcoco	110	54	49.1	59	27.8	44.1
Teotihuacan	201	30	14.9	198	70.0	4.5
Cuauhtitlan	326	32	9.8	139	75.0	15.1
Temascalapa	168	6	3.6	77	83.3	6.5
Zumpango	302	2	0.7	213	0.0	0.0
Total	1,560	264	16.9	835	33.0	9.5

a. Listed south to north

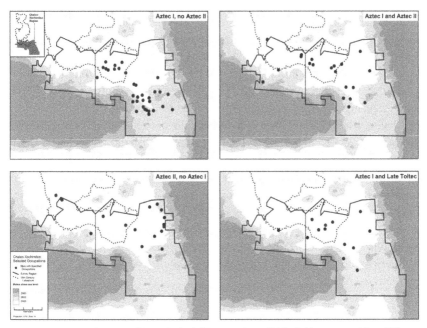

FIGURE 4.4. *Distributions of Aztec I Black/Orange, Aztec II Black/Orange, and Late Toltec (Mazapan-like Red/Buff) surface pottery in the Chalco-Xochimilco Region, southeastern Basin of Mexico.*

overlies a very substantial epiclassic (Coyotlatelco) occupation (Parsons, Brumfiel, Parsons, and Wilson 1982; Parsons, Brumfiel, Parsons, Popper, and Taft 1982; Parsons et al. 1985)—a situation seemingly analogous to what Noguera (1935) encountered at Tenayuca, except that at Tenayuca there was Aztec II B/O overlying the Epiclassic, with both Mazapan Red/Buff and Aztec I B/O present only in trace amounts.

In the Ixtapalapa region, Aztec I B/O has been found in quantity only at the large site of Culhuacan at the western end of the Ixtapalapa peninsula (Blanton 1972), a site where, like Chalco, Aztec II B/O also occurs, along with Mazapan Red/Buff pottery in trace quantities. Apart from Culhuacan, there is little Aztec I B/O anywhere in the western Ixtapalapa region. Farther east on the Ixtapalapa peninsula, Aztec I B/O occurs slightly more frequently in settlements and sometimes sparsely in off-site locations (Richard E. Blanton, personal communication 2006). Mazapan Red/Buff is abundant throughout the Ixtapalapa region (e.g., Tovalín 1998), as it is from there northward in the Basin of Mexico, where Aztec I B/O occurs only in trace quantities—except at Xaltocan in the north-central Basin, where Aztec I B/O is very abundant and where Mazapan-Tollan Red/Buff pottery is scarce (Brumfiel 2005a:133, 137).

Thus, in the southern Basin of Mexico we confront a complicated situation in which Aztec I B/O and Mazapan-like Red/Buff sometimes co-occur in significant quantities in surface collections at the same sites, although these are often spatially separated (but usually not by much distance), and where the two major Aztec I B/O centers, Chalco and Culhuacan, feature only trace amounts of Mazapan pottery even though smaller settlements only a few kilometers away have substantial quantities of both Mazapan-related Red/Buff and Aztec I B/O pottery. As noted earlier, a unique situation exists at Xico, just 3 kilometers west of Chalco, where closely spaced, but physically detached, large concentrations of Mazapan-related Red/Buff and Aztec I and II B/O ceramics occur.

The occasional co-occurrence, in some combination, of Mazapan Red/Buff, Aztec I B/O, and Aztec II B/O in the southern Basin of Mexico contrasts sharply with the extreme discontinuity among these pottery types in the Zumpango region, although there are also relatively low levels of continuity in the Teotihuacan and Temascalapa regions in the northeast. What might be the implications for the Zumpango region of these ceramic distributions in the southern Basin? We can think of three possibilities (which are not necessarily mutually exclusive):

1. There is only partial chronological overlap between Mazapan and Aztec I in the southern Basin, and the Mazapan-related Red/Buff pottery in that region represents an early phase of the Early Postclassic period, which was superseded by an Aztec I ceramic assemblage during the middle and late portions

of that period. Available radiocarbon dates (see tables 4.3 and 4.4) make this alternative unlikely, as Aztec I B/O seems to appear as early as Mazapan Red/Buff within the Basin as a whole. However, because there are still no radiocarbon dates clearly associated with Mazapan-related Red/Buff pottery from the southern Basin, the precise chronological relationships between Aztec I B/O and Mazapan-related Red/Buff in that region remain uncertain.

2. Mazapan Red/Buff and Aztec I B/O ceramic distributions reflect the presence of coeval but culturally and sociopolitically different groups who occupied the same general area but had limited interaction with each other. The concept of multi-group (or multi-ethnic) co-occupation of a single region has been discussed in ethnohistorically based studies in the Basin of Mexico (e.g., Carrasco 1999; Hodge 1984; Jiménez 1954). However, archaeologists have had limited success in assessing *ethnicity* based on material remains.

3. The observed interdigitation of Mazapan-related and Aztec I occupations in the southern Basin may reflect a kind of Mesoamerican *verticality*, analogous to the better-known Andean example (e.g., Murra 1972), in which settlements dependent on different core polities may occupy the same region to exploit resources and/or sociopolitical considerations that complement or extend those of the polities' core areas. Based on ethnohistoric sources, Carrasco (1980) argued that a comparable multi-niche, or archipelago-like, adaptive strategy characterized Late Postclassic highland Mexico. If the interdigitation of Aztec I and Mazapan-related settlements in the Chalco region reflects some sort of multi-ethnic/multi-polity arrangement during the Early Postclassic, then such an archipelago-like arrangement appears to have been abandoned, or much altered, by Middle Postclassic times, when Aztec II B/O pottery is widespread in the southern Basin following the collapse of Tula.

4. Because Aztec II B/O is comparatively rare in the southern Basin of Mexico relative to its greater abundance in the central Basin, and because Aztec I and II frequently co-occur in the southern Basin, "there does not appear to be a distinct phase of Aztec II B/O in the south" and "within the Basin as a whole, . . . these Early Aztec types (Az I and Az II B/O) are largely, if not wholly, contemporaneous" (Minc et al. 1994:140). Considered in this light, scarcity of Aztec II B/O in the northern Basin might reflect forces similar to, but less extreme than, those that produced the relatively weak development of Aztec II B/O in the southern Basin.

RECENT STUDIES

Radiocarbon Dates

Over the past few decades, several radiocarbon dates from Tula and the Basin of Mexico have become available (see tables 4.3 and 4.4). Generally speaking, and ignoring several outliers, these dates suggest that (1) Mazapan-Tollan Red/Buff

TABLE 4.3. Summary of radiocarbon dates. The two Phase 2 dates from Xaltocan (mixed Az I and Az II B/O) are not included in this tabulation.

Phase	Number of Dates	Range of Mid-Point Dates	Median Mid-Point Date (with one standard deviation)
Mazapan-Tollan	11	882–1166 CE	941 ± 58 CE
Aztec I[a]	17	880–1390 CE	1092 ±157 CE
Aztec II[b]	20	1331–1437 CE	1358 ± 73 CE

a. Three extreme outliers have been eliminated (690, 1415, 1425 CE).

b. One extreme outlier has been eliminated (1035 CE).

and Aztec I B/O came into use and were approximately coeval during the tenth and eleventh centuries; (2) Aztec I B/O continued in use into the thirteenth century, while Mazapan-Tollan Red/Buff ceased being produced sometime during the twelfth century; (3) Aztec II B/O began to be used during the later thirteenth century (ignoring the outlying date of 1035 CE from Otumba); and (4) Aztec I B/O and Aztec II B/O overlapped for a short period during the late thirteenth century, while Aztec II B/O continued into the fifteenth century. These dates also suggest that Aztec II B/O had a much shorter duration of use than either Aztec I B/O or Mazapan-related Red/Buff. The lack of Mazapan-related dates from the southern Basin prevents us from establishing precise chronological relationships between Mazapan-related Red/Buff and Aztec I B/O in that region, where the two ceramic types co-occur.

Stylistic, Stratigraphic, Neutron-Activation, and Distributional Studies

Aztec I B/O: Stylistic analyses have indicated that there are three regional variants of Aztec I B/O in the Basin of Mexico: Chalco, Mixquic, and Culhuacan (Hodge 1998; Hodge and Minc 1991; Minc et al. 1994). These variants were previously subsumed within a general Culhuacan type. Stylistic and neutron activation analyses show that in the southern Basin Aztec I B/O was produced and distributed primarily within local marketing areas, thus accounting for the predominance of local stylistic variants within different subregions (Hodge and Minc 1991). However, at Xaltocan in the north-central Basin, most Aztec I B/O pottery corresponds to the Culhuacan variant and was imported from production zones well south of Xaltocan (Brumfiel 2005b; Hodge and Neff 2005). Thus, Xaltocan is unusual both in its location at the extreme northern edge of where Aztec I B/O pottery occurs in quantity and in imported pottery from well outside the local area. Brumfiel (2005b) suggested that this importation probably reflects the need of Xaltocan elites to establish alliances with counterparts in polities further south in the Basin.

Stratigraphic excavations at Xaltocan (Brumfiel 2005a) show that Aztec I B/O preceded Aztec II B/O at that site for a considerable time prior to a substantial

TABLE 4.4. Calibrated radiocarbon dates (mid-points only) from Tula and the Basin of Mexico for Mazapan/Tollan, Aztec I, and Aztec II sites. The Tlalpizahuac site is situated north of Chalco, near the northeastern shore of Lake Chalco. For multiple-intercept dates, only the central intercept is shown and is indicated as "ca."

Site[a]	Mazapan-Tollan (CE)	Aztec I B/O (CE)	Aztec II B/O (CE)	Reference
Tula	ca. 1110			García 2004:366–67
Tula	1166			García 2004:366–67
Xaltocan (Phase 1)[b]		880		Parsons et al. 1996:225
Xaltocan (Phase 1)[b]		960		Parsons et al. 1996:225
Xaltocan (Phase 1)[b]		970		Parsons et al. 1996:225
Xaltocan (Phase 1)[b]		990		Parsons et al. 1996:225
Xaltocan (Phase 2)[b]		1235 (mixed Az I & Az II)		Parsons et al. 1996:225
Xaltocan (Phase 2)[b]		1300 (mixed Az I & Az II)		Parsons et al. 1996:225
Xaltocan (Phase 3)[b]			1395	Parsons et al. 1996:225
Xaltocan (Phase 3)[b]			1425	Parsons et al. 1996:225
Cuauhtitlan	896			García 2004:366–67
Cuauhtitlan			ca. 1331	García 2004:366–67
Cuauhtitlan			1437	García 2004:366–67
Cuauhtitlan			1437	García 2004:366–67
Tenayuca			1230	García 2004:366–67
Teotihuacan			1422	García 2004:366–67
Teotihuacan	1007			García 2004:366–67
Teotihuacan	1012			García 2004:366–67
Teotihuacan	1020			García 2004:366–67
Otumba			1035	Charlton et al. 2000:258; Nichols and Charlton 1996:237
Otumba			1300	Charlton et al. 2000:258; Nichols and Charlton 1996:237
Otumba			1270	Charlton et al. 2000:258; Nichols and Charlton 1996:237
Otumba			1285	Charlton et al. 2000:258; Nichols and Charlton 1996:237
Texcoco			1411	García 2004:366–67
Culhuacan			1262	García 2004:366–67
Culhuacan			1282	García 2004:366–67

continued on next page

TABLE 4.4.—*continued*

Site[a]	Mazapan-Tollan (CE)	Aztec I B/O (CE)	Aztec II B/O (CE)	Reference
Culhuacan			1418	García 2004:366–67
Chimalhuacan			ca. 1365	García 2004:366–67
Tlalpizahuac	882			García 2004:366–67
Tlalpizahuac	894			García 2004:366–67
Tlalpizahuac	896			García 2004:366–67
Tlalpizahuac	ca. 902			García 2004:366–67
Tlalpizahuac	956			García 2004:366–67
Chalco			1282	García 2004:366–67
Chalco			1400	García 2004:366–67
Chalco			1455	García 2004:366–67
Chalco		ca. 1100		Parsons et al. 1996:221
Chalco		1210		Parsons et al. 1996:221
Chalco		1290		Parsons et al. 1996:221
Xico		976		García 2004:366–67
Xico		999		García 2004:366–67
Xico		1262		García 2004:366–67
Ch-Az-195		690		Parsons et al. 1996:223
Ch-Az-195		960		Parsons et al. 1996:223
Ch-Az-195		1035		Parsons et al. 1996:223
Ch-Az-195		ca. 1075		Parsons et al. 1996:223
Ch-Az-195		1290		Parsons et al. 1996:223
Ch-Az-195		1395		Parsons et al. 1996:223
Ch-Az-195		1415		Parsons et al. 1996:223
Tlalmanalco			1403	García 2004:366–67

a. Listed north to south

b. For Xaltocan dates, Phase 1=Pure Aztec I B/O, Phase 2=Mixed Aztec I B/O and Aztec II B/O; Phase 3=Pure Aztec II B/O.

chronological overlap between Aztec I and II near the end of the Aztec I sequence there. As noted, radiocarbon dates from Xaltocan indicate that Aztec I B/O may have first appeared as early as the tenth century, and probably continued well into the fourteenth century before it was entirely replaced by Aztec II B/O (Brumfiel 2005a; Parsons et al. 1996).

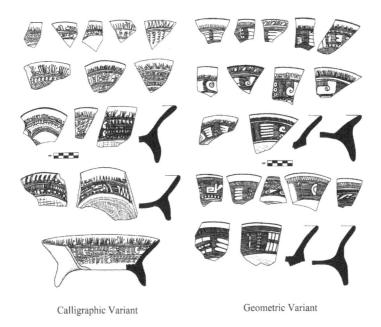

Calligraphic Variant   Geometric Variant

FIGURE 4.5. *Calligraphic and Geometric variants of Aztec II Black/Orange. Adapted from Minc et al. (1994:146–47, figures 6.5, 6.6).*

The Xaltocan sequence thus replicates the general stratigraphic relationships between Aztec I B/O and Aztec II B/O that were revealed earlier in excavated sequences at Chalco (Hodge 2008; O'Neill 1962; see also Parsons et al. 1996) and at Culhuacan (Séjourné 1970, 1983) in the southern Basin: a long period of Aztec I B/O without Aztec II B/O and only traces of Mazapan-Tollan Red/Buff, overlain by a shorter period with both Aztec I B/O and Aztec II B/O, which is then overlain by levels of only Aztec II B/O of relatively short duration. Furthermore, as noted earlier, both Xaltocan and Culhuacan occur in areas surrounded by settlements with abundant Mazapan-Tollan Red/Buff pottery, and with only traces of Aztec I B/O. Even in the Chalco region, where Aztec I B/O occurs widely in small settlements well away from the Chalco center, there is significant Mazapan-related Red/Buff pottery.

As previously noted, Mazapan-Tollan–phase pottery is scarce at Xaltocan. Thus, during much (perhaps most) of the Early Postclassic, Xaltocan was a sociopolitical *island* whose inhabitants used Aztec I B/O ceramics and only traces of Mazapan pottery. Many contemporary surrounding settlements, which used Mazapan/Tollan-phase ceramics and only trace amounts of Aztec I B/O pottery (see figures 4.1 and 4.2a), were just a few kilometers distant. Just as striking, during the earlier part of the subsequent Middle Postclassic, inhabitants of Xaltocan possibly continued to use Aztec I B/O, gradually replacing this pottery with Aztec II B/O at a time when massive depopulation may have been happening just a few kilometers to the north.

Aztec II B/O: Within the Basin of Mexico, Aztec II B/O pottery is now known to vary in style and place of production. Using samples selected from the original survey collections from the Texcoco, Ixtapalapa, and Chalco regions, Hodge and Minc (1991) distinguished two main stylistic variants within the broad Aztec II (Tenayuca) B/O category: Calligraphic and Geometric (see figure 4.5). These apparently coeval variants partially overlap spatially within the Basin, although they tend to be differentially distributed to some extent:

> Geometric Black-on-Orange is primarily concentrated within the northern Texcoco survey region; occurrences outside this zone are fairly low density. Calligraphic Tenayuca shows a marked concentration closely confined to . . . the area of Culhuacan; lower density occurrences are found throughout the Texcoco and Chalco Regions as well. (Hodge and Minc 1991:156–57).

On the basis of their neutron-activation analysis, Minc and colleagues (1994:158) found that, in contrast to the variants of Aztec I B/O, which show relatively localized distributions within the Basin, ". . . the Calligraphic and Geometric types [of Aztec II B/O] apparently circulated through spatially more extensive market networks. The market territories of these two types overlapped to a considerable extent . . ."

The Minc and colleagues (1994) study indicates a strong contrast between the more local exchange systems of the Early Postclassic regional economies that distributed Aztec I B/O pottery and the more expansive and broadly overlapping Middle Postclassic exchange networks that distributed Aztec II B/O pottery. This implies that if there were any significant number of people in the Zumpango region during the Middle Postclassic, Aztec II B/O pottery should have found its way to them in quantities proportionate to the size and density of the consuming population.

In his overview of Early and Middle Postclassic ceramics in the Basin of Mexico, García (2004) distinguishes four regional variants of the Aztec II ceramic assemblage (including B/O and other ceramic types): (1) the northern Basin (primarily the Cuauhtitlan region), (2) the south-central Basin (the Culhuacan area), (3) the eastern Basin (mainly the Texcoco region), and (4) the southeastern Basin (mainly the Chalco region). In his view, these distributions reflect the existence of four separate regional polities. García's spatial divisions of Aztec II ceramic assemblages are suggestive of larger economic and sociopolitical forces that might have operated during the Middle Postclassic. However, we are presently unable to relate them clearly to the calligraphic and geometric groupings proposed by Minc and colleagues (1994). It is notable in this regard that analysis by Minc and colleagues

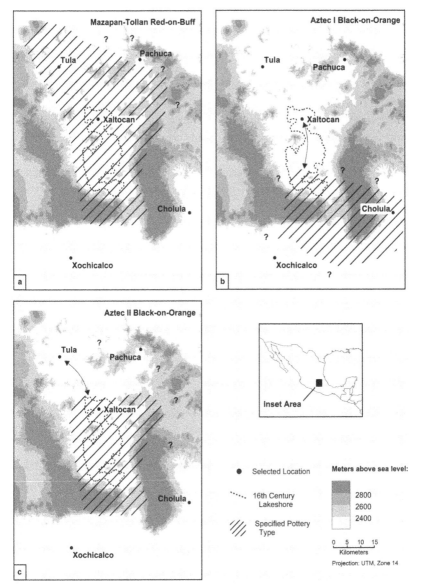

FIGURE 4.6. *Distributions of Mazapan-Tollan Red/Buff (a), Aztec I Black/Orange and closely related types (b), and Aztec II Black/Orange (c) in and around the Basin of Mexico.*

relied on samples from the eastern and southern Basin of Mexico and, unlike García's, did not include sherds from the northern or western Basin.

Whatever the case, a large, dense, and seemingly politically centralized Aztec II occupation has been noted by García, Brumfiel, and ourselves in the Cuautitlan region, at Xaltocan, and along the eastern shore of Lake Xaltocan (see figure 4.4). Geographically, within the Basin of Mexico, this occupation appears to have extended up to, *but not beyond*, the northern shores of Lake Xaltocan-Zumpango.

Aztec I B/O and Aztec II B/O outside the Basin of Mexico: The geographic distribution of Mazapan-Tollan Red/Buff, Aztec I-related B/O, and Aztec II B/O pottery in neighboring regions around the Basin of Mexico helps explain the distribution of these styles in the Basin of Mexico (see figure 4.6). In particular, we note occurrences north of the Basin, in and around Tula and Pachuca, as well as occurrences south at Cholula and at sites in Morelos.

McCafferty (2001) has shown that his "Chalco Black/Orange," a local variant of Aztec I B/O from Cholula (see figure 4.1), constituted a minor sub-type within his Cocoyotla Black-on-Natural ceramic type characteristic of the Middle and Late Tlachihualtepetl phase (roughly corresponding to Early Postclassic in the Basin of Mexico). The presence of Aztec I B/O pottery, or of closely related ceramics, in western Puebla outside Cholula itself, remains to be fully defined, although Plunket (1990) has reported closely related pottery in the Atlixco Valley of southwestern Puebla.

Although excavations at Chalcatzingo in eastern Morelos have revealed significant quantities of Aztec I B/O (Norr 1987), excavations and surveys at Xochicalco and Yautepec in western Morelos, have found only trace amounts of it (Hare and Smith 1996; Smith 2000). However, at Yautepec, Smith notes an abundance of what he calls Tepozteco Black-on-White, "which is like Aztec I in vessel form and design motifs, but decorated in black on white" (Michael Smith, personal communication 2006). Smith also reports substantial quantities of a very similar type that he calls Morelos-Puebla Black-on-Orange at the Teopanzolco site in northwestern Morelos, "which is exactly like Aztec I in everything but paste."

These studies indicate that there is a broad band of pottery closely related to Aztec I B/O immediately south and southeast of the Basin of Mexico, extending from western Morelos eastward into southwestern Puebla. The stylistic variability of this pottery within this Morelos-Puebla region is probably generally comparable to that observed by Minc and colleagues (1994) for Aztec I B/O within the Basin. The variability of Aztec I-like B/O pottery throughout the southern Basin of Mexico, Morelos, and southwestern Puebla probably reflects localized exchange networks embedded within small regional polities who shared certain broad traditions of ceramic production and decoration during the Early Postclassic.

Surveys and excavations in the Toluca and Tula Regions (Cobean and Mastache 1999; Mastache and Crespo 1974; Mastache et al. 1982, 2002; Michael Smith personal communication 2006; Sugiura 2005; Yoko Sugiura personal communication 2006) have revealed only trace amounts of Aztec I B/O. Although some Aztec II B/O has long been known at Tula, investigations there suggest that this pottery type may occur primarily in restricted localities within a Middle Postclassic center that was much reduced in size and importance relative to its Early Postclassic peak (Mastache et al. 2002:42). With the apparent exception of Tula, Aztec II B/O pottery in significant quantities apparently occurs exclusively within the Basin of Mexico and at the Teopanzolco site in northwestern Morelos (Michael Smith, personal communication 2006). Interestingly, Norr (1987:406) found no Aztec II B/O at Chalcatzingo in eastern Morelos, a locality where Aztec I B/O is abundant (but where Mazapan-like Red/Buff is absent). In other surrounding regions, Aztec II B/O is quite scarce (Yoko Sugiura, personal communication 2006, regarding the Toluca Region; Geoffrey McCafferty, personal communication 2006, regarding Cholula; Kenneth Hirth, personal communication 2006, regarding western Puebla and eastern Morelos). At present, we have no information about the occurrence of Aztec II B/O in Tlaxcala, east of the Basin.

The apparent absence of significant quantities of Aztec II B/O pottery outside the Basin of Mexico, except nearby Tula and Teopanzolco, suggests that the Middle Postclassic exchange networks that distributed Aztec II B/O widely within the Basin did not extend much beyond the Basin itself (unlike those of the Late Postclassic). Also apparently absent were the kind of shared cultural norms which seem to have produced generic similarities that during Early Postclassic times linked (1) Aztec I B/O with coeval pottery in the Morelos-southwestern Puebla region to the south and southeast of the Basin of Mexico; and (2) Mazapan-Tollan Red/Buff with (still poorly defined) regions to the north and west of the Basin.

CONCLUSIONS

In the preceding pages, we considered implications of the absence of Aztec II B/O pottery in the Zumpango region given available information on the distributions in time and space of Mazapan-Tollan Red/Buff, Aztec I B/O, and Aztec II B/O ceramics, both within the Basin of Mexico and in other parts of Central Mexico that hosted Early and Middle Postclassic occupations. Recent stratigraphic, stylistic, radiocarbon, and geochemical studies complement older settlement pattern data from the Basin and help to resolve (though also complicate) some uncertainties about chronological, spatial, and cultural relationships among these three ceramic types.

Our study considered some old problems and raised some new ones:

1. The lack of Aztec II B/O pottery in the Zumpango region represents a virtual absence of population there during the Middle Postclassic. It is likely that there were also significant population losses in the northeastern Basin of Mexico (Temascalapa and Teotihuacan regions) and probably in the adjacent Tula region as well. This Middle Postclassic population loss in the northern Basin contrasts with the southern and central Basin where substantial occupation persisted from Early Postclassic through Late Postclassic, and where a

generally higher degree of settlement continuity suggests a greater degree of overall sociopolitical stability.

2. Available radiocarbon dates suggest that the span of absolute time when Aztec II B/O was used may have been little more than a century, from the early-mid-fourteenth century into the mid-fifteenth century. This contrasts with the apparently much longer time spans of both Mazapan-Tollan Red/Buff and Aztec I B/O. Thus, the Middle Postclassic depopulation of the northwestern Basin may not have lasted much more than three generations. If Aztec II-III (Var. D) B/O is late Middle Postclassic in age, the regional population abandonment may have endured no more than two generations.

3. Radiocarbon dates suggest that Mazapan-Tollan Red/Buff and Aztec I B/O pottery largely overlap in time, although Aztec I B/O seems to persist longer, overlapping for a short period near the end of its use with Aztec II B/O.

   The geographic distribution of Mazapan-Tollan Red/Buff, Aztec I-related B/O, and Aztec II B/O pottery in and around the Basin of Mexico suggests two Early Postclassic sociocultural *spheres*: (a) a northern sphere, identified archaeologically by the distribution of Tollan-Mazapan Red/Buff; and (b) a southern sphere, identified archaeologically by the distribution of Aztec I-related B/O pottery. There is a projection of Aztec I B/O from its core region in the southeastern Basin northward into Xaltocan during the Early Postclassic, and a similar northward projection of Aztec II B/O into Tula during the Middle Postclassic. By the Middle Postclassic both of the Early Postclassic ceramic spheres had disappeared, with Aztec II B/O everywhere replacing Mazapan-Tollan Red/Buff and Aztec I B/O, although the distribution of Aztec II B/O outside the Basin of Mexico is apparently quite restricted.

4. The implications of these ceramic distributions remain to be more fully ascertained, but the southeastern Basin of Mexico stands out as a sociocultural frontier between the northern and southern spheres. The most significant *players* in this macro-regional configuration were probably Tula and Teotihuacan in the north, and Cholula and Xochicalco (or one of the other Morelos centers) in the south. Recent estimates of Teotihuacan's Mazapan-phase population (15,233, Gorenflo and Sanders 2007:218 [based on an estimate by Ian Robertson]; 30,000, Cowgill 1996:330) indicate that this center was more important during Early Postclassic times than previously thought.

5. The southeastern Basin of Mexico shows a spatial association of Mazapan Red/Buff and Aztec I B/O, in both urban and rural settlements, that exists nowhere else in the Basin. If these two ceramic complexes were coeval in the southeastern Basin, then some form of multi-polity/multi-ethnic use of that region possibly occurred there (perhaps analogous to Andean verticality). During the Early Postclassic, Xaltocan was a densely settled island where Aztec I B/O pottery was abundant in a region where Mazapan-Tollan Red/

Buff pottery predominated elsewhere. This configuration might indicate that, as in the southeastern Basin, some sort of multi-group occupation had also occurred in the northern Basin during the Early Postclassic. In this setting, Tula and Xaltocan would have played complementary roles, with Xaltocan controlling direct access to lacustrine resources at the southern edge of Tula's dominance, but lacking direct access to the rich lime and mineral resources of localities in the north controlled by Tula. In this scenario, the collapse of Tula in the twelfth century would have removed a major component in such an arrangement and could have led to the collapse of an entire regional economic structure, especially in a comparatively arid region (like the far northern Basin of Mexico) that may have depended on access to food resources from more humid zones farther south.

6. Although, strictly speaking, we lack good population estimates for the Early Aztec occupation in the Basin of Mexico,[2] the number of sites where Early Aztec archaeological remains occur provide a sense of the magnitude of population decline during this period (see table 4.2). An analysis of the finalized settlement pattern data for the Basin argued that for the region as a whole, major demographic events—changes that would introduce a large imbalance between fertility and mortality, or massive migration into or out of the Basin—would not have been necessary to account for the estimated shifts in population (Gorenflo 2015). But that study focused solely on periods for which more precise population estimates exist. Introducing substantial Middle Postclassic depopulation likely would change that conclusion, particularly in the Zumpango region, where there was virtually no Early Aztec occupation.

7. We have discussed the Middle Postclassic population decline in the Basin of Mexico in general, and in the Zumpango region in particular, as associated with the fall of Tula, located ca. 20 km to the northwest. We suggested that pre-Columbian occupation in the northern third of the Basin would have been risky for an economy based largely on intensive agriculture, owing largely to the low rainfall that tends to occur in the region, ranging from about 680 mm annually in the southern part of the Zumpango region to less than 500 mm per year in the northeastern Temascalapa region (Sanders et al. 1979:map 2). Other research proposes that any substantial population in these parts of the Basin of Mexico would have required some sort of adaptive specialization consistent with low precipitation and integrated within a broader regional market system that provided access to other resources not locally available (Gorenflo 2015).

The Late Postclassic regional settlement system, dominated by Tenochtitlan with its city-state building blocks, provided the basis for broad economic inte-

---

2 Early Aztec populations are difficult to estimate because Early Aztec ceramic types are typically found within larger and more densely occupied Late Aztec sites where they are often obscured on the surface by heavy admixture with Late Aztec pottery.

gration during a time when the Zumpango region was densely occupied. The Early Postclassic regional settlement system in the northwestern Basin, dominated by nearby Tula, likely provided an integrated regional economic system as well, and during that period the northern Basin hosted considerable occupation. The intervening Middle Postclassic, a period after the demise of Tula but before the full emergence of the Triple Alliance that administered the Aztec empire, likely lacked such regional economic integration, especially within a region previously dominated by Tula. The relatively wetter southern Basin of Mexico, a region of persisting Middle Postclassic occupation, would have provided broader and lower-risk opportunities for agriculture, and a higher degree of self-sufficiency, not present in the north. The relatively drier northern Basin could not have met subsistence demands for any substantial occupation.

In sum, we envision the abandonment of the Zumpango region during Middle Postclassic times as a comparatively short-lived phenomenon caused by a combination of ecological and sociopolitical factors. The far northwestern Basin of Mexico was occupied by large, dense populations only when centralized polities provided an overarching organizational framework that integrated specialized producers of complementary products. Hence, the Zumpango region was sparsely occupied during periods of relatively weak or uncentralized polities (Formative, Epiclassic, and Middle Postclassic), and much more densely occupied during periods of relative strong, centralized polities (Classic, Early Postclassic, Late Postclassic).

Acknowledgments. We are grateful to several colleagues who have provided us with important information about archaeological ceramics in their study areas: Richard Blanton, Elizabeth Brumfiel, Robert Cobean, Destiny Crider, Raul García, Chris Garraty, Dan Healan, Kenneth Hirth, Geoffrey McCafferty, Leah Minc, Chris Morehart, Deborah Nichols, Michael Smith, Barbara Stark, and Yoko Sugiura. Mark Denil provided several extremely useful recommendations on map design.

REFERENCES

Acosta, José. 1940. "Exploraciones en Tula, Hidalgo, 1940." *Revista mexicana de estudios antropológicos* 4:172–94.

Acosta, José. 1941. "Los últimos descubrimientos arqueológicos en Tula, Hidalgo, 1941." *Revista mexicana de estudios antropológicos* 5:239–43.

Acosta, José. 1944. "La tercera temporada de exploraciones arqueológicas en Tula, Hgo., 1942." *Revista mexicana de estudios antropológicos* 6:125–64.

Acosta, José. 1945. "La cuarta y quinta temporada de exploraciones arqueológicas en Tula, Hgo." *Revista mexicana de estudios antropológicos* 7:23–64.

Acosta, José. 1952. "Review of Griffin and Espejo (1947, 1950)." *Boletín bibliográfico de antropología americana* 15:76–77.

Blanton, Richard E. 1972. *Prehispanic Settlement Patterns of the Ixtapalapa Peninsula Region, Mexico.* Occasional Papers in Anthropology, no. 6. Department of Anthropology, The Pennsylvania State University, University Park.

Boas, Frans, and Manuel Gamio. 1921. *Album de colecciones arqueológicas.* Museo Nacional de Arqueología, História y Etnografía, Mexico City, Mexico. Reprinted 1990, Instituto Nacional de Antropología e Historia, Mexico City.

Brenner, Anita. 1931. *The Influence of Technique on the Decorative Style in the Domestic Pottery of Culhuacan.* Columbia University Contributions to Anthropology, vol. 13. Reprinted in 1969 by AMS Press, New York.

Brumfiel, Elizabeth M. 2005a. "Opting in and Opting Out: Tula, Cholula, and Xaltocan." In *Settlement, Subsistence, and Social Complexity: Essays Honoring the Legacy of Jeffrey R. Parsons,* edited by Richard E. Blanton, 63–88. Cotsen Institute of Archaeology, University of California, Los Angeles.

Brumfiel, Elizabeth M. 2005b. "Ceramic Chronology at Xaltocan." In *Production and Power at Postclassic Xaltocan,* edited by Elizabeth M. Brumfiel, 117–52. Serie Arqueología de México, University of Pittsburgh and Instituto Nacional de Antropología e Historia, Pittsburgh, Pennsylvania, and Mexico City.

Carrasco, Pedro. 1980. "La aplicabilidad a Mesoamérica del modelo andino de verticalidad." *Revista de la Universidad Complutense* 117:237–43.

Carrasco, Pedro. 1999. *The Tenocha Empire of Ancient Mexico: The Triple Alliance of Tenochtitlan, Tetzcoco, and Tlacopan.* University of Oklahoma Press, Norman.

Charlton, Thomas H., Deborah L. Nichols, and Cynthia Otis Charlton. 2000. "Otumba and Its Neighbors: Ex Oriente Lux." *Ancient Mesoamerica* 11:247–65.

Cobean, Robert H. 1978. "The Pre-Aztec Ceramics of Tula, Hidalgo, Mexico." PhD dissertation, Department of Anthropology, Harvard University, Cambridge, MA.

Cobean, Robert H. 1990. *La cerámica de Tula, Hidalgo.* Instituto Nacional de Antropología e História, Mexico City.

Cobean, Robert H., and Alba Guadalupe Mastache. 1999. *Tepetitlán: A Rural Household in the Toltec Heartland.* Serie Arqueología de México, University of Pittsburgh and Instituto Nacional de Antropología e Historia, Pittsburgh, Pennsylvania, and Mexico City.

Cowgill, George L. 1996. "Discussion." *Ancient Mesoamerica* 7:325–31.

Franco, José Luís. 1945. "Comentarios sobre tipología y filogenía de la decoración negro sobre color natural del barro en la cerámica 'Azteca II.'" *Revista mexicana de estudios antropológicos* 7:163–86.

Franco, José Luís. 1949. "Algunos problemas relativos a la cerámica Azteca." *El México antiguo* 7:162–208.

Franco, José Luís, and Frederick A. Peterson. 1957. *Motivos decorativos en la cerámica azteca.* Serie Científica, no. 5. Museo Nacional de Antropología, Mexico City.

García, Raúl Ernesto. 2004. "De Tula a Azcapotzalco: Caracterización arqueológica de los Altepetl de la Cuenca de México del Posclásico Temprano y Medio, a través del estudio cerámico regional." Tesis de doctorado, Facultad de Filosofía y Letras, División de Posgrado, Universidad Nacional Autónoma de México, Mexico City.

Gorenflo, L. J. 2015. "Compilation and Analysis of Pre-Columbian Settlement Data in the Basin of Mexico." *Ancient Mesoamerica* 26:197–212.

Gorenflo, L. J., and William T. Sanders. 2007. *Prehispanic Settlement Pattern Data from the Cuautitlan, Temascalapa, and Teotihuacan Regions, Mexico.* Occasional Papers in Anthropology, no. 30. Department of Anthropology, The Pennsylvania State University, University Park.

Griffin, James B., and Antonieta Espejo. 1947. "La alfarería correspondiente al último período de ocupación nahua del Valle de México, I." *Memorias de la Academia Mexicana de la Historia* 6(2):3–20.

Griffin, James B., and Antonieta Espejo. 1950. "La alfarería correspondiente al último período de ocupación nahua del Valle de México, II." *Memorias de la Academia Mexicana de la Historia* 9(1):3–54.

Hare, Timothy S., and Michael E. Smith. 1996. "A New Postclassic Chronology for Yautepec, Morelos." *Ancient Mesoamerica* 7:281–97.

Hodge, Mary G. 1984. *Aztec City States.* Memoirs of the Museum of Anthropology, no. 18. University of Michigan, Ann Arbor.

Hodge, Mary G. 1998. "Archaeological Views of Aztec Culture." *Journal of Archaeological Research* 6:197–238.

Hodge, Mary G., ed. 2008. *Place of Jade: Society and Economy in Ancient Chalco.* Serie Arqueología de México, University of Pittsburgh and Instituto Nacional de Antropología e Historia, Pittsburgh, Pennsylvania, and Mexico City.

Hodge, Mary G., and Leah D. Minc. 1991. *Aztec-Period Ceramic Distribution and Exchange Systems.* Report submitted to the National Science Foundation. National Science Foundation, Washington, DC.

Hodge, Mary G., and Hector Neff. 2005. "Xaltocan in the Economy of the Basin of Mexico: A View from Ceramic Tradewares." In *Production and Power at Postclassic Xaltocan*, edited by Elizabeth M. Brumfiel, 319–48. Serie Arqueología de Mexico, University of Pittsburgh and Instituto Nacional de Antropología e Historia, Pittsburgh, Pennsylvania, and Mexico City.

Jiménez, Wigberto. 1954. "Síntesis de la historia precolonial del Valle de México." *Revista mexicana de estudios antropológicos* 14:1:219–36.

Mastache, Alba Guadalupe, and Ana María Crespo. 1974. "La ocupación prehispánica en el área de Tula, Hgo." In *Proyecto Tula*, edited by Eduardo Matos Moctezuma, pt. 1, 71–104. Instituto Nacional de Antropología e Historia, Mexico City.

Mastache, Guadalupe, Ana María Crespo, Robert H. Cobean, and Dan M. Healan. 1982. *Estudios sobre la antigua ciudad de Tula.* Instituto Nacional de Antropología e Historia, Mexico City.

Mastache, Alba Guadalupe, Robert H. Cobean, and Dan M. Healan. 2002. *Ancient Tollan: Tula and the Toltec Heartland*. University Press of Colorado, Boulder.

Mayer-Oakes, William J. 1959. "A Stratigraphic Excavation at El Risco, Mexico." *Proceedings of the American Philosophical Society* 103(3):332–73.

McCafferty, Geoffrey G. 2001. *Ceramics at Postclassic Cholula, Mexico: Typology and Seriation of Pottery from the UA-1 Domestic Compound*. Monograph no. 43. Cotsen Institute of Archaeology, University of California, Los Angeles.

Minc, Leah D., Mary G. Hodge, and M. James Blackman. 1994. "Stylistic and Spatial Variability in Early Aztec Ceramics: Insights into Pre-Imperial Exchange Systems." In *Economies and Polities in the Aztec Realm*, edited by Mary G. Hodge and Michael E. Smith, 133–73. Institute for Mesoamerican Studies, State University of New York, Albany.

Müller, Florencia. 1952. "Las cerámicas del horizonte-culturales locales." In *The Civilizations of Ancient America: Selected Papers of the 29th International Congress of Americanists*, edited by Sol Tax, 43–51. University of Chicago Press.

Müller, Florencia. 1978. *La alfarería de Cholula*. Instituto Nacional de Antropología e Historia, Mexico City.

Murra, John V. 1972. "El 'control vertical' de un máximo de pisos ecológicos en la economía de las sociedades andinas." In *Visita de la Provincia de León de Huánuco en 1562. I: Ortiz de Zuñiga, Visitador*, edited by John V. Murra, vol. 2, 427–76. Universidad Nacional Hermilio Valdizán, Huánuco, Peru.

Nichols, Deborah L., and Thomas H. Charlton. 1996. "The Postclassic Occupation at Otumba: A Chronological Assessment." *Ancient Mesoamerica* 7:231–44.

Noguera, Eduardo. 1935. "La cerámica de Tenayuca y las excavaciones estratigráficas." In *Tenayuca*, 141–201. Secretaría de Educación Pública, Departamento de Monumentos, Mexico City.

Noguera, Eduardo. 1954. *La cerámica arqueológica de Cholula*. Editorial Guarania, Mexico City.

Norr, Lynette. 1987. "Postclassic Artifacts from Tetla." In *Ancient Chalcatzingo*, edited by David C. Grove, 525–46. University of Texas Press, Austin.

O'Neill, George Caracena. 1962. "Postclassic Ceramic Stratigraphy at Chalco in the Valley of Mexico." PhD dissertation, Department of Anthropology, Columbia University. University Microfilms, Ann Arbor.

Parsons, Jeffrey R. 1966. "The Aztec Ceramic Sequence in the Teotihuacan Valley, Mexico." PhD dissertation, Department of Anthropology, University of Michigan, Ann Arbor.

Parsons, Jeffrey R. 1971. *Prehistoric Settlement Patterns in the Texcoco Region, Mexico*. Memoirs of the Museum of Anthropology, no. 3. University of Michigan, Ann Arbor.

Parsons, Jeffrey R. 2008. *Prehispanic Settlement Patterns in the Northwestern Valley of Mexico: The Zumpango Region*. Memoirs of the Museum of Anthropology, no. 45. University of Michigan, Ann Arbor.

Parsons, Jeffrey R., Elizabeth M. Brumfiel, and Mary G. Hodge. 1996. "Developmental Implications of Earlier Dates for Early Aztec in the Basin of Mexico." *Ancient Meso-america* 7:217–30.

Parsons, Jeffrey R., Elizabeth M. Brumfiel, Mary Hrones Parsons, and David J. Wilson. 1982. *Prehispanic Settlement Patterns in the Southern Valley of Mexico: The Chalco-Xochimilco Region.* Memoirs of the Museum of Anthropology, no. 14. University of Michigan, Ann Arbor.

Parsons, Jeffrey R., Elizabeth M. Brumfiel, Mary Hrones Parsons, Virginia Popper, and Mary Taft. 1982. *Late Prehispanic Chinampa Agriculture on Lake Chalco-Xochimilco, Mexico.* Preliminary report submitted to the National Science Foundation the Instituto Nacional de Antropología e Historia. Museum of Anthropology, University of Michigan, Ann Arbor.

Parsons, Jeffrey R., Mary Hrones Parsons, Virginia Popper, and Mary Taft. 1985. "Chinampa Agriculture and Aztec Urbanization in the Valley of Mexico." In *Prehistoric Intensive Agriculture in the Tropics*, edited by I. S. Farrington, 49–96. BAR International Series, no. 232. British Archaeological Reports, Oxford.

Plunket, Patricia. 1990. "Arqueología y etnohistoria en el Valle de Atlixco." *Notas Meso-americanas* 12:3–18.

Sanders, William T. 1965 *The Cultural Ecology of the Teotihuacan Valley, Mexico.* Department of Sociology and Anthropology, The Pennsylvania State University, University Park.

Sanders, William T., ed. 1986. "The Toltec Period Occupation of the Valley," pt. 1: "Excavations and Ceramics." In *The Teotihuacan Valley Project Final Report*, vol. 4. Occasional Papers in Anthropology, Department of Anthropology, The Pennsylvania State University, University Park.

Sanders, William T., Jeffrey R. Parsons, and Robert S. Santley. 1979. *The Basin of Mexico: Ecological Processes in the Evolution of a Civilization.* Academic Press, New York.

Séjourné, Laurette. 1970. *Arqueología del Valle de México*, vol. 1: *Culhuacán.* Instituto Nacional de Antropología e Historia, Mexico City.

Séjourné, Laurette. 1983. *Arqueología e história del Valle de México, de Xochimilco a Ameca-meca.* Siglo Veintiuno, Mexico City.

Smith, Michael E. 1983. "Postclassic Culture Change in Western Morelos, Mexico: The Development and Correlation of Archaeological and Ethnohistorical Chronologies." PhD dissertation, Department of Anthropology, University of Illinois, Champaign/Urbana. University Microfilms, Ann Arbor.

Smith, Michael E. 2000. "Postclassic Developments at Xochicalco." In *Archaeological Research at Xochicalco*, vol. 2: *The Xochicalco Mapping Project*, edited by Kenneth G. Hirth, 167–83. University of Utah Press, Salt Lake City.

Sugiura, Yoko. 2005. *Historia de los asentamientos en el Valle de Toluca.* Instituto de Investigaciones Antropológicas, Universidad Nacional Autónoma de México, Mexico City.

Tolstoy, Paul. 1958. "Surface Survey in the Northern Valley of Mexico: The Classic and Postclassic Periods." *Transactions of the American Philosophical Society* 48(5):1–101.

Tovalín, Alejandro. 1998. *Desarrollo arquitectónico del sitio arqueológico de Tlalpizahuac.* Serie Arqueología, Instituto Nacional de Historia y Anthropología, Mexico City.

Vaillant, George C. 1938. "A Correlation of Archaeological and Historical Sequences in the Valley of Mexico." *American Anthropologist* 40:535–73.

5

A Study of Non-Metric Skull Traits from Tlatilco and Xico, in Relation to Classic Teotihuacan

ABIGAIL MEZA-PEÑALOZA, FEDERICO ZERTUCHE, AND RAÚL GARCÍA CHÁVEZ

INTRODUCTION

One of the academic concerns of Jeffrey Parsons was related to the settlement patterns and demography of the Basin of Mexico. In this work we present a bio-distance analysis among some populations settled in the Basin of Mexico from the Early Formative (ca. 1500–1000 BCE) to the Early Postclassic (ca. 950–1150 CE). To achieve this goal, we make use of the analysis of non-metric anatomical variables that occur in the skull, also known as categorical epigenetic features.

Within their diversity, the anatomical variables in the skull include persistence of sutures, bones in the place of fontanelles, expression or absence of canals, foramina, and tubercles. They also have an important application to the studies of hominid fossils, including those of non-human primates. In the human species, as among other vertebrates, there is an unequal distribution of the manifestation of these and other morphological variables. This does not necessarily imply that they are under evolutionary selection pressure. However, the laws that govern their inheritance allow us to find affinities between populations (Berry and Berry 1967; Buikstra and Ubelaker 1994; Hauser and De Stefano 1989; McGrath et

https://doi.org/10.5876/9781646424078.c005

al. 1984; Pink et al. 2016). Furthermore, in the Basin of Mexico, biological affinities have been found by using these techniques (Beekman and Christensen 2003; Christensen 1997; Meza-Peñaloza et al. 2019). In this work, we analyze morphological affinities among the inhabitants of Teotihuacan and their surrounding areas in a diachronic context. The basic idea of this approach is to understand what kind of migrations could have settled in the area after the fall of Teotihuacan.

We test our hypothesis through a statistical study of cranial non-metric traits of osteological samples from three Classical Teotihuacan neighborhoods (Ventilla B, Ventilla 92–94 and San Sebastián Xolalpan) in relation to five rural neighboring populations (Preclassic to Postclassic Xico, Preclassic Tlatilco, and Epiclassic Xaltocan).

MIGRATIONS FROM NEIGHBORING RURAL ZONES TO TEOTIHUACAN

The apogee of Teotihuacan occurs during the Classic period of Mesoamerica (ca. 150–650 CE), though settlement began during the first millennium BCE. The city was located in the northeastern Basin of Mexico. During the Terminal Preclassic period (ca. 300–100 BCE), Teotihuacan became the main competitor of Cuicuilco (Manzanilla 2015). A number of authors have presented exhaustive analyses of the formation and economic development of Teotihuacan (Cowgill 1997; Kurtz et al. 1987; Manzanilla 2015; Millon 1972, 1981; Nichols 2016). According to these studies, Teotihuacan was a stratified society with classes of priests, military, merchants, artisans, and peasants. In addition to this social division, the design, construction, and operation of the city required economic specialization; engineers, architects, and builders likely were in charge of obtaining and transferring the raw materials necessary for building, and those who produced goods likely exchanged them in markets and paid taxes or tribute with craft items. In summary, Teotihuacan has been considered the main center of a state that dominated the surrounding settlements of Mexico's Basin, politically and economically. Its relationships with subordinate settlements, however, are still not fully understood.

Since its origins, Teotihuacan became a multi-ethnic settlement, and many groups of different origins settled on the periphery of the metropolis (Álvarez-Sandoval et al. 2015; Manzanilla 2015, 2017). The city was likely made up of permanent residents, temporary residents (including probable ambassadors or representatives of other cities), and transients (travelers, merchants, temporary workers, etc.). Indeed, mobility was a hallmark of Teotihuacan influence, and, as some evidence shows, movement to Teotihuacan occurred from distant provinces in the Maya area, the Gulf Coast, the west and Oaxaca (Álvarez-Sandoval et al. 2015; Cowgill 2008; Nichols 2016). Nevertheless, little information exists on the nature or extent of bi-directional rural-to-urban/urban-to-rural movement between Teotihuacan and the surrounding communities and how such movements affected the population dynamics of the Central Highlands. Moreover, few studies have explored the ethnic and genetic relationships of peripheral or rural sites, both on their own terms and in terms of broader transformations in the political landscape, such as the development and collapse of major states, including Teotihuacan. In response, this chapter uses material from different archaeological sites and periods of time to examine regional and historical population dynamics, including Classic period Teotihuacan, Preclassic to Postclassic Xico, Preclassic Tlatilco, and Epiclassic Xaltocan.

THE OSTEOLOGICAL SAMPLE

To examine our hypothesis, we studied osteological material that date from the Early Preclassic period (ca. 1500–1000 BCE) to the Early Postclassic period (ca. 950–1150 CE) from five sites in the Basin of Mexico and three neighborhoods at Teotihuacan occupied during the Classic period (see figure 5.1). The osteological sample under study consists of 363 adult skulls.

The Teotihuacan sample consists of materials from La Ventilla 92–94, San Sebastián Xolalpan, and La Ventilla B. The materials from La Ventilla 92–94 were excavated between 1992 and 1994 (Cabrera 1996). Archaeologists have interpreted the area as a residential complex (Cabrera 2003; Gómez and Núñez 2003). We analyzed sixty skeletons from Frente 3, identified as a housing complex of artisans. The burials are estimated to correspond to the Terminal Preclassic to Early Classic period—Early Tlamimilolpa phase (ca. 250–350 CE), a period of major growth at Teotihuacan (Cowgill 2015).

The materials analyzed from San Sebastián Xolalpan correspond to an archaeological rescue operation and also date to the Tlamimilolpa phase (Ortega-Cabrera 2000). The remains were recovered from public, ritual contexts (altars and temples), where community events were likely held. The individuals buried might have had a degree of social recognition, given their funerary contexts. The studied sample from this locality consisted of six individuals.

La Ventilla B is interpreted as a residential complex inhabited from the Early Tlamimilolpa to the Metepec phase. This locality is considered one of the first structures in Ventilla B (Serrano and Lagunas 2003). It consisted of rooms around small patios and a series of disturbed architectural elements, including three staircases that probably gave access to three temples. Its inhabitants have been interpreted as artisans who specialized in painting and had possible affinities to the Maya and Gulf Coast regions (Piña-Chan 1963; Rattray 1978). The studied sample from this locality consisted of forty-eight individuals described in Spence's (1974) report.

For Xico, we examined a sample spanning three periods: Late Preclassic (ca. 750–100 BCE), Epiclassic (ca. 600–900 CE), and Early Postclassic (ca. 950–1150 CE).

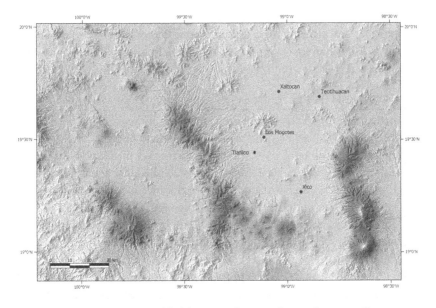

FIGURE 5.1. *Digital elevation model of the Basin of Mexico, showing locations of sites included in this study.*

Given the long period of occupation at Xico, these samples offer a unique opportunity to examine the movement in the context of settlement continuity, particularly the possible relationships to Teotihuacan prior to and after its collapse. The importance of Xico is reflected in the historical sources (Cuauhtlehuanitzin 1997; Velázquez and León-Portilla 2019). The site has been absorbed by the urban growth of greater Mexico City, and most of the data comes from salvage archaeological excavations (García Chávez 2004; García Chávez and Vélez 2008). We were able to analyze seven individuals from the Preclassic, five from the Epiclassic, and forty-one from the Early Postclassic.

We include samples from Tlatilco and Xaltocan to have a better frame of reference to examine regional dynamics across time. The Xaltocan samples were excavated by Morehart in 2007 and 2012 (Morehart 2009, 2015; Morehart et al. 2012). The excavations uncovered the remains of at least three hundred individuals, all of which consist of crania or cranial fragments. Many of the crania were intact enough to be used to measure their cranial non-metric traits, so we were able to include the analysis of 118 individuals.

For Tlatilco, we used the database obtained by Vargas (1973) in his master's thesis. Tlatilco was one of the first villages in Central Mexico (ca. 1500–1000 BCE). It is located in the western region of the Basin of Mexico in the municipality of San Bartolo Naucalpan, State of Mexico. The settlement was on fluvial terraces, well suited for agriculture, and near forests and lakes with their different natural resources. It is speculated that Tlatilco had strong Olmec influences (García-Moll et al. 1991; Piña-Chan 1958). We were able to obtain a sample of seventy-eight individuals from Vargas's sources (Vargas 1973).

CRANIAL NON-METRIC TRAITS

Non-metric traits (NMT) have been used for about fifty years. It has been shown that they are transmitted by genetic means (Berry and Berry 1967; Hauser and De Stefano 1989; Pink et al. 2016). Although their exact mechanisms of biological transmission are not yet clear, it has been established that cranial NMT allow intergroup comparisons of variation that are indicative of migration, gene flow, founder effect, and reproductive isolation (Hauser and De Stefano 1989; Pink et al. 2016). Another advantage is that cranial NMT are easy to measure in contrast to other techniques, such as geometric morphometry and the like, since NMT traits can be measured on incomplete or poorly preserved skeletal samples. The range of NMT available for study allows researchers to select those traits that cannot be distorted by other sources of physical variation, such as cranial modification. We measured twelve NMT of the facial and basal region of the skull, as artificial modification may change the NMT of the vault. Since the number of samples of many populations are too small for a standard statistical analysis (see table 5.1), we resample the data using a parametric bootstrapping technique, as we explain below.

We recorded the variables following methods proposed by Hauser and De Stefano (1989), Buikstra and Ubelaker (1994), Hanihara and Hajime (2002) and Pink and colleagues (2016). Additionally, we used the individual count method of Scott and Turner (1997) for bilateral traits, where the maximum expression of a trait is counted, regardless of the side of the skull where it is expressed. We selected this method instead of arbitrarily analyzing only one side, since it maximizes the number of observable traits in fragmented or damaged skulls.

The protocols employed for counting the twelve NMT under study include:

1. Metopic suture: only the complete expression was considered present; the partial expression of it was included in the absent category.
2. Supraorbital foramen: any foramen in the supraorbital open margin that goes through the orbit was recorded as such.
3. Multiple infraorbital foramen: this foramen is usually unique, but may be internally divided by a bone bridge; a bristle was used verify the communication of the foramina with the orbital floor.
4. Zygomaticofacial foramen absence.
5. Parietal foramen: its presence was recorded if it crossed the internal table.
6. Patent condylar canal: its presence behind the occipital condyle was recorded using a bristle.

TABLE 5.1. Counts of non-metric traits (NMT) for the eight populations under study. Population sample names are listed in the far-left column, indicating the values of measures and presences of each of the twelve traits recorded. Refer to the text for a description of the twelve traits. Numerical values for measures represent $N^{\mu i}$ (number of measures of the i-trait in the μ-population); numerical values for presences represent $K^{\mu i}$ (number of counts where the i-trait is present). See the beginning of the section on statistical analysis for details.

NMT	1	2	3	4	5	6	7	8	9	10	11	12
Tlatilco												
Measures	77	78	74	63	78	75	78	56	53	78	78	78
Presences	3	52	10	14	66	34	11	3	5	9	16	43
Preclassic Xico												
Measures	7	7	6	6	7	5	5	5	5	7	7	7
Presences	1	7	0	0	7	4	0	1	2	2	1	3
Ventilla 92–94												
Measures	27	27	12	7	22	15	12	10	9	14	14	15
Presences	0	15	12	0	15	1	1	5	5	1	0	1
Ventilla B												
Measures	14	31	31	30	32	12	14	14	17	19	48	38
Presences	0	23	7	29	22	0	1	0	1	0	1	37
Xolalpan												
Measures	6	5	3	3	6	6	4	5	4	4	4	6
Presences	0	1	3	0	3	0	0	4	4	3	0	0
Epiclassic Xico												
Measures	5	5	5	5	5	4	4	3	4	5	5	5
Presences	0	5	0	2	5	3	0	2	2	4	1	1
Xaltocan												
Measures	93	95	82	80	106	94	94	95	95	116	116	116
Presences	0	77	10	49	68	65	25	8	51	32	8	80
Postclassic Xico												
Measures	41	41	37	35	40	30	29	34	34	40	40	40
Presences	0	40	1	13	27	22	9	9	11	17	6	14

7. Divided hypoglossal canal: only the complete division of this was recorded as present.
8. Foramen ovale incomplete.
9. Foramen spinosum incomplete: it was considered if it had a partial or null formation of bone that joined them to the foramen lacerum.

10. Tympanic dehiscence: the presence of perforations in the tympanic plate was recorded with a magnifying lens to determine whether it was the effect of postmortem damage.

11. Auditory exostosis.

12. Mastoid foramen: it was recorded as present if it traversed the internal table.

STATISTICAL METHODS

We use the mean measure of divergence (MMD) to analyze biodistance, which is the standard method used for assessing the NMT (Berry and Berry 1967; De Souza and Houghton 1977; Edgar 2017; Harris and Sjøvold 2004). MMD biodistance can be easily tested for statistical significance and is an unbiased estimator of the real value (De Souza and Houghton 1977). We labeled the $P = 8$ populations with the Greek subscripts μ and ν. Let M = 12 denotes the number of NMT under study and let the subindex i ($i = 1, 2, \ldots, M$) denotes the traits. Let N_μ designate the size of the μ-population sample. Non-metric traits are categorical variables coded as 'o' (absent), '1' (present), and '?' (the trait was not able to be measured). In the latter, no count is done in the database. For each μ-population and each i-trait, let: $K^{\mu i}$ and $N^{\mu i}$ let: and denote the number of counts where the i-trait is present, and the number of measures of the i-trait in the μ-population, respectively. From these definitions, $K^{\mu i} \leq N^{\mu i} \leq N^{\mu}$, since it may happen that the i-trait was not able to be measured in all of the μ-population sample (i.e., some '?' were found).

The MMD biodistance among two populations μ and ν is given by (De Souza and Houghton 1977; Nikita 2015)

$$MMD(\mu, \nu) = \frac{1}{M} \sum_{i=1}^{M} \left\{ (\theta_{\mu i} - \theta_{\nu i})^2 - \frac{1}{N_{\mu i} + 1/2} - \frac{1}{N_{\nu i} + 1/2} \right\} \quad ,$$

where the angle angle $\theta_{\mu i}$ is measured in radians ($-$<pi> ($-\pi/2 < \theta_{\mu i} < \pi/2$), and is given by the Anscombe's transformation

$$\theta_{\mu i} = \sin^{-1}\left(1 - 2\,\frac{K_{\mu i} + 3/8}{N_{\mu i} + 3/4}\right),$$

(Anscombe 1948; Nikita 2015; Zertuche and Meza-Peñaloza 2020). Under the *null hypothesis of random behavior*, $\theta_{\mu i}$ follows nearly a normal distribution 0, $\sigma^2_{\mu i}$, where the standard deviation is given by

$$\sigma_{\mu i} = \frac{1}{\sqrt{N_{\mu i} + 1/2}} \,.\, (1)$$

The variance of the *MMD* under the *null hypothesis* was calculated by De Souza and Houghton (1977) with the result

$$\sigma^2(\mu, \nu) = \frac{2}{M^2} \sum_{i=1}^{M} \left\{ \frac{1}{N_{\mu i} + 1/2} + \frac{1}{N_{\nu i} + 1/2} \right\}^2 .$$

If the MMD(μ, v) results ≤ 0, then $MMD(\mu, v)$ is set to zero. If $MMD>0$ one must establish if the value is statistically significant. To test for significance, it is better to work with standardized MMS biodistance defined by

$$stMMD(\mu, v) = MMD(\mu, v) / \sigma(\mu, v).$$

This approach has the advantage that the standardized mean measure of distance (*stMMD*) nearly follows an $N(0, 1)$ distribution under the *null hypothesis* (De Souza and Houghton 1977). If $stMMD(\mu, v)>2$, its significance level is $\alpha \leq 0.05$.

Given the small number of individuals in some of the samples (Xico Preclassic, San Sebastian Xolalpan, and Xico Epiclassic), calculating the stMMD will not necessarily demonstrate statistically significant results. In fact, some results might give $MMD = 0$. So, we use a parametric bootstrap (PB) procedure to statistically increment the samples' sizes (Zertuche and Meza-Peñaloza 2020).

Since, under the *null hypothesis of random fluctuations*, the probabilistic distribution of $\theta_{\mu i}$ is the normal N $\boldsymbol{N}(0, \sigma_{\mu i}^2)$ with $\sigma \mu i$ given by (1), it is possible to apply a PB approach in order to increase the representability of the biodistance data. This procedure must be done for all of the populations, regardless of their number of samples, which is the case for any bootstrapping procedure, whether or not it is parametric or non-parametric Devore and Berk 2012; Efron 1979; Lupton 1993; Zertuche and Meza-Peñaloza 2020. Essentially, parametric procedure are more powerful than non-parametric ones Devore and Berk 2012; Lupton 1993. Also, note that any bootstrap method increases the sample size, and, as a result, increases the distance among the groups. Therefore, large biodistance values should appear due to the PB procedure. From 1, and the fact that $\theta_{\mu i} \sim \boldsymbol{N}(0, \sigma_{\mu i}^2)$, $N^{\mu i}$ variates $\theta_{\mu i}^{(s)}$ (s=1,2, . . . ,$N^{\mu i}$) are extracted from $\boldsymbol{N}(0, \sigma_{\mu i}^2)$, obtaining new standard deviations $\sigma_{\mu i}^*$ through

$$\sigma_{\mu i}^* = \sqrt{\frac{1}{N_{\mu i} - 1} \sum_{s=1}^{N_{\mu i}} \left\{ \theta_{\mu i}^{(s)} - <\theta_{\mu i}> \right\}^2}, (2)$$

where

$$<\theta_{\mu i}> = \frac{1}{N_{\mu i}} \sum_{s=1}^{N_{\mu i}} \theta_{\mu i}^{(s)}.$$

The procedure can be repeated B times (b = 1, 2, . . . , B) by doing new extractions and using (2). So, we get the set

$$\left\{ \sigma_{\mu i}^{*(b)} \right\}_{b=1}^{B}.$$

Then, a bootstrapped value $\Sigma \mu i$ of $\sigma \mu i$ is obtained through

$$\Sigma_{\mu i} = \sqrt{\frac{1}{B-1} \sum_{b=1}^{B} \left\{ \sigma_{\mu i}^{*(b)} - < \sigma_{\mu i}^{*} > \right\}^2} \ ,$$

where

$$< \sigma_{\mu i}^{*} > = \frac{1}{B} \sum_{b=1}^{B} \sigma_{\mu i}^{*(b)} .$$

Now, a bootstrapped value for: MMD^B is given by

$$MMD_B(\mu, \nu) = \frac{1}{M} \sum_{i=1}^{M} \left\{ \left(\theta_{\mu i} - \theta_{\nu i} \right)^2 - \Sigma_{\mu i}^2 - \Sigma_{\nu i}^2 \right\},$$

with its associated standard deviation σ^B,

$$\sigma_B(\mu, \nu) = \sqrt{\frac{2}{M^2} \sum_{i=1}^{M} \left\{ \Sigma_{\mu i}^2 + \Sigma_{\nu i}^2 \right\}^2}$$

and the standardized $stMMD^B$

$$stMMD_B(\mu, \nu) = MMD_B(\mu, \nu) \, / \, \sigma_B(\mu, \nu) \, , (3)$$

are finally constructed. In general, a value of $B = 500$ is adequate, and the results will not change by increasing it (Devore and Berk 2012; Zertuche and Meza-Peñaloza 2020). All the results that follow will be expressed by (3) with $B = 500$ iterations.

Note that: $\sigma_{\mu i}$ given by (1) decreases with sample size by orders $\sigma_{\mu i} \sim \left(1 / \sqrt{N_{\mu i}} \right)$. While $\Sigma_{\mu i}$ shrinks as $\sigma_{\mu i} \sim O \, 1 \, / \, N^{\mu i}$ or more due to the Central Limit Theorem (Zertuche and Meza-Peñaloza 2020). As a result, big values of the $stMMD^B$ (3) are expected. This effect will also happen when using the unweighted pair group method with arithmetic mean (UPGMA). The interested reader can find a careful explanation of the PB in Zertuche and Meza-Peñaloza (2020).

For the analysis of the distance matrix, we use the UPGMA (Sokal and Michener 1958). Numerical calculations were done using PAST 3.21, GNUPLOT 5.0, and self-made programs in C computational language (Press et al. 1996).

RESULTS AND DISCUSSION

The non-metric counts of the populations appear in table 5.1, and the resulting distance matrix is obtained from (3) in table 5.2. Figure 5.2 displays the graphical results of the biodistance analysis using UPGMA. According to the data, it does not appear that there was a close relationship between the Preclassic

TABLE 5.2. Distance matrix for the eight populations in table 5.1

μ \ ν	1	2	3	4	5	6	7	8
1	0.00	36.67	406.69	661.03	89.15	38.47	3254.27	1242.94
2	36.67	0.00	121.07	164.24	63.96	10.04	54.59	28.85
3	406.69	121.07	0.00	568.92	18.79	71.34	513.74	500.81
4	661.03	164.24	568.92	0.00	134.10	95.40	686.28	999.13
5	89.15	63.96	18.79	134.10	0.00	37.96	86.97	87.29
6	38.47	10.04	71.34	95.40	37.96	0.00	30.52	12.63
7	3254.27	54.59	513.74	686.28	86.97	30.52	0.00	750.09
8	1242.94	28.85	500.81	999.13	87.29	12.63	750.09	0.00

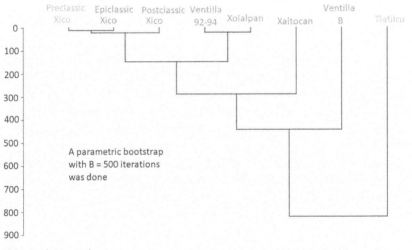

FIGURE 5.2. *A dendrogram of the distance matrix in table 5.2.*

inhabitants of Xico and Tlatilco. The settlement in Xico during this period did not exceed one hundred people (Sanders et al. 1979) and we do not know their ancestral affiliation.

The studies of ancient populations in the Central Highlands have been focused on the power relations exercised by urban settlements, characterized by the presence of ceremonial centers and exchange networks (Cowgill 1997, 2008). In this work, we used Xico Island as an example because of its particular location, which allows us to use it as a model to explain the development of a community and the possible influences that its location could have marked the behavior of its inhabitants.

When Teotihuacán was at its peak, there was a decrease in population in Xico, most likely because some of the inhabitants migrated to Teotihuacan. Toward the Epiclassic period, the site became a local center, with an astonishing increase in population. It has been estimated that more than 1,000 people lived on the island (Sanders et al. 1979). During the Postclassic, population growth continued (Sanders et al. 1979). Our results indicate that Xico's population remained almost unchanged at the phenotypic level across its history of occupation. Therefore, its population's behavior over time differed from other settlements that exhibit more direct influence from Teotihuacan's expansion, at least biologically.

A variety of explanations have been proposed to explain the extraordinary growth of Teotihuacan. Millon (1981) suggested that the exploitation of agricultural resources could have been the main attraction for the development of the settlement. Throughout its history of occupation, the city was characterized by a constant migratory flow. In some cases, the marriage unions occurred within the complexes, where the population was of local origin, although in some neighborhoods the population could have been of mixed origin (Álvarez-Sandoval et al. 2015). For example, the *Barrio de los Comerciantes* maintained constant communication with people from the Gulf of Mexico and Maya areas, and isotopic analyses have pointed toward a possible matrilocal residence system (Spence et al. 2005). In the La Ventilla and Tlajinga neighborhoods, however, no geographical differences between men and women have been observed in place of residence, which could translate into a lower frequency of immigration at least in these two places of the city (Nado et al. 2017; White et al. 2004). The closeness among the inhabitants of La Ventilla and San Sebastián Xolalpan may indicate that, during Teotihuacan's Classic period, inhabitants of different parts of the city interacted more intensively than others. The observed cluster distance (see figure 5.2) between La Ventilla B and other Teotihuacan neighborhoods, however, may reflect the possibility that the inhabitants of this neighborhood maintained strong connections with the Gulf Coast (Rattray 1978).

Although there exists extensive regional information for the Basin of Mexico regarding settlement patterns (Parsons et al. 1982; Sanders et al. 1979), there are few details about the size of the populations, the kinship relationships, and demographic exchange between the different settlements. Given the wide sphere of influence of Teotihuacan within the cultural development of the central highlands and the territorial proximity of the rural populations to the city, it would be natural to infer a close biodistance among the eight populations under study. Nevertheless, this is not what the biodistance analysis of NMT presented in the dendrogram in figure 5.2 shows. We consider that the results presented in this work represent an important contribution toward using biodistance analysis at a macro-regional and temporal scale to understand past population dynamics.

CONCLUSIONS

Given the great apogee of Teotihuacan over a period of nearly five hundred years (ca. 150–650 CE) one would expect a nearby biodistance among it and their close neighborhoods. Yet we found, using non-metric traits analysis, that this is not the case. More explicitly, from the dendrogram in figure 5.2 we can see that even in the very same city of Teotihuacan there were different kinds of biological affinities: while the neighborhoods of La Ventilla 92–94 and San Sebastián Xolalpan have a small biodistance; the other neighborhood analyzed (La Ventilla B) has much longer distances.

These results lead us to hypothesize that there existed a complex behavior of migrations from different parts in the Basin of Mexico. This is the case not only in the Classical period, but in all of the periods, and settlements, that we analyzed, running from the Early Formative (ca. 1500–1000 BCE) to the Early Postclassic (ca. 950–1150 CE). We see no reason to infer that other settlements than those analyzed here would exhibit this kind of behavior. We hope to be able, in the nearby future, to analyze other materials to obtain a deeper understanding of these migrations.

Acknowledgments. The authors would like to thank Pilar López Rico for her informatics services and Gerardo Giménez for the elaboration of figure 5.1. We also acknowledge our source of funding from the grant UNAM-PAPIIT IN402720.

REFERENCES

Álvarez-Sandoval, Brenda, A., Linda Manzanilla, Mercedes González-Ruiz, Assumpció Malgosa, and Rafael Montiel. 2015. "Genetic Evidence Supports the Multiethnic Character of Teopancazco, a Neighborhood Center of Teotihuacan, Mexico (AD 200–600)." *PLOS ONE* 10(7):1–19.

Anscombe, Francis J. 1948. "The Transformation of Poisson, Binomial, and Negative-Binomial Data." *Biometrika* 35:246–54.

Beekman, Christopher S., and Alexander F. Christensen. 2003. "Controlling for Doubt and Uncertainty through Multiple Lines of Evidence: A New Look at the Mesoamerican Nahua Migrations." *Journal of Archaeological Method and Theory* 10(2):111–64.

Berry, Caroline, and R. J. Berry. 1967. "Epigenetic Variation in the Human Cranium." *Journal of Anatomy* 101(2):361–79.

Buikstra, Jane, and Douglas H. Ubelaker. 1994. *Standards for Data Collection from Human Skeletal Remains.* Arkansas Archaeological Survey Research Series, no. 44. Arkansas Archeological Survey, Fayetteville, AR.

Cabrera, Rubén. 1996. "Las excavaciones en La Ventilla." *Revista mexicana de estudios antropológicos* 42:5–30.

Cabrera, Rubén. 2003. "Las prácticas funerarias de los antiguos teotihuacanos." In *Prácticas funerarias en la Ciudad de los Dioses: Los enterramientos humanos de la antigua*

Teotihuacan, edited by L. Manzanilla and C. Serrano, 503–39. IIA, DGAPA, UNAM, Mexico City.

Christensen, Alexander, F. 1997. "Cranial non-metric variation in North and Central Mexico." *Anthropologischer Anzeiger* 55(1):15–32.

Cowgill, George. 1997. "State and Society at Teotihuacan, México." *Annual Review of Anthropology* 26:129–61.

Cowgill, George. 2008. "Teotihuacan as an Urban Place." In *El urbanismo en Mesoamerica / Urbanism in Mesoamerica*, edited by R. H. Cobean, A. G. Mastache, Á. G. Cook and K. G. Hirt, vol. 2, 85–112. Instituto Nacional de Antropología e Historia and Pennsylvania State University, Mexico City and University Park.

Cowgill, George. 2015. *Ancient Teotihuacan: Early Urbanism in Central Mexico*. Cambridge University Press, Cambridge.

Cuauhtlehuanitzin, Chimalpahin Domingo Francisco de San Antón Muñón. 1997. *Primer amoxtli libro: 3A relación de las différentes histoires originales*. Electronic document. https://historicas.unam.mx/publicaciones/publicadigital/libros/329/amoxtli.html, accessed October 20, 2022.

De Souza, Peter, and Philip Houghton. 1977. "The Mean Measure of Divergence and the Use of Non-Metric Data in the Estimation of Biological Distances." *Journal of Archaeological Science* 4(2):163–69.

Devore, Jay L., and Kenneth N. Berk. 2012. *Modern Mathematical Statistics with Applications*. Springer, New York.

Edgar, Heather. 2017. *Dental Morphology for Anthropology: An Illustrated Manual*. Taylor & Francis, Albuquerque, NM.

Efron, Bradley. 1979. "Bootstrap Methods: Another Look at the Jackknife." *Annals of Statistics* 7(1):1–26.

García Chávez, Raúl. 2004. "De Tula a Azcapotzalco: Caracterización arqueológica de los altepetl de la Cuenca de México del Posclásico Temprano y Medio, a través del estudio cerámico regional." Tesis Doctorado en Antropología, Facultad de Filosofía y Letras, Universidad Nacional Autónoma de México, Mexico City.

García Chávez, Raúl, and Nadia Vélez. 2008. "Informe final de las excavaciones del Proyecto de Salvamento Arqueológico en el Cerro de la Mesa y San Martín Xico." Estado de México, Instituto Nacional de Antropología e Historia, Mexico City.

García-Moll, Roberto, Daniel Cossio, Carmen Piojan-Aguade, and María Elena Salas-Cuesta. 1991. *Catálogo de entierros de San Luis Tlatilco, México, Temporada IV*. Instituto Nacional de Antropología e Historia, Mexico City.

Gómez, Sergio, and Jaime Núñez. 2003. "Análisis preliminar del patrón y la distribución espacial de entierros en el Barrio de La Ventilla." In *Prácticas funerarias en la Ciudad de los Dioses: Los enterramientos humanos de la antigua Teotihuacan*, edited by L. Manzanilla and C. Serrano, 81–147. IIA, DGAPA, UNAM, Mexico City.

Hanihara, Tsunehiko, and Ishida Hajime. 2002. "Frequency Variations of Discrete Cranial Traits in Major Human Populations. IV. Vessel and Nerve Related Variations." *Journal of Anatomy* 196:273–87.

Harris, Edward F., and Torstein Sjøvold. 2004. "Calculation of Smith's Mean Measure of Divergence for Intergroup Comparisons Using Nonmetric Data." *Dental Anthropology.* 17:55–62.

Hauser, Gertrud, and Gian Franco De Stefano. 1989. *Epigenetic Variants of the Human Skull.* E. Schweizerbartsche Verlagsbuchhandlung, Stuttgart.

Kurtz, Donald, Thomas H. Charlton, James F. Hopgood, Stephen A. Kowaleski, Deborah Nichols, Robert. S. Santley, Marc J. Swartz, and Bruce G. Trigger. 1987. "The Economics of Urbanization and State Formation at Teotihuacan (and Comments and Reply)." *Current Anthropology* 28(3):329–53.

Lupton, Robert. 1993. *Statistics in Theory and Practice.* Princeton University Press, Princeton, NJ.

Manzanilla, Linda. 2015. "Cooperation and Tensions in Multiethnic Corporate Societies Using Teotihuacan, Central Mexico, as a Case Study." *Proceedings of the National Academy of Sciences* 112(30):9210–15.

Manzanilla, Linda. 2017. *Teotihuacan, ciudad excepcional de Mesoamérica.* El Colegio Nacional, Mexico City.

McGrath, Janet W., James M. Cheverud, and Jane E. Buikstra. 1984. "Genetic Correlations between Sides and Heritability of Asymmetry for Nonmetric Traits in Rhesus Macaques on Cayo Santiago." *American Journal of Physical Anthropology* 64(4):401–11.

Meza-Peñaloza, Abigail, Federico Zertuche, María García-Velasco, and Christopher Morehart. 2019. "A Non-Metric Traits Study of Skulls from Epiclassic Xaltocan in Relation to Other Mesoamerican Cultures." *Journal of Archaeological Science: Reports.* 23:559–66.

Millon, René. 1972. "El valle de Teotihuacan y su entorno." In *Teotihuacan, XI mesa redonda*, 326–38. Sociedad Mexicana de Antropología, Mexico City.

Millon, René. 1981. "Teotihuacan: City, State, and Civilization." In *Supplement to the Handbook of Middle American Indians*, edited by R. Bricker, 198–243. University of Texas Press, Austin.

Morehart, Christopher T. 2009. "Proyecto chinampero Xaltocan: Informe de la temporada de campo 2007–2008." Report on File. Instituto Nacional de Antropología e Historia, Mexico City.

Morehart, Christopher T. 2015. "Excavaciones en No-Cuadrícula 4." In *Proyecto de ecología histórica del norte de la Cuenca de México: Informe de la temporada de campo junio-agosto 2012*, edited by Christopher T. Morehart, 6–35. Report on File, Instituto Nacional de Antropología e Historia, Mexico City.

Morehart, Christopher T., Abigail Meza-Peñaloza, Carlos Serrano Sánchez, Emily McClung de Tapia, and Emilio Ibarra Morales. 2012. "Human Sacrifice during the Epiclassic Period in the Northern Basin of Mexico." *Latin American Antiquity* 23(4):426–48.

Nado, Kristin L., Natalya Zolotova, and Kelly Knudson. 2017. "Paleodietary Analysis of the Sacrificial Victims from the Feathered Serpent Pyramid, Teotihuacan." *Archaeological and Anthropological Sciences* 9(1):117–32.

Nichols, Deborah. 2016. "Teotihuacan." *Journal of Archaeological Research* 24:1–74.

Nikita, Efthymia. 2015. "A Critical Review of the Mean Measure of Divergence and Mahalanobis Distances Using Artificial Data and New Approaches to the Estimation of Biodistances Employing Nonmetric Traits." *American Journal of Physical Anthropology* 157(2):284–94.

Ortega-Cabrera, Verónica. 2000. "El Barrio en Teotihuacan: Un análisis arqueológico." Licenciatura en arqueología, Escuela Nacional de Antropología e Historia, Mexico City.

Parsons, Jeffrey. R., Elizabeth Brumfiel, Mary H. Parsons, and David J. Wilson. 1982. *Prehispanic Settlement Patterns in the Southern Valley of Mexico: The Chalco-Xochimilco Region*. Memoirs of the Museum of Anthropology, no. 14. University of Michigan, Michigan.

Piña-Chan, Román. 1958. *Tlatilco*. Instituto Nacional de Antropología e Historia, Mexico City.

Piña-Chan, Román. 1963. "Excavaciones en el Rancho La Ventilla." In *Teotihuacan*, edited by I. Bernal, 50–52. Instituto Nacional de Antropología e Historia, Mexico City.

Pink, Christine M., Christopher Maier, Marin Pilloud, and Joseph T. Hefner. 2016. "Cranial Nonmetric and Morphoscopic Data Sets." In *Biological Distance Analysis*, edited by Marin A. Pilloud and Joseph T. Hefner, 91–107. Academic Press, London.

Press, William H., Saul A. Teukolsky, William T. Vetterling, and Brian P. Flannery. 1996. *Numerical Recipes in C*. Cambridge University Press, Cambridge.

Rattray, Evelyn C. 1978. "Los contactos Teotihuacan-Maya visto desde el centro de México." *Anales de antropología* 15:33–52.

Sanders, William T., Jeffrey R. Parsons, and Robert S. Santley. 1979. *The Basin of Mexico: Ecological Processes in the Evolution of a Civilization*. Studies in Archaeology. Academic Press, New York.

Scott, G. Richard, and Christy G. Turner. 1997. *Anthropology of Modern Human Teeth*. Cambridge University Press. Cambridge University Press, Cambridge.

Serrano, Carlos, and Zaíd Lagunas. 2003. "Prácticas mortuorias prehispánicas en un barrio de artesanos ('La Ventilla B'), Teotihuacan." In *Prácticas funerarias en la Ciudad de los Dioses: Los enterramientos humanos de la antigua Teotihuacan*, edited by L. Manzanilla and C. Serrano, 35–79. IIA, DGAPA, UNAM, Mexico City.

Sokal, Robert, and Charles Michener. 1958. "A Statistical Method for Evaluating Systematic Relationships." *University of Kansas Science Bulletin* 38:1409–38.

Spence, Michael W. 1974. "Residential Practices and the Distribution of Skeletal Traits in Teotihuacan, Mexico." *Man* 9(2):262–73.

Spence, Michael W., Christine D. White, Evelyn C. Rattray, and Fred J. Longstaffe. 2005. "Past Lives in Different Places: The Origins and Relationships of Teotihuacan's Foreign Residents." In *Settlement, Subsistence, and Social Complexity: Essays Honoring the Legacy of Jeffrey R. Parsons*, edited by R. E. Blanton, 155–97. Cotsen Institute of Archaeology, University of California, Los Angeles.

Vargas, Luis A. 1973. "Estudio de los caracteres craneanos discontinuos en la población de Tlatilco." Tesis maestría en Antropología física, Escuela Nacional de Antropología e Historia, Mexico City.

Velázquez, Primo F., and Miguel León-Portilla. 2019. *Códice Chimalpopoca: Anales de Cuauhtitlan y Leyenda de los Soles*. UNAM, Mexico City.

White, Christine D., Rebecca Storey, Fred J. Longstaffe, and Michael W. Spence. 2004. "Immigration, Assimilation, and Status in the Ancient City of Teotihuacan: Stable Isotopic Evidence from Tlajinga 33." *Latin American Antiquity* 15(2):176–98.

Zertuche, Federico, and Abigail Meza-Peñaloza. 2020. "A Parametric Bootstrap for the Mean Measure of Divergence." *International Journal of Biostatistics* 16(2):20190117.

6

Mind the Gaps

*Thoughts on the Merits of Exploring between the Archeological
Sites Discovered by the Basin of Mexico Survey*

CHARLES D. FREDERICK

INTRODUCTION

Archeological surveys, as the starting point for most archaeological endeavors, define the places where subsequent investigations will be performed. Typically, such subsequent work is focused on ancient settlements, and it is logical that this occurs in the locations where the densest evidence of settlement exists. However, complex landscapes such as the Basin of Mexico (BOM) include extensive off-site features of archaeological interest, which present a unique problem for archaeological surveys. Many of these features are exquisitely complex anthropogenic built environments that are as interesting as the settlements identified by survey but, alas, are not settlements as defined by the BOM surveys.

The areas between the sites identified by the surveys, or the non-site areas described here as "gaps," have the potential to contain significant evidence of concealed remains of past settlements and their former agricultural areas. The goal of this paper is to highlight the importance of the non-site or gap areas in the evaluation of the archaeological record of the BOM.

https://doi.org/10.5876/9781646424078.c006

ANTECEDENTS

I had my first chance to work in the Basin of Mexico during the early summer of 1990, while a graduate student at the University of Texas. I spent the last half of May that year working with Liz Brumfiel at Xaltocan, driving around the northern Basin surrounding the site, aerial photographs and the maps from the Green Book (Sanders et al. 1979) in hand, trying to come to grips with the geomorphology, late Quaternary stratigraphy, and archaeology. At the end of the first week of June, I was about to depart for the Bajío, my doctoral research field area, when Liz mentioned that Jeff Parsons would be dropping by Xaltocan for a visit in a couple of weeks. At that point I had lots of questions for him and figured the 2-hour drive from Guanajuato was a lot shorter than a drive from Austin to Ann Arbor, so I began making plans to come back to meet Jeff and ask him about the survey and what I had been seeing in the landscape around Xaltocan. That would turn out to be one of the better decisions I made as a graduate student.

At the top of my list of questions for Jeff was why an amazing site I had found on the lakebed between Xaltocan and Tonanitla was not in the Basin of Mexico survey. The site, a multi-mound complex that Jeff immediately identified as a Postclassic salt production site, was obvious and I was confused how it had not been included in the survey maps. I could envision numerous ways such a site might be missed, but his answer caught me off guard: "We did not think anybody would have lived on the lakebed so we only surveyed down to the 2,240 m contour" (see also comment in Parsons 2015:189). They quickly learned the error of this omission, but the die had been cast for that particular survey. That said, John Millhauser (2012, this volume) carried out an intensive program of excavations at the site. Jeff spent many years in the field, and wrote of correcting this on subsequent surveys in the Basin, most notably the survey of the southern Basin and his last field effort in the Basin with Luis Morett on the Texcoco lakebed (Parsons 2015; Parsons and Morett 2004).

My assumption, that the survey had recorded all of the visible archaeological sites, which with the benefit of hindsight was rather typical of a green, naïve graduate student, was probably not unique to me. Indeed, a more literal reading of the survey documents would have revealed the specific detail that I had missed. Nevertheless, this was my first experience with an area between the dots (the archaeological sites) that retained features of archaeological significance, and caused me to look more closely at processes associated with survey methodology, human behavior (ancient and modern), and geomorphology that might result in significant discoveries occurring between the sites identified by the survey. After thirty years of field experience in areas examined by the BOM surveys and working with their published and unpublished data, I identified several issues that archeologists working in the BOM should be aware of when evaluating land within the surveys.

Simply put, the areas between the archaeological sites identified by the BOM surveys are what I am referring to as "the gaps." The methods employed by the BOM surveys have been described in various places (e.g., Parsons 2008:52–57). In general, estimates of artifact density, codified as one of six categories ranging from nothing (*nada*) to heavy, were recorded for discrete parcels of land after they had been traversed, and these observations were directly recorded onto 1:5,000 scale aerial photographs (Sanders et al. 1979:23). Sites were typically defined out of the field using a combination of discrete clusters of surface pottery (in excess of a "light" density) and/or architectural remains. These field observations can be used to portray the archaeological survey results in a variety of ways, and here the emphasis is on the gaps or spaces between the sites.

These gaps can be construed as two different things: actual gaps and conceptual gaps. Actual gaps (also referred to here as the "nada" gaps) are places where the survey recorded no artifacts visible on the surface. These places were never formally published as part of the survey documents, but are easily seen as the "nada" areas on the primary survey records (the aerial photos and derivative products such as the compiled tracings of the artifact density[1]). It is the "nada" gaps that drew Carlos Cordova and I to examine the primary survey data in the southeastern Basin, in an effort to delineate places where archaeological visibility had been compromised by sedimentation (see Frederick and Cordova 2019 for more discussion of this point). Figure 6.1 is a simplified rendition of the raw survey data designed to highlight the nada gaps in the southeastern Basin near Chalco, specifically displaying survey data for the Lake Chalco lakebed and the lakeshore plain immediately to the east. The orange tone shows the areas where sherd scatters occurred, as well as areas not shaded orange were where nothing was observed by the survey (nada areas).

Contemplating figure 6.1, however, leads one to ponder another kind of gap, what I call the conceptual gap, which arose from the synthesis of the raw survey data. Unknown to those unfamiliar with the primary survey data, the spatial distribution of actual sites is considerably smaller than the footprint of the scatters that were recorded (see figure 6.1). Most consumers of the survey data only know the "dots" or sites that the surveyors distilled from the larger artifact scatters. In the maps published by Sanders, Parsons, and Santley (1979) these dots appear as different icons linked to different categories of settlements based on

---

1 Jeff Parsons provided us access to the primary survey data for the Chalco-Xochimilco region in the early 1990s. The most useful products at that time were compiled tracings of the raw survey data that were in the form of large photocopied strips (~1 m wide by as much as 4 m long). These maps are now available as part of the Jeffrey R. Parsons papers: 1960–2013 (bulk 1966–1992), which are curated at the Bentley Historical Library, University of Michigan, Ann Arbor (https://quod.lib.umich.edu/b/bhlead/umich-bhl-2012180).

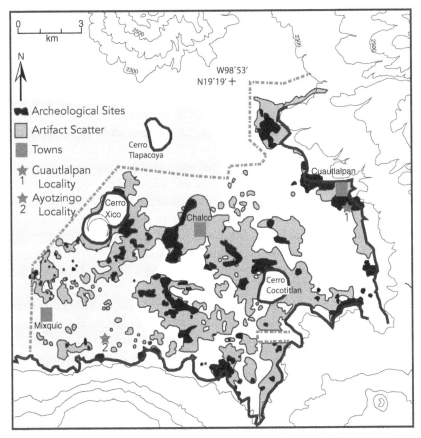

FIGURE 6.1. *A binary rendition of the spatial variation in artifacts recorded by the Chalco-Xochimilco survey in the southeastern Basin of Mexico, where the orange tone denotes artifact densities in excess of a very light scatter. The survey data has been clipped to the show only the lakeshore plain (the limits of which are the heavy black line) and lakebed. Black dots are all of the sites delineated within the artifact scatter. The red stars indicate the location of the Cuautlalpan and Ayotzingo locations discussed in the text. The white areas between the orange tones are the actual gaps, and the areas of orange surrounding the sites are what I am calling the conceptual gaps.*

estimated population. In other cases, such as in maps of some of the regional survey reports (e.g., Parsons 2008; Parsons et al. 1982), sites appear as the tracings of the actual site boundaries.

That the sites are merely geographic subsets of larger artifact scatters suggests that settlement was more broadly dispersed in some places than the sites imply, and/or that post-depositional processes have dispersed the artifacts. On sloping lands such as the piedmonts, overland flow in tandem with widespread erosion and cultivation may have extended the spatial extent of the scatters. But on low gradient surfaces like the lakeshore plain east of Chalco, this pattern hints at a broader, more dispersed settlement.

NADA INTERESTING HERE?

Subsurface exploration of the "nada" gaps in the southeastern Basin (Chalco and Xochimilco survey regions) revealed that many of these are areas of alluvial sedimentation. Depositional environments we observed in these areas range from the floodplains of gently incised alluvial valleys to broad plains where sedimentation more closely resembled alluvial fans, to actual stream deltas that prograded directly into the lakes. Backhoe trenching of these areas has encountered a variety of buried archaeological sites/features, ranging from occupational surfaces, to post-Conquest furrowed agricultural fields, to *chinampas*. Such dynamic depositional environments provide a range of archaeological opportunities depending on the prehistoric activities occurring at the time and the rate of sedimentation.

As might be expected, the sedimentation rate strongly conditions the nature of preservation and here I distinguish three categories: rapid (or obrution deposits), episodic, and incremental. *Obrution* refers to the burial of a surface by a single sudden depositional event (Brett et al. 1997; Kidwell and Bosence 1991:177); it is applied by paleontologists to fossil assemblages that are exceptionally well resolved temporally (hours to days) and thus offer brief "snapshots" of ancient conditions (the frozen moment) and communities. Although often associated with Pompeiian-like qualities, these rapidly buried or obrution surfaces can be single, short-lived occupation surfaces or almost any kind of time-averaged surface and therefore do not necessarily afford exemplary preservation or interpretive insight (Simoes et al. 1998). Beyond the realms of archaeology and paleontology, the obrution concept can be found in other disciplines, such as soil science. Thus, the Soil Survey Staff (1999:10) defines a fossil soil or paleosol, as a soil buried by 50 cm or more, which assumes that the burial occurred rapidly, or at least at a rate greater than the rate of soil development.

Episodic sedimentation, as used here, refers to the repeated and rapid deposition of a significant amount of sediment (~>10 cm) but in intervals widely spaced in time. Sedimentation of this type may not necessarily be perceived as a recurring threat to settlement, and sites in these settings are often subsequently re-occupied. Incremental sedimentation, on the other hand, refers to the gradual addition of very thin amounts of sediment, which is often incorporated into the soil profile so slowly that is often difficult to detect stratigraphically. The rate and magnitude of sedimentation conditions the manner in which preexisting surfaces are preserved in the archaeological record.

THREE EXAMPLES

To illustrate how some of the gaps in the survey may hide things of inter-est, I will present three examples, all from the southern Basin. The first two are from work Carlos Cordova and I did together in collaboration with Mary Hodge in the southeastern Basin near Chalco (Frederick and Cordova 2019) (see figure 6.1). The last is from subsequent work done exploring the origins of *chinampa* agriculture in the southern Basin with Virginia Popper and Luis Morett. Although it would be nice to say that we explored these gaps in the survey intentionally, in the first two cases the work was more broadly focused on understanding landscape dynamics and human interaction, while the third was a fortuitous discovery associated with exploring the antiquity of *chinampa* agriculture.

The Tlalmanalco River Valley, Southeastern Basin near San Martin Cuautlalpan

The valley of the Tlalmanalco River, where it traverses the lakeshore plain north and east of Lake Chalco is a relatively flat surface (see figure 6.1). This area has been extensively mined for earth to make bricks, resulting in vast exposures of the alluvial deposits that provide a highly variable but informative window into the subsurface. One particular brickyard located south and east of San Martin Cuautlalpan (Frederick and Cordova 2019, Locality 37) exposed a dramatic exam-ple of the contrasting preservational opportunities present at the margins of the Tlalmanalco river valley, where the BOM survey identified site Ch-MF-5 on the upland where it met the alluvial valley floor (Parsons et al. 1982; and unpublished data). Ch-MF-5 was classified as a large, nucleated village with no preserved structural remains. Tolstoy (1975) examined the assemblage from this site and concluded that it spanned the early Formative (Manantial phase) to late Middle Formative (La Pastora/Cuatepec phases). At the time of our fieldwork in the early 1990s, the upland was largely denuded to tepetate and strewn with Formative pottery. The brickyards, however, were cut into a floodplain that exhibited no artifacts on the surface, but examination of the deposits revealed that it had experienced repeated episodic occupation and sedimentation during the Middle Formative, when it was aggrading at an average rate of about 1 cm per year between approximately 814 and 913 cal BCE.

The photograph in figure 6.2 shows a 5.2-meter-high, excavated exposure in one brickyard, where six discrete occupation surfaces of Middle Formative age (see table 6.1 for the radiocarbon dates) are discernible. At a larger scale, all of these occupation surfaces compress to form the single Middle Formative occu-pation surface on the upland, where the only substantial archaeological features preserved now are negative relief features such as pits. Virtually none of the site on the upland retains significant deposits capable of reconstructing Middle Formative lifeways, but the adjacent alluvial lowlands, paradoxically just outside

FIGURE 6.2. *Photograph of a brickyard exposure southeast of San Martin Cuautlalpan. The red lines on the wall denote discrete Middle Formative occupation surfaces stratified within floodplain deposits of the Tlalmanalco River that were buried between 913 and 814 cal BCE.*

TABLE 6.1. Radiocarbon ages from the Cuautlalpan East Locality 37 (Frederick and Cordova 2019). Calibrated in Calib 8.2 using the IntCal20 data set (Reimer et al. 2020).

Lab No.	Material Dated	Conventional Age	Calibrated Age 2 sigma	Comment
OS-9493	charcoal	2650±35	898–860 BCE (16%) 843–778 BCE (84%)	Uppermost occupation surface
OS-9967	charcoal	2770±30	996–832 BCE (100%)	Lowest occupation surface
OS-10174	charcoal	4160±120	3085–3059 BCE (0.7%) 3030–2451 BCE (98.3%) 2421–2406 BCE (0.04%) 2377–2351 BCE (0.07%)	Occupation debris within mud flow.

the site boundary identified during the survey, provide ample opportunities to examine relatively short time windows into this period.

Delta of the Amecameca River, Rancho Mondragón, near Ayotzingo

One of the largest actual gaps in the Chalco-Xochimilco survey occurs along the leading edge of the lakeshore plain south of Chalco, where the Amecameca River entered Lake Chalco (see figures 6.1 and 6.3). The survey identified no settlements in this area but did record numerous small isolated low-density scatters of sherds. Subsurface exploration of this area by backhoe trenching has revealed that the relative absence of artifacts is due to the deposition of an extensive amount of

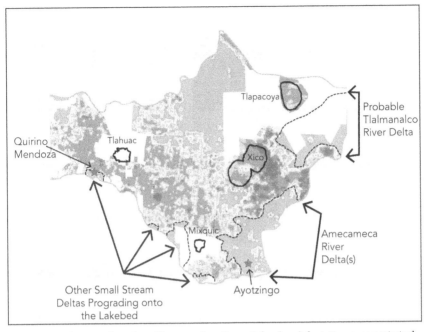

FIGURE 6.3. *Annotated version of figure 5.3 from Luna Golya (2014) depicting a geostatistical surface (inverse distance weighted) of Aztec-period population density. The lowest population density areas near Ayotzingo and Quirino Mendoza are confirmed delta deposits that have prograded onto the lakebed. Several other possible deltas southwest of Mixquic are highlighted. A key for the depiction of the survey data is provided on figure 6.4.*

sediment by deltas of the Amecameca River. The most dramatic illustration of this was the discovery of a deeply buried suite of *chinampas* that were exposed by a trench at Rancho Mondragón, near San Pablo Ayotzingo (Frederick and Cordova 2019, figure 14, Locality 14). The relatively rapid and deep burial of the fields near Ayotzingo appears to be an obrution event, which resulted in excellent preservation of both the field morphology and the organic remains therein. Pollen from the Ayotzingo locality was studied by Silva (2003) and macrobotanical results are briefly discussed by McClung and Acosta Ochoa (this volume).

Interestingly, Jeff Parsons (2019:272–73, figures 15.18 and 15.19) published a photo of a canal exposing a buried *chinampa* landscape close to and east of Mixquic (the precise location of which is unknown; Jeffrey Parsons 2002, personal communication). The appearance of these fields are very similar to the Ayotzingo locality, but the *chinampas* are buried by only a meter of silt. Parsons (2019) interpreted the sediment burying the *chinampas* as windblown silt, but this is much more likely to be pro-delta deposit derived from the Amecameca River. The full extent of this buried *chinampa* landscape is unknown, but it likely

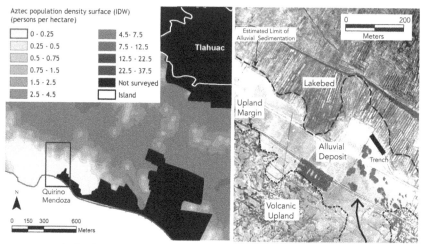

FIGURE 6.4. *Left: Plot of the spatial variation in artifact density rendered as a population density surface from Luna Golya (2014) for the Lake Xochimilco lakebed near Quirino Mendoza. The lowest category (0–0.25) represents the areas where nothing was observed on the ground surface (the "nadas"). The black rectangle is the location shown in the aerial photograph, right. Right: A 1955 aerial of the Quirino Mendoza locality annotated to show the southern shore of Lake Xochimilco (the upland margin), the lakebed, which is populated with* chinampas, *and the alluvial apron that has buried the* chinampas *at the margin of the lake.*

contains numerous small settlements once inhabited by the *chinampa* farmers, similar to those documented on the Xochimilco lakebed to the west by Parsons and colleagues (1982) and shown in more detail by Luna Golya (2014).

Southern Rim of the Xochimilco Lakebed, Colonia Quirino Mendoza (Tulyehualco)

The Quirino Mendoza locality lies on the southern edge of the bed of Lake Xochimilco, close to where the Basin floor meets the lavas of the Sierra de Chichinautzin. The BOM survey data in this area reveals a conspicuous absence of artifacts immediately adjacent to the lake edge (see figure 6.4). Fortuitous examination of a wastewater utility trench in 2002 revealed that this area was occupied by *chinampa* farmers, but that evidence was buried by alluvium deposited on the lakebed by a small stream that emerges from the uplands immediately to the south. Analysis of the profile of a part of this trench revealed an enlightening sequence of events that records the back-and-forth adaptation of *chinampa* farmers to evolving conditions, most likely in the post-Conquest period.

The sequence of events is interpreted from the stratigraphy in a stepwise fashion on figure 6.5. The starting point for this record (Phase 0) is a long succession of very slowly aggrading lacustrine deposits on the floor of Lake Xochimilco. About

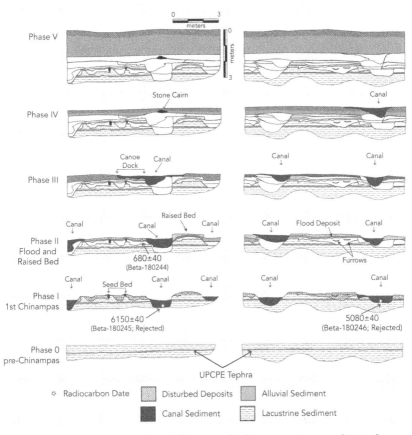

FIGURE 6.5. *Stepwise reconstruction of* chinampa *development as it occurred in tandem with alluvial sedimentation in the Postclassic and Postconquest periods at the Quirino Mendoza locality.*

a meter of black gyttja-like sediment was exposed by the trench and in the middle of this was a thin white tephra that is inferred to be correlative with the Upper Pre-Ceramic Plinian Eruptive Sequence (UPCPES) attributed to Popocatepetl (Siebe and Macías 2006), which dates to around 5,000 years BP. The initial phase of *chinampa* cultivation begins with ditched fields, where the ditches were cut into the preexisting lacustrine deposits by more than half a meter, often cross-cutting the UPCPES tephra. The ground between the ditches (the *chinampas*) exhibited evidence of agricultural disturbance to depths between 10 and 30 centimeters. These early *chinampas* measured between 2 and 4 meters wide. Features observed within the deposits of these early fields include a seed bed (*almácigo*) that consisted of a slightly concave surface almost a meter wide that was bordered by masses of hard clay, several shallow pits, and one planting surface with

TABLE 6.2. Radiocarbon ages from the Quirino Mendoza Locality. Calibrated in Calib 8.2 using the IntCal20 data set (Reimer et al. 2020)

Lab No.	Material Dated	Conventional Age	Calibrated Age 2 sigma	Comment
Beta-80244	Conifer, c. pine	680±40	1269–1327 cal CE (58.9%) 1348–1395 cal CE (41.1%)	flood deposit that buries earliest *chinampa*
Beta-180245	monocot	6150±40	5214–4988 cal BCE (99.7%) 4962–4960 cal BCE (3%)	lowest fill in earliest canal (rejected as an accurate depositional age)
Beta-180246	monocot	5080±40	3968–3781 cal BCE	lowest fill in earliest canal (rejected as an accurate depositional age)

preserved traces of two furrows that were about 40 centimeters wide, and separated by about 30 centimeters. Three pieces of charcoal were collected from the earliest canal deposits (see table 6.2), but only one yielded an age consistent with Early to Late Postclassic use of the field (1269–1395 cal CE; Beta 180244). The other two samples are interpreted as redeposited and not accurate ages for the time of sedimentation. At some point (Phase II; around 1269–1395 cal CE) a flood buried these *chinampas* with a thin (~5 cm) drape of sand, and immediately after this the beds appear to have been raised between 15 to 30 centimeters by the addition of new sediment, with the edges bordering the canals squared off. From this point onward, alluvium periodically filled the canals, requiring cleaning, and occasionally inundated and buried the fields. In Phase III, the *chinampa* width appears to have become more standardized at about 4 meters, and one field exhibited a shallow 1.5-m-wide bench that was inset below the cultivation surface but adjacent to a deeper canal; we interpreted this feature as a canoe dock.

By phase IV, renewed sedimentation had buried all of the previous *chinampas*, yet one canal remained in the nearly 25-meter exposure illustrated in figure 6.5. This dramatic increase in *chinampa* width is consistent with previous observations by Ávila López (1991, 2006). Interestingly, one of the most persistent canals in the examined profile had been completely filled by this time but was marked by a stone cairn or bank (or probably a continuous bank of rocks), as if this ditch were important for some reason other than water (e.g., a property boundary). In Phase V, alluvial sedimentation had filled in all of the previous canals, and if this landscape were still being used for *chinampa* agriculture, the field width is much greater than all of the Prehispanic antecedents.

It is important to note that in this particular instance, the sedimentation was episodic and, as a result, it preserves incremental changes in the agricultural landscape through the period of sedimentation. In contrast, long-term changes in agricultural landscapes on geomorphically stable surfaces are much more difficult to resolve as they are constantly plowed or modified every growing season.

DISCUSSION

The presentation of the survey results by Sanders, Parsons, and Santley (1979) as well as the various regional surveys such as the Chalco-Xochimilco survey discussed here (Parsons et al., 1982) are typical for most archaeological surveys, with the majority of the emphasis on loci of intense concentrations of artifacts. This traditional approach, despite the authors' keen awareness of the vast, complex anthropogenic landscape at hand, results in the binary situation of sites and non-site areas. It has been my experience that the results of such surveys become simplified with subsequent use, which is ever more tightly focused on the sites, while the intervening gaps are progressively ignored. That may be acceptable for hunter-gatherer archaeology, where traces of human activities away from the sites are negligible, but it is much less so for complex archaeological landscapes like the BOM.

It is unfortunate that depiction of the raw survey data was beyond the methods available at the time, as access to this information is critical to being an informed user of the BOM survey data. Nevertheless, the nature of the data collection employed by the BOM surveys continues to provide new and useful ways of viewing Prehispanic settlement and land use. In particular, the initial collection of spatially discrete observations of artifact/ceramic density has proven useful in translating these observations into Geographic Information Systems (GIS; see Hirth et al. 2009; Luna Golya 2014), which can be readily statistically manipulated and portrayed graphically in myriad ways. Simplistic pre-GIS attempts to exploit these data, such as the binary representation (artifact scatters, as opposed to "nada") of the southeastern BOM landscape, provides a basic view of the archaeological landscape that was intended to highlight areas of probable geological bias in artifact/site visibility. This is the case of the Amecameca Delta area (see, e.g., figure 6.1; see also Frederick and Cordova 2019:112, figure 4) and its subsequent testing by backhoe trenching, which confirmed the suspicions of Parsons and colleagues (1982:4) of where their survey data yielded an inaccurate portrayal of the actual archaeological landscape, owing to site burial due to sedimentation.

In contrast, Luna Golya's (2014) presentation and analysis of the survey data for the southern Basin lakebed (i.e., the *chinampa* landscape) leverages the best aspects of the BOM survey data with historic aerial photographs and geoinformatics to provide an entirely new view of this cultural landscape in its continuous complexity. In specifics, his comparison of the sites identified by the Chalco-Xochimilco survey with the spatial variation in ceramic density and the location of relic mounds identified from historic aerial photos (Luna

Golya 2014:136, figure 6-3) reveals a much truer image of Prehispanic occupation of the lakebed than any of the BOM survey reports. It also exposes the limitations of the site concept in such densely settled/manipulated landscapes, and how the binary site/non-site distinction hides/omits or downplays vast areas of Prehispanic human activity. Parsons and colleagues (1982) were keenly aware of how the assumptions that underpinned their fieldwork limited their interpretations (Parsons 2015), and it is to our benefit that they maintained their devotion to "the big picture" and emphasized spatial coverage at the expense of more detailed examination of sites, as well as made spatial point observations on the density of artifacts. However, maps such as Luna Golya's clearly reveal the landscape diversity of the areas "between the gaps" and how perilous it can be to consider these areas unworthy of archaeological attention.

Given the conversations I had with Jeff Parsons over the decades since 1990, it is my opinion that little of what I have said here would come as a surprise to him. His retrospective on the BOM surveys (Parsons 2015), as well as his last fieldwork in the Basin (Parsons and Morett 2004), clearly show that he came around to seeing that the areas between the sites, although subtle and not necessarily exhibiting activity that fit within the settlement-driven framework of the BOM surveys, preserve useful details about the past (see also Morehart and Crider 2016). The emphasis on the Texcoco lakebed as a relatively undisturbed place to examine such localities, while undoubtedly true, tacitly downplays the potential of off-site archaeology elsewhere in the Basin. Although I have no concrete examples to offer here, I suspect that many of the off-site areas that fall within the artifact scatters identified by the surveys contain evidence of more domestic and/or agrarian activities. The surficial presentation of these off-site areas may be underwhelming, but their subsurface or stratigraphic records may reveal evidence of domestic settlement. Granted, all of these areas have to be evaluated on a per-case basis.

CONCLUSION

The Basin of Mexico surveys have provided myriad details about the archaeological landscape, some of which are only now coming into focus with the application of GIScience to the raw field observations. This paper has chosen to examine the merits of two kinds of gaps, places where the survey did not find artifacts on the surface (the "nada" gaps), and the areas between the sites as defined by the survey (i.e., the "conceptual" gaps). The "nada" gaps, where they correspond with dynamic depositional environments such as river valleys and lake margins, are often a by-product of sedimentation, and the lack of artifacts on the surface does not mean these areas were not settled in the past. Instead, these are areas with compromised archaeological visibility. Hence, the gap areas may contain exquisitely preserved evidence of ancient settlement and/

or agrarian activities, albeit buried by alluvia. The nature of the preservation in these locations will, to some extent, be conditioned by the sedimentation rate, with rapid deposition and or episodic sedimentation providing repeated opportunities to observe long-term change in land use. Given the continued expansion of the urban environment, these places of often deep sedimentation may preserve the best long-term record of the Prehispanic past well into the future.

Conversely, close examination of the raw survey data reveals that the areas between the sites were often littered with artifacts, and, in less complex landscapes, many of these areas would have been considered sites. It is likely that in some places these "conceptual gaps" in the survey may harbor myriad archaeological features, albeit somewhat disturbed by more recent land use. Unfortunately, until the GIS database compiled by Kenneth Hirth (Hirth et al. 2009; NSF Grant Award Number 0609926 "GIS Data Base and Spatial Analysis of the Basin of Mexico") becomes more widely available, understanding the location of conceptual gaps will be difficult, if not impossible, for most researchers. Alternatively, they can avail themselves of the Jeffrey R. Parsons Papers curated at the Bentley Historical Library at the University of Michigan (https://quod.lib .umich.edu/b/bhlead/umich-bhl-2012180) where all of the raw data is accessible in person.

Acknowledgments. Jeff Parsons graciously offered access to the raw survey data from the Chalco-Xochimilco survey region, and these data proved to be of more use than initially expected. The work at the Quirino Mendoza locality was supported by grants from the National Geographic Society (no. 7195-02) to Charles D. Frederick (CDF), Virginia Popper (VP), Luis Morett (LM), and Fernando Sánchez Martínez (FSM); UC-Mexus-Conacyt (2001) to VP and LM, and was done in collaboration with CDF, VP, LM, and Nicholas James. The Chalco study was funded by a 1993 grant from the Texas Higher Education Coordinating Board Advanced Research Program to Dr. Mary Hodge (MH); fieldwork was performed by CDF, MH and Carlos Cordova. GIS illustrations of the survey data in figures 6.3 and 6.44 were provided by Dr. Gregory Luna Golya.

REFERENCES

Ávila López, Raúl. 1991. *Chinampas de Iztapalapa*. D.F. Instituto Nacional de Antropología e Historia, Mexico City.

Ávila López, Raúl. 2006. *Mexicaltzingo: Arqueología de un reino culhua-mexica*. 2 vols. Instituto Nacional de Antropología e Historia, Mexico City.

Brett, Carlton E., Godron C. Baird, and Stephen E. Speyer. 1997. "Fossil Lagerstätten: Stratigraphic Record of Paleontological and Taphonomic Events." In *Paleontological Events: Stratigraphic, Ecological, and Evolutionary Implications*, edited by Carlton Eliot Brett, and Gordon C. Baird, 3–40. Columbia University Press, New York.

Frederick, C. D., and Carlos E. Cordova. 2019. "Prehispanic and Colonial Landscape Change and Fluvial Dynamics in the Chalco Region, Mexico." *Geomorphology* 331:107–26. https://doi.org/10.1016/j.geomorph.2018.10.009.

Hirth, Kenneth, Gregory Luna Golya, and Peter van Rossum. 2009. *Methodology: Building the Basin of Mexico GIS Database*. The Pennsylvania State University, University Park.

Kidwell, Susan M., and Daniel W. J. Bosence. 1991. "Taphonomy and Time Averaging of Marine Shelly Faunas." In *Taphonomy: Releasing the Data Locked in the Fossil Record*, edited by Peter A. Allison and Derek E. G. Briggs. Topics in Geobiology, vol. 9. Plenum Press, New York.

Luna Golya, Gregory Gerard. 2014. "Modeling the Aztec Agricultural Waterscape of Lake Xochimilco: A GIS Analysis of Lakebed Chinampas and Settlement." PhD dissertation, The Pennsylvania State University, University Park.

Millhauser, John K. 2012. "Saltmaking, Craft, and Community at Late Postclassic and Early Colonial San Bartolome Salinas, Mexico." PhD dissertation, Northwestern University, Evanston, IL.

Morehart, Christopher T., and Destiny L. Crider. 2016. "Low-intensity Investigations at Three Small Sites along Lake Xaltocan in the Northern Basin of Mexico." *Latin American Antiquity* 27(2):257–63.

Parsons, Jeffrey R. 2008. *Prehispanic Settlement Patterns in the Northwestern Valley of Mexico: The Zumpango Region*. Memoirs of the Museum of Anthropology, no. 45. University of Michigan, Ann Arbor.

Parsons, Jeffrey R. 2015. "An Appraisal of Regional Surveys in the Basin of Mexico, 1960–1975." *Ancient Mesoamerica* 26(1):183–96.

Parsons, Jeffrey R. 2019. *Remembering Archaeological Fieldwork in Mexico and Peru, 1961–2003: A Photographic Essay*. Special Publication of the Museum of Anthropology, no. 3. The University of Michigan, Ann Arbor.

Parsons, Jeffrey R., and Luis Morett A. 2004. "Recursos acuáticos en la subsistencia azteca: Cazadores, pescadores y recolectores." *Arqueología mexicana* 12(68):38–43.

Parsons, Jeffrey R., Elizabeth Brumfiel, Mary H. Parsons, and David J. Wilson. 1982. *Prehispanic Settlement Patterns in the Southern Valley of Mexico: The Chalco-Xochimilco Region*. Memoirs of the Museum of Anthropology, no. 14. University of Michigan, Ann Arbor.

Reimer, Paula J., William E. N. Austin, Edouard Bard, Alex Bayliss, Paul G. Blackwell, Christopher Bronk Ramsey, Martin Butzin, Hai Cheng, R. Lawrence Edwards, Michael Friedrich, Pieter M. Grootes, Thomas P. Guilderson, Irka Hajdas, Timothy J. Heaton, Alan G. Hogg, Konrad A. Hughen, Bernd Kromer, Sturt W. Manning, Raimund Muscheler, Jonathan G. Palmer, Charlotte Pearson, Johannes van der Plicht, Ron W. Reimer, David A. Richards, E. Marian Scott, John R. Southon, Christian S. M. Turney, Lukas Wacker, Florian Adolphi, Ulf Büntgen, Manuela Capano, Simon M.

Fahrni, Alexandra Fogtmann-Schulz, Ronny Friedrich, Peter Köhler, Sabrina Kudsk, Fusa Miyake, Jesper Olsen, Frederick Reinig, Minoru Sakamoto, Adam Sookdeo, and Sahra Talamo. 2020. "The IntCal20 Northern Hemisphere radiocarbon age calibration curve (0–55 cal kB)." *Radiocarbon* 62(4):725–57. https://doi.org/10.1017/RDC.2020.41.

Sanders, William T., Jeffrey R. Parsons, and Robert S. Santley. 1979. *The Basin of México: Ecological Processes in the Evolution of a Civilization*. Academic Press, New York.

Siebe, C., and Macías, J. L. 2006. "Volcanic Hazards in the Mexico City Metropolitan Area from Eruptions at Popocatépetl, Nevado de Toluca, and Jocotitlán Stratovolcanoes and Monogenetic Scoria Cones in the Sierra Chichinautzin Volcanic Field." In *Neogene-Quaternary Continental Margin Volcanism: A Perspective from Mexico, GSA Special Papers 402*, edited by C. Siebe, J. L. Macías, and G. J. Aguirre-Díaz, 253–329. Geological Society of America, Boulder, CO.

Silva, María Gabriela. 2003. *Análisis palinológico del perfil de una antigua chinampa en Ayotzingo, Chalco, Edo. de México*. Maestría en Biología Vegetal, Facultad de Ciencias, Universidad Nacional Autónoma de México, Mexico City.

Simoes, M. G., M. Kowalewski, F. F. Torello, and L. E. Anelli. 1998. "Long-Term Time-Averaging despite Abrupt Burial: Paleozoic Obrution Deposits from Epeiric Settings of Parana Basin, Brazil" (abstract). Paper presented to the Geological Society of America Annual Meeting. http://www.geo.arizona.edu/ceam/gsa98ms.html, accessed October 16, 2022.

Soil Survey Staff. 1999. *Soil Taxonomy: A Basic System of Soil Classification for Making and Interpreting Soil Surveys*, 2nd ed. Agricultural Handbook, no. 436. United States Department of Agriculture, Natural Resources Conservation Service. U. S. Government Printing Office, Washington, DC.

Tolstoy, P. 1975. "Settlement and Population Trends in the Basin of Mexico (Ixtapaluca and Zacatenco Phases)." *Journal of Field Archaeology* 2:97–104.

7

Modern Regional Demographics and Land Use in the Basin of Mexico

Insights from and Impacts on the Archaeological Record

L. J. GORENFLO

". . . we should stress a critical factor of immediate and overwhelming concern: Time is rapidly running out *as archaeological remains are daily consumed and forever obliterated by the astonishing, and accelerating, industrial and urban growth of modern Mexico City." (Sanders et al. 1979:411)*

INTRODUCTION

Although primarily focused on studying the past, archaeology also connects to the present in important ways. One potential link is using research on the past to comprehend key characteristics of the present and near-term future. Archaeological inquiries help to understand efforts by sociocultural systems to adapt to physical and cultural geographies of the past, revealing both successes and failures that may help us grasp key challenges of the Anthropocene. Archaeology often lacks detail, even on fundamental aspects of earlier times such as the routine activities of daily life. But this area of research can yield insights on change over time, broad patterns of cultural behavior, and possible

https://doi.org/10.5876/9781646424078.c007

long-term implications of that behavior (Redman 2005). In many cases, such understanding provides a useful perspective from which to evaluate modern socio-ecological systems. A second potential link between archaeology and the present is how current activity affects the archaeological record. Extracting insights from archaeological data requires the availability of those data. To enable its collection and analysis, archaeological evidence must survive all socio-cultural systems after its creation, including those existing now.

One geographic area where linking the present with the prehistoric past involves both of these types of past-present connection is the Basin of Mexico. For centuries, this region hosted complex societies that, like many modern societies, would have challenged the capacity of natural systems to support them. In pre-Columbian times, the Basin was a cradle of civilization, one of a handful of regions in the world that witnessed the emergence of a pristine state (Wright 1977). It also hosted the core of the Aztec empire, a polity that not only controlled much of Mesoamerica in the fifteenth and sixteenth centuries, but also had many of its characteristics documented when conquered by Spanish invaders and their indigenous allies in 1521 (Carrasco 1999; Sahagún 1950, 1982). The Basin's prominence continued into the Colonial period as the center of New Spain into the early nineteenth century (Gibson 1964; Lockhart 1992). Occupying much of the modern Basin of Mexico, Mexico City, has dominated the region as the political, economic, and demographic hub of Mexico since the Spanish conquest. Rapid population growth during the second half of the twentieth century has made it one of the largest cities on Earth (Kandell 1988). The persisting importance of this region in prehistoric and historic times has generated remarkable sociocultural systems *and* has attracted considerable attention from both administrators and scholars, the latter providing a wealth of information on the Basin throughout its past and into the present. Unfortunately, centuries of considerable human presence have been a two-edged sword. The economic and political importance of the region generates efforts to document its evolution, but also development that has consumed key evidence of that very same evolution.

This chapter addresses two issues related to Basin of Mexico archaeology. One is the degree to which patterns of regional adaptation in the archaeological past help us understand similar issues in the modern Basin. Much of this is predicated on our understanding of prehistoric settlement in the region, first synthesized in detail in the landmark volume by William Sanders, Jeffrey Parsons, and Robert Santley (1979). The second is the degree to which modern human actions in the Basin have compromised the very archaeological data that might provide clues to understanding past *and current* occupations of the region. The chapter begins by first discussing in broad terms what we know about resident prehistoric cultures through archaeological settlement pattern surveys and studies of resulting data. It then examines modern regional demographics and, where possible, modern land use in the Basin of Mexico, presenting a story of slow, steady population growth into the second half of the twentieth century followed by decades of rapid population increase that began to push what once was widespread crop production to the geographic margins of the region. Examining archaeological survey data in the context of 1970 and 2018 landscapes reveals how recent settlement and land use have greatly affected the prehistoric record. The chapter closes by exploring options for maintaining important parts of an irreplaceable archaeological record amid expanding settlement, mechanized agriculture, and other changes that have already damaged or destroyed much of that record.

PRE-COLUMBIAN REGIONAL SETTLEMENT PATTERNS IN THE BASIN OF MEXICO

Between 1960 and 1975, archaeologists conducted settlement pattern surveys of eight subsections of the Basin of Mexico (Sanders et al. 1979): the Teotihuacan region (1960–1966; Sanders 1965), the Texcoco region (1967; Parsons 1971), the Ixtapalapa region (1969; Blanton 1972), the Chalco region (1969; Parsons et al. 1982), the Xochimilco region (1972; Parsons et al. 1982), the Zumpango region (1973; Parsons 2008), the Cuautitlan region (1974; Sanders and Gorenflo 2007), and the Temascalapa region (1974–1975; Gorenflo and Sanders 2007). These projects sought to locate all archaeological sites in non-urbanized portions of the Basin of Mexico, though with a clear emphasis on sites with ceramics, to help us understand the evolution of complex societies in the region. Using intensive surface survey guided by 1:5000 (usually) aerial photographs, field crews identified, mapped, and recorded select archaeological and environmental information on all pre-Columbian archaeological sites in each survey region. The result was the discovery and documentation of more than 3,900 sites dating between 1500 BCE and 1519 CE (Gorenflo 2015). Although the surveys did not systematically assess site function, they often considered location in conjunction with the archaeological remains encountered to assign a basic type for each site.

Survey results enabled researchers to map pre-Columbian settlement in the Basin of Mexico for eight major time periods: Early, Middle, Late, and Terminal Formative; Teotihuacan period; Early and Late Toltec; and Late Aztec. Figures 7.1 and 7.2 show maps from three different periods as examples. Some general patterns emerge. One is the presence of settlement hierarchies, a characteristic frequently encountered in the regional arrangement of communities where each settlement is both a separate entity and part of a multi-settlement system consisting of places with different sizes and roles (Haggett 1965). Another pattern is a tendency to favor certain sections of the Basin or environmental zones. As discussed in detail elsewhere (Gorenflo 2015; Sanders et al. 1979), the geographic arrangement of settlement varied throughout the pre-Columbian past, likely reflecting differences in the adaptive strategies and sociopolitical realities

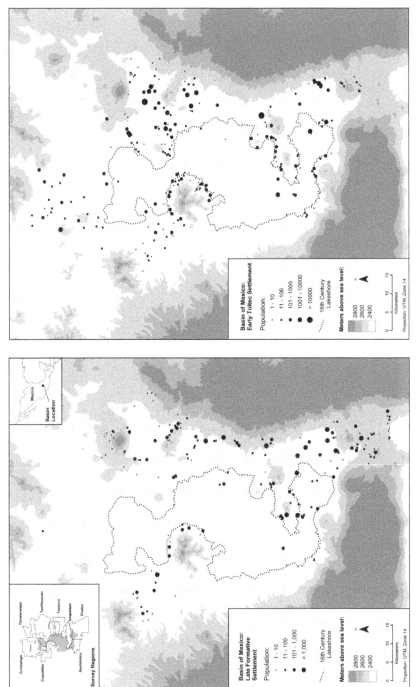

FIGURE 7.1. Settlement patterns in the Basin of Mexico based on archaeological survey data: Late Formative (a) and Early Toltec (b) periods.

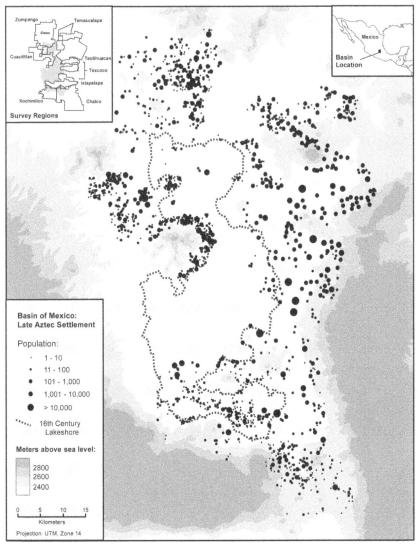

FIGURE 7.2. *Settlement patterns in the Basin of Mexico, based on archaeological survey data: Late Aztec period.*

of various time periods. Nevertheless, archaeological evidence of prehistoric occupation of the Basin indicates remarkable success over about three millennia, with regional population possibly reaching 1.0 million or more at the time of the Spanish Conquest in 1519 (Sanders et al. 1979:184).

Prehistoric settlement tended to favor the southern part of the Basin of Mexico when dense regional population and sociocultural conditions did not lead to occupations further north. This general pattern probably related to rainfall, which is markedly higher in the southern Basin, making agriculture for many of the key pre-Columbian crops much riskier in the north, in the absence of systematic water control (Gorenflo 2015; cf. Evans 1992; Nichols 1987, 2015). Other broad patterns that emerge from archaeological settlement data indicate the possible influence of dominant environmental features. This is the case of the central lake system, which represented the key resources and energetically efficient means of transportation, as well as of the lower piedmont, which featured soils particularly suitable for agriculture (Gibson 1964; Gorenflo 2015; Millhauser 2017; Parsons 2005, 2006; Sanders and Santley 1983; Sanders et al. 1979). Elaborate modifications of the environment for crop production, such as *chinampa* agriculture (Armillas 1971; Parsons 1976; Rojas Rabiela 1988; Sanders 1965), also affected prehistoric settlement in the Basin of Mexico. In addition, the presence of large administrative centers during certain periods seemed to influence the geographic arrangement of communities, such as Teotihuacan and Tula, probably *attracting* settlement toward the northern portion of the Basin during the Teotihuacan and Late Toltec periods of occupation (Parsons 2008; Sanders et al. 1979). The influence of water was likely an important factor during prehistoric times, not surprisingly for generally agrarian sociocultural systems in a region where some areas may have received on average less than 500 mm of rainfall annually (Sanders et al. 1979:map 2). Parts of the region were too risky for certain crops in the absence of water control, which certainly affected settlement. The tendency to emphasize the southern Basin for settlement, to engage in limited economic pursuits in the north, and to rely on irrigation for certain crops in particular parts of the region persisted through the historic past and into modern times.

DRAMATIC DEMOGRAPHIC AND LAND USE CHANGE IN THE TWENTIETH-CENTURY BASIN OF MEXICO

Population and land use patterns in the Basin of Mexico changed markedly over the course of the twentieth and into the twenty-first century. To summarize this, I present population density maps for *municipios* (administrative units below the level of state) found at least partially inside the Basin. The maps represent three particular years: 1900, the year of the second census in Mexico; 1960, the year Sanders began the Teotihuacan region settlement survey; and 2010, the year of the most recently available census data when preparing this manuscript.

Population densities for each year appear in figures 7.3 and 7.4 and reveal some striking changes, as total population in these *municipios* grew from 781,000 in 1900 to 5,887,000 in 1960, and then to 20,699,000 in 2010, an increase of nearly twenty-seven times in barely one century. In 1900, none of the *municipios* examined (including Mexico City) had a population greater than 370,000; by 2010 the population of thirteen *municipios* (including Mexico City) exceeded that number. Beyond overall population growth, the largest single-decade increases occurred between 1960–70 (3.9 million people) and 1970–80 (5.8 million), precisely when the archaeological settlement pattern surveys were underway (see figure 7.5). With more people added during the 1960s than lived in all Basin *municipios* in 1900, and nearly half of the 2010 total population for those *municipios* added during the 1960s and 1970s, it appears that archaeologists began to document prehistoric settlement patterns precisely when modern population growth began to threaten evidence for those patterns throughout much of the region.

The demographic history of the Basin of Mexico during the twentieth century underscores the importance of not conducting settlement pattern surveys any later than they occurred. Sanders visited the Basin for the first time in 1951, when the total population of the Basin *municipios* was about 3.7 million and when a simple agrarian economy based mostly on subsistence agriculture dominated the region. Much of his understanding of land use and the cultural ecology of the Basin emerged in 1953–54, influenced as much by his study of *campesino* agriculture and contemporary land use as by ethnohistoric and archaeological data, as described in his doctoral dissertation a few years later (Sanders 1957). When the Teotihuacan region survey began in 1960, Sanders and his crews—including Parsons as a crew member—encountered a dispersed agrarian economy in that region and throughout much of the Basin of Mexico (Sanders 1965).

Field crews in the early 1960s examined archaeological landscapes that in many ways had been minimally affected by settlement or destructive land use since the Spanish Conquest. Archaeologists encountered the remains of prehistoric settlements with extant domestic architecture: the remains of small house mounds on otherwise well-preserved archaeological sites. Many of the crops grown in the first half of the 1960s—maize, beans, squash, amaranth, maguey, nopal—were grown in pre-Columbian times and used low-impact techniques broadly similar to what the Spanish had encountered in the early sixteenth century, apart from plow cultivation using draft animals (Sanders 1965; Sanders et al. 1979). Rural settlements occupied largely by subsistence agriculturalists tended to be small and sparsely arranged over the landscape in the early 1960s, with higher settlement density often supported by irrigation systems that helped reduce risk and increase productivity (Gamio 1922; Palerm 1973). Other activities persisted as well. Observing traditional cultural behavior with pre-Columbian roots during those early years of fieldwork would inspire Parsons to conduct two classic ethnoarchaeological studies, one of traditional salt-making (Parsons 2001) and one of lake-resource exploitation (Parsons 2006).

Despite massive changes in population and its geographic arrangement, much of the Basin of Mexico was still involved in agriculture during the second decade of the twenty-first century (see figure 7.4b). Persistence in crop

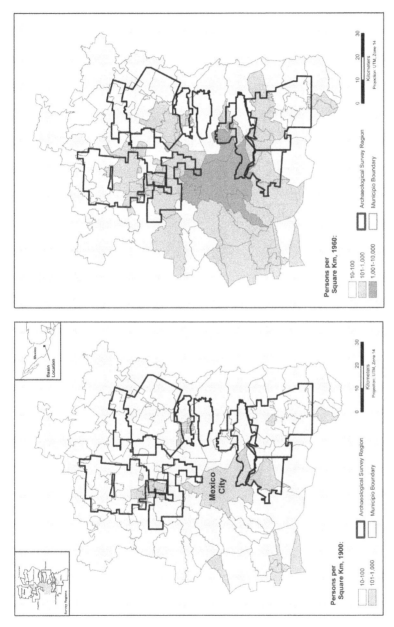

FIGURE 7.3. *Population density for municipios lying at least partially in the Basin of Mexico: 1900 (a) and 1960 (b). Note: Municipio boundaries for 2010 used for 1900 and 1960 population data to enable comparisons over time, with populations for earlier years allocated to the 2010 municipio area. Data sources: Dirección General de Estadística 1901a, 1901b, 1901c, 1963a, 1963b, 1963c.*

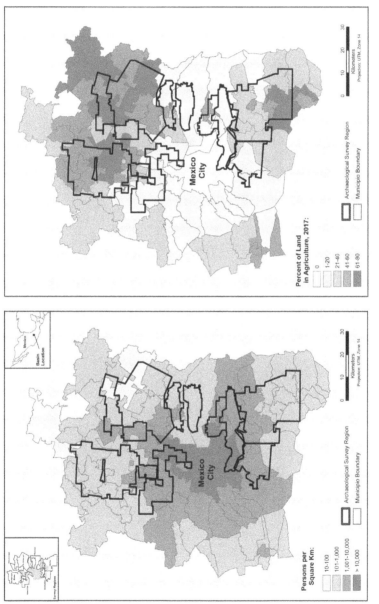

FIGURE 7.4. *Population density and crop production for municipios lying at least partially in the Basin of Mexico: Population per square mile, 2010 (a); percentage of land used for agriculture, 2017 (b). Data sources: Instituto Nacional de Estadística y Geografía 2013; Servicio de Información Agroalimentaria y Pesquera 2019.*

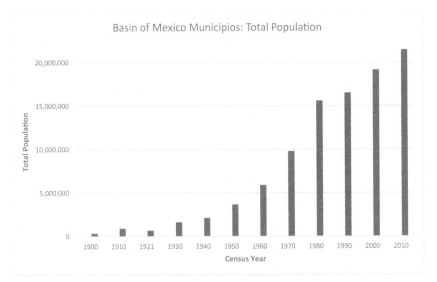

FIGURE 7.5. *Total population in* municipios *lying at least partially within the Basin of Mexico, 1900–2010. Data sources: Dirección General de Estadística 1901a, 1901b, 1901c, 1928, 1934, 1941, 1943a, 1943b, 1952a, 1952b, 1963a, 1963b, 1963c, 1973; Instituto Nacional de Estadística, Geografía e Informática 1990a, 1990b, 1990c, 1992a, 1992b, 1992c, 2002a, 2002b, 2002c; Instituto Nacional de Estadística y Geografía 2013; Secretaría de Agricultura y Fomento 1918.*

production continues the rich heritage of an economic activity established during pre-Columbian times, though with some important changes. Many crops prior to European arrival continue—maize, beans, squash, tomatoes, tomatillos, chilis, amaranth, avocadoes, maguey, nopal, etc.—though the Basin hosts other crops as well. Barley, wheat, oats, carrots, cucumbers, potatoes, spinach, cauliflower, walnuts, broccoli, cabbage, lettuce, peaches, plums, apples, pears, and other cultigens all occur in the Basin in different locations and varying amounts (Servicio de Información Agroalimentaria y Pesquera 2019). Much of modern crop production is mechanized, signaling an important change over a few decades. Furthermore, farming has expanded markedly in the northeastern Basin of Mexico, that part of the region with the lowest rainfall and traditionally an area of high agricultural risk, though the nopal that dominates agriculture in that area requires much less water than virtually any other cultigen grown in the region. Not surprisingly, one sees a generally inverse relationship between the population density of *municipios* and the percentage of land used to produce crops, with high values of the former (often closer to Mexico City) understandably precluding high values of the latter (see figures 7.4a, 7.4b). But considerable amounts of crop production persist in some densely populated *municipios*, maintaining a connection with a past both distant and recent.

One portion of the Basin of Mexico that archaeologists surveyed amid many of the rapid demographic changes that occurred during the 1970s was the Cuautitlan region (Sanders and Gorenflo 2007). When fieldwork occurred in 1974, land use in this survey region—on the northern edge of the Mexico City sprawl at the time—was in transition from agrarian to urban. Survey crews found large areas plotted for development. Many archaeological sites remained, though most were deflated from modern activities and little architecture occurred apart from large mounds. Although Sanders, Santley, Deborah Nichols, Richard Diehl, and other archaeologists who worked on that project recognized coming changes, it would have been difficult to envision their magnitude. For example, Cuautitlan Izcalli Municipio, which contained more than 511,000 people in 2010 (Instituto Nacional de Estadíscica y Geografía 2013) did not even exist in 1970; created in 1973 from parts of three other *municipios* because of rapid population growth (Sanders and Gorenflo 2007:18–20), by 1980 it contained nearly 174,000 people (Instituto Nacional de Estadística, Geografía e Informática 1990c). Some links to the pre-Columbian past had persisted through the mid-twentieth century in the Basin of Mexico. Mexico City occupied the ruins of Aztec Tenochtitlan, modern towns covered many of the Late Aztec city-states, and small-scale agriculture dominated much of the rural landscape. But by 1970 things had begun to change in the Cuautitlan region, the sprawl of Mexico City overrunning pre-Columbian settlement, houses and other infrastructure replacing agricultural fields. Certainly, these sorts of changes had occurred in other portions of the Basin close to the city, but the pace of change in the Cuautitlan region was particularly alarming. And connections with the prehistoric past, where a large urban area and dispersed smaller settlements occurred in a landscape largely dominated by small-scale crop production, were disappearing rapidly amid increasingly expanding human settlement and industrialization. These changes would not only decouple modern land use from its pre-Columbian past, but also destroy much of the archaeological record in the process.

RECENT IMPACTS ON THE PRE-COLUMBIAN ARCHAEOLOGICAL RECORD IN THE BASIN OF MEXICO

I was fortunate to work with Sanders and Parsons for many years. Both had witnessed the changes discussed above first hand, changes that I suppose they long feared but probably could never fully envision. Working on the database of archaeological sites in the three regions that Sanders surveyed—Teotihuacan, Cuautitlan, and Temascalapa—provided ample time to discuss many of his concerns about the region, concerns amplified on several trips to the Basin together beginning in the early 1990s. More recent forays in the Basin with Parsons between 2008 and 2019, to examine the condition of archaeological sites, brought more conversations about what the region had looked like in the 1960s and how much it had changed. Those conversations made me recall Parsons commenting in 1979 on a magazine article about the growth of Mexico City, noting how modern development was consuming much of the areas he had surveyed less than a decade earlier.

As one would expect, given the discussion above, increasing modern settlement and changing land use have broadly compromised the archaeological record in the Basin of Mexico. Aerial imagery, complementing the maps of population density and agriculture presented in the last section, tells much of the story of a changing landscape that often does not accommodate the region's prehistory. A 1970 aerial photograph of the area immediately west of the settlement of Ecatepec, in the Guadalupe Range of mountains, shows a locality dominated by open fields a few years before the Cuautitlan settlement survey of 1974 (see figure 7.6). In 1970, the population of Ecatepec was about 12,000 people (Dirección General de Estadística 1973). The large Late Aztec sites in the piedmont near the center of the photo were largely intact, as were the smaller sites in the northeastern quadrant extending into the old Lake Texcoco lakebed. In contrast, 2018 high-resolution satellite imagery available through Google Earth Pro reveals a landscape dominated by modern settlement. By 2010, Ecatepec had become a city of nearly 1.7 million inhabitants (Instituto Nacional de Estadística y Geografía 2013), explaining the dramatic difference in the two images. Virtually all archaeological sites discovered by the settlement survey were covered by the sprawl of Ecatepec and nearby communities, the buildings and streets leaving little hope for any of the pre-Columbian sites found earlier.

In contrast, imagery of the northeastern Basin of Mexico indicates considerably less modern impact, at least from settlement. A 1970 aerial photograph from the Teotihuacan survey region north of Cerro Gordo, showing Late Aztec sites, depicts the small town of San Juan Teacalco and surrounding terrain, the latter primarily comprising agricultural fields (see figure 7.7). Teacalco was a clearly defined community, though sparsely settled and with a population only 750 (Dirección General de Estadística 1973). Fields surrounding Teacalco that hosted Late Aztec sites featured little modern infrastructure, providing good visibility of surface remains. At first glance, in 2018, Teacalco and the fields surrounding it seemed broadly similar to those seen in 1970. However, closer examination reveals that Teacalco had both infilled and expanded over the preceding five decades, observations consistent with the community's population having increased to nearly 3,000 by 2010 (Instituto Nacional de Estadística y Geografía 2013). Surrounding fields outside of the town featured more disturbance compared to 1970, including terracing, suggesting more intensive crop production, though it was possibly not entirely inhospitable to archaeological remains apart from the construction of terrace systems and deeper plowing. Much of the northeastern Basin of Mexico, including portions of the Temascalapa and Teotihuacan survey regions, remained sparsely settled as late as 2010, though

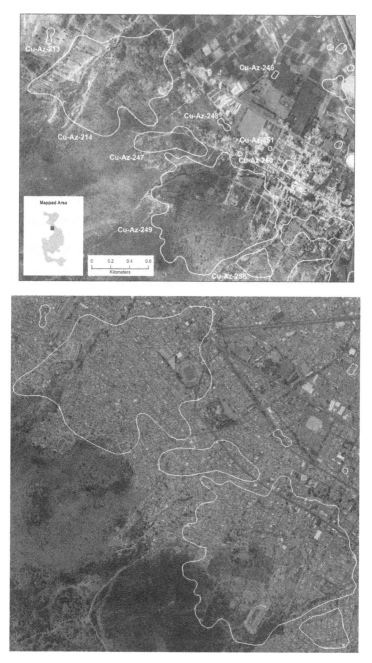

FIGURE 7.6. *Portion of the Cuautitlan survey region, on the western edge of Ecatepec de Morelos, showing sites on (a) a 1970 aerial photograph and (b) 2018 high-resolution imagery from Google Earth Pro.*

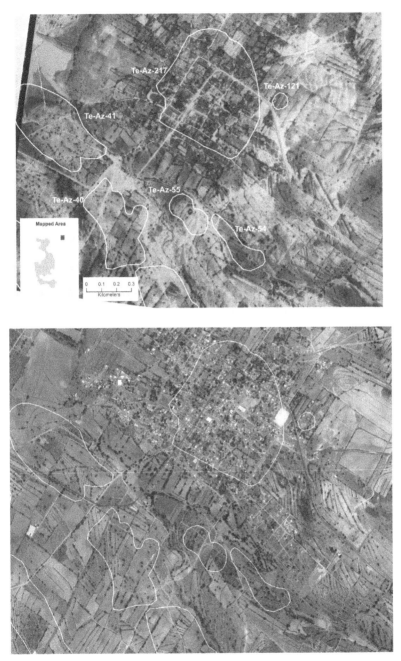

FIGURE 7.7. *Portion of the Teotihuacan survey region, in the vicinity of San Juan Teacalco, showing sites on (a) a 1970 aerial photograph and (b) 2018 high-resolution imagery from Google Earth Pro.*

it contained fairly dense agriculture (see figures 7.4a and 7.4b), likely damaging the archaeological record though contrasting greatly with the destruction in the Cuautitlan region only a few dozen kilometers to the southwest.

Although many see expanding human settlement as the main threat to the archaeological record in the Basin of Mexico, modern agricultural technology has also had an adverse impact on archaeological sites (Morehart and Millhauser 2016). Much of the crop production during the early years of the archaeological surveys, particularly in rural areas, used a simple plow similar to that introduced centuries earlier by the Spanish and pulled by animals to prepare fields, coupled with hand cultivation (Sanders 1965; Sanders et al. 1979). The result was limited site destruction—tilling occurred several times during the cultivation cycle but was shallow and avoided domestic mounds and other small architectural features. But more recent agriculture is often mechanized. Tractor plowing to prepare fields for planting enables destruction of all but quite large pre-Columbian architecture, while chisel-plowing to break up calcareous bedrock and restore minimal fertility to heavily eroded fields can completely destroy an archaeological site. Mechanized plowing minimally *smears* a site horizontally while increasing plow zone depth, in the worst cases altering sites so dramatically that further investigation becomes useless. One example of how modern agriculture can affect the prehistoric record is Te-Az-91, a Late Aztec site in the east-central part of the Teotihuacan survey region (see figure 7.8). Viewed from a distance, land use in 2018 appears to have had minimal impact on the archaeological record, the presence of a few modern structures and roads affecting little of the 80-ha site. However, a closer view reveals pockets of extremely dense crops (mainly nopal) that would have been planted in fields plowed by machines, the quantity of plants and the development of thick root systems adding to the destruction of archaeological remains from field preparation.

By examining portions of the Cuautitlan and Teotihuacan survey regions with aerial photographs and satellite imagery, one sees how a connection between modern land use and the pre-Columbian past persisted until 1970 in certain areas, and how that link was weakened or lost only a few decades later. The degree of impact varies considerably. However, all the sites discussed have been adversely affected to at least some degree. Although small-scale agriculture enabled maintenance of certain connections with the prehistoric past while minimally affecting the archaeological record, most crop production in the twenty-first century is different. Even in the agriculturally marginal northeastern Basin of Mexico, what is now largely commercial crop production compromises archaeological sites. Although agriculture has long been the salvation for evidence of prehistoric occupation in the Basin—probably second only to an absence of modern use—current farming no longer plays that role, as increased mechanization and intensification expand into new areas and compromise the archaeological record.

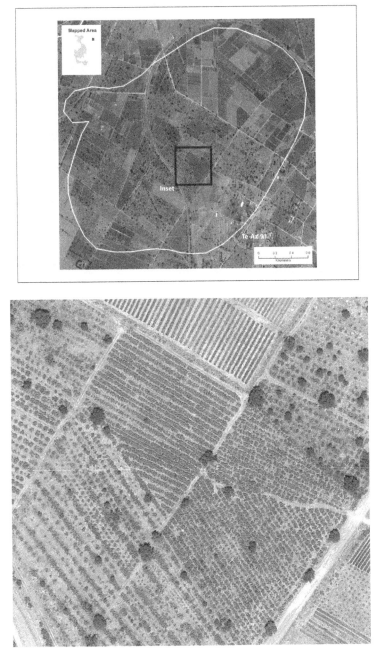

FIGURE 7.8. *Agricultural impacts on Te-Az-91, a Late Aztec site in the east-central part of the Teotihuacan survey region, shown on 2018 high-resolution imagery from Google Earth Pro: (a) overall site and (b) close-up of area under intense agriculture.*

CONCLUSIONS

The prehistory and history of the Basin of Mexico tell fascinating tales of a remarkable region. Most people today probably do not think about linking the current Basin with its prehistoric past, but some key researchers in the region certainly did only a few decades ago. Sanders built parts of his interpretations of pre-Columbian cultural ecology in the Basin on campesino behavior he observed during the 1950s and 1960s. Parsons focused ethnoarchaeological inquiries on behavior he witnessed in the 1960s that were remnants of a distant past. But in recent years, the connection with pre-Columbian times has become much more tenuous. Many of those old lifeways with prehistoric roots are now gone; many of the archaeological sites that served as their prehistoric antecedents are gone as well. Recalling how two archaeologist colleagues and I encountered a golf course in the arid Temascalapa region while revisiting Teotihuacan period sites during the 1990s makes such disconnection with the past both real and personal.

As an archaeologist, it is easy to despair at the changes that have occurred in the Basin of Mexico over the past several decades. As a citizen of the planet, it is easy to become alarmed at the amount of growth in a fragile natural setting, with large-scale environmental degradation and resource extraction in the Basin undoubtedly straining the capacity of natural systems. Probably the only time in the pre-Columbian past that the region experienced such widespread pressure on the environment was during the Late Aztec occupation, when a large urban center and settlement throughout the region survived by carefully manipulating a heavily modified landscape. Systematic attention to managing regional hydrology, recycling waste, and maintaining soil capacity to produce crops was essential to sustaining an enormous preindustrial population in the region (Candiani 2014; Díaz del Castillo 1956; Rojas 2012; Tellman et al. 2018). Might the attention to purposeful management of the environment inspire strategies useful—indeed, *necessary*—in the Basin of Mexico in the early twenty-first century? Or will the inclination of many modern humans to be reactive instead of proactive preclude any large-scale efforts before it is too late for residents of the region, which is already suffering from widespread contamination, water shortages, and other environmental maladies (Simon 1997)?

One important question is whether anything can be done to conserve what remains of the pre-Columbian past in the Basin of Mexico. Ideally, future development could simply avoid key sites that persist, or at worst promote land use that would minimize impacts, though neither of these solutions appear to be feasible given the widespread destruction of the archaeological record over recent decades, coupled with increased pressure on remaining *undeveloped* land. Revisiting known sites throughout the Basin in recent years has revealed massive loss of the archaeological record, with a few notable exceptions, the latter including a few larger sites on the edges of rural settlements. Ultimately, establishing some type of formal protection from infrastructure construction and other damaging development may be the only practical solution to conserve what remains of these glimpses into the pre-Columbian past, a suggestion made in Sanders, Parsons, and Santley (1979:418), but unfortunately never pursued. The opportunity for broad conservation of the prehistoric record is lost. But it may not be too late to protect some select sites meeting certain criteria—say, larger sites with noteworthy architecture that date to what we believe are key periods of sociocultural evolution—that have somehow been spared the bulldozer and chisel plow. Such protection would enable future excavations to study those sites more carefully and understand the processes underlying sociocultural evolution and the emergence of complex societies, the type of investigation still lacking in so much of the region.

In attracting various pre-Columbian cultures, conquistadores, the colonial government and economy, and modern development, the Basin of Mexico became an amazingly rich archaeological research setting and historical landscape. But as population grew and destructive land uses expanded during the second half of the twentieth century, they began to compromise many links to the past—both removing the prehistoric record *and* some of the utility of studying that record to understand the present. Sanders, Parsons, Santley, and colleagues conducted seminal research based largely on intensive archaeological surveys conducted over less than two decades, documenting pre-Columbian regional settlement in one of the key regions for the evolution of complex societies. Archaeology is extremely fortunate they began when they did. The main portion of the Basin they did not survey, covered by development in and around Mexico City in the 1960s, was a preview of *coming attractions*. Little could they have known that the conditions that had them avoid the area near Mexico City would, in fairly short time, come to characterize so much of the entire Basin.

REFERENCES

Armillas, P. 1971. "Gardens on Swamps." *Science* 174:653–61.

Blanton, Richard E. 1972. *Prehispanic Settlement Patterns of the Ixtapalapa Peninsula Region, Mexico*. Occasional Papers in Anthropology, no. 6. Department of Anthropology, The Pennsylvania State University, University Park.

Candiani, Vera S. 2014. *Dreaming of Dry Land: Environmental Transformation in Colonial Mexico City*. Stanford University Press, Redwood City, CA.

Carrasco, Pedro. 1999. *The Tenocha Empire of Ancient Mexico: The Triple Alliance of Tenochtitlan, Tetzcoco, and Tlacopan*. University of Oklahoma Press, Norman.

Díaz del Castillo, Bernal. 1956. *The Discovery and Conquest of Mexico*. Translated by A. P. Mautslay. Derrar, Strauss, and Cudahy, New York.

Dirección General de Estadística. 1901a. *Censo general de la República Mexicana: Distrito Federal*. Oficina Tip. de la Secretaría de Fomento, Mexico City.

Dirección General de Estadística. 1901b. *Censo general de la República Mexicana: Estado de Hidalgo*. Oficina Tip. de la Secretaría de Fomento, Mexico City.

Dirección General de Estadística. 1901c. *Censo general de la República Mexicana: Estado de México*. Oficina Tip. de la Secretaría de Fomento, Mexico City.

Dirección General de Estadística. 1928. *Resumen del censo general de habitantes de 30 de noviembre de 1921*. Talleres Gráficos de la Nación, Mexico City.

Dirección General de Estadística. 1934. *Quinto censo de población 15 de mayo de 1930*. Secretaría de la Economía Nacional, Dirección de Estadística, Mexico City.

Dirección General de Estadística. 1941. *6° censo de población 1940: Distrito Federal*. Secretaría de la Economía Nacional, Dirección de Estadística, Mexico City.

Dirección General de Estadística. 1943a. *6° censo de población 1940: Hidalgo*. Secretaría de la Economía Nacional, Dirección de Estadística, Mexico City.

Dirección General de Estadística. 1943b. *6° censo de población 1940: México*. Secretaría de la Economía Nacional, Dirección de Estadística, Mexico City.

Dirección General de Estadística. 1952a. *Integración territorial de los Estados Unidos Mexicanos: Séptimo censo general de población, 1950*. Dirección General de Estadística, Mexico City.

Dirección General de Estadística. 1952b. *Séptimo censo general de población, 6 de junio de 1950: Parte especial*. Dirección General de Estadística, Mexico City.

Dirección General de Estadística. 1963a. *VIII censo general de población, 1960, 8 de junio de 1960: Distrito Federal*. Dirección General de Estadística, Mexico City.

Dirección General de Estadística. 1963b. *VIII censo general de población, 1960, 8 de junio de 1960: Estado de Hidalgo*. Dirección General de Estadística, Mexico City.

Dirección General de Estadística. 1963c. *VIII censo general de población, 1960, 8 de junio de 1960: Estado de México*. Dirección General de Estadística, Mexico City.

Dirección General de Estadística. 1973. *IX censo general de población, 1970: 28 de enero de 1970; Localidades por entidad federativa y municipio con algunas características de su población y vivienda*. Secretaría de Industria y Comercio, Dirección General de Estadística, Mexico City.

Evans, Susan Toby. 1992. "The Productivity of Maguey Terrace Agriculture in Central Mexico During the Aztec Period." In *Gardens of Prehistory: The Archaeology of Settlement Agriculture in Greater Mesoamerica*, edited by T. W. Killion, 117–32. University of Alabama Press, Tuscaloosa.

Gamio, Manuel. 1922. *La población del Valle de Teotihuacan*. Secretaría de Agricultura y Fomento, Mexico City.

Gibson, Charles. 1964. *The Aztecs under Spanish Rule*. Stanford University Press, Redwood City, CA.

Gorenflo, L. J. 2015. "Compilation and Analysis of Pre-Columbian Settlement Data in the Basin of Mexico." *Ancient Mesoamerica* 26:197–212.

Gorenflo, L. J., and William T. Sanders. 2007. *Archaeological Settlement Pattern Data from the Cuautitlan, Temascalapa, and Teotihuacan Regions, Mexico*. Occasional Papers in Anthropology, no. 30. Department of Anthropology, The Pennsylvania State University, University Park.

Haggett, Peter. 1965. *Locational Analysis in Human Geography*. Edward Arnold, London.

Instituto Nacional de Estadística y Geografía. 2013. *Censo de población y vivienda 2010*. Instituto Nacional de Geografía e Estadísticas, Mexico City. Electronic document. https://www.inegi.org.mx/programas/ccpv/2010/default.html#Datos_abiertos, accessed April 18, 2020.

Instituto Nacional de Estadística, Geografía e Informática. 1990a. *X censo general de población y vivienda: Integración territorial, Distrito Federal*. Instituto Nacional de Estadística, Geografía, e Informática, Aguascalientes.

Instituto Nacional de Estadística, Geografía e Informática. 1990b. *X censo general de población y vivienda: Integración territorial, Estado de Hidalgo*. Instituto Nacional de Estadística, Geografía, e Informática, Aguascalientes.

Instituto Nacional de Estadística, Geografía e Informática. 1990c. *X censo general de población y vivienda: Integración territorial, Estado de México*. Instituto Nacional de Estadística, Geografía, e Informática, Aguascalientes.

Instituto Nacional de Estadística, Geografía e Informática. 1992a. *Distrito Federal, perfil sociodemográfico: XI censo general de población y vivienda, 1990*. Instituto Nacional de Estadística, Geografía, e Informática, Aguascalientes.

Instituto Nacional de Estadística, Geografía e Informática. 1992b. *Estado de Hidalgo, perfil sociodemográfico: XI censo general de población y vivienda, 1990*. Instituto Nacional de Estadística, Geografía, e Informática, Aguascalientes.

Instituto Nacional de Estadística, Geografía e Informática. 1992c. *Estado de México, perfil sociodemográfico: XI censo general de población y vivienda, 1990*. Instituto Nacional de Estadística, Geografía, e Informática, Aguascalientes.

Instituto Nacional de Estadística, Geografía e Informática. 2002a. *Sistema para la consulta de información censal 2000: XII censo general de población y vivienda 2000. Distrito Federal*. Compact disk. Instituto Nacional de Estadística, Geografía, e Informática, Aguascalientes.

Instituto Nacional de Estadística, Geografía e Informática. 2002b. *Sistema para la consulta de información censal 2000: XII censo general de población y vivienda 2000. Estado de México*. Compact disk. Instituto Nacional de Estadística, Geografía, e Informática, Aguascalientes.

Instituto Nacional de Estadística, Geografía e Informática. 2002c. *Sistema para la consulta de información censal 2000: XII censo general de población y vivienda 2000. Estado de Hidalgo*. Compact disk. Instituto Nacional de Estadística, Geografía, e Informática, Aguascalientes.

Kandell, Jonathan. 1988. *La Capital: The Biography of Mexico City*. Random House, New York.

Lockhart, James. 1992. *The Nahuas after the Conquest: A Social and Cultural History of the Indians of Central Mexico, Sixteenth through Eighteenth Centuries.* Stanford University Press, Redwood City, CA.

Millhauser, John K. 2017. "Aztec Use of Lake Resources in the Basin of Mexico." In *The Oxford Handbook of the Aztecs,* edited by D. L. Nichols and E. Rodríguez-Alegría, 301–18. Oxford University Press, New York.

Morehart, Christopher T., and John K. Millhauser. 2016. "Monitoring Cultural Landscapes from Space: Evaluating Archaeological Sites in the Basin of Mexico Using Very High Resolution Satellite Imagery." *Journal of Archaeological Science: Reports* 10:363–76.

Nichols, Deborah L. 1987. "Risk and Agricultural Intensification during the Formative Period in the Northern Basin of Mexico." *American Anthropologist* 89:596–616.

Nichols, Deborah L. 2015. "Intensive Agriculture and Early Complex Societies of the Basin of Mexico: The Formative Period." *Ancient Mesoamerica* 26:407–21.

Palerm, A. 1973. *Obras hidráulicas prehispánicas en el sistema lacustre del Valle de México.* Instituto Nacional de Antropología e Historia, Mexico City.

Parsons, Jeffrey R. 1971. *Prehistoric Settlement Patterns in the Texcoco Region, Mexico.* Memoirs of the Museum of Anthropology, no. 3. University of Michigan, Ann Arbor.

Parsons, Jeffrey R. 1976. "The Role of Chinampa Agriculture in the Food Supply of Aztec Tenochtitlan." In *Cultural Change and Continuity: Essays in Honor of James Bennett Griffin,* edited by Charles Cleland, 233–62. Academic Press, New York.

Parsons, Jeffrey R. 2001. *The Last Saltmakers of Nexquipayac, Mexico: An Archaeological Ethnography.* Anthropological Papers, no. 92. Museum of Anthropology, University of Michigan, Ann Arbor.

Parsons, Jeffrey R. 2005. "The Aquatic Components of Aztec Subsistence: Hunters, Collectors, and Fishers in an Urbanized Society." *Michigan Discussions in Anthropology* 15:49–89.

Parsons, Jeffrey R. 2006. *The Last Pescadores of Chimalhuacan, Mexico: An Archaeological Ethnography.* Anthropological Papers, no. 96. Museum of Anthropology, University of Michigan, Ann Arbor.

Parsons, Jeffrey R. 2008. *Prehispanic Settlement Patterns in the Northwestern Valley of Mexico: The Zumpango Region.* Memoirs of the Museum of Anthropology, no. 45. University of Michigan, Ann Arbor.

Parsons, Jeffrey R., Elizabeth M. Brumfiel, Mary H. Parsons, and David J. Wilson. 1982. *Prehispanic Settlement Patterns in the Southern Valley of Mexico: The Chalco-Xochimilco Region.* Memoirs of the Museum of Anthropology, no. 14. University of Michigan, Ann Arbor.

Redman, C. L. 2005. "Resilience Theory in Archaeology." *American Anthropologist* 107:70–77.

Rojas Rabiela, T. 1988. *Las siembras de ayer: La agricultura indígena del siglo XVI.* Secretaría de Educación Pública / Centro de Investigaciones y Estudios Superiores de Antropología Social Mexico City.

Rojas, J. L. de. 2012. *Tenochtitlan: Capital of the Aztec Empire*. University Press of Florida, Gainesville.

Sahagún, Bernardino de. 1950. *Florentine Codex: General History of the Things of New Spain*, translated by Charles E. Dibble. School of American Research, Santa Fe, NM.

Sahagún, Bernardino de. 1982. *Dibble and A. J. O. Anderson*. University of Utah Press, Salt Lake City.

Sanders, William T. 1957. "Land and Water." PhD dissertation, Department of Anthropology, Harvard University.

Sanders, William T. 1965. *The Cultural Ecology of the Teotihuacan Valley, Mexico*. Department of Sociology and Anthropology, The Pennsylvania State University, University Park.

Sanders, William T., and L. J. Gorenflo. 2007. *Prehispanic Settlement Patterns in the Cuautitlan Region, Mexico*. Occasional Papers in Anthropology, no. 29. Department of Anthropology, The Pennsylvania State University, University Park.

Sanders, William T., and Robert S. Santley. 1983. "A Tale of Three Cities: Energetics and Urbanization in Prehispanic Central Mexico." In *Prehistoric Settlement Patterns: Essays in Honor of Gordon R. Willey*, edited by Evon Z. Vogt and Richard M. Leventhal, 243–92. University of New Mexico Press, Albuquerque.

Sanders, William T., Jeffrey R. Parsons, and Robert S. Santley. 1979. *The Basin of Mexico: Ecological Processes in the Evolution of a Civilization*. Academic Press, New York.

Secretaría de Agricultura y Fomento. 1918. *Tercer censo de población de los Estados Unidos Mexicanos*. Oficina Impresora de la Secretaría de Hacienda, Departamento de Fomento, Mexico City.

Servicio de Información Agroalimentaria y Pesquera. 2019. "Estadística de la producción agrícola de 2017." Servicio de Información Agroalimentaria y Pesquera, Mexico City. Electronic document. http://infosiap.siap.gob.mx/gobmx/datosAbiertos.php, accessed April 6, 2019.

Simon, Joel. 1997. *Endangered Mexico: An Environment on the Edge*. Sierra Club Books, San Francisco, CA.

Tellman, B., J. C. Bausch, H. Eakin, J. M. Anderies, M. Mazari-Hirart, D. Manuel-Navarrete, and C. L. Redman. 2018. "Adaptive Pathways and Coupled Infrastructure: Seven Centuries of Adaptation to Water Risk and the Production of Vulnerability in Mexico City." *Ecology and Society* 23(1):1. https://doi.org/10.5751/ES-09712-230101.

Wright, H. T. 1977. "Recent Research on the Origin of the State." *Annual Review of Anthropology* 6:379–97.

New Approaches to Studying Processes of Environmental Change across Space and Time

8

The Prehispanic Soil Cover of the Basin of Mexico

Its Potential as a Natural Resource in the Teotihuacan Valley

ELIZABETH SOLLEIRO-REBOLLEDO,
SERAFÍN SÁNCHEZ-PÉREZ,
GEORGINA IBARRA-ARZAVE, SERGEY SEDOV,
FRANK LEHMKUHL, PHILIPP SCHULTE,
AND DAISY VALERA-FERNÁNDEZ

INTRODUCTION

Studies on human-environment relations are essential for understanding cultural development (Klepeis and Turner 2001). This is particularly true of landscape changes, which are driven by land-cover transformations related to the environmental processes that accompany the rise and decline of ancient civilizations (Dunning et al. 2002). In Mesoamerica, particularly in the Basin of Mexico, the first stage of sedentarism was influenced by the richness and variety of natural resources. Among these resources were the mixed forest, with a variety of oak, alder, elm, ash, walnut, maples and sweet gum, and grasslands formed on alluvial bottoms. This biological diversity also provided animal protein from terrestrial and aquatic ecosystems (Cubero 2018; Niederberger-Betton 1979). These resources were important for the development of the Playa phase (6000—4500 BCE), defined as a pre-ceramic, pre-agricultural, and sedentary period of time focused on the exploitation of the Basin's various biotopes.

Sedentary communities comprised of pottery-making farmers existed during the subsequent Nevada phase (1700—1500 BCE) (Niederberger-Betton 1979).

https://doi.org/10.5876/9781646424078.c008

Human populations grew, and, consequently, pressure on resources within the Basin increased (Cubero 2018). Soils represented an important resource for the development of sedentary societies dependent on agroecosystems. Furthermore, soils were also used as a raw material for the production of ceramics and for architecture, including construction fill and the manufacture of adobes and *bajareque* (Barba 1995; Gendrop 2001; Moya-Rubio 1982; Rice 1987). Soils of this region were diverse, and their usefulness for construction, agriculture, or ceramic production depended on the local environmental and soil-forming characteristics, namely parent material, organisms, climate, relief, and time (Dokuchaev 1967).

Because the Basin of Mexico is located in the Trans-Mexican Volcanic Belt, a large part of the geological material that constitutes its soils is volcanic. The oldest rhyolitic, andesitic, and dacitic emissions are found in the northern limit of the Basin, represented by the Middle Miocene Sierras de Pachuca and Guadalupe (Lozano-Barraza 1968). During the Pliocene and Pleistocene, an intensive volcanic activity was responsible for the formation of andesitic and basaltic rocks at the mountains surrounding the central lowlands of the Basin, thus forming the Sierra de las Cruces to the west, Sierra Nevada to the east, and Sierra Patlachique, directly south of the Teotihuacan Valley (Mooser et al. 1974). During the Pleistocene, vulcanism of the Sierra Chichinautzin, whose materials include lava flows and pyroclastic deposits, closed the southward drainage of the Basin of Mexico (Arce et al. 2013; García-Palomo et al., 2002; Mooser 1975; Vázquez-Sánchez and Jaimes-Palomera 1989).

Precipitation in the Basin of Mexico increases progressively from north to south, varying from the semi-arid climates of the north to the sub-humid climates of the south (García 1988). Although the south receives more rainfall, higher mean annual temperatures occur in the north (García 1988). Vegetation types also co-vary with climate, resulting in high regional biodiversity (Palma-Mardocheo et al. 2001). The northern areas are characterized by more xerophytic vegetation whereas mixed forest is more widely distributed in the south.

The modern soil cover of the Basin of Mexico is also diverse. In the north, there are Phaeozems, Calcisols and Vertisols, while in the south, it is common to find Andosols (INEGI 2001). However, research has recorded a different soil cover in the past: in some localities, soils classified as Fluvisols, Regosols, or Cambisols show vertic features in their profiles, suggesting that their predecessors were different (Ibarra-Arzave et al. 2019; Rivera-Uria et al. 2007; Sánchez-Pérez et al. 2013; Solleiro-Rebolledo et al. 2006, 2011). Furthermore, the abrupt topography has favored erosion and mass removal processes, resulting in the burial of valley bottom paleosols by colluvial sediments and pedosediments (Cordova 1997; Solleiro-Rebolledo et al. 2011; see Frederick, this volume).

For just over two decades, paleosol studies in the Basin have increased knowledge about the evolution of the landscape (Cabadas-Báez et al. 2005; Ibarra-Arzave et al. 2019; Solleiro-Rebolledo et al. 2006, 2011). This paleopedological research has allowed the reconstruction of the soil cover during the Teotihuacan period (Sánchez-Pérez et al. 2013) and the effect of soil exploitation on environmental degradation (Rivera-Uria et al. 2007). Although Ibarra-Arzave and colleagues (2019) proposed a preliminary vision of the Holocene paleosol cover distribution in the Basin of Mexico, no assessment of the soil as a resource for ancient populations exists. Thus, the purpose of this chapter is to reconstruct the distribution of paleosols in the Basin during the Prehispanic periods, to explore its potential as an agricultural resource, as a raw material for the elaboration of ceramics, and as construction material. We present evidence of human impact in the soils, by presenting a new set of analytical data that sheds light on the origin and evolution of the Black San Pablo Paleosol—the key component of the soil mantle of Teotihuacan Valley during the Formative and Classic periods.

WHAT IS KNOWN ABOUT THE SOILS OF THE BASIN OF MEXICO IN PREHISPANIC TIMES?

Systematic work on the paleoecological environment in the north-central Basin of Mexico has been carried out over the last two decades. Several case studies have explored paleoenvironmental features, human-environment relationships, and the use of natural resources, providing knowledge for the Formative and Classic periods (approximately 400 BCE to 650 CE). This approach has modified the suggestion made by Sanders (1976) and Sanders, Parsons, and Santley (1979), who stated that the landscape of the Prehispanic Teotihuacan Valley was somewhat similar to the present one. To the contrary, our work shows a strong modification of the Formative and Classic paleosol cover because of land-use change that promoted erosion and sedimentation processes, covering the bottom of the Teotihuacan Valley (McClung de Tapia et al. 2005; Rivera-Uria et al. 2007; Sedov et al. 2010; Solleiro-Rebolledo et al. 2011). Records of these ubiquitous erosion-sedimentation processes are found inside and outside the Basin, such as in Texcoco (Cordova and Parsons 1997) and Tlaxcala (Borejsza et al. 2008; Heine 2003). Erosion-sedimentation processes resulted in the burial of paleosols dating to Prehispanic times under several meters of sediments, pedosediments, and other paleosols (McClung de Tapia et al. 2005). Thanks to this burial process, however, it is possible to recognize a set of features that make a paleoenvironmental reconstruction feasible.

Charlton (1970) and Nichols (1987) first observed a paleosol with a chronological relation to the Teotihuacan period, but it was not until later that Rivera-Uria and colleagues (2007) studied it in detail in a soil profile exposed in the ravine of the San Pablo River. Our team recognized the Teotihuacan paleosol buried under more than a meter of alluvial sediments and poorly developed Fluvisols. The sequence of horizons observed at the key section in the San Pablo River is Ap-AC-2A-2AC-2C-3A-3C-4A-4C-5AE-5aBti-5Bk-5Ck (Sánchez-Pérez et al. 2013), where the paleosol corresponding to the Teotihuacan period appears in the fifth cycle (5AE-5aBti-5Bk-5Ck) (see figure 8.1). In addition to its high degree of development in the sequence, the main characteristic that distinguishes the paleosol is its black color, particularly in the 5aBti horizon, hence its denomination as Black San Pablo Paleosol (BSPP) (Sánchez-Pérez et al. 2013). Besides the black color, the 5aBti horizon shows vertic features; it is clayey, has an angular blocky structure whose blocks are very hard, and exhibits friction surfaces and vertical fissures. The 5AE horizon is clearer and siltier than the 5aBti horizon. The 5Bk horizon is very hard, with abundant secondary carbonates filling fissures, with a predominantly horizontal orientation. BSPP appears in various localities along the Teotihuacan Valley, and it has been observed under excavated buildings at Teotihuacan (Sánchez-Pérez 2015; Sánchez-Pérez et al. 2013). Nevertheless, some variations in its characteristics have been noted, depending on the BSPP landscape position. For instance, the 5AE horizon has been observed at the bottom of the valley, but not at higher elevations, and has been associated with irrigation canals and therefore with the intensive use of the soil by agriculture. On the slopes of the foothills, between 2,280 and 2,380 meters above sea level, the BSPP "zone," has no pale horizon. In these places, the BSPP is buried by pedosediments or appears on the surface, where it has been incorporated into modern agricultural activity (Sánchez-Pérez et al. 2013).

The BSPP was classified as a calcic Vertisol. The dates obtained by Rivera-Uria and colleagues (2007), Solleiro-Rebolledo and colleagues (2011) and Sanchez-Pérez and colleagues (2013) allow us to chronologically position the BSPP at the end of the Formative and beginning of the Classic. Because archaeological reports often describe the occurrence of a black surface (the 5aBti horizon) and a tepetate (5Bk horizon) at the bottom of their excavations, the BSPP can be used as a stratigraphic and chronological marker.

In the northern region of the Basin, where a semi-arid environment dominates, vertic features dominate in the BSPP, while other variations appear farther south. In Texcoco, for instance, Cordova (1997, 2017) reports several alluvial units where a soil, identified as S3, occurs with evidence of human occupation. This S3 soil correlates with the BSPP. However, in the areas near the former Texcoco Lake, as in Tepexpan, its presence is unclear because paleosols that have been documented are less developed and have strong fluvial characteristics (Sedov et al. 2010). Furthermore, in the south of the Basin, the main soil type is an Andosol that reflects the influence of continuous sedimentation of pyroclastic materials (Ibarra-Arzave et al. 2019). The palaeosol is commonly beneath the Xitle lava flow (see figure 8.1). Outside the Basin of Mexico, the "black" palaeosol

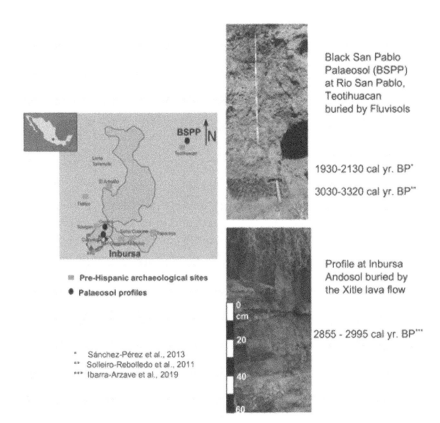

FIGURE 8.1. *(a) Map of the study area in the Basin of Mexico, showing the extension of the ex-lakes, the location of the Prehispanic sites during the Formative period, and the location of the palaeosols mentioned; (b) Black San Pablo Palaeosol (BSPP) in Teotihuacan; (c) andosol buried by the Xitle volcanic eruption in Copilco-Cuiculco area.*

also correlates with a very dark and clayey soil dated to the Formative period, located in the northeast of the state of Tlaxcala (Borejsza et al. 2008).

MATERIALS AND METHODS

This work presents new data on the BSPP in the floodplain of the Teotihuacan Valley. In our earlier publications, we proposed that the pale-horizon 5AE formed due to the alteration caused by agricultural activity carried out by the ancient Teotihuacans (Rivera-Uria et al. 2007; Sánchez-Pérez et al. 2013; Solleiro-Rebolledo et al. 2011). In the approach presented here, we try to identify specific properties and features that help in understanding the pedogenic as well as the sedimentation processes (cultural or natural) responsible for the paleosol formation. We examine the indicators of ancient soil use.

Sampling of the BSPP

Bulk samples from every horizon of the BSPP were taken for laboratory analyses. The 5AE horizon was sampled in more detail: two samples were obtained, one from the upper part and the other from the lower one. For micromorphological analyses, unaltered blocks of 10 × 10 cm were obtained from each horizon and were wrapped in aluminum foil, to prevent the block from breaking. In addition, a monolith 20 cm wide by 60 cm long and 15 cm deep was extracted for detailed geochemical analysis.

Laboratory Analyses

For micromorphological analysis, the samples were impregnated at room temperature with a resin, Cristal MC-40. Thin sections (30 μm thick) were produced and studied under a petrographic microscope Olympus BX 51, in plane-polarized (PPL) and crossed-polarized (XPL) light. The descriptions were made following Bullock's (1985) terminology.

The particle size distribution was measured using a Laser Diffraction Particle Size Analyzer (Beckman Coulter LS 13 320), at the Department of Geography, RWTH Aachen University, Germany. Organic matter was removed by treating the samples with 0.70 ml 30 percent H_2O_2 at 70 °C for several hours. To keep particles dispersed, the samples were treated with 1.25 milliliters $Na_4P_2O_7$ (0.1 mol*l-1) for twelve hours on an overhead shaker (ISO 2020; Schulte et al. 2016). The grain size distribution was determined by applying the Mie theory (Fluid RI: 1.33; Sample RI: 1.55; Imaginary RI: 0.1; Özer et al. 2010; cf. Schulte and Lehmkuhl 2018) and is given as the particle size frequency of 116 classes within a size range of 0.04–2000 μm.

The bulk chemical composition (major elements) was evaluated by X-ray fluorescence using a portable Thermo Scientific brand, Model Niton XL3t, calibrated with a blank and then with a CCRMP—Till—four standard and three filters were used. Twenty measurements were made along the extracted monolith from the BSPP, which included the 4C-5AE-5aBti horizons, starting at 1 centimeter from the base and the subsequent readings were taken every 3 centimeters.

RESULTS

Micromorphological Observations

The micromorphological characteristics of the 5aBti horizon demonstrates a microstructure of very compact, dark angular blocks, pigmented by humus, and separated by fissures (see figure 8.2a-c). Continuous illuvial clay coatings with relatively high interference colors cover the block surfaces (see figure 8.2c). Some of the coatings are laminated, and some of the microlayers are impure, containing a mixture of humus and fine silt particles (see figure 8.2b). On the other hand, in the 5AE horizon, the number of textural pedofeatures decreases, including illuvial clay coatings (see figure 8.2d) and humus pigmentation. Some

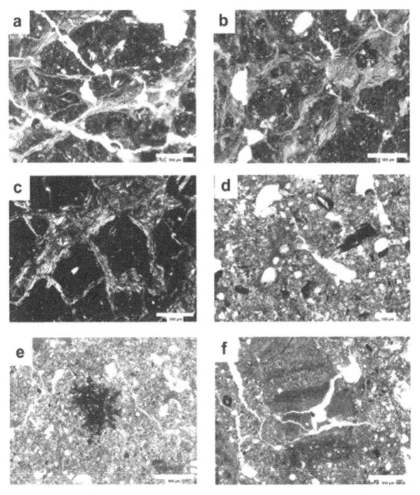

FIGURE 8.2. *Microphotographs of the Black San Pablo Palaeosol (Plane Polarizer Light [PPL]; Cross Polarizer Light [XPL]). The aBti horizon: (a) angular blocky structure; illuvial clay coatings on the compact dark aggregates and fissures separating the aggregates (PPL); (b) thick and laminated clay coatings—some of the microlayers are impure, with a mixture of humus and fine silt particles (PPL). (c) clay coatings with high interference colors (XPL). The 5AE horizon: (d) bleached areas among zones impregnated with humus (PPL). (e) rounded and compound Fe—nodules in a bleached matrix (PPL); (f) surface crust fragments associated with charred material (PPL).*

areas are thus dark, and some are bleached (see figure 8.2d-e). The structure is poorly developed, and silt and sand fractions are dominant (see figure 8.2e). Rounded and compound ferruginous nodules are frequent only in this horizon (see figure 8.2e), small, elongated charcoal fragments are common and a few larger charred fragments with apparent wood structure are also present. Surface crust fragments are also commonly observed (see figure 8.2f), associated with vegetation burning, surface clearance, and soil mass dispersion.

Grain Size Distribution

The results of the texture analysis are shown in figure 8.3a. The distribution of the particles is very similar in the 4C and 5AE horizons, particularly in the upper part of the latter. Although the 4C horizon has a similar distribution, it differs in the proportion of fine and medium silt. In contrast, the 5Bk horizon shows a different behavior: it has less clay and fine and medium silt and more coarse silt (29.2 vol%) and fine sand (11.5 vol%). The amount of fine and medium clay is generally very limited (see figure 8.3a). However, the 5ABti horizon shows a clear peak in the medium clay range. This fraction has a grain-size frequency of 12.8 vol percent, almost three times higher than in all the other samples.

Geochemical Analysis

From the major elements, only the Ti and Zr are selected, as they are very stable in the soil and can help in the identification of discontinuities in the profile. The idea of using the Ti/Zr index is to identify a possible modification in the 5AE horizon due to the intensive use of the soil by the ancient Teotihuacanos and/or due to the accumulation of sediments.

As shown in figure 8.3b, the 4C horizon displays the lowest Ti/Zr value (mean value of 7.99) which clearly increases in the 5AE horizon where the highest ratio is detected (mean value of 15.07), evidencing the discontinuity between the two horizons. When comparing the 5AE and the 5ABti horizons, we observe a decrease in the Ti/Zr ratio (mean value 9.15), which can be interpreted as evidence of a discordance between the components that constitute the two horizons.

DISCUSSION

The BSPP as Evidence of Intensive Cultivation

Macromorphologically, the 5AE horizon is characterized by its pale color, due to redox conditions, and by its poorly developed blocky structure. The micromorphological features: bleached areas (see figure 8.2d, 8.2e), presence of rounded and compound ferruginous nodules (see figure 8.2e), and a higher amount of medium and coarse silt fractions (see figures 8.2e, 8.3a) clearly evidence the eluvial and reductomorphic processes that gave rise to the horizon. On the other hand, the macromorphological features observed in the 5ABti horizon, particularly the black color and the well-developed angular blocky structure (see figure 8.3b), clearly indicate a vertic character (Kovda and Mermut 2018). Several characteristics document illuvial processes in this horizon, including the micromorphological and textural features as oriented clay materials, clay and

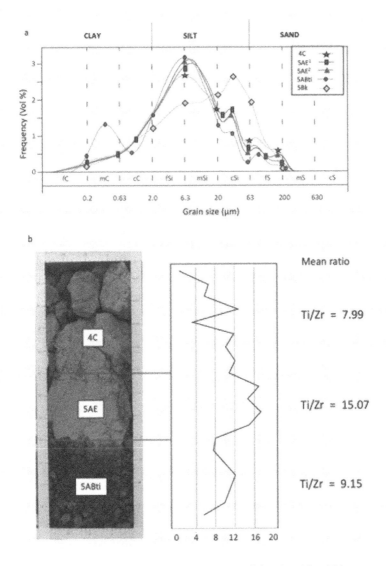

FIGURE 8.3. *(a) Grain size distribution of the 4C horizon and the BSPP. The 5AE horizon is divided into 5AE superior and 5AE inferior. (b) Ti/Zr ratio obtained in a monolith, collected in the key section of the BSPP. fC, fine clay; mC, medium clay; cC, coarse clay; fSi, fine silt; mSi, medium silt; cSi, coarse silt; fS, fine sand; mS, medium sand; cS, coarse sand.*

silt coatings (see figure 8.2b, 8.2c), and impure coatings on the vertic structures (see figure 8.2a, 8.2c), as well as a higher amount of medium clay fraction.

Despite the differences between the 5AE and 5ABti horizons, we suggest that both horizons belong to the same soil formation cycle, and that the diversity of pedofeatures is due to eluviation and illuviation processes. The excess of water causes the loss of materials from the 5AE horizon; they are deposited in the 5ABti horizon in the form of impure coatings. Previous studies in the Teotihuacan area during the Formative and Classic periods suggest a semi-arid environment (McClung de Tapia 2012; Sánchez-Pérez et al. 2013; Solleiro-Rebolledo et al. 2011). Consequently, the waterlogging in the soil profiles can be attributed to the irrigation of crop fields, causing a reductomorphic environment in the topsoil (5AE horizon) that promoted the formation of Fe nodules and bleached areas (see figure 8.2d, 8.2e) that give the horizon a paler color (Kovda and Mermut 2018).

The differences in the Ti/Zr index in the 4C and 5AE horizons from the mean value of 7.99 to 15.09 indicate a variation in the composition, attributed to a discontinuity since they belong to different pedogenetic cycles. Even more, the Ti/Zr values in the 4C horizon show abrupt changes related to its fluvial character (see figure 8.3b). However, the difference in this ratio between the 5AE horizon and the 5ABti also reveals a discontinuity, going from a mean value of 15.09 in the 5AE to 9.15 in the 5ABti horizon. In particular, the highest variation is shown in the transition between these two horizons. Accordingly, the higher ratio, which reflects a relative enrichment of Ti content, originated from material suspended in irrigation water or from some type of fertilizer used in agricultural production. However, the granulometric similarity between the 5AE and 5ABti suggests that the major part of the mineral material of the former is derived from the latter. However, a sharp contrast, both textural and geochemical (Ti/Zr index), between 5ABti and 5Bk horizons (see figure 8.3a, 8.3b) indicates that the diagnostic black horizons of BSPP (5ABti horizon) may have a partly allochthonous, depositional origin. A large gap between the radiocarbon dates of humus in 5ABti horizon (about 3ka BP) and neoformed carbonates in the Bk horizon (21 ka BP, Sánchez-Pérez et al. 2013) supports this conclusion.

Based on these results, we conclude that the 5AE horizon is the result of intense agricultural activity carried out by the Teotihuacanos during much of the Classic period and represents one of the first lines of evidence of soil degradation that resulted from its exploitation.

The Potential Use of the Different Types of Soils in the Valley

In the Basin of Mexico, soils have been transformed by long-term, intensive agriculture activities (e.g., McClung de Tapia 2012; Nichols 1987; Nichols et al. 1991; Rivera-Uria et al. 2007), by extraction of raw materials for construction (Barba 1995, 2005; Guillén 2018; Rivera-Uria et al. 2007), including the manufacture of

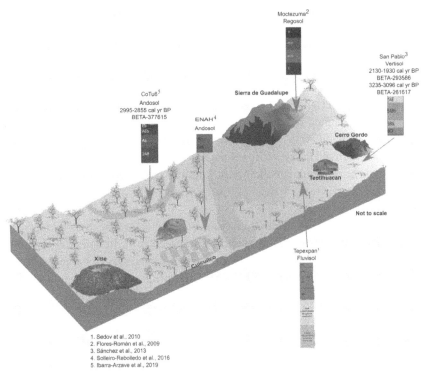

FIGURE 8.4. *Schematic model of Prehispanic soil distribution in the Basin of Mexico.*

adobes and *bajareque* (Ibarra-Arzave 2015), and for raw material for ceramic making (Alex et al. 2012).

The Prehispanic soil identified in the Teotihuacan Valley (BSPP) and at various points in the north of the Basin of Mexico, is a calcic Vertisol (see figure 8.4). This soil has high agricultural potential due to the following properties: elevated proportions of clay and organic carbon promoting a high cation-exchange capacity, a strong stable structure, low salinity, and a high water-holding capacity (Sánchez-Pérez et al. 2013). However, hydraulic conductivity tests indicate the soil has low permeability, which increases its saturation rate (Rivera-Uria et al. 2007; Sánchez-Pérez et al. 2013). Currently, Vertisols are an important agricultural resource worldwide (Coulombe et al. 1996) and among the most productive in Mexico, but they require complex techniques for their exploitation, including irrigation, mechanization, and fertilization (Torres-Guerrero et al. 2016).

In Prehispanic times, the evidence indicates that intensive agricultural practices were applied using irrigation and some type of fertilizer (Rivera-Uria et al. 2007; Sánchez-Pérez et al. 2013). The soil exploitation has caused the formation of an eluvial horizon (5AE), considered to be some of the first evidence of soil degradation by human activity in Prehispanic times. In the Cuicuilco-Copilco area, the studied Andosols also have AE horizons (see figure 8.4), which are also associated with changes caused by cultivation (Ibarra-Arzave et al. 2019).

Regarding the use of Prehispanic soils as constructive materials, Barba (1995, 2005) has documented the presence of soils in the interior of the Sun Pyramid, while Rivera-Uria and colleagues (2007) and Sánchez-Pérez and colleagues (2013) have identified remains of the BSPP inside the Moon Pyramid covering the talus of the different building stages. Guillén (2018) has also observed fragments of a dark soil in several Teotihuacan structures. All these findings suggest that the large ceremonial buildings of Teotihuacan were constructed through large-scale destruction of the BSPP soil, despite its importance as an agricultural resource.

The use of soils for the manufacture of architecture, such as adobes and *bajareques*, is global (Moya-Rubio 1982). The selection of the soil often depends on its accessibility. However, one of the most necessary characteristics is plasticity, a condition produced via the relative proportions of clay and silt fractions. Plasticity is a basic, necessary attribute for modeling the cubic structures of adobes or the shapes of walls (Gendrop 2001). In the case of the *bajareque*, the materials should have a better adhesiveness than the adobes to support the weave of vegetable structures and the wall itself. In most of the Teotihuacan houses, both *bajareque* and adobe have been used (Millon 1973; Morelos-García 1993). The calcic Vertisol (BSPP) that dominates the Holocene soil cover in the northern center of the Basin (Sánchez-Pérez et al. 2013; Solleiro-Rebolledo et al. 2015) has the basic qualities to be used as raw material. Its high percentage of clay, which is mainly a non-expanding mineral, increases its plasticity (Sánchez-Pérez 2015).

In the case of ceramic production, artisans prefer a raw material with high plasticity and a very low amount of organic matter because this component makes ceramic firing difficult (Rice 1987). Soils are the main source of this raw material, particularly those of B horizons, which have the highest concentration of clay and less organic matter. Although the calcic Vertisols in the northern center of the Basin are abundant, they seem too problematic for ceramic production because the organic matter content is high. Solleiro-Rebolledo and colleagues (2006) report the presence of reddish Luvisols with an elevated clay content and a minimum of organic matter in the talus of the Sierra Patlachique and Cerro Gordo. These Luvisols are more convenient for ceramic production. Rattray (2001) and López-Valenzuela and colleagues (2010) identified the typical mineralogical assemblage of the soils and volcanic sediments of the region (amphiboles, plagioclases, and Fe and Ti oxides), which coincides with the mineral determinations made by Solleiro-Rebolledo and colleagues (2011) for the soils of Teotihuacan Valley's surrounding hills.

How Are the Prehispanic Soils Found Today?

The Prehispanic soil cover has experienced many modifications over time, due to both natural and cultural processes. One of the first modifications in the southern Basin of Mexico was caused by the eruption of the Xitle volcano (245–315 CE, Siebe 2000). The former Andosols (developed from much earlier volcanic ejections), were buried by the lava, leaving an unfertile landform where no soil or water was available (Cordova et al. 1994; Ibarra-Arzave et al. 2019; Solleiro-Rebolledo et al. 2016).

In the northern central part of the Basin, the Prehispanic Vertisols in the floodplain are buried by sediments and pedosediments. The erosion-sedimentation processes begin toward the end of the Classic period and continue throughout the Colonial period to the present day (Cordova 1997; Cordova and Parsons 1997; González-Arqueros et al. 2017; Rivera-Uria et al. 2007). This is why it is common to find the Teotihuacan soil buried by under sedimentary layers in the valley bottom or beneath ancient structures (Sánchez-Pérez et al. 2013). In some flat areas, at the base of foothills or even on the slopes of the Sierra Patlachique and Cerro Gordo, relict Vertisols have been identified on the surface and are being exploited today for agriculture (Sánchez-Pérez 2015; Solleiro-Rebolledo et al. 2015).

It is worth mentioning that there are other soils that were built by the ancient inhabitants of the Basin of Mexico in order to intensify the agriculture production, especially the *chinampas* constructed in the lacustrine bodies. *Chinampa* construction by Prehispanic societies is evidence of a high degree of knowledge about the properties of the soil and its relationship with the growth of cultivated plants (Frederick 2007; McClung de Tapia and Acosta Ochoa, this volume). As human-made soils, *chinampa* soils are nowadays designated as technosols (IUSS Working Group WRB 2014).

CONCLUSIONS

Micromorphological observations, grain-size distribution and geochemical analysis have demonstrated that the BSPP was intensively cultivated. The eluvial and illuvial pedofeatures found in its 5AE and 5ABti horizons, respectively, are interpreted as waterlogging conditions attributed to the irrigation of crop fields. The similar granulometric distribution among the horizons supports the conclusion that they belong to the same pedogenetic cycle and that the relative enrichment of Ti content in the 5AE horizon is due to the use of a kind of fertilizer.

Besides the agricultural practices conducted on the BSPP, there is also evidence of its intensive use as a constructive material. The ceremonial buildings of Teotihuacan incorporated fragments of the paleosol, which was the dominant soil cover during the late Holocene in the north-center of the Basin, causing large-scale destruction, despite its importance as an agricultural resource. The high percentage of non-expanding clay in the BSPP-5Bt horizon favored its use as raw material for ceramic production, due to its high plasticity and its very low amount of organic matter.

Finally, the BSPP is nowadays not found in the surface of the Teotihuacan area, as sedimentation and erosional processes have buried the paleosurface. Therefore, in the valley bottom, the BSPP is covered by more than a meter of sediments and pedosediments. This situation should be taken into account when archaeological excavations are conducted.

Acknowledgments. This work is the product of several years of study in the Basin of Mexico (Teotihuacan and Copilco-Cuiculco). During this time, we have had the support and collaboration of colleagues who led archaeological projects. Particularly, we are deeply grateful to Emily McClung de Tapia, who invited us to discover the fascinating world of the Teotihuacan palaeosols. We also acknowledge the "Proyecto Arqueológico Cuicuilco" and "Proyecto Copilco: un sitio arqueológico del Pedregal de San Angel." Thanks also to everyone who helped with and supported the investigations in the Basin of Mexico: Jaime Díaz-Ortega, René Alcalá, Yazmín Rivera-Uria, Elena Luciano, Karla Guillén, and René Alcalá.

REFERENCES

Alex, Bridget A., Deborah L. Nichols, and Michael D. Glascock. 2012. "Complementary Compositional Analysis of Formative Period Ceramics from the Teotihuacan Valley." *Archaeometry* 54(5):821–34.

Arce, José Luis, Paul W. Layer, Eric Morales-Casique, Jeff A. Benowitz, Elizabeth Rangel, and Oscar Escolero. 2013. "New Constraints on the Subsurface Geology of the Mexico City Basin: The San Lorenzo Tezonco Deep Well, on the Basis of 40ar/39ar Geochronology and Whole-Rock Chemistry." *Journal of Volcanology and Geothermal Research* 266(1):34–49.

Barba, Luis. 1995. "El impacto en la paleogeografía de Teotihuacan." PhD dissertation, Facultad de Filosofía y Letras. Universidad Nacional Autónoma de México, Mexico City.

Barba, Luis. 2005. "Materiales, técnicas y energía en la construcción." In *Arquitectura y urbanismo: Pasado y presente de los espacios en Teotihuacan*, edited by María Elena Ruiz-Gallut and Jesús Torres-Peralta, 211–30. Memoria de la Tercera Mesa Redonda. Instituto Nacional de Antropología e Historia, Mexico City.

Borejsza, Alexander, Isabel Rodríguez-López, Charles D. Frederick, and Mark D. Bateman. 2008. "Agricultural Slope Management at La Laguna, Tlaxcala, Mexico." *Journal of Archaeological Science* 35:1854–66.

Bullock, Peter. 1985. *Handbook for Soil Thin Section Description.* Waine Research Publications, Wolverhampton, UK.

Cabadas-Báez, Héctor, Elizabeth Solleiro-Rebolledo, Jorge E. Gama-Castro, Sergey Sedov, and Emily McClung de Tapia. 2005. "Paleosuelos como indicadores de cambio ambiental en el Cuaternario Superior: El caso del valle de Teotihuacan." In *Arquitectura y urbanismo: Pasado y presente de los espacios en Teotihuacan*, Memoria de la Tercera Mesa Redonda, edited by María Elena Ruiz-Gallut and Jesús Torres-Peralta, 75–95. Instituto Nacional de Antropología e Historia, Mexico City.

Charlton, Thomas H. 1970. "Contemporary Agriculture of the Valley." In *The Natural Environment, Contemporary Occupation and Sixteenth-Century Population of the Valley. The Teotihuacan Valley Project: Final Report*, edited by William T. Sanders, Amy Kovar, Thomas H. Charlton and Richard A. Diehl, vol. 1, 253–383. Occasional papers in Anthropology, no. 3. Department of Anthropology, The Pennsylvania State University, University Park.

Cordova, Carlos E. 1997. "Landscape Transformation in Aztec and Spanish Colonial Texcoco, Mexico." PhD dissertation, Department of Geography, University of Texas, Austin.

Cordova, Carlos E. 2017. "Pre-Hispanic and Colonial Flood Plain Destabilization in the Texcoco Region and Lower Teotihuacan Valley, Mexico." *Geoarchaeology* 32:64–89.

Cordova, Carlos E., and Jeffrey R. Parsons. 1997. "Geoarchaeology of an Aztec Dispersed Village on the Texcoco Piedmont of Central Mexico." *Geoarchaeology* 12(3):177–210.

Cordova, Carlos E., Ana Lillian Martín del Pozzo, and Javier López-Camacho. 1994. "Palaeolandforms and Volcanic Impact on the Environment of Prehistoric Cuicuilco, Southern Mexico City." *Journal of Archaeological Science* 21:585–96.

Coulombe, Clement E., Larry P. Wilding, and Joe B. Dixon. 1996. "Overview of Vertisols: Characteristics and Impacts on Society." In *Advances in Agronomy*, edited by D. L. Sparks, vol. 57, 289–375. Academic Press, New York.

Cubero, José Ignacio. 2018. *Historia general de la agricultura: De los pueblos nómadas a la biotecnología*. Editorial Guadalmazán, Córdoba, Spain.

Dokuchaev, Vasily V. 1967. "Russian Chernozem." Translated from Russian by N. Kaner. Israel Program of Scientific Translations, Jerusalem.

Dunning, Nicholas P., Sheryl Luzzadder-Beach, Timothy Beach, John G. Jones, Vernon Scarborough, and Patrick T. Culbert. 2002. "Arising from the Bajos: The Evolution of a Neotropical Landscape and the Rise of Maya Civilization." *Annals of the Association of American Geographers* 92(2):267–83.

Frederick, Charles D. 2007. "Chinampa Cultivation in the Basin of Mexico: Observations on the Evolution of Form and Function." In *Seeking a Richer Harvest*, edited by Timothy L. Thurston and Christopher T. Fisher, 107–24. Studies in Human Ecology and Adaptation, vol. 3. Springer, Boston, MA.

García-Palomo, Armando, José Luis Macías, Gustavo Tolson, Gabriel Valdez, and Juan Carlos Mora. 2002. "Volcanic Stratigraphy and Geological Evolution of the Apan

Region, East Central Sector of the Mexican Volcanic Belt." *Geofísica international* 41(2):133–50.

García, Enriqueta. 1988. "Modificaciones al sistema de clasificación climática de Köpen: Instituto de Geografía." Universidad Nacional Autónoma de México, Mexico City.

Gendrop, Paul. 2001. *Diccionario de arquitectura mesoamericana*. Editorial Trillas, Mexico City.

González-Arqueros, Lourdes, Lorenzo Vázquez-Selem, Jorge Gama-Castro, and Emily McClung de Tapia. 2017. "Late Holocene Erosion Events in the Valley of Teotihuacan, Central Mexico: Insights from a Soil-Geomorphic Analysis of Catenas." *Catena* 158:69–81.

Guillén, Karla. 2018. "Caracterización geoquímica de estucos y morteros de la zona arqueológica de Teotihuacán con una perspectiva de restauración y preservación." Undergraduate thesis. Facultad de Ciencias, Universidad Nacional Autónoma de México, Mexico City.

Heine, Klaus. 2003. "Paleopedological Evidence of Human-Induced Environmental Change in the Puebla–Tlaxcala Area (Mexico) during the Last 3,500 Years." *Revista mexicana de ciencias geológicas* 20:235–44.

Ibarra-Arzave, Georgina. 2015. "Reconstrucción paleoambiental en el sur de la Cuenca de México, y su relación con la distribución de los sitios Formativos." MSc thesis. Posgrado en Ciencias de la Tierra, Universidad Nacional Autónoma de México, Mexico City.

Ibarra-Arzave, Georgina, Elizabeth Solleiro-Rebolledo, Sergey Sedov, and Daniel Leonard. 2019. "The Role of Pedogenesis in Palaeosols of Mexico Basin and Its Implication in the Paleoenvironmental Reconstruction." *Quaternary International* 502:267–79.

INEGI (Instituto Nacional de Estadística, Geografía e Informática). 2001. "Síntesis de información geográfica del Estado de México." Instituto Nacional de Estadística, Geografía e Informática, Aguascalientes.

ISO (International Organization for Standardization). 2020. "ISO 11277:2020. Soil Quality—Determination of Particle Size Distribution in Mineral Soil Material—Method by Sieving and Sedimentation." German Institute for Standardisation (Deutsches Institut für Normung). Electronic document. https://www.iso.org/standard/69496.html, accessed October 17, 2022.

IUSS Working Group WRB (International Union of Soil Sciences Working Group World Reference Base for Soil Resources). 2014. "International Soil Classification System for Naming Soils and Creating Legends for Soil Maps." World Soil Resources Reports, no. 106. FAO, Rome.

Klepeis, Peter, and Billie L. Turner II. 2001. "Integrated Land History and Global Change Science: The Example of the Southern Yucatán Peninsular Region Project." *Land Use Policy* 18:272–309.

Kovda, Irina, and Ahmet R. Mermut. 2018. "Vertic Features." In *Interpretation of Micromorphological Features of Soils and Regoliths*, 2nd ed., edited by Georges Stoops, Florias Mees, and Vera Marcelino, 605–32. Elsevier, London.

López-Valenzuela, Ramón, José Antonio López-Palacios, Melania Jiménez-Reyes, G. Cataño, and Dolores Tenorio. 2010. "Characterization of Ceramic Ornaments of a Theatre-like Incense Burner." *Journal of Radioanalytical and Nuclear Chemistry* 283(3):675–81.

Lozano-Barraza, Luis. 1968. "Geología de la Sierra de Guadalupe, México, D. F." Undergraduate thesis, Escuela Superior de Ingeniería y Arquitectura, Instituto Politécnico Nacional, Mexico City.

McClung de Tapia, Emily. 2012. "Silent Hazards—Invisible Risks: Prehispanic Erosion in the Teotihuacan Valley, Central, Mexico." In *Surviving Sudden Environmental Change: Understanding Hazards, Mitigating Impacts, Avoiding Disasters*, edited by Jago Cooper, and Payson Sheets, 139–61. University Press of Colorado, Boulder.

McClung de Tapia, Emily, Irma Domínguez Rubio, Jorge Gama Castro, Elizabeth Solleiro-Rebolledo, and Sergey Sedov. 2005. "Radiocarbon Dates from Soil Profiles in the Teotihuacan Valley, Mexico: Indicators of Geomorphological Processes." *Radiocarbon* 47(1):159–75.

Millon, René. 1973. *Urbanization at Teotihuacan, Mexico*, vol. 1, pt. 1: *The Teotihuacan Map*, University of Texas Press, Austin.

Mooser, Federico. 1975. "Historia geológica de la Cuenca de México." In *Memoria de las obras del sistema de drenaje profundo del Distrito Federal*, Vol. I: 7–38. Departamento del Distrito Federal, Mexico City.

Mooser, Federico, Alan E. M. Nair, and Jörg F. W. Negendank. 1974. "Paleomagnetic Investigations of Tertiary and Quaternary Igneous Rocks; vii, a Paleomagnetic and Petrologic Study of Volcanics of the Valley of Mexico." *Geologische Rundschau* 63:451–83.

Morelos García, Noel. 1993. "Procesos de producción de espacios y estructuras en Teotihuacan." Colección Científica, no. 274. Instituto Nacional de Antropología e Historia, Mexico City.

Moya-Rubio, Víctor José. 1982. *La vivienda indígena de México y del mundo: Coordinación de humanidades*. Universidad Nacional Autónoma de México, Mexico City.

Nichols, Deborah L. 1987. "Prehispanic Irrigation at Teotihuacan, New Evidence: The Tlajinga Canals." In *Teotihuacan: Nuevos datos, nuevas síntesis, nuevos problemas*, edited by Emily McClung de Tapia and Evelyn C. Rattray, 133–60. Instituto de Investigaciones Antropológicas, Universidad Nacional Autónoma de México, Mexico City.

Nichols, Deborah L., Michael Spence, and Mark D. Borland. 1991. "Watering the Fields of Teotihuacan: Early Irrigation at the Ancient City." *Ancient Mesoamerica* 2:119–29.

Niederberger-Betton, Christine. 1979. "Early Sedentary Economy in the Basin of Mexico." *Science* 203:131–42.

Özer, Mustafa, Metin Orhan, and Nihat S. Isik. 2010. "Effect of Particle Optical Proper-ties on Size Distribution of Soils Obtained by Laser Diffraction." *Environmental and Engineering Geoscience* 16:163–73.

Palma-Mardocheo, Francisco J. Romero, and Alejandro Velázquez. 2001. "La Cuenca de México: Una revisión de su importancia biológica. Comisión Nacional para el Conocimiento y Uso de la Biodiversidad, CONABIO." *Biodiversitas* 37:12–14.

Rattray, Evelyn C. 2001. *Teotihuacan: Ceramics, Chronology, and Cultural Trends.* Instituto Nacional de Antropología e Historia, Mexico City.

Rice, Prudence M. 1987. *Pottery Analysis: A Sourcebook.* 1987. University of Chicago Press.

Rivera-Uria, María Yazmín, Sergeu Sedov, Elizabeth Solleiro-Rebolledo, Julia Pérez-Pérez, Emily McClung de Tapia, Arelia González, and Jorge Gama-Castro. 2007. "Degradación ambiental en el valle de Teotihuacan: Evidencias geológicas y paleope-dológicas." *Boletín de la Sociedad Geológica Mexicana* 59(2):203–17.

Sánchez-Pérez, Serafín. 2015. "Los paleosuelos 'negros' como indicadores de cambios ambientales naturales e inducidos por el hombre en el periodo de ocupacion teoti-huacano." PhD dissertation, Posgrado en Ciencias de la Tierra, Universidad Nacional Autónoma de México, Mexico City.

Sánchez-Pérez, Serafín, Elizabeth Solleiro-Rebolledo, Sergey Sedov, Emily McClung de Tapia, Alexandra Golyeva, Blanca Prado, and Emilio Ibarra-Morales. 2013. "The Black San Pablo Paleosol of the Teotihuacan Valley, Mexico: Pedogenesis, Fertility, and Use in Ancient Agricultural and Urban Systems." *Geoarchaeology* 28:249–67.

Sanders, William T. 1976. "The Agricultural History of the Basin of Mexico." In *The Valley of Mexico: Studies in Pre-Hispanic Ecology and Society*, edited by Eric R. Wolf, 101–59. School of American Research, University of New Mexico Press, Albuquerque.

Sanders, William T., Jeffrey R. Parsons, and Robert S. Santley. 1979. *The Basin of Mexico: Ecological Processes in the Evolution of a Civilization.* Academic Press, New York.

Schulte, Phillipp, and Frank Lehmkuhl. 2018. "The Difference of Two Laser Diffraction Patterns as an Indicator for Post-Depositional Grain Size Reduction in Loess-Paleosol Sequences." *Palaeogeography, Palaeoclimatology, Palaeoecology* 509:126–36.

Schulte, Phillipp, Frank Lehmkuhl, Florian Steininger, David Loibl, Gregory Lockot, Jens Protze, Peter Fischer, and Georg Stauch. 2016. "Influence of HCl Pretreat-ment and Organo-Mineral Complexes on Laser Diffraction Measurement of Loess-Paleosol-Sequences." *Catena* 137:392–405.

Sedov, Sergey, Socorro Lozano-García, Elizabeth Solleiro-Rebolledo, Emily McClung de Tapia, Beatriz Ortega-Guerrero, and Susana Sosa-Nájera. 2010. "Tepexpan Revis-ited: A Multiple Proxy of Local Environmental Changes in Relation to Human Occupation from a Lake Shore Section in Central Mexico." *Geomorphology* 122:309–22.

Siebe, Claus. 2000. "Age and Archaeological Implications of Xitle Volcano, Southwest-ern Basin of Mexico City." *Journal of Volcanology and Geothermal Research* 104:45–64.

Solleiro-Rebolledo, Elizabeth, Sergey Sedov, Emily McClung de Tapia, Héctor Cabadas, Jorge E: Gama-Castro, and Ernestina Vallejo-Gómez E. 2006. "Spatial Variability of Environment Change in the Teotihuacan Valley during Late Quaternary: Paleopedological Inferences." *Quaternary International* 156–57:13–31.

Solleiro-Rebolledo, Elizabeth, Svetlana Sycheva, Sergey Sedov, Emily McClung de Tapia, Yazmín Rivera-Uria, César Salcido-Berkovich, and Alexandra Kuznetsova. 2011. "Fluvial Processes and Paleopedogenesis in the Teotihuacan Valley, México: Responses to Late Quaternary Environmental Changes." *Quaternary International* 233:40–52.

Solleiro-Rebolledo, Elizabeth, Sergey Sedov, Svetlana Sycheva, Serafín Sánchez-Pérez, Konstantin Pustovoitov, and Daniela Sauer. 2015. "Influencia de los paleosuelos en los procesos exógenos modernos en la porción noreste de la Cuenca de México." *Boletín de la Sociedad Geológica Mexicana* 67(2):255–72.

Solleiro-Rebolledo, Elizabeth, Margit Straubinger, Birgit Terhorst, Sergey Sedov, Georgina Ibarra-Arzave, José Ignaico Sánchez-Alaniz, Carmen Solanes, and Ema Marmolejo. 2016. "Paleosols beneath a Lava Flow in the Southern Basin of Mexico: The Effect of Heat on the Paleopedological Record." *Catena* 137:622–34.

Torres-Guerrero, Carlos A., Carmen Gutiérrez-Castorena, Carlos A. Ortiz-Solorio, and Edgar V. Gutiérrez-Castorena. 2016. "Manejo agronómico de los vertisoles en México: Una revision." *Terra latinoamericana* 34:457–66.

Vázquez-Sánchez, Eliseo, and Jaimes-Palomera, Ricardo. 1989. "Geología de la Cuenca de México." *Geofísica internacional* 28(2), 133–90.

9

Ancient Settlements, Sediments, and Prehistoric Lacustrine Dynamics in Lake Texcoco

CARLOS E. CORDOVA

INTRODUCTION

Lake Texcoco was the largest and lowest of the five interconnected lakes of the Basin of Mexico. Over the course of the past four centuries, the lake gradually disappeared through systematic drainage and desiccation, leaving a vast salt flat with scattered small artificial and seasonal ponds. Although Mexico City grew over this vast flat territory, the eastern part of the former lakebed remained largely untouched by urban sprawl. This area includes the land owned and managed by the federal government, known as "El Vaso del Antiguo Lago de Texcoco" and the collectively held *ejido* lands of several towns and villages (see figure 9.1).

At the time of the Basin of Mexico surveys in the 1960s and 1970s, technical difficulties in surveying the lakebed and the idea that the center of the lake had previously held deep water not suitable for settlement led to the decision not to survey the vast plain of former Lake Texcoco (Sanders et al. 1979:62). Thus, the surveys focused only on areas considered to have once been on the "lakeshore," as shown by the extent of the Texcoco Regional survey (Parsons 1971), the Iztapalapa Region survey (Blanton 1972), the Teotihuacan Valley survey (Sanders

https://doi.org/10.5876/9781646424078.c009

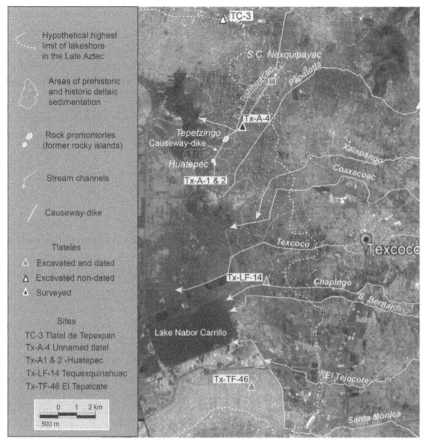

FIGURE 9.1. *Eastern part of former Lake Texcoco bed on Google Earth with surface sediment and sites mentioned in the text. The inset map shows the location of the Google Earth image in relation to Basin of Mexico surveys.*

1975, 1987, 1994), and the Cuautitlan Region survey (Cordova and Morehart, this volume, figure 1.1; Sanders and Gorenflo 2007). However, a more recent survey of the north-central part of the lake, named the Lake Texcoco Region (Parsons and Morett 2004), produced in-situ archaeological surface materials, proving that even areas far away from the shore experienced forms of human activity.

Based on the description of sites in the surveys, it is evident that most prehistoric settlements on the lakebed and lakeshore areas comprise insular settlements of the *tlatel* type (Parsons 1971; Sanders 1994). A tlatel (from the Nahuatl, *tlaltelli*, stone and earth mound) is a constructive mound built on a permanently or seasonally inundated surface (Cordova 2022). Although many have been associated with salt procurement, others may have had other functions within the various niches of the lakeshore ecosystems (Cordova 2022; Cordova et al. 2022).

Constellations of tlateles also developed into connected systems of settlement, usually a precursor of lacustrine urban settlements and in some cases connected with associated with other cultural features (dikes, causeways, canals, etc.) (Cordova 2022). Therefore, the understanding of the building and distribution of tlatel-type settlements in the lakes of the Basin of Mexico is important for reconstructing lacustrine dynamics and environments.

In general, the term "lacustrine dynamics" refers to changes occurring in a lake over different timescales. I divide them into seasonal, short-, and long-term changes. The seasonal changes influenced the type of activities that took place in the lake over the course of a year. Short-term changes, taking place over years and decades, demarcated and shaped the areas that could be settled more permanently and determined the types of structures that would have to be built. Long-term changes, over decades and centuries, affected the regional settlement pattern as seen from the point of view of the archaeological chronologies employed by the surveys.

The term "lacustrine environments" refers to areas dominated by distinct geomorphic and sedimentary processes, which in turn determine lake water quality—including its salinity and turbidity—as well as soils and vegetation communities that develop at lake margins. In this sense, lacustrine dynamics and lacustrine environments are interrelated, providing different choices for resource utilization and settlement. This chapter presents different types of lacustrine environments that existed along the eastern shores of Lake Texcoco, and the dynamics associated with some of the lacustrine sites.

THE NATURE AND GEOGRAPHY OF THE LAKES OF THE BASIN OF MEXICO

The nature and geography of the ancient lakes of the Basin of Mexico have often been misrepresented, despite the numerous descriptions in the chronicles of the Conquest and other written and pictorial documents of the sixteenth century. One of the misrepresentations is the exaggerated extent of the lakes in many twentieth-century maps, including those of Sanders, Parsons, and Santley (1979) and all of the Basin of Mexico survey reports. This overestimate tends to connect all water bodies from Zumpango to Chalco into one lake, which contradicts the maps and descriptions of the early Colonial period and does not even match the topography and distribution of subsurface sediments of the Basin.

A careful look at the Map of Uppsala and other maps dated to the mid-1500s (León Portilla and Aguilera 2016) reveals aspects of the lacustrine landscape that have been overlooked by modern cartographic recreations of the appearance of the Basin at that time. Even though the maps provide an idea of the lakeshore configuration, we must not forget that this was a moving target for cartographers, as the lakes underwent tremendous seasonal and short-term changes. These fluctuations are clear in the history of events that led to the *desagüe* projects aimed at draining the lakes by providing an artificial outlet for the naturally closed Basin (Candiani 2014).

The misrepresentation of the former lakes is also due to the idea that they were stable bodies of water. In part, this false idea comes from the modern usage of the word *lago* in place names such as Lago de Chalco, Lago de Texcoco, or Lago de Xaltocan, in contrast to *laguna*, used in maps and documents of the Colonial period. Although the two words translate into English as *lake*, in Spanish they designate bodies of water of different characteristics. The word *lago* evokes a stable, deep, and large lake, while *laguna* refers to a shallow and widely fluctuating lake, a distinction made both by modern geographers (Ortiz Pérez 1975) and dictionaries as old as the *Tesoro de la Lengua Española* of 1611 (Covarrubias 1611:512–13).

The first written document that referred to the lakes of the Basin as *lagos* was the *Historia Antigua de México* by Francisco Javier Clavijero, a translation from Italian into Spanish, though the original Spanish version published edited by Mariano Cuevas in the twentieth century had the word *lago* (see Clavijero 1974). It is, however, not clear if the word was changed in the editing, or if Clavijero used it in the original. The untranslated map in Italian meant to accompany this work also bears the word *Lago di Tetzcuco*. In Italian *lago* has the same meaning as "lake" in English, while *laguna* refers only to lagoon (coastal body of water). Some maps in French in the 1700s and 1800s use the word *lac* to refer to the lakes of the Basin (see the maps in the collections by Apenes 1947; Lombardo de Ruiz 1996), a word that would translate into Spanish as *lago*. However, *lac* in French has the same meaning as *lago* in Italian, with the words *lagune* and *lagon* referring to bodies of water in an atoll or along the coast, respectively. Thus, the trend for translators is to render the Italian *lago* and the French *lac* as *lago* in Spanish, which perhaps influenced scholars to use *lago* to designate the former lakes of the Basin.

The first official document related to the lakes in independent Mexico uses the words *lago* and *laguna* interchangeably (Mora 1823). However, by the middle of the nineteenth century, as literature on the *desagüe* begins to appear, the word *lago* becomes fully established. From then on, terms such as *Laguna de Texcoco*, *Laguna de Chalco*, and the like disappear completely from the literature. With the lakes having completely disappeared in the twentieth century, scholars have begun to reconstruct the ancient lakes with the idea of *lagos* (large, stable, and permanent lakes), overestimating their extent and misunderstanding their dynamics.

Although descriptions of the conquest are contradictory, Hernán Cortés (1985), Bernal Díaz del Castillo (1982) and Francisco López de Gómara (2006), among others, provide some idea of the dynamics of the lakes. Furthermore, descriptions of the lakes in the sixteenth century, often related to floods, provide an idea of the threats Mexico City faced from short- and long-term changes (see

Candiani 2014; Palerm 1973), as well as the series of colonial maps in some collection works (e.g., Apenes 1947; Lombardo Ruiz 1996).

After the early seventeenth century, as the original extent of the lakes began to diminish due to the drainage projects, the original dynamics of the lakes began to be forgotten, except for some descriptions of the remaining lakes in the south (Chalco and Xochimilco), north (Zumpango, Xaltocan, and San Cristóbal), and a much-reduced Lake Texcoco. Although important descriptions of the remaining bodies of water in the nineteenth century still reveal interesting aspects of their dynamics (Garay 1888; Humboldt 1811; Orozco y Berra 1864), many of these have been overlooked. Historians, archaeologists, and other scholars preferred to view the ancient lakes as large and stable bodies of water, thus distorting reconstructions of the lacustrine environments of the Basin (Cordova 2022).

Cartographic misrepresentations appear for good during the twentieth century, when many of the lakes had disappeared. Notable among them is the configuration of the lakes proposed by Ángel Palerm (1973), whose maps show lakes much larger than those that would have existed, merging the two northern lakes (Zumpango and Xaltocan) into a single body of water. A similar configuration, though exaggerating the size of the northern lakes to a lesser degree, appears in the maps published in Sanders, Parsons, and Santley's (1979) book. These reconstructions find no support in any description or map prior to the twentieth century. In the already mentioned 1554 Map of Uppsala, the northern lakes appear as small and separate bodies of water connected to each other and to Lake Texcoco by a stream. Moreover, a large single lake in the north would have been impossible in view of the estimated 6-meter difference in water level between Lakes Zumpango and Texcoco (Orozco y Berra 1864). Had these two maintained the same level, so would have all the other lake basins, keeping underwater cities like Azcapotzalco, Texcoco, Coyoacan, and Chalco, all of which lie below the contour of Lake Zumpango.

Beyond the historical descriptions, the sedimentary record attests to the shallow nature of the lakes. Of particular relevance is the observation that many Pleistocene sediments are almost at the modern ground surface, covered only by discontinuous thin layers of Holocene sediments (Cordova 2022). Another contributing factor would have been sediment resuspension, a process typical of shallow lakes. This would have reduced deposition on the lakebed, except in vegetated areas (Hamilton and Mitchell 1996; James and Barko 1994). The geoarchaeological examples presented in the next section illustrate the unstable and shallow nature of Lake Texcoco.

REVISITING SITES AND OFF-SITE LOCALITIES

As in the rest of the Texcoco area, the majority of the settlements that the Texcoco regional survey (TRS) identified in the lacustrine plain date to the Late

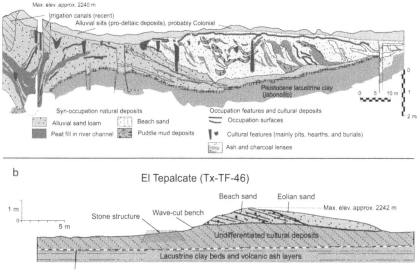

a

Tlatel de Tequexquinahuac (Tx-LF-14)

Max. elev. approx. 2240 m

Irrigation canals (recent)
Alluvial silts (pro-deltaic deposits), probably Colonial

Pleistocene lacustrine clay
(Jaboncillo)

0   5   10 m

0

1

2 m

Syn-occupation natural deposits

Alluvial sand loam

Peat fill in river channel

Beach sand

Puddle mud deposits

Occupation features and cultural deposits

Occupation surfaces

Cultural features (mainly pits, hearths, and burials)

Ash and charcoal lenses

b

El Tepalcate (Tx-TF-46)

Beach sand   Eolian sand

1 m

0

5 m

Stone structure   Wave-cut bench

Max. elev. approx. 2242 m

Undifferentiated cultural deposits

Lacustrine clay beds and volcanic ash layers

Typha sp.(cattail) layer

FIGURE 9.2. *Stratigraphy of two* tlateles: *(a) Tlatel de Tequexquinahuac and (b) El Tepalcate (after Cordova et al. 2022). See locations in figure 9.1.*

Postclassic (Parsons 1971). However, earlier periods such as the Late Toltec and the Late and Terminal Formative had substantial settlements, including some that were re-occupied in the Late Aztec period (see maps in Parsons 1971).

Of the lacustrine sites in the eastern part of Lake Texcoco, only a few have been further excavated and investigated (see figure 9.1). These sites include El Tepalcate (Tx-TF-46) and Tlatel de Tequexquinahuac (Tx-LF-14), for which there is dated information on the stratigraphy of natural and cultural sediments. Other excavated sites produced interesting sequential information with no absolute dates, as is the case of Tlatel de Tepexpan. Other sites, such as the area of site Tx-A-4 and Huatepec Hill (Tx-A 1 & 2) have been partially studied through fortuitous exposures in brickyards and other openings of the grounds, soil studies, and historical maps and documentation.

The main occupation of the Tlatel de Tequexquinahuac, or site Tx-LF-14, dates to the Late Formative period, although features of the Classic also exist within its bounds (Morett Alatorre et al. 1999). The settlement developed on the levees of a deltaic channel where occupations are interbedded with alluvial deposition (Fig. 9.2a). The occupation extended temporarily to a beach that formed on the side of the levee. However, rising lake levels most likely forced its settlers to abandon it sometime before 200 BCE (Cordova et al. 2022). There seem to be similar sites in the area, suggesting perhaps a community occupying deltaic islands (Luis Morett, personal communication).

El Tepalcate, or site Tx-TF-46 in the TRS, is an islet in the now completely urbanized southwestern part of the lake (see figure 9.1). Ola Apenes (1943) and Eduardo Noguera (1943) were the first to record the site, which Parsons (1971) later described and recorded as part of the TRS. Lorena Gámez-Eternod (2005) excavated it, confirming its Late Formative age and possible importance as a settlement devoted, among other things, to salt production. The geoarchaeological analysis of the site (Cordova 1997; Cordova et al. 2022) revealed the relations of the layers shown in figure 9.2b to the wider site context. The site was established on a stand of cattail (*Typha* sp.) in an area probably flooded, at least seasonally. With a location on a lakebed higher than Tequexquinahuac, the inhabitants of the site were able to maintain it above the rising lake levels by elevating its height with materials imported from the mainland. However, the site seems to have been abandoned in the Classic due to a further rise of lake levels, attributed to increasing atmospheric moisture on the basis of site stratigraphy (Cordova et al. 2022) and independent proxies of climate change (Lachniet et al. 2012, 2017). Thereafter, lower and more stable lake levels led to the formation of a beach bar, with ephemeral occupations during the Late Aztec period.

Excavation of the Tlatel de Tepexpan, or site TC-3 in the Teotihuacan Region survey (Sanders 1994) by Jaime Litvak King (1964) revealed several occupation layers, with the Classic one being the most important. Minor settlements existed in the same place during the Late Toltec and Late Aztec. Layers V and IV are the pre-settlement lacustrine and palustrine deposits (see figure 9.3). Layer V seems to be an indurated layer, possibly the same as the one reported by De Terra (1949). This natural layer may have enabled settlement growth in this place. Cultural layers III and II contain predominantly early Classic artifacts, though with intrusions of younger materials. Layer I has a mixture of Classic, Toltec, and Late Aztec materials (Litvak King 1964). When compared to the *tlateles* of Tequexquinahuac and El Tepalcate, it is evident that elevation made a big difference to the settlement at the Tlatel de Tepexpan (Cordova et al. 2022). The consistently high lake levels during the Classic period made the procurement of salt possible only at a higher elevation, in areas that at other periods would have been farther inland.

Site Tx-A-4 is a small *tlatel* apparently adjoined to a former causeway dike (see figure 9.4a). The dominant ceramics at the site are Late Aztec, but the lack of Texcoco-fabric-marked ceramics suggests that it was not a salt production station (Parsons 1971). However, its association with a Late Aztec causeway dike and a layer of underlying peat suggests other activities, perhaps including wetland agriculture. Today, most of its surroundings are covered by recent deposits of silt (*lama*) produced by a technique called *entarquinado*, or the deliberate flooding of

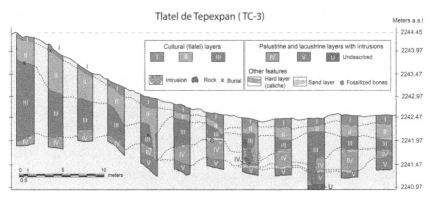

FIGURE 9.3. *Tlatel de Tepexpan (after Litvak King 1964). See location in figure 9.1.*

fields with nutrient-laden silt from the San Juan Teotihuacan River (see figure 9.4a). This technique was brought from Spain and have been practiced widely in the Bajío of Guanajuato and Michoacan (Sánchez Rodríguez 2009), though in many parts of the Basin of Mexico, where it has caused drying of the lakebed (Candiani 2014). However, soil studies (Gutiérrez Castorena et al. 2005, 2006) and a geoarchaeological reconnaissance of the area, including its former brickyards (Cordova et al. 2022), suggest a complex system of natural and human-made or managed lacustrine ecosystems.

Huatepec Hill is a rock promontory and a former island linked by a Late Aztec causeway to a larger promontory (Tepetzingo), which is in turn connected to the causeway associated with site Tx-A-4 (see figure 9.1). The hill corresponds to the location of sites Tx-A-1 and Tx-A-2 identified in the TRS (Parsons 1971). It seems to be an important area of Late Aztec occupation partially concealed by recent alluvial sedimentation, particularly by the deliberate flushing of sediments from the canals. An excavation aimed at studying Pleistocene occupations at the base of Huatepec (Morett Alatorre 2001) also produced important information about the Postclassic configuration of the lakeshore near this small island (see figure 9.4b). It documents the establishment of a settlement on a stable rock surface surrounded by a saline lake. There is no information on possible springs, as occurred on similar rocky islands elsewhere, such as Peñón de los Baños and Tlapacoya (González et al. 2015; Lorenzo and Mirambell 1986). However, no detailed geological study of Huatepec and Tepetzingo has yet been conducted.

Ceramics embedded in the youngest beach deposit at the foot of Huatepec Hill (see figure 9.4, sites Tx-A-1 & 2), suggest that its formation occurred in the Late Aztec period, and can be correlated with the beach ridge on top of the *tlatel* at El Tepalcate (see figure 9.2b). The elevation of both beaches suggest that they mark the high-level stand proposed by Lachniet and colleagues (2017) for the Aztec Pluvial, centered in the early to middle fifteenth century.

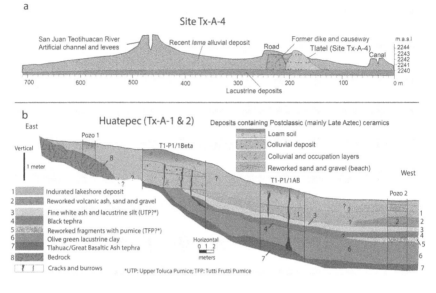

FIGURE 9.4. *(a) General stratigraphy around Site Tx-A-4 (Cordova et al. 2022) and (b) the western shoreline of Huatepec Hill (Morett Alatorre 2001). See locations in figure 9.1.*

Localities studied in other parts of Lake Texcoco and in other lakes of the Basin provide information regarding the use of the lacustrine environment for settlement. El Risco, for example, a *tlatel* with Classic, Epiclassic, Late Toltec and Late Aztec occupations, was apparently devoted to the procurement of salt (Mayer-Oakes 1959), but no details of its stratigraphy have been published. The cultural material collected in the north-central part of Lake Texcoco, within the area covered by the Lake Texcoco survey (see figure 9.1), suggests that localities far from the shore were also important in terms of resource procurement. Although there is no clear evidence of permanent settlements, or even salt-production sites, this most recent survey proves that the lakebed had a complex relief but was generally shallow, and that there was intense cultural activity in every part of the lake. The recurrence of *palafitte*-like structures, formed by stakes planted in the ground, is often associated with ceramics and figurines, suggestive of ceremonial activities (Parsons and Morett 2004). Despite this use, Parsons (2001, 2006) does not rule out that some of these shallow areas may have been used for setting nets for trapping birds.

Many *tlateles* in the northern lakes seem to be salt production sites (Parsons 2008; Sanders and Gorenflo 2007). However, large *tlateles* with permanent settlements also exist, the largest being Xaltocan and Tonanitla (Frederick et al. 2005). The southern lakes, although remarkably different from Lake Texcoco in terms of salinity and vegetation, also inform the interpretations presented here, particularly in terms of the use of lacustrine spaces and resources. Tlapacoya and Xico are good examples of shoreline occupations on stable rock structures, though at a larger scale than that reported for Huatepec Hill above. Terremote-Tlaltenco is an example of small, *tlatel*-type settlement established in a shallow, near-shore lacustrine environment with dense aquatic vegetation (McClung et al. 1986; Serra Puche 1988).

LAKE TEXCOCO: ENVIRONMENTAL CONTEXT AND DYNAMICS

The majority of Prehispanic settlements reported in the eastern part of Lake Texcoco correspond to islets of the *tlatel* type. Many were salt-production stations, a few were residential settlements, and many apparently had multiple purposes (Cordova 2022; Cordova et al. 2022; Parsons 1971). Evidently, these settlements were not established haphazardly; they had to follow certain preexisting natural features and adjust to lacustrine dynamics.

The geomorphic settings of the settlements described above (see figures 9.2, 9.3, and 9.4) showcase the diversity of resource-rich lacustrine spaces apt for settlement. They can be viewed as lacustrine ecological niches, each of which with a specific set of lacustrine processes (i.e., lacustrine dynamics). With this picture in mind, it is possible to visualize the different lacustrine niches that can be subsequently transformed or utilized for resource exploitation and settlement (see figure 9.5). The natural lacustrine dynamics would have created a variety of environments in Lake Texcoco, depending on the gradient of the lakeshore and the lakebed, the influence of incoming rivers, and the presence of springs, which sometimes present certain advantages for seasonal or permanent settlement. At a more advanced stage of managing the lacustrine environment, dikes and canals could help control the flows of saline and fresh water. Consequently, the transformation of each of these natural environments into different areas of settlement and economic activities would augment the natural diversity of lacustrine environments, providing further possibilities for settlement, both permanent and seasonal. In some cases, and with the help of dikes mitigating the fluctuations of lake levels, settlements could develop into a complex network of platforms, *tlateles*, and *chinampas*. Unfortunately, many of these complexes, many of which have been reconstructed from historic sources, have no representation in the archaeological record (see Borejsza, this volume). However, numerous scattered salvage excavations in Mexico City have exposed some pieces of information about parts of these large complexes (see Sánchez-Vázquez et al. 2007).

Lakeshores characterized by ample mud flats, salt flats, and associated silt dunes (see figure 9.5, model 1) may be ideal for the exploitation of salt, *tequesquite*, bird hunting, and the gathering of insects and algae, as shown in ethnohistoric and ethnographic examples (Parsons 2001, 2006). This was the case at El Tepalcate during the Terminal Formative and Late Aztec, and most probably also at the Tlatel de Tepexpan during the Classic, Late Toltec, and Late Aztec (see figure 9.3). With dikes, it would be possible to dam the incoming fresh water from streams and springs in a manner similar to the dike associated with site Tx-A-4 (see figure 9.4).

Near-shore areas at river mouths would present a diversity of ecological niches, with fresh, brackish, and saline water (see figure 9.5, model 2). Initially, settlers could establish temporary dwellings on the islands, with permanent settlements gradually developing in the higher areas, as on the Tlatel de Tequexquinahuac in the Terminal Formative (see figure 9.2). However, such settlements lacked dikes and *bordos* (small earthen dams) that would regulate flows of saline and freshwater and protect settlements with floods as seen around those in the Late Postclassic in the lacustrine realm of the Basin. This would create more space for permanent settlement, even of an urban nature complex with the possibility of *chinampa* agriculture (see figure 9.5, model 2, transformed). This would not have been the situation in the western part of Texcoco, but it was in the areas of Tenochtitlan and stretching toward Iztapalapa and Mexicaltzingo (see Ávila-López 2006).

Shoreline areas connected to *bajadas* (alluvial-fan slopes) reaching from the foothills into the lakebed would also have been ideal for establishing stations for salt production and the gathering of other lacustrine resources (see figure 9.5, model 3). This is the setting of many settlements at the foot of the Sierra de Guadalupe, in El Risco, and in many localities along the shores of Chiconautla, Chimalhuacan, and the Iztapalapa Peninsula (Cordova 2022). Rock promontories are similar to the *bajada* setting, but they have the advantage of a shorter transition between the stable rocky ground and the lakebed, permitting permanent settlement closer to the lake (see figure 9.5, model 4), the Tx-A-1 and Tx-A-2 sites at the base of the Huatepec Hill being good examples (see figure 9.2).

Open-lake areas were perhaps not suitable for salt production, but may have been ideal for bird catching, fishing, and probably ceremonial activities (see figure 9.5, model 5), as documented by the archaeological contexts identified in the north-central part of Lake Texcoco (Parsons and Morett 2004). These areas would have been extremely shallow, but largely featureless, and structures for water flow control would probably be difficult to build and maintain. At low lake levels, these areas may have become swampy, making them equally difficult to reach by canoe and on foot.

POTENTIAL RESEARCH ISSUES AND AREAS

The settlement data from the TRS and the geoarchaeological research reviewed in this chapter are the basis for a deeper study of the dynamics of lacustrine settlements on the eastern shore of former Lake Texcoco. Three geographical areas stand out as having a high potential for a regional study of Prehispanic

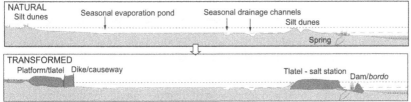

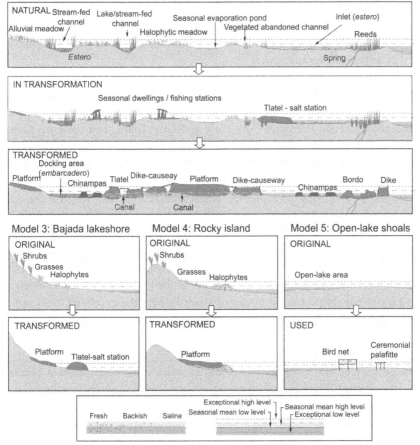

FIGURE 9.5. *Schematic models of lacustrine environments and their transformation for resource utilization in Lake Texcoco.*

settlement. The first lies within the Nexquipayac-Tepetzingo-Hautepec-Atenco-Nexquipayac polygon, which encompasses a transitional area between fluvial and lacustrine environments, with some areas of swamps known to have been transformed during the Late Aztec period on the basis of historical documents.

Within this polygon, incoming fresh water could have been contained before reaching the saline lake by building dikes and dams; these would have, at the same time, prevented the inflow of saline water. The area could have been used for some form of raised-field agriculture of the type Ángel Palerm (1973:21) called *chinampas de tierra adentro*. The existence of beach deposits on the small islands could also help us understand the dynamics of the lake over time.

A second area lies west and southwest of Texcoco, along the shoreline extending from Tocuila, across Santa Cruz de Abajo, and into the fields of the former Hacienda de Chapingo, now belonging to ejidos and the Universidad Autónoma Chapingo. This area also witnessed important development during the Late Aztec and perhaps even earlier; post-Aztec fluvial sedimentation has drawn a veil of sediment over many sites.

A third area of great interest is the former mouths of the Chapingo and San Bernardino rivers, which most likely formed a deltaic complex, as shown by the study of the Tlatel de Tequexquinahuac. The TRS recorded here sites of the Late and Terminal Formative, the Early and Late Toltec, and the Late Aztec, suggesting a persistent interest in the area, probably due to the potential that the incoming fresh water and several natural islands and abandoned channels presented in terms of resources other than salt.

To the west of these areas lies the ample federal zone mentioned at the outset, where airport construction was halted in 2018 to make room for a planned Lake Texcoco Ecological Park. Perhaps there are places in this area where some research is still possible, as shown by the results of Parsons and Morett's (2004) surveys. With the planned restoration or re-creation of wetlands and small ponds, perhaps this area also holds potential for experimental archaeological and geoarchaeological research, aimed at testing hypotheses related to the building of *tlateles*, the use of salt, *tequesquite*, and other lacustrine resources.

CONCLUSIONS

The geographic misrepresentations of the lacustrine realm of the Basin of Mexico and the practical difficulties of surveying a lakebed led the early archaeological surveys to skip most of the non-urbanized area formerly occupied by Lake Texcoco. As a result, areas that could have produced important information were left to be destroyed by the expansion of the urban areas and an airport construction project that was halted only after substantial damage had been wrought. However, an examination of the stratigraphy and geomorphic setting of some surveyed sites and new information from surveys in the center of the lake provide information about the variety of settlements in the various ecological niches of the lake.

The eastern part of Lake Texcoco, where urbanization and infrastructure development has not completely destroyed sites, has areas with great potential to help us understand the Prehispanic habitation and use of resources in this saline lake. Examples from the studied sites presented and discussed in this chapter showcase the complexity of lacustrine settlements in the context of natural lacustrine dynamic processes and the different structures built by ancient settlers.

Future research in key areas of the eastern part of former Lake Texcoco could provide additional information on the process of adaptation to this large saline lake and its eventual control. This information could also be of importance in understanding the development of Prehispanic settlement and hydraulic control in other parts of the lake, namely areas within and around the Aztec capital of Tenochtitlan, as well as neighboring Iztapalapa.

REFERENCES

Apenes, Ola. 1943. "The 'Tlateles' of Lake Texcoco." *American Antiquity* 9:29–32.

Apenes, Ola. 1947. *Mapas antiguos del Valle de México*. Universidad Nacional Autónoma de México, Mexico City.

Ávila-López, Raúl. 2006. *Mexicaltzingo: Arqueología de un reino culhua-mexica*. 2 vols. Instituto Nacional de Antropologia e Historia-Consejo Nacional de la Cultura y las Artes, Mexico City.

Blanton, Richard Edward. 1972. *Prehispanic Settlement Patterns of the Ixtapalapa Peninsula Region, Mexico*. Occasional Papers in Anthropology, no. 6. University Park, The Pennsylvania State University.

Candiani, Vera S. 2014. *Dreaming of Dry Land: Environmental Transformation in Colonial Mexico City*. Stanford University Press, Redwood City, CA.

Clavijero, Francisco Javier. 1974. *Historia antigua de México*. Porrúa, Mexico City.

Cordova, Carlos E. 1997. "Landscape Transformation in Aztec and Spanish Colonial Texcoco." PhD dissertation, Department of Geography, University of Texas at Austin.

Cordova, Carlos E., Luis Morett Alatorre, Charles Frederick, and Lorena Gámez Eternod. 2022. "Lacustrine Dynamics of Tlatel-Type Settlements from Middle Formative to Late Aztec in the Eastern Part of Lake Texcoco, Mexico." *Ancient Mesoamerica* 33(2):211–26. https://doi.org/10.1017/S0956536120000322.

Cordova, Carlos E. 2022. *The Lakes of the Basin of Mexico: Dynamics of a Lacustrine System and the Evolution of a Civilization*. Springer, New York.

Cortés, Hernán. 1985. *Cartas de relación*. 2nd ed. Editores Mexicanos Unidos, Mexico City.

Covarrubias, Sebastián de. 1611. *Tesoro de la lengua Castellana o Española*. Luis Sanchez, Impresor del Rey, Madrid.

De Terra, Helmut. 1949. "Early Man in Mexico." In *Tepexpan Man*, edited by Helmut de Terra, Javier Romero, and T. D. Stewart, 13–86. Monograph in Viking Fund Publications in Anthropology, vol. 11. Viking Fund, New York.

Díaz del Castillo, Bernal. 1982. *Historia verdadera de la conquista de la Nueva España*. Edition by C. Senz de Santa María. Instituto Fernández de Oviedo, CSIC, Madrid.

Frederick, Charles David, Barbara Winsborough, and Virginia S. Popper. 2005. "Geoarchaeological Investigations in the Northern Basin of Mexico." In *Production and Power at Postclassic Xaltocan*, edited by Elizabeth Brumfiel, 71–115. University of Pittsburgh and Instituto Nacional de Antropología e Historia, Mexico City.

Gámez-Eternod, Lorena. 2005. "El Tepalcate: Una aldea del Formativo terminal en la ribera oriental del Lago de Texcoco." In *IV Coloquio Pedro Bosch Gimpera*, edited by Ernesto Vargas-Pacheco, 221–51. Instituto de Investigaciones Antropológicas-Universidad Nacional Autónoma de Mexico, Mexico City.

Garay, Francisco. 1888. *El Valle de México: Apuntes sobre su hidrografía*. Oficina Tipográfica de la Secretaría de Fomento, Mexico City.

González, Silvia, David Huddart, Isabel Israde-Alcántara, Gabriela Domínguez-Vázquez, James Bischoff, and Nicholas Felstead. 2015. "Paleoindian Sites from the Basin of Mexico: Evidence from Stratigraphy, Tephrochronology and Dating." *Quaternary International* 363:4–19.

Gutiérrez-Castorena, María del Carmen, Georges Stoops, G., Carlos A. Ortiz-Solorio, and Guillermo López-Ávila. 2005. "Amorphous Silica Materials in Soils and Sediments of the Ex-Lago de Texcoco, Mexico: An Explanation for Its Subsidence." *Catena* 60:205–26.

Gutiérrez-Castorena, María del Carmen, Georges Stoops, Carlos A. Ortiz-Solorio, and Patricio Sánchez-Guzmán. 2006. "Micromorphology of Opaline Features in Soils on the Sediments of the Ex-Lago de Texcoco, México." *Geoderma* 132:89–104.

Hamilton, David P., and Stuart F. Mitchell. 1996. "An Empirical Model for Sediment Resuspension in Shallow Lakes." *Hydrobiologia* 317(3):209–20.

Humboldt, Alexander von. 1811. *Political Essay of the Kingdom of New Spain*. Longman Hurst, London.

James, William F., and John W. Barko. 1994. "Macrophyte Influences on Sediment Resuspension and Export in a Shallow Impoundment." *Lake and Reservoir Management* 10(2):95–102.

Lachniet, Matthew S., Juan Pablo Bernal, Yemane Asmerom, Victor Polyak, and Dolores Piperno. 2012. "A 2400 Year Mesoamerican Rainfall Reconstruction Links Climate and Cultural Change." *Geology* 40:259–62.

Lachniet, Matthew S., Yemane Asmerom, Ictor Polyak, and Juan Pablo Bernal. 2017. "Two Millennia of Mesoamerican Monsoon Variability Driven by Pacific and Atlantic Synergistic Forcing." *Quaternary Science Reviews* 155:100–13.

León-Portilla, Miguel, and Carmen Aguilera. 2016. *Mapa de Mexico Tenochtitlan y sus contornos hacia 1550*. Ediciones Era-Secretaría de Cultura-El Colegio Nacional, Mexico City.

Litvak King, Jaime. 1964. *Estratigrafía cultural y natural en un tlatel en el Lago de Texcoco*. Instituto Nacional de Antropología e Historia, Mexico City.

Lombardo de Ruiz, Sonia. 1996. *Atlas histórico de la Ciudad de México*, vol. 1. Instituto Nacional de Antropología e Historia and Consejo Nacional para la Cultura y las Artes, Mexico City.

López de Gómara, Francisco. 2006. *Historia de la conquista de México*. 4th ed. Porrúa, Mexico City.

Lorenzo, Jose Luis, and Lorena Mirambell. 1986. *Tlapacoya: 35,000 años de historia del Lago de Chalco*. Instituto Nacional de Antropología e Historia, Mexico City.

Mayer-Oakes, William J. 1959. "A Stratigraphic Excavation at El Risco, Mexico." *Proceedings of the American Philosophical Society* 103(3):332–73.

McClung de Tapia, Emily, Mari Carmen Serra Puche, and Amy Ellen Limón de Dyer. 1986. "Formative Lacustrine Adaptation: Botanical Remains from Terremote-Tlaltenco, D.F., Mexico." *Journal of Field Archaeology* 13:99–113.

Mora, José María Luis. 1823. *Memoria que para informar sobre el origen y estado actual de las obras emprendidas para el desagüe de las lagunas del Valle de México*. Imprenta del Águila, Mexico City.

Morett Alatorre, Luis, Fernando Sánchez Martínez, and Lorena Mirambell. 1999. "El islote de Tequexquinahuac: Proyecto de investigación arqueológico." Unpublished technical report, Archivo Técnico, Instituto Nacional de Antropologia e Historia, Mexico City.

Morett Alatorre, Luis. 2001. "Huatepec-Tepetzingo/Atenco; Lago de Texcoco; Playas pleistocénicas." Unpublished technical report, Archivo General, Universidad Autónoma Chapingo, Texcoco.

Noguera, Eduardo. 1943. "Excavaciones en el Tepalcate, Chimalhuacan, Mexico." *American Antiquity* 9:33–43.

Orozco y Berra, Manuel. 1864. *Memoria para la carta hidrográfica del Valle de México*. Imprenta de A. Boix, Mexico City.

Ortiz Pérez, Mario Arturo. 1975. "Algunos conceptos y criterios de clasificación de los medios lacustres." *Anuario de Geografía* 15:129–38.

Palerm, Ángel. 1973. *Obras hidráulicas prehispánicas en el sistema lacustre del Valle de México*. Instituto Nacional de Antropología e Historia, Mexico City.

Parsons, Jeffrey R. 1971. *Prehispanic Settlement Patterns in the Texcoco Region, Mexico*. Memoirs of the Museum of Anthropology, no. 3. University of Michigan, Ann Arbor.

Parsons, Jeffrey R. 2001. *The Last Saltmakers of Nexquipayac, Mexico: An Archaeological Ethnography*. Anthropological Papers, no. 92. Museum of Anthropology, University of Michigan, Ann Arbor.

Parsons, Jeffrey R. 2006. *The Last Pescadores of Chimalhuacan, Mexico: An Archaeological Ethnography*. Anthropological Papers, no. 96. Museum of Anthropology, University of Michigan, Ann Arbor.

Parsons, Jeffrey R. 2008. *Prehispanic Settlement Patterns in the Northwestern Valley of Mexico: The Zumpango Region*. Memoirs of the Museum of Anthropology, no. 45. University of Michigan, Ann Arbor.

Parsons, Jeffrey R., and Luis Morett. 2004. "Recursos acuáticos en la subsistencia azteca: Cazadores, pescadores y recolectores." *Arqueología mexicana* 12(68):38–43.

Sánchez Rodríguez, Martín. 2009. "Entarquinamiento: Vestigios de una técnica de riego en México." In *Espacios y patrimonios*, edited by Nelly Sigaut, 41–56. Universidad de Murcia, Murcia, Spain.

Sánchez-Vázquez, Martín, P. F. Sánchez-Nava, and R. A. Cedillo-Vargas. 2007. "Tenochtitlan y Tlatetlolco durante el Posclásico Tardío." In *Ciudad excavada: Veinte años de arqueología de salvamento en la Ciudad de México y área metropolitana*, edited by Luis A. López-Wario, 145–87. Instituto Nacional de Antropología e Historia, Mexico City.

Sanders, William T., ed. 1975. *The Teotihuacan Valley Project Final Report*, vol. 2: *The Formative Period Occupation of the Valley*, pt. 1: *Texts and Tables*. Occasional Papers in Anthropology, no. 10. The Pennsylvania State University, University Park.

Sanders, William T., ed. 1987. *The Teotihuacan Valley Project Final Report*, vol. 4: *The Toltec Period Occupation of the Valley*. Occasional Papers in Anthropology, no. 13. Pennsylvania State University, University Park.

Sanders, William T., ed. 1994. *The Teotihuacan Valley Project Final Report*, vol. 3: *The Teotihuacan Period Occupation of the Valley*, pt. 3: *The Surface Survey*. Occasional Papers in Anthropology, no. 21. Pennsylvania State University, University Park.

Sanders, William T., and Larry J. Gorenflo. 2007. *Prehispanic Settlement Patterns in the Cuautitlan Region, Mexico*. Occasional Papers in Anthropology, no. 29. Department of Anthropology, Pennsylvania State University, University Park.

Sanders, William T., Jeffrey R. Parsons, Jeffrey, and Robert S. Santley. 1979. *The Basin of Mexico: Ecological Processes in the Evolution of a Civilization*. Academic Press, New York.

Serra Puche, Mari Carmen. 1988. *Los recursos lacustres de la Cuenca de México durante el Formativo*. Instituto de Investigaciones Antropológicas, Universidad Nacional Autónoma de México, Mexico City.

PART IV

New Observations on Resource Exploitation

10

From *Tlacolol* to *Metepantle*

A Reappraisal of the Antiquity of the Agricultural Niches of the Central Mexican Symbiotic Region

ALEKSANDER BOREJSZA

INTRODUCTION: THE CONCEPT OF AGRICULTURAL NICHE

Modern archaeological practice approaches the study of ancient agriculture from two complementary angles. One involves the study of food remains, typically found at settlements, and uses them to inventory the crops and animals that people raised. With the aid of ethnographic and historical analogy, it makes more indirect inferences about where people practiced agriculture and how. The bulk of the practitioners of this approach self-identify as archaeobotanists or archaeozoologists. The other one involves studying what remains of ancient fields or livestock enclosures, typically some distance away from human dwellings. In this case, the order of inference is reversed: the answer to the "where" question is self-evident, whereas the "how" and "what" questions require increasing doses of analogy. The majority of the practitioners of this approach are to be found among geoarchaeologists and landscape archaeologists.

The concept of "agricultural niche" seems useful in that it unites both approaches to the study of ancient agriculture. Doolittle and Mabry (2006:109) define it as:

https://doi.org/10.5876/9781646424078.c010

a specialized strategy of food production based on one or more farming systems (combinations of crop plants, technologies, and techniques), with the optimum location for a specific strategy having a combination of landform, soil, and micro-climate in which subsistence goals are most closely and predictably achieved.

They go on to discuss the rainfed, dry, runoff, flood, irrigated, and water-table farming techniques practiced in certain locations in the prehistoric American Southwest, as well as the races of maize associated with them. One of their major concerns is establishing and explaining the chronological order in which the different niches were filled (see also Mabry 2005). The term "agricultural niche" is evidently modeled on the term now in common parlance, "ecological niche," transposing it to settings in which the farmer's routines are the decisive factor molding landforms, biotic communities, and the interactions between species. An ecological niche is not just a place, but also a set of relationships uniting different organisms and inanimate objects. Similarly, in order to define satisfactorily an agricultural niche, it is not sufficient to delimit a suitable location in space. It is also necessary to describe the crops and other living organisms present, their mutual relations, the interactions between biotic and physical elements, and certain sets of behavioral patterns, with the greatest emphasis falling, in this case, on the farmer's cyclical activities, such as tillage, weeding, or the maintenance of field boundaries. Following Doolittle's (2006a:179) dictum that "farmland does not exist until it is made," there are no vacant agricultural niches waiting to be occupied by agricultural colonists, though every agricultural niche obviously tends to replace certain types of natural niches.

The purpose of this chapter is to offer an up-to-date review of what archaeological research has revealed regarding the chronological order in which the major types of agricultural niches of Prehispanic Central Mexico were constructed. Simplifying Doolittle and Mabry's (2006) definition, it is possible to reduce the concept of agricultural niche to the sum of optimal (1) location, (2) techniques, (3) crops, and (4) tools. The amount of information at our disposal decreases dramatically from the first to the last member of the sum. As a result, I focus below on location and technique, with only scant and tentative references to associated crops. My ultimate aim is to elucidate the reasons why agricultural niches should be constructed in a particular order, though I recognize that the available dataset does not allow more than the formulation of a few working hypotheses.

THE BASIN OF MEXICO SURVEY AND THE ORDER OF AGRICULTURAL NICHE CONSTRUCTION

The term "agricultural niche" may be a recent addition to archaeological vocabulary, but similar research problems have busied the minds of several Mesoamericanists from the mid-twentieth century onward (e.g., Armillas 1949;

Flannery 1983; McClung 1979; Palerm 1952, 1955; Whitmore and Turner 2001; Woodbury and Neely 1972), taking a particular impetus from the cultural ecology fathered by Julian Steward (1955). In Central Mexico, the most wide-ranging and ambitious discussions of the options available to Prehispanic farmers and of their decision-making were the work of archaeologists associated with the Basin of Mexico survey (BMS), a series of projects that set out to walk every field of the then still-extensive countryside of this region (for retrospective overviews, see Charlton and Nichols 2005; Mastache et al. 1996; Nichols 2006; Parsons 2015; Sanders 1997; Webster and Evans 2008). The surveys were organized around the concept of "archaeological site," focusing on the identification of surface concentrations of artifacts usually indicative of the location of former human dwellings rather than agricultural fields, but several participant teams also took considerable pains to record abandoned agricultural features visible on the surface—for example, terrace walls or aqueducts—that could reasonably be expected to pre-date the Spanish conquest. William Sanders also set out a template whereby archaeological surveys were preceded or accompanied by in-depth ethnographic studies of modern (i.e., mid-twentieth century) settlement patterns and agricultural systems, as well as the consultation of published early-Colonial sources that threw some light on the kind of agriculture practiced in the Basin on the eve of Conquest.

Very early on, Sanders (1956:116) identified a triad of intensive farming techniques—hillslope terraces, canal-irrigated fields, and raised wetland fields (*chinampas*)—as crucial in structuring the settlement patterns of state-level societies in a geographic area that he termed the "Central Mexican Symbiotic Region" (see figure 10.1). Sanders contrasted them with extensive techniques that relied on direct rainfall only and did not strive to permanently modify the natural topography of the field. In subsequent publications, he singled out among the latter a form of swiddening that he referred to as *tlacolol* (Sanders 1965:155–57; Price 1971:7, 11–12, 18–19; Sanders and Price 1968:123–25, 133–34, 145–46), a term borrowed from Oscar Lewis's (1951, 1960) ethnographic descriptions of a specific niche observed in Tepoztlan, but referred to by this name throughout the hot country of both Morelos and Guerrero. I have adopted the term *tlacolol* and the mentioned triad as the four categories that structure this review, and use the Central Mexican Symbiotic Region (CMSR)—roughly coterminous with Eric Wolf's (1959:7) "central highland"—to delimit its geographic scope. It is possible and desirable to define agricultural niches at a much finer resolution, distinguishing, for example, between different kinds of rainfed cultivation depending on the length of fallow, or different kinds of canal irrigation depending on the source of water and the seasonality of its application. High-quality excavation data that bear on such distinctions, however, are so few and far between that splitting the four basic categories would, at present, defeat the purpose of a synthetic review.

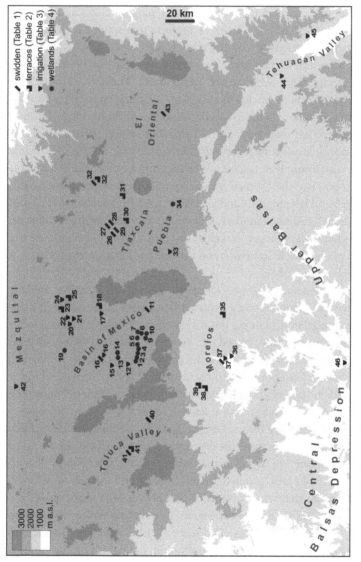

FIGURE 10.1. *The Central Mexican Symbiotic Region. For the key to sites, see tables 10.1–10.4.*

Different publications of the BMS ranked the four categories (or their subdivisions) in quasi-evolutionary sequences. The most obvious criterion was their productivity, expressed as maize yields per surface area, with estimates derived from a number of agronomic studies on traditional agriculture in Mexico and Guatemala (Logan and Sanders 1976:table 2). They were also ranked more subjectively by their perceived labor requirements and technological sophistication. Solid data on labor inputs in traditional agriculture are hard to come by even today (see Wilken 1987 as a rare exception) and it seems that these were assumed to be highly correlated with yield. Technological sophistication is of course a subject even less amenable to quantification. Sanders and associates were wary of viewing any of the essential elements of the farming techniques that they discussed as "inventions" requiring the protracted historical maturation of technological know-how (e.g., Sanders et al. 1979:383), a contentious issue over which they were taken to task by Doolittle (1990). Their criteria resulted in a rather consequent ordering, in which swidden was ranked lowest, followed by terracing, irrigation, and *chinampas*. It does not seem gratuitous that, for the intensive triad, this is the order of presentation followed in the grand synthesis of the BMS (Sanders et al. 1979).

By the 1970s, Boserup's (1965) ideas on population growth and technological change in agriculture loomed large over the theoretical models drawn on by the BMS (Logan and Sanders 1976; Sanders et al. 1979:359–85). Consequently, it seemed that the ranking just mentioned should also be, *grosso modo*, the chronological order of agricultural niche construction (e.g., Sanders et al. 1979:382–84). This was made explicit, for example, in discussing how farmers took on the heavier chores of terracing and irrigation only once *tlacolol* was no longer viable because of rising population numbers and accrued soil degradation. It was implicit, for example, in discussions of *chinampa* agriculture as the culmination of agricultural intensification in the Basin that allowed it to feed the metropolis of Tenochtitlan (Parsons 1976).

The BMS by and large modeled the kind of agriculture practiced by the inhabitants of any particular site in any particular phase on site location with respect to land optimal for the construction of this or that niche, as well as from the amount of "room" left for agriculture by the spacing of houses within sites and the spacing and distribution of sites within the different subregions of the Basin, that is, from both intra- and intersite settlement patterns. This indirect reasoning was supplemented, wherever possible, by observations on the proximity of abandoned agricultural features to the same sites. Sanders, Parsons, and Santley (1979:249–81,383) fully acknowledged the difficulties of dating the remains of terraces, canals, or *chinampas* by this kind of surface association. They ventured nonetheless to offer predictions on where and when the different farming techniques first appeared and where and when they became widespread. I start the discussion of each agricultural niche below by summarizing these predictions, cognizant of course that I am condensing much more elaborate and nuanced arguments by a large team of archaeologists who need not have agreed on every point and whose published ideas evolved over several decades.

REAPPRAISAL IN VIEW OF STRATIGRAPHICALLY CONSTRAINED DATA

In the last forty years, excavation has replaced surface survey as the primary mode of archaeological exploration in Central Mexico. Explosive urban and suburban development has devoured much of the countryside and many archaeological sites identified in surface surveys. Consequently, several discoveries of buried agricultural features have been the work of salvage projects, whose results are not always publicly shared in Spanish, and which rarely make it into English-language syntheses. As of today, many subregions of the CMSR can boast published archaeological surveys, but only those in the Tehuacan Valley (MacNeish et al. 1975; Woodbury and Neely 1972) and Tlaxcala (Abascal Macías 1980; García Cook 1976; Merino Carrión 1989) can rival the BMS in the degree of attention to agricultural features and the fervor brought to theoretical discussions of Prehispanic subsistence. The work in Tehuacan has focused strongly on irrigation, somewhat to the exclusion of alternative agricultural niches. Regarding the surveys of agricultural features in Tlaxcala, I share the reservations of Doolittle (1990:9, 29–30; 2006b) and have voiced my own (Borejsza 2006, 2014:15; Borejsza and Lesure 2014; Borejsza et al. 2021:252–53,295n6,315n123). In this situation, the predictions of the BMS remain the only baseline to which one can productively compare the discoveries made throughout the CMSR. Conversely, the unparalleled degree to which the archaeological record of the Basin has been ravaged by development means that insights into the functioning of Prehispanic agricultural systems are more likely to be gained in the somewhat less urbanized neighboring valleys.

This is why I feel justified in ranging more widely in contrasting survey data from the Basin with those recovered in stratigraphic context and assigned an absolute age, usually on the basis of radiometric assays. Tables 10.1 to 10.4 summarize the finds that I consider indicative of the four categories of agricultural niche, all of them keyed to the map in figure 10.1. The antiquity of different niches being the main concern, I have been rather strict in my criteria for including a particular site in the listings, excluding those for which a Prehispanic age can be put in doubt, as well as those for which dating relies exclusively on regional survey. I also excluded sites whose age can be corroborated with a reasonable degree of confidence by references in early Colonial documents, but which have not been ground-truthed. The bulk of bibliographic referencing is contained in the tables.

Swidden on Slopes (*Tlacolol*)

Swidden, broadly synonymous with slash-and-burn and shifting agriculture, is something normally associated with hot and relatively humid settings, where it is facilitated by the rapid regeneration of tropical forests. There is no ethnographic or historical record of swidden in the northern belt of the CMSR above 2000 meters above sea level, dominated by pine-oak woodland before agriculture. This is why, in his search for appropriate analogies for the extensive farming techniques of the earliest farmers in the Basin, Sanders turned to the tropical deciduous forest zone of Morelos. He maintained across several publications that *tlacolol* was the preferred technique of Formative-period agricultural colonists of the Basin. He thought, in particular, that the soil erosion inflicted by *tlacolol* on the unterraced slopes of the Teotihuacan Valley explained the frequent relocation of settlements from one ceramic phase to another, as well as the eventual shift to the valley floor by ca. 200 BCE (Sanders 1965:153–56). However, there seem to have been doubts about the usefulness of the analogy among the members of the BMS. As a result, the final project syntheses (Parsons et al. 1982; Sanders et al. 1979; Wolf 1976) barely mentioned *tlacolol*, preferring more generic references to rainfed (*temporal*) cultivation. By the following decade, one of Sanders's students was explicitly questioning the appropriateness of the analogy and doubted *tlacolol* could have been practiced in the Basin for any length of time (Nichols 1982:142, 1987b:609–10).

Geoarchaeological research is now reviving and vindicating Sanders's original ideas (see table 10.1). The most conclusive evidence comes not from the Basin, but from Tlaxcala, where alluvial fills contain hundreds of laminae saturated in charcoal, as well as reworked peds of surface and subsurface soil horizons (see figure 10.2a). The fills in question have been deposited by gullies or small streams with catchments no larger than 5 km², making it relatively easy to pinpoint the source areas of sediment and to compare them to coeval settlement patterns. The great thickness of these fills (reaching 10 meters in some cases), the preservation of fluvial sedimentary structures, and the radiocarbon chronology make clear that they were deposited very rapidly, fed by a thorough stripping of the natural soil cover. The charcoal laminae reflect the annual burning of secondary vegetation in different parts of the catchment, ahead of the planting of crops on unterraced slopes. Recent excavations at five Formative villages and the resulting refinements of the regional ceramic periodization confirm the picture of relatively short-lived settlements, occupied for a few human generations (Borejsza et al. 2010; Lesure 2014a; Lesure et al. 2013). A decisive factor in their abandonment was land degradation, corroborated both by on-site erosional unconformities and the local depletion of game observed in the faunal assemblages (Borejsza et al. 2014b; Lesure et al. 2006). The swiddening of slopes persisted in some places until as late as 1100 CE. Rather than awakening a conservationist ethic, the degradation

TABLE 10.1. Stratigraphic sequences suggestive of swidden agriculture and related erosion of unterraced slopes

No.	Location	Area	Timespan	Observations	References
11	Cuautlalpan	Basin of Mexico	1900–800 BCE	Massive mudflows in the foothills of the Iztaccihuatl volcano coincide in time with Formative agricultural colonization. Finer-grained rapid aggradation separating several occupation surfaces between 900 and 800 BCE.	Borejsza et al. 2014a:286–88; Frederick 1997; Frederick and Cordova 2019
37	Ticumán	Morelos	ca. 1000 BCE–?	Shift to coarser-grained and more rapid aggradation on the floodplain of the Yautepec river roughly coincides in time with Formative agricultural colonization. Poor chronological resolution.	Borejsza et al. 2014a:289; Morett Alatorre et al. 2000
40	Laguna de Chignahuapan	Toluca Valley	ca. 1000 BCE– ca. 1000 CE	Increased inputs of exogenic sediment and charcoal in lake coincide with appearance of disturbance taxa and agricultural colonization of the Toluca Valley. Poor chronological resolution due to slow sedimentation.	Caballero et al. 2002; Lesure 2008:116–7; Lozano García et al. 2005; Metcalfe et al. 1991
16	Santa Clara Coatitlan	Basin of Mexico	ca. 900–700 BCE	Rapid aggradation at the foot of the Guadalupe Range separating several generations of Formative irrigation canals.	Nichols 1982; Sanders and Santley 1977
32	La Laguna	Tlaxcala	ca. 500–300 BCE	Erosional unconformity separating two Formative occupations on slopes. Colluvial deposits in areas of reduced gradient. A second, less well-dated erosional episode at ca. 1–100 CE.	Borejsza 2006:168–270, 365–84; Borejsza and Carballo 2014; Borejsza and Rodríguez López 2014; Borejsza et al. 2008
28	Barranca Xilomantla	Tlaxcala	300 BCE–400 CE	Charcoal laminae in rapidly aggraded alluvium. Deposition of charcoal-rich alluvium may have continued until 1300 CE, but is not as well dated.	Borejsza 2006:298–320, 384–99; Borejsza et al. 2011

continued on next page

TABLE 10.1.—*continued*

No.	Location	Area	Timespan	Observations	References
29	La Concepción	Tlaxcala	200 BCE–300 CE	Charcoal-rich alluvium with redeposited peds of soil A horizons.	Borejsza et al. 2010, 2017
43	Aljojuca	El Oriental	200–1200 CE	Increased inputs of charcoal in maar coincide with regional population increase, but also with more arid climate. No pollen evidence of deforestation.	Bhattacharya and Byrne 2016
27	La Ladera	Tlaxcala	400–900 CE	Charcoal laminae in gully fill and corresponding erosional unconformity upslope.	Borejsza 2006:320–42, 384–99; Borejsza et al. 2011
41	Calixtlahuaca	Toluca Valley	400–1100 CE	Accelerated slope erosion expressed in erosional unconformities, gully fill, and alluvial fan deposits; some of the latter rich in charcoal.	Borejsza 2011; Borejsza et al. 2015, 2021:132–38, 255
26	Las Minas	Tlaxcala	600–1100 CE	Charcoal laminae in rapidly aggraded alluvium.	Borejsza et al. 2010, 2017

seems to have motivated the farmers to repeat the same destructive cycle in as yet untouched or perhaps partially recovered drainages.

Elsewhere, the evidence is more equivocal, usually consisting of only one member of the equation: either accelerated transfers of sediment from slopes to valley floors, or increased inputs of charcoal in alluvial or lacustrine sediment sinks. Both phenomena have plausible alternative causes, many of them unrelated to agriculture, but it is striking that the earliest hints at land degradation should come precisely from those areas—Morelos and the southeastern Basin of Mexico—where settlement surveys and excavations have identified some of the earliest sedentary villages (Grove 2000:130–33; Parsons et al. 1982; Plunket and Uruñuela 2012:6–12). I have omitted many other sedimentary records of accelerated erosion, including some from the piedmonts above Texcoco and Teotihuacan where Sanders's ideas first crystallized, either because they lack sufficient chronological control and clear links to archaeological-survey and excavation data, or because there are good reasons to doubt that swidden agriculture was the primary cause of erosion. I anticipate that future research will find additional evidence of swidden in alluvial sequences, such as those examined by Cook (1949)

FIGURE 10.2. *Archaeological evidence of various agricultural niches. (a) Las Minas: A cut-bank with charcoal laminations indicative of swidden agriculture. Six meters of alluvium rich in charcoal and redeposited soil were deposited at this location from the seventh through the eleventh centuries CE, from a catchment of only 0.5 km². (b) Superimposed terracing systems exposed by excavation at Calixtlahuaca. The lower level of stone masonry is Aztec, the upper level and the berms planted in maguey date to the nineteenth and twentieth centuries. (c) The Purrón Dam (in-between the arrows), now dated to 1100 BCE or earlier. (d) Charles Frederick examining* chinampa *stratigraphy exposed in the Quirino Mendoza utility trench. Many discoveries of Prehispanic agricultural features have been made in salvage contexts.*

before the advent of radiocarbon dating and settlement survey, or those dated by means of ceramic inclusions by Heine (1976, 1978, 1983, 2003).

Hillslope Terracing

In the Basin of Mexico, Puebla-Tlaxcala, and the Toluca Valley, actively cultivated and abandoned hillslope terraces of different morphologies are so ubiquitous that many observers find it difficult to imagine that dense Prehispanic populations could have done without them. The BMS publications repeatedly commented on how the settlement patterns of the Late Horizon (1350–1520 CE) were associated with and conditioned by hillslope terracing extending over practically the entire surveyed piedmont (Sanders et al. 1979:242–52). With house foundations of that age often visible at the modern ground surface and resting on still-extant terrace treads, there was no doubt that the terraces were at least as old. At the same time, the extremely dispersed nature of Late Horizon settlement meant there was ample tread space available for cultivation between the houses. Surveys in neighboring Puebla-Tlaxcala revealed similar patterns (Abascal Macías 1980; Borejsza 2014; García Cook 1976; Merino Carrión 1989). For earlier periods, especially those characterized by nucleated settlement, Sanders, Parsons, and Santley (1979:383) acknowledged the difficulties of using sherd scatters to date vestiges of terracing, as well as those of establishing an agricultural rather than exclusively residential purpose of terracing. They were nonetheless quite confident that for two phases (300–100 BCE and 950–1150 CE) characterized by dispersed settlement, they had identified terraces that, at the very least, supported "small kitchen gardens," as well as terraces of uncertain purpose as old as 650–300 BCE. In short, the expectation was that future excavation would confirm the considerable antiquity of terracing as a farming technique.

This has not occurred. The number of sites where hillslope terraces have been excavated is embarrassingly small (see table 10.2). There are only two pre–1200 CE entries in the table. The explorers of the fortified Epiclassic hilltop city of Xochicalco are adamant that its shallow soils were singularly ill-suited to agriculture and that its terrace treads—some of them carved into bedrock—were densely built-up with houses and other structures. At Chalcatzingo, the excavators seem to have used terrace risers and other field boundaries visible at the modern ground surface to structure their intensive survey and excavation (Grove and Cyphers Guillén 1987). According to their reconstructions, the slope was terraced at ca. 1300 BCE and each large tread was occupied by a single house surrounded by cultivation surfaces (Prindiville and Grove 1987:79–80). However, the scarcity of published stratigraphic information casts doubt on the premise that Formative terrace boundaries should have persisted at the ground surface until the present (see also Doolittle 1990:22). I do not doubt that the houses of

TABLE 10.2. Locations with Prehispanic hillslope terraces and research carried beyond the stage of regional survey

No.	Location	Area	Antiquity	Observations	Sources
35	Chalcatzingo	Morelos	1300 BCE	Relationship between modern and ancient terracing unclear. Little stratigraphic detail. Terraces primarily residential?	Grove 1987
38	Xochicalco	Morelos	600 CE	Soils unsuitable for agriculture. Terraces supported residences and public buildings.	González Crespo et al. 1995; Hirth 2000a, 2000b; Hirth and Cyphers Guillén 1988
41	Calixtlahuaca	Toluca Valley	1200 CE	261 m of slope-parallel stratigraphic sections, 55 radiometric dates. Two superimposed stages of stone-faced terracing, the first dated to 1200–1500 CE, the second post-dating 1800 CE.	Borejsza 2011; Borejsza et al. 2015, 2021; Huster and Smith 2015; Smith et al. 2013
30	Tlaxcallan	Tlaxcala	ca. 1200 CE	Mapped and surface-collected. No stratigraphic data.	Borejsza 2006:159–65, 2014; Fargher et al. 2010, 2011; García Cook and Mora López 1974; López Corral et al. 2016
25	Cihuatecpan	Basin of Mexico	ca. 1300 CE	Shallow extensive excavation privileged. Published sections show only extent of excavation units and location of house foundations. No trenches breaching risers and showing relationship of modern terraces to their Aztec predecessors. No radiometric dates.	Evans 1988, 1990, 1991, 1996, 2000b, 2005; Pérez Pérez 2006, 2013; Pérez Pérez et al. 2012

continued on next page

Formative Chalcatzingo stood on terraces, but I am not convinced that they also served agricultural purposes.

I can think of many other excavated sites in the CMSR with occupations that pre-date 1200 CE that are *presently* located on terraced slopes. Unfortunately,

TABLE 10.2.—*continued*

No.	Location	Area	Antiquity	Observations	Sources
32	La Laguna	Tlaxcala	ca. 1300 CE	107 m of slope-parallel stratigraphic sections, 49 radio-metric dates. Most excavated terraces date to the eighteenth century or later and are of the ditch-and-berm variety. Aztec-period stone-faced terraces more limited in extent.	Borejsza 2006:168–270; Borejsza and Carballo 2014; Borejsza and Rodríguez López 2014; Borejsza et al. 2008; Carballo 2014; Lesure et al. 2014; Trautmann 1981:55
31	Amoltepec	Tlaxcala	ca. 1300 CE	Mapped only. No stratigraphic data.	Borejsza 2006:154–59, 2014
18	Olopa	Basin of Mexico	ca. 1400 CE	Stratigraphy of ter-race fills examined in erosional pedestals. No controlled excava-tion. One radiometric date.	Cordova 1997:183–227; Cordova and Parsons 1997; Parsons 1971:132–33
23	Cerro Gordo South Slope	Basin of Mexico	ca. 1400 CE	Mapped in detail. No stratigraphic data.	Evans 1985, 2000a
39	Cuexcomate	Morelos	ca. 1400 CE	12 m of slope-parallel stratigraphic sections exposed. No radio-metric dates. Several cross-channel ter-races excavated and radiocarbon-dated at Cuexcomate and nearby Capilco.	Price and Smith 1992; Smith 1992, 2014; Smith and Doershuk 1991; Smith and Price 1994

most archaeologists privilege extensive over stratigraphic excavation, place units in the middle of terrace treads, and studiously avoid the breaching of terrace ris-ers and removal of trees and perennial crops growing along them, thus missing most opportunities to ascertain the existence and morphology of *ancient* terrac-ing, and its relationship to the terracing expressed at the modern ground surface.

This leaves us with no excavated *agricultural* terrace dated to earlier than 1200 CE. The pattern cannot be blamed on an excavation bias favoring Aztec-period occupations. The two largest samples of excavated terraces come from multi-component sites, Calixtlahuaca (see figure 10.2b) and La Laguna, where agriculture and habitation have a much longer history. La Laguna's most con-spicuous occupations date in fact to the Formative and both the modern ground surface and the excavated terrace fills are dominated by artifacts of that period.

Small areas of the slope were leveled for habitation in the Formative. The terrace morphology perceptible at the modern ground surface, however, largely post-dates 1700 CE, with remnants of Aztec-period terraces preserved in only one circumscribed portion of the site. The excavations teach us that, where terraces are still in cultivation (Calixtlahuaca, Cihuatecpan, La Laguna, Amoltepec), their surface morphology is a highly unreliable guide to what the slope may have looked like in the Aztec period. Natural decay and intentional destruction, followed by the re-shaping of treads and refurbishment of stone walls in the past five hundred years must be assumed *unless* excavation proves otherwise.

The ethnographic component of the BMS has consecrated an important distinction between two contrasting morphologies of terrace risers: stone walls as opposed to ditches paired with earthen berms planted in maguey. The archaeological and geographical literature refers to the latter morphology by the terms *bancal*, *zanja-bordo*, or *metepantle* and correctly associates it with more moderate reductions of slope gradient (LaFevor 2014; Patrick 1977; West 1970; Whitmore and Turner 2001:136–43). All precisely mapped or excavated Aztec-period terraces turn out to be of the stone-faced variety and have substantially flattened treads. This does not seem to be a preservation bias, as the infilled ditches have a relatively high preservation potential; several post–1700 CE specimens have been excavated at La Laguna. In an independent study of archival sources, Skopyk (2010, 2017) demonstrated that, in Tlaxcala at least, *metepantles* boomed only from the seventeenth century onward. Both the archaeological and archival findings chime with other comments in the literature (e.g., Kaerger 1986:241–44, 264–65) to suggest that the development of *metepantles* was powerfully aided by the introduction of the plow and the ease of transporting pulque to urban markets on muleback and later by train. I am thus beginning to doubt whether contoured ridges planted in maguey were a common sight in the Prehispanic countryside.

Another important insight of the excavations is that Aztec terrace fills usually rest on top of erosional unconformities that run through indurated soil B or C horizons. This means that, rather than gradually intensifying prior techniques of farming slopes, terrace builders created a completely new agricultural niche amid eroded badlands. The Late Horizon expansion onto "marginal" land (Sanders et al. 1979:177), often achieved by granting property rights to non-Nahuatl speaking minorities displaced by warfare (Borejsza 2006:98, 371–74, 392, 427–28; Borejsza et al. 2017:56; 2021:252–56; Evans 2001), was in many places an expansion onto land that had been rendered near-useless by agricultural activity in the previous 2,000 years. In other words, Sanders was essentially correct in viewing the introduction of terracing as remediation of the damage wrought by swidden, but he underestimated the time lag after which it had occurred.

Canal Irrigation

Besides Boserup, the other and earlier source of theoretical inspiration for the BMS were the ideas of Wittfogel (1957, 1972) regarding irrigation as a catalyst in the development of state-level social organization. Their ultimate origin lay in a few embryonic opinions expressed by Marx, and their lasting popularity in Mexico was in no small measure due to the Marxist sympathies of a number of anthropologists who can be credited with the earliest studies of Prehispanic irrigation (Friedman 1987; González Jácome 2007; Palerm 1969–70; Rojas Rabiela 1991). The early expectation was therefore that irrigation and other forms of "hydraulic" agriculture flourished concurrently with the rise of Teotihuacan, the first prominent and undisputed state in the CMSR. The shift in settlement patterns toward the floor of the Teotihuacan Valley near the end of the Formative fueled that expectation. By the late 1970s, however, direct evidence of Formative irrigation in the valley was limited to a small floodwater system at Otumba, far upstream from the ancient city (see table 10.3). Conversely, a re-routed stream and a set of canals dated to 900 BCE discovered at Santa Clara Coatitlan seemed precocious and without obvious consequences in stimulating greater social complexity. Members of the BMS recognized that it did not fit their prior theories and asked whether small irrigation systems could have developed early in the more arid parts of the Basin to allay the risk of losing the maize crop to drought, rather than as an expression of agricultural intensification in response to population pressure (Nichols 1987b, 1989; Sanders and Nichols 1988; Sanders et al. 1979:384). It also provided fodder to detractors of the BMS keen on demonstrating the primacy of social over demographic pressures (Feinman and Nicholas 1989; responses to Sanders and Nichols 1988).

The task of assessing the antiquity and development of canal irrigation in the light of more recent discoveries is made easy by the pan-Mexican and pan-Mesoamerican reviews by Doolittle (1990, 2006b) and Neely (2005, in press), which critically evaluate nearly all the literature listed in table 10.3. It is by now clear that the Santa Clara canals were by no means a precocious anomaly. New finds and the radiometric dating of previously known features converge on 1000 BCE as the approximate date at which irrigation systems flourished in several locations across the highlands of Western Mesoamerica. Their distribution in time and space decisively disassociates the origins of irrigation from those of the state, suggesting that even the largest and most complex water management systems, such as those of the Tehuacan Valley, grew out of incremental and uncoordinated efforts by families or small communities of Formative farmers. In this respect, Mesoamerica adds to the worldwide archaeological falsification of Wittfogel's "hydraulic hypothesis" (e.g., Billman 2002; Hunt 1988; Kirch 1994).

The available data do not yet allow us to reject any of the scenarios of the origins of irrigation discussed by Doolittle (1990:136–43). New descriptions of

TABLE 10.3. Locations with Prehispanic irrigation canals and research carried beyond the stage of regional survey. All locations presented and analyzed by Doolittle (1990, 2006b) or Neely (2005, in press).

No.	Location	Area	Antiquity	Observations	Sources
46	Teopante-cuanitlan	Middle Balsas	ca. 1200 BCE	Dam and stone-lined canal. No radiometric dates. Age of dam and agricultural purpose of canal in dispute.	Martínez Donjuán 1986, 1994; Niederberger 1996
45	Arroyo Lencho Diego	Tehuacan Valley	1100 BCE	A complex of superimposed prehistoric dams, fields, and habitation areas. One of 10 radiometric dates suggests origins in 3rd millennium BCE. The Purrón Dam grew in the Formative to become the largest known water management feature in Mesoamerica. Functioning and association with irrigation not entirely clear, as only preserved canal bypasses dam and seems to be Classic in age. No preserved canals or prehistoric fields downstream of dam.	Aiuvalasit et al. 2010; Caran and Neely 2006; Neely 2005, 2016; Neely and Castellón Huerta 2014; Neely et al. 2015; Spencer 1979; Woodbury and Neely 1972
36	Las Estacas	Morelos	1000 BCE	Infilled canal exposed in river cutbank downstream of major spring. One radiocarbon date. Permanent irrigation from spring-fed perennial stream.	Borejsza et al. 2014a:287–89; Morett Alatorre et al. 2000; Nichols et al. 2006
16	Santa Clara Coatitlan	Basin of Mexico	900 BCE	Multiple primary and secondary canals buried within rapidly aggraded barranca floodplain. Floodwater irrigation. No radiometric dates.	Nichols 1982; Sanders and Santley 1977
44	Tehuacan	Tehuacan Valley	700 BCE	Spring-fed canals precipitated in travertine. Five "systems" mapped in detail in the valley. Seven published radiocarbon dates come from those near the city of Tehuacan and San Marcos Necoxtla. Other more cursorily mentioned dates could push antiquity to 2nd or 3rd millennium BCE.	Caran and Neely 2006; Neely 2001, 2005, 2016; Neely and Castellón Huerta 2003, 2014; Smith 1965; Spencer 1979; Winsborough et al. 1996; Woodbury and Neely 1972
37	Ticumán	Morelos	400 BCE	Multiple canals buried within the floodplain of the Yautepec River, some precipitated in travertine. Placed by 11 radiocarbon dates and artifact inclusions in the Formative, Classic, Epiclassic, and Colonial periods. Permanent irrigation from perennial river or springs.	Borejsza et al. 2014a:287–89; Frederick et al. 2008; Morett Alatorre et al. 1999, 2000; Nichols et al. 2006
24	Otumba	Basin of Mexico	300 BCE	Floodwater irrigation canals, rebuilt and expanded until the Late Aztec period.	Charlton 1977, 1978, 1979a, 1979b, 1990

continued on next page

TABLE 10.2.—continued

No.	Location	Area	Antiquity	Observations	Sources
12	Cuicuilco	Basin of Mexico	ca. 300 BCE	Canals buried under lava, of indubitable antiquity, but never studied in detail. Controversies regarding eruption date may mean canals are a few centuries younger than 300 BCE.	Cordova et al. 1994; González et al. 2000; Lugo Hubp et al. 2001; Palerm 1961; Siebe 2000; Urrutia Fucugauchi 1996
33	Tetimpa	Valley of Puebla	1 CE	Furrowed fields buried under pumice from an eruption of Popocatepetl volcano. The furrows functioned to distribute water, but its ultimate source (irrigation canals as opposed to direct rainfall) is not entirely clear. The date is that of the eruption, the furrows may have been in existence earlier. A second set of furrows buried by Epiclassic eruption.	Hirth 2013; López Corral 2000, 2006; Plunket and Uruñuela 1998a, 1998b, 2000, 2005:98–99, 2008; Seele 1973
22	Barrio Oaxaqueño	Basin of Mexico	100 CE	Secondary floodwater canals buried by Classic residential architecture.	Nichols et al. 1991
21	Tlajinga	Basin of Mexico	300 CE?	Straightened barranca reaches and floodwater irrigation canals of at least late Aztec antiquity. Dating and inferring the function of the different constituents of the system difficult because of shallow burial.	Nichols 1987a, 1988
20	Maravilla	Basin of Mexico	800 CE?	Rerouted floodwater channel reach and irrigation canal.	Armillas et al. 1956; Millon 1957
42	Tula	Mezquital?	1100 CE?	A set of parallel furrows suggesting an irrigated field.	Peña Castillo and Rodríguez 1976
15	Chapultepec	Basin of Mexico	1400 CE	Aqueduct carrying water from springs, over a dike in Lake Texcoco, and to urban houses, gardens, and chinampas.	Braniff and Cervantes 1966, 1967; Bribiesca Castrejón 1958
17	Tezcotzingo	Basin of Mexico	1300 CE?	Aqueduct several kilometers in length, carrying water to royal retreat equipped with stone-lined reservoirs. Relationship to nearby terraces and remains of Formative and later settlement unclear. Mapped in detail, never excavated.	Cordova 1997:169–76; Hicks 2001; Medina 1997; Palerm and Wolf 1961; Parsons 1971; Wolf and Palerm 1955

the complex of agricultural features along Arroyo Lencho Diego (Aiuvalasit et al. 2010; Neely et al. 2015) still do not provide clear evidence that the original and principal function of the dams was to impound water to be conveyed by canals to fields farther downstream. An alternative hypothesis would be that the complex started out as a series of cross-channel terraces built to create cultivable surfaces with high water tables *upstream* of the obstruction and only later coalesced into the monumental feature known as the Purrón Dam (see figure 10.2c). The cross-channel terrace is a niche very different from the hillslope terraces discussed above, not only in its functioning but also its history (Pérez Rodríguez and Anderson 2013; Rogé and Astier 2015; Spores 1969). New evidence collected only some 50 kilometers south of the CMSR places their antiquity at 1700 BCE (Leigh et al. 2013), making them coeval with the first sedentary villagers. This throws a favorable light on theories viewing the impoundment of water and digging of canals as a historical outgrowth of certain forms of floodwater farming (Doolittle 1990:140–42).

The Formative-age features listed in table 10.3 also seem to dispel any notion of an orderly progression from small to large features, and from floodwater to permanent irrigation. Among the earliest dated canals are examples that drew water from large permanent rivers and large-volume springs (Las Estacas, Tehuacan-Necoxtla, Ticuman), as well as ephemeral streams both small and large (Santa Clara and perhaps Arroyo Lencho Diego). Many early canals have rather large cross-sectional areas. In irrigation, larger does not necessarily mean more advanced—well-engineered smaller canals can be more efficient at preventing water loss in transit and reducing the velocity of flow. Coarse-textured fills reported for several early canals suggest that they were still mimicking the morphology of natural stream channels. To compound untested hypotheses regarding the Purrón Dam, I wonder whether it was not a feature that "grew out of control" as farmers tried to correct problems that accrued in the system due to temporary fixes introduced by their predecessors, along the lines described—in the general, not the specific case—by Doolittle (1990:150–54). The dam would end up impounding water on a scale that nobody had originally planned for, by gravity rather than by virtue of technologically more sophisticated solutions (see Doolittle 1990:159–61).

The entries in table 10.3 give chronological preeminence to the southern, lower-altitude belt of the CMSR, in keeping with the idea that the first farmers came from that direction, with those from Morelos, for example, colonizing the Basin of Mexico. There is no pattern, however, associating early irrigation with greater risk of crop loss to drought, as the entries range from the arid Tehuacan Valley to areas of Morelos and Guerrero receiving relatively abundant rainfall.

The characteristics of later systems make clear that, despite the truly "formative" nature of the Formative as far as irrigation is concerned, farmers had not mastered all aspects of the technique by the end of this period, and the irrigation niche continued to expand and evolve, as originally emphasized by Doolittle (1990). Stratigraphically and radiometrically constrained studies of later Prehispanic canals are few, but the features in operation at Conquest—known mostly through survey and archival research—reveal that irrigation had changed in both quantitative and qualitative ways, incorporating technological solutions previously unknown or not used in agriculture, such as stone masonry, stuccoed surfaces, aqueducts and, perhaps, clay pipes. This suggests that, as one begins to focus on the detail of one of the major categories of agricultural niche—the others have yet to receive a book-length treatment—there is indeed room for "invention," a notion that jars with the emphasis that New Archaeology put on the primacy of process over historical contingency.

Wetland Fields (*Chinampas*)

The wetland fields known as *chinampas* are recognized as the pinnacle of Prehispanic agricultural achievement, whether measured by productivity, technological sophistication, or modern concepts of "sustainability." Their surviving remnants in Lake Xochimilco have been celebrated for their aesthetic qualities, too, and are on the UNESCO world heritage list. Their antiquity role in Tenochtitlan's food supply were among the research priorities of the BMS, which consequently recognized former lakebeds as zones to be surveyed. Archaeologists were aware that the *chinampa* zone had shrunk since the Colonial period (Armillas 1971) and were therefore attuned to the possibility of discovering *chinampas* in areas where none remained in cultivation.

We can abstract a three-stage model of *chinampa* development from BMS publications. Before the Epiclassic, it was thought, a few lakebed and lakeshore villages had probably experimented with small-scale wetland agriculture (Armillas 1971:657–58; Sanders 1976:135–36). Some project members also posited the existence of Classic-period *chinampas* on the floodplain downstream from historic Teotihuacan, on the basis of the kind of agriculture practiced there in the mid-twentieth century, a peak in sedge in an undated pollen diagram, and representations of a paradisiacal watery landscape in the Tepantitla murals (Sanders 1965:44–45, 159–60, figure 16). In a second stage, beginning in the Epiclassic (750–950 CE), the existence of *chinampas* was considered almost certain, especially in view of dense settlement on Xico Island, thought unsustainable without wetland agriculture (Parsons et al. 1985:92; Sanders et al. 1979:281). In the third stage, corresponding to the Late Horizon, the evidence for a vast *chinampa* landscape stretching from Lake Chalco to the very center of Tenochtitlan was incontrovertible, on the basis of archaeological explorations and written testimony.

Outside the Basin of Mexico, wetland management failed to make an impression on early Spanish chroniclers, but a more involved examination of archival sources and ethnographic research testify to the feasibility and former importance of wetland agriculture on the plains bordering the Zahuapan and Atoyac rivers (González Jácome 1999, 2008; Trautmann 1973, 1981:55–59; Wilken 1967, 1969, 1987). The fields documented there, however, are different from modern *chinampas* in that they are "drained" rather than "raised," a distinction with implications for both farming technique and the expected stratigraphic record. There is also documentary evidence of the Conquest-era cultivation of wetlands along the Lerma River and the large shallow lakes in its headwaters (Albores Zárate 1998; Archivo General de la Nación 1549–1586).

Since 1979, several academic projects have set themselves the goal of searching for pre-Aztec wetland fields, and more broadly of exploring prehistoric subsistence options in the wetlands of the Basin of Mexico (in addition to table 10.4, McClung et al. 1986; Parsons 2001, 2006; Serra Puche 1988), Tlaxcala (Lesure et al. 2006; Lesure 2014a; Serra Puche 1998; Serra Puche and Lazcano Arce 2008, 2011), and the Toluca Valley (Sugiura Yamamoto 2009; Sugiura Yamamoto et al. 1983, 1994, 1998). In the Basin, they were joined by a flurry of salvage excavations. The efforts outside the Basin have so far failed to produce a shred of stratigraphically constrained evidence of Prehispanic wetland cultivation. The only possible exception are the Amalucan canals, initially thought to have served irrigation, but subsequently re-interpreted (Doolittle 1990:56–7) in terms bringing them closer to the drained fields known ethnographically from nearby Tlaxcala. Excavations in the Toluca Valley (Sugiura Yamamoto 2009) and at Terremote-Tlaltenco in the Basin of Mexico (Serra Puche 1988) revealed that their respectively Classic- and Formative-period inhabitants had mastered the technology required to raise large permanent platforms in lake waters. They did not translate that know-how into raising cultivation beds, however, with both communities specializing in the exploitation of wild wetland resources instead.

Excavations in the Basin have confirmed the ubiquity of *chinampas* (see table 10.4; figure 10.2d). Of the five interconnected lakes, only Zumpango remains without archaeological evidence of *chinampas*. Excavations documented the tremendous amount of earth moved in Prehispanic times by canoe, for *chinampa* construction, as architectural fill, and in the form of adobe brick. All three involved the inadvertent redeposition of older ceramic sherds. Some of the small pre-Aztec "hamlets" identified on the lakebed and originally thought to have cultivated *chinampas* may therefore be accidental sherd scatters created by Aztec farmers or builders (Parsons et al. 1985:92). Intense development and salvage excavations at Xico (Lechuga García and Rivas Castro 1994; Lechuga García et al. 1995; Pulido Méndez 1993; Pulido Méndez and Ortuño Cos 1994) did not bring to light any Epiclassic *chinampas*.

While ubiquitous, *chinampas* are not particularly old. The dates of initial construction listed in table 10.4 are my conservative estimates. They are based

TABLE 10.4. Locations with Prehispanic wetland fields and research carried beyond the stage of regional survey

No.	Location	Area	Antiquity	Observations	Sources
34	Amalucan	Puebla	ca. 300 BCE	Field system interpreted by discoverer as involving both canal irrigation and drainage. Re-interpreted (Doolittle 1990:54–7) as drained wetland fields. Eight radiocarbon dates spanning Formative and Classic.	Fowler 1969, 1987
5	Acatla	Basin of Mexico	ca. 1100 CE	Lake Xochimilco. Canal and *chinampas* exposed by extensive excavation, associated with Aztec I pottery.	Ávila López 1998, 2006
13	Mexicaltzingo	Basin of Mexico	ca. 1100 CE	Lake Texcoco. Multiple *chinampas* exposed by extensive excavation, constructed by dredging and mounding, frequently over a tephra bed.	Ávila López 2006
19	Xaltocan	Basin of Mexico	ca. 1200 CE	Lake Xaltocan. Multiple excavation units exposing *chinampas*. Eleven radiocarbon dates. Fields raised by dredging and mounding. The system relied on input of fresh water by means of irrigation canals and was abandoned in the 15th century.	Brumfiel and Frederick 1992; Frederick et al. 2005; McClung and Martínez Yrizar 2005; Morehart 2010, 2012, 2014, 2016, 2018; Morehart and Eisenberg 2010; Morehart and Frederick 2014; Nichols and Frederick 1993
10	Ayotzingo	Basin of Mexico	1200 CE	Lake Chalco. Two *chinampa* beds separated by canal, exposed in test trench. Four radiocarbon dates. Sediment imported from elsewhere to raise fields.	Frederick 1997, 2007; Frederick and Cordova 2019; Frederick et al. 2000

continued on next page

mostly on time-diagnostic sherds reported by the authors, as only Xaltocan and Ayotzingo can boast a number of radiocarbon dates commensurate with the number of fields that were exposed. Ávila López (2006) places the origins of *chinampas* in the southern Basin as early as 900–1000 CE, but he does so mostly on the basis of Aztec I sherds, which span the 900–1250 CE interval (Brumfiel 2005; Morehart and Frederick 2014:539; Parsons et al. 1996) and, strictly speaking,

TABLE 10.4.—*continued*

No.	Location	Area	Antiquity	Observations	Sources
14	Iztapalapa	Basin of Mexico	ca. 1300 CE	Lake Texcoco. Multiple *chinampas* exposed by extensive excavation, constructed by dredging and mounding.	Ávila López 1991, 1995, 2006
4	Quirino Mendoza	Basin of Mexico	ca. 1300 CE	Lake Xochimilco. Several *chinampas* exposed by utility trench. Three radiocarbon dates. Four construction phases, changing from ditching to importation of non-local sediment.	Frederick et al. 2002, ca. 2003, 2007
2	El Japón	Basin of Mexico	ca. 1300 CE	Lake Xochimilco. Multiple *chinampas* exposed by extensive excavation, some buried under Late Aztec cemetery.	Acosta Ochoa et al. 2017; Ávila López 1995; Parsons et al. 1982:228–29, 1985; this volume
1	Ejido Xochimilco	Basin of Mexico	ca. 1400 CE	Lake Xochimilco. Multiple *chinampas* exposed by extensive excavation, constructed by gradual additions of lake mud and organic amendments.	Serra Puche 1994
3	Acuexcomatl	Basin of Mexico	ca. 1400 CE	Lake Xochimilco. Multiple *chinampas* exposed by extensive excavation, constructed by dredging and mounding over a diatomite bed.	Ávila López 1998, 2006
9	Mixquic	Basin of Mexico	ca. 1400 CE	Lake Chalco. Twenty *chinampas* exposed in modern drainage ditch. 2-m-long segment studied in detail, constructed by gradual additions of lake mud and organic amendments.	Parsons et al. 1985
8	Ch-LT-77	Basin of Mexico	ca. 1400 CE	Lake Chalco. *Chinampa* exposed in 2 m × 2 m test pit.	Parsons et al. 1985
6	Ch-Az-236	Basin of Mexico	ca. 1400 CE	Lake Chalco. Burrowed and fragmentarily exposed *chinampa* in 2 m × 2 m test pit.	Parsons et al. 1985
7	Besana de San Martín	Basin of Mexico	?	Lake Chalco. Several *chinampa* beds exposed in test trench. Heavily burrowed.	Frederick et al. ca. 2003

provide only a *terminus post quem* for *chinampa* construction. Morehart and Frederick are more circumspect regarding *chinampa* beginnings at Xaltocan, considering a pre–1150 CE date possible, but placing the most conspicuous expansion between 1250 and 1350 CE. It is my impression therefore that *chinampas* became common only after 1200 CE. Most scholars agree, moreover, that *chinampa* construction received a substantial boost from the large-scale waterworks undertaken by Aztec emperors from the 1430s onward (e.g., Ávila López 2006; Parsons 1976).

Excavations also reveal the limitations of ethnographic and historical analogies in reconstructing aspects of construction technique, morphology, crop choice, cultivation, maintenance, and abandonment. Both Ávila López (2006) and Frederick (2007) comment extensively on the mismatch between the "standard" account of raising the beds in shallow water by layered additions of lake mud and vegetation mats, and the much more diverse archaeological reality, which included the dredging of canals at low lake stands, the judicious placement of planting beds over porous substrates such as diatomite or tephra, and the importation of non-local sediment. The finely bedded *chinampas* seem to appear late in the sequence. The archaeological *chinampas* of Prehispanic age are far narrower on average than their Colonial or ethnographic counterparts. Echoing my comment on maguey-planted berms in terracing, Frederick (2007) begins to doubt whether the Prehispanic *chinampa* landscape had room for the willows (*ahuejotes*) that now line most field edges. A careful reading of Ávila López's (2006) account of the distribution of his four types of *chinampas* in time and space suggests that he, too, views the willow-less models as the Prehispanic norm.

The final insight of *chinampa* excavations is the renewed emphasis on the challenges of maintaining an adequate distance between cultivation surface and water level. A residential platform could be raised well above the highest remembered lake stand; in the case of a cultivation surface, this approach would have been counterproductive. The productivity of *chinampas* came at the cost of vulnerability to (1) fluctuations in lake levels; (2) incursions of saltwater from Lake Texcoco; (3) excessive upward growth due to the frequent addition of mud and green manure; (4) salinization of stable cultivation surfaces; (5) siltation of canals due to the decay or intentional scraping of *chinampas*; or (6) burial of lake-edge fields and canals by alluvium. The last problem is evident, for example, in the three reconstruction stages of the Quirino Mendoza fields. The first problem was apparently dealt with in the south by means of dikes separating lakes Chalco, Xochimilco, and Texcoco into different compartments. With the exception of the historically attested causeways leading into Tenochtitlan, however, the archaeological vestiges of such dikes, hypothesized by Parsons and colleagues (1985:88, 90), have yet to be located. The construction of a small planting bed in the lake was perhaps within the ken of a Formative farmer, but the hydraulic works required to make *chinampa* agriculture viable had to wait for state-sponsored Aztec engineers.

In the north, the problem of fluctuating lake levels was controlled by channeling water from the Chiconautla springs or from the Cuautitlan River, into Lake Xaltocan. The re-routing of the river for irrigation in the fifteenth century meant the demise of the *chinampas* of Xaltocan and may have been a deliberate political act. It is here that the histories of different agricultural niches meet. In many locations there may be difficult tradeoffs between irrigation and wetland agriculture. Accelerated sedimentary inputs into many lakes provoked by slope cultivation may have had deleterious effects at the lake edge, as in the Quirino Mendoza example. Elsewhere, erosion may have raised lakebeds to the point where *chinampa* construction became practicable. This long-term enabling effect of slope swiddening and erosion (see Kirch 1994) should perhaps be entertained as a hypothesis to be tested in the CMSR. Conversely, the still unexcavated and undated cross-channel terraces of the Xochimilco piedmont, which Armillas (1987) guessed to be Aztec, may have reduced or delayed the discharge of water and sediment into the *chinampa* zone.

CONCLUSIONS: THE LOGIC OF AGRICULTURAL NICHE CONSTRUCTION

On- and off-site excavations of the last forty years have forced significant shifts in our appreciation of the antiquity of different archaeological niches with respect to the survey-based synthesis of Sanders, Parsons, and Santley (1979). We now have archaeological confirmation of swiddening and a drastic loss of cultivable acreage in the CMSR from at least 1000 BCE to at least 1000 CE. Irrigation turns out to be more ancient and its earliest forms more sophisticated than thought in 1979. The earliest dates cluster around 1000 BCE. On the other hand, widespread hillslope terracing and raised-field agriculture in wetlands turn out to be much later than previously thought (see also McClung 2015:384). Both seem to be singular achievements of the Aztec period, largely post-dating 1200 CE.

Almost any aspect of this synthesis can of course be countered by saying that absence of evidence is not evidence of absence, and that earlier examples of every type of agricultural niche still await discovery. This is of course true of almost any category of archaeological evidence, but—taking the BMS as a shining example—it should not prevent us from formulating theories that future generations will have the opportunity to pick apart. The critical mass of research now available in the Basin of Mexico and the severe limitations to future exploration make it the area of the CMSR where a complete revision of the proposed sequence of niche construction seems unlikely. Puebla-Tlaxcala, Morelos, and the Tehuacan Valley are also relatively well explored, though they no doubt still hold many surprises. The Oriental Basin, the Toluca Valley, and the hot country of the Upper to Middle Balsas (see figure 10.1) are badly neglected areas where the possible scenarios are still wide open. The omission of the latter area is of particular concern, because the biogeography of teosinte (Sánchez González et al. 2018), lake-based palaeoenvironmental proxies (Piperno et al. 2007), and a host of agro-ecological considerations suggest that both maize and the earliest farmers came from that direction.

It is by now clear that Boserupian intensification in response to demographic growth cannot alone explain the order of agricultural niche construction in the Basin of Mexico, let alone the entire CMSR. Following Nichols's (1987b) lead, it will be important to explore the tradeoffs between energy efficiency (ratios of yield to labor inputs) and risk in different agricultural niches, distinguishing between variance-adverse and variance-prone risk management strategies (see Mabry 2005:135). Both energetic and risk considerations, however, still leave us in the realm of explanations that emphasize synchronic ecological processes to the almost complete exclusion of diachronic contingency. The most convincing explanations of agricultural change integrate both process and history (Kirch 1994:321–23) and several observations made above point to the need to devote more thought to historical trajectories.

The long-term limiting and enabling impacts of agricultural land degradation are the most obvious example. It seems perilous to attempt to explain the appearance of terraces or wetland fields in any particular drainage at 1200 CE in terms of timeless ecological choice, without giving thought to the impact of the preceding two or three millennia of agricultural activity on soil fertility, hydrology, and the sediment budgets between slopes and valley floors. In other words, projects that wish to understand Prehispanic agriculture while focusing narrowly on one or two ceramic phases are probably ill-advised.

Another example is the cumulative nature of agro-technological knowledge emphasized by Doolittle (1990:3) and summarized by his quote of Sauer's dictum that "ideas must build upon ideas." Formative and Classic-period villagers built platforms for habitation by leveling sloping land or mounding earth on a lakebed, yet did not adapt that technology for agricultural purposes. Some may take this as an indication that there was a latent pool of "traditional" technological know-how waiting for the right demographic or social pressures. The mentioned platforms, however, are circumscribed in time and space, and it seems justified to ask whether there is a historical link between them and later agricultural terraces and *chinampas*. The great lacunae in the archaeological record aside, we have probably not paid sufficient attention to the technological intricacies and labor costs of transferring these technologies from house to field.

Perhaps we also exaggerate the degree to which ecology constrained pre-industrial agriculture, and underestimate migrant farmers' determination to replicate the agricultural niches of their original homeland, even when this went against the laws of minimum effort or came at the expense of lasting land degradation. Iberian immigrants to Colonial Mexico are commonly accused of or celebrated for such stubbornness in trying to re-create Mediterranean agricultural niches (Butzer 1988, 1991, 1992, 1996; Butzer and Butzer 1995; Melville 1994), while Prehispanic farmers are denied similar instincts and generally credited with a perfect understanding of the most "appropriate" ecological and economic choices and their long-term ramifications. I would like to speculate that there are at least two major junctures in the agricultural history of the CMSR at which migration and tradition played an important role, in one case negative, in the other largely positive.

The origins of agriculture and sedentism in the northern belt of the CMSR seem to obey the logic of village fissioning and gradual migration of farmers between ca. 1700 and 900 BCE, rather than the adoption of new lifeways by autochthonous foragers (Lesure 2008, 2014b; Lesure et al. 2006; Parsons et al. 1982:365–66; Plunket and Uruñuela 2012:10). The homeland of these farmers seems to have been located in southwestern Puebla, Morelos, and Guerrero, areas where swiddening was followed by relatively rapid regeneration of tropical deciduous forest. It is conceivable that these farmers introduced swidden, without much adaptation, to the pine-oak woodland belt with its more erodible pyroclastic substrates.

At the second juncture, between ca. 900 and 1200 CE, waves of migrants from the arid northern frontier of Mesoamerica streamed into the same areas. Recent research has debunked the myth of these being savage hunter-gatherer groups (Beekman and Christensen 2003; Braniff 2000; Faugère 2007). They were more likely people who had farmed for many generations in environments requiring greater labor inputs and more risk taking than was the norm in the CMSR. Some of these places, in the Bajío, the "Gran Tunal," or southern Zacatecas, were perhaps more extreme versions of Parsons's (2010) "pastoral niche," where water- and soil-conserving farming techniques were used to grow not only maize, but also amaranths and a range of xerophytic plants (e.g., Nelson 1992; Trombold and Israde Alcántara 2005). The Aztec-period agricultural florescence, which included the reclamation of *tepetates* by means of terracing, the development of *chinampa* agriculture, and significant advancements in irrigation technology, followed in the wake of these migrations. Though no doubt powerfully driven by demographic growth and some involvement of state institutions, this florescence may have benefited from the technological know-how and cultural norms of people accustomed to farming much closer to the economic margin.

The final set of considerations sorely lacking from most explanations offered to date brings us back to the definition of an agricultural niche. It concerns its biotic aspects, that is, the suite of crops optimal for a swiddened slope or the water-saturated soil of a *chinampa*. We know little about the crop complexes associated with each niche in Prehispanic times, and next to nothing about the historical trajectories of their selection and dispersal. The long shadow cast by the spectacular Archaic-period finds in the dry caves of Tehuacan and Oaxaca (Byers and MacNeish 1967–75; Flannery 1986) apparently leads many researchers to assume that the evolution of Mesoamerican cultivars was essentially complete on the threshold of the Formative. Part of the problem seems to lie in the fact that the selection of crops appropriate for different agricultural niches often operates at the infraspecific level, very difficult to document in fragmentary and usually charred plant remains. The classification system and challenges charted out by Benz (1994a, 1994b; 1999) for the archaeobotanical recovery and identification of different race complexes of maize have failed to resonate among younger researchers. Throughout Western Mesoamerica, flotation is still seen as a costly whim by most field archaeologists and actively publishing scholars devoted full-time to archaeobotany can be counted on the fingers of one hand.

And yet it is the appearance of certain crop varieties at certain points in time that may hold some of the keys to understanding the order of agricultural niche construction. The date of ca. 1000 BCE mentioned above in connection with the oldest irrigation systems in the highlands, for example, is also that proposed recently for the shift from mixed subsistence systems exploiting a variety of wild resources, to full dependence on maize as a staple in the lowlands (Arnold 2009; Cyphers et al. 2013; Rosenswig 2006; Webster 2011). We may therefore ask whether, instead of some notional threshold in maize cob size and yield according to Kirkby's (1973) endlessly misapplied curve, the date of 1000 BCE marks the appearance of a race of maize better adapted to the application of irrigation waters. Similarly, the development of frost-resistant conical cobs (see McClung 1977), may have been a pre-requisite for the development of the more frost-exposed agricultural niches of the northern belt of the CMSR. Finally, to return to one of the concerns already raised by Sanders, Parsons, and Santley (1979:233–36, 290, 375–76), we need to abandon the fixation on the ecology of maize as the only measure of agricultural potential and success, and seek to understand both the ecological preferences and the historical origins of staples such as beans, amaranth, and *chia*, whose importance on the eve of Conquest is widely attested in written sources.

Acknowledgments. I wish to single out Charles Frederick and Luis Morett Alatorre as my physical and intellectual guides to countless agricultural niches spread throughout the Central Mexican Symbiotic Region over the past twenty years. Arthur Joyce, Richard Lesure, Emily McClung, James Neely, and Michael Smith provided other crucial opportunities to be in the field or discuss Mesoamerican agriculture.

REFERENCES

Abascal Macías, Rafae. 1980. "Riego y control de agua en los cultivos prehispánicos de Tlaxcala." *Revista mexicana de estudios antropológicos* 26:115–67.

Acosta Ochoa, Guillermo, Emily McClung, Gerardo Jiménez, and Víctor Hugo García. 2017. "El empleo de fotogrametría mediante vehículos aéreos no tripulados (VANT / dron) como herramienta de evaluación del patrimonio en riesgo: Chinampas arqueológicas de Xochimilco." *Revista española de antropología americana* 47:185–97.

Aiuvalasit, Michael J., James A. Neely, and Mark D. Bateman. 2010. "New Radiometric Dating of Water Management Features at the Prehistoric Purrón Dam Complex, Tehuacán Valley, Puebla, México." *Journal of Archaeological Science* 37:1207–13.

Albores Zárate, Beatriz. 1998. *Origen pre-mexica de las chinampas de la zona lacustre del Alto Lerma mexiquense.* Colegio Mexiquense, Zinacantepec.

Archivo General de la Nación 1549–1586. Hospital de Jesús, leg. 413, exp. 3 AGN, Mexico City.

Armillas, Pedro. 1949. "Notas sobre sistemas de cultivo en Mesoamérica: Cultivos de riego y humedad en la Cuenca del Río Balsas." *Anales del Instituto Nacional de Antropología e Historia* 3:85–113.

Armillas, Pedro. 1971. "Gardens on Swamps." *Science* 174:653–61.

Armillas, Pedro. 1987. "El paisaje agrario azteca." In *La aventura intelectual de Pedro Armillas*, edited by José Luis Rojas, 66–107. Colegio de Michoacán, Zamora.

Armillas, Pedro, Ángel Palerm, and Eric R. Wolf. 1956. "A Small Irrigation System in the Valley of Teotihuacan." *American Antiquity* 21:396–99.

Arnold, Philip J. III. 2009. "Settlement and Subsistence among the Early Formative Gulf Olmec." *Journal of Anthropological Archaeology* 28:397–411.

Ávila López, Raúl. 1991. *Chinampas de Iztapalapa, D.F.* Instituto Nacional de Antropología e Historia, Mexico City.

Ávila López, Raúl. 1995. "Excavaciones arqueológicas en San Gregorio Atlapulco, Xochimilco." Report on file at the Archivo Técnico, Instituto Nacional de Antropología e Historia.

Ávila López, Raúl. 1998. "Investigaciones del Proyecto Arqueológico San Luis Tlaxialtemalco, 6 vols." Report on file at the Archivo Técnico, Instituto Nacional de Antropología e Historia.

Ávila López, Raúl. 2006. *Mexicaltzingo: Arqueología de un reino culhua-mexica.* 2 vols. Instituto Nacional de Antropología e Historia, Mexico City.

Beekman, Christopher S., and Alexander F. Christensen. 2003. "Controlling for Doubt and Uncertainty through Multiple Lines of Evidence: A New Look at the Mesoamerican Nahua Migrations." *Journal of Archaeological Method and Theory* 10:111–64.

Benz, Bruce F. 1994a. "Can Prehistoric Racial Diversification be Deciphered from Burned Corn Cobs?" In *Corn and Culture in the Prehistoric New World*, edited by Sissel Johannessen and Christine A. Hastorf, 23–33. Westview Press, Boulder, CO.

Benz, Bruce F. 1994b. "Reconstructing the Racial Phylogeny of Mexican Maize: Where Do We Stand." In *Corn and Culture in the Prehistoric New World*, edited by Johannessen Sissel and Christine A. Hastorf, 157–79. Westview Press, Boulder.

Benz, Bruce F. 1999. "On the Origin, Evolution, and Dispersal of Maize." In *Pacific Latin America in Prehistory: The Evolution of Archaic and Formative Cultures*, edited by Michael Blake, 25–38. Washington State University Press, Pullman.

Bhattacharya, Tripti, and Roger Byrne. 2016. "Late Holocene Anthropogenic and Climatic Influences on the Regional Vegetation of Mexico's Cuenca Oriental." *Global and Planetary Change* 138:56–69.

Billman, Brian R. 2002. "Irrigation and the Origins of the Southern Moche State on the North Coast of Peru." *Latin American Antiquity* 13:371–400.

Borejsza, Aleksander. 2006. "Agricultural Slope Management and Soil Erosion in Tlaxcala, Mexico." PhD dissertation, University of California, Los Angeles.

Borejsza, Aleksander. 2011. "Excavaciones de terrazas y geoarqueología." In *Proyecto Calixtlahuaca: Organización de un centro urbano posclásico; Informe técnico parcial, temporada de 2007*, edited by Michael E. Smith, C1-C184. Report on file at the Archivo Técnico, Instituto Nacional de Antropología e Historia, Mexico City.

Borejsza, Aleksander. 2014. "Village and Field Abandonment in Post-Conquest Tlaxcala: A Geoarchaeological Perspective." *Anthropocene* 3:9–23.

Borejsza, Aleksander, and David M. Carballo. 2014. "La Laguna: Overview of Site." In *Formative Lifeways in Central Tlaxcala*, vol. 1: *Excavations, Ceramics, and Chronology*, edited by Richard G. Lesure, 83–88. Cotsen Institute of Archaeology Press, Los Angeles.

Borejsza, Aleksander, and Richard G. Lesure. 2014. "A Wider Context for Studying Formative Resource Exploitation in Tlaxcala." Chapter draft for *Formative Lifeways in Central Tlaxcala*, vol. 2: *The Foundations of Early Sedentary Life*, edited by Aleksander Borejsza and Richard G. Lesure. Manuscript in possession of the author.

Borejsza, Aleksander, and Isabel Rodríguez López. 2014. "La Laguna: Formative Contexts Away from the Site Center." In *Formative Lifeways in Central Tlaxcala, vol. 1: Excavations, Ceramics, and Chronology*, edited by Richard G. Lesure, 113–67. Cotsen Institute of Archaeology Press, Los Angeles.

Borejsza, Aleksander, Isabel Rodríguez López, Charles D. Frederick, and Mark D. Bateman. 2008. "Agricultural Slope Management and Soil Erosion at La Laguna, Tlaxcala, Mexico." *Journal of Archaeological Science* 35:1854–66.

Borejsza, Aleksander, Isabel Rodríguez López, Emily McClung de Tapia, Lorenzo Vázquez Selem, and Cristina Adriano Morán. 2010. "Informe técnico del proyecto geoarqueológico 'Agricultura prehispánica y la degradación del medio ambiente en Tlaxcala.'" Report on file at the Archivo Técnico, Instituto Nacional de Antropología e Historia.

Borejsza, Aleksander, Charles D. Frederick, and Richard G. Lesure. 2011. "Swidden Agriculture in the *Tierra Fría*? Evidence from Sedimentary Records in Tlaxcala." *Ancient Mesoamerica* 22:91–106.

Borejsza, Aleksander, Charles D. Frederick, Luis Morett Alatorre, and Arthur A. Joyce. 2014a. "Alluvial Stratigraphy and the Search for Preceramic Open-Air Sites in Highland Mesoamerica." *Latin American Antiquity* 25:278–99.

Borejsza, Aleksander, Richard G. Lesure, Thomas A. Wake, Víctor Emmanuel Salazar Chávez, Gilberto Pérez Roldán, and María Teresa Gómez Lomelí. 2014b. "Animal Bones as Remains of Food and Indicators of Site Environment." Chapter draft for *Formative Lifeways in Central Tlaxcala*, vol. 2: *The Foundations of Early Sedentary Life*, edited by Aleksander Borejsza and Richard G. Lesure. Manuscript in possession of the author.

Borejsza, Aleksander, Isabel Rodríguez López, and Charles D. Frederick. 2015. "Informe de los análisis de laboratorio del Proyecto Calixtlahuaca, 2007–2015." Report on file at the School of Human Evolution and Social Change, Arizona State University.

Borejsza, Aleksander, Emily McClung de Tapia, Lorenzo Vázquez Selem, Cristina Adriano Morán, Renato Castro Govea, and Isabel Rodríguez López. 2017. "Changing Rural Landscapes of the Last Three Millennia at Santiago Tlalpan, Tlaxcala, Mexico." *Geoarchaeology* 32:36–63.

Borejsza, Aleksander, Isabel Rodríguez López, Charles D. Frederick, and Michael E. Smith. 2021. *From Ancient Matlatzinco to Modern Calixtlahuaca: The Geoarchaeology of a Terraced Landscape*. University of Utah Press, Salt Lake City.

Boserup, Ester. 1965. *The Conditions of Agricultural Growth: The Economics of Agrarian Change under Population Pressure*. Aldine, Chicago.

Braniff, Beatriz. 2000. "La frontera septentrional de Mesoamérica." In *Historia antigua de México*, vol. 1: *El México antiguo, sus áreas culturales, los orígenes y el horizonte Preclásico*, edited by Linda Manzanilla and Leonardo López Luján, 159–90. Instituto Nacional de Antropología e Historia, Mexico City.

Braniff, Beatriz, and María Antonieta Cervantes. 1966. "Excavaciones en el antiguo acueducto de Chapultepec I." *Tlalocan* 5:161–68.

Braniff, Beatriz, and María Antonieta Cervantes. 1967. "Excavaciones en el antiguo acueducto de Chapultepec II." *Tlalocan* 5:265–66.

Bribiesca Castrejón, José Luis. 1958. "El agua potable en la República mexicana: Los abastecimientos en la época prehispánica." *Ingeniería hidráulica en México* 12(2):69–82.

Brumfiel, Elizabeth M. 2005. "Ceramic Chronology at Xaltocan." In *Production and Power at Postclassic Xaltocan*, edited by Elizabeth M. Brumfiel, 117–52. University of Pittsburgh, Pittsburgh, PA.

Brumfiel, Elizabeth M., and Charles D. Frederick. 1992. "Xaltocan: Centro regional de la Cuenca de México." *Boletín del Consejo de Arqueología* 1991:24–30.

Butzer, Karl W. 1988. "Cattle and Sheep from Old to New Spain: Historical Antecedents." *Annals of the Association of American Geographers* 78:29–56.

Butzer, Karl W. 1991. "Spanish Colonization of the New World: Cultural Continuity and Change in Mexico." *Erdkunde* 45:205–19.

Butzer, Karl W. 1992. "Spanish Conquest Society in the New World: Ecological Read-aptation and Cultural Transformation." In *Person, Place and Thing: Interpretive and Empirical Essays in Cultural Geography*, edited by Shue Tuck Wong, 211–42. Department of Geography and Anthropology, Louisiana State University, Baton Rouge.

Butzer, Karl W. 1996. "Ecology in the Long View: Settlement Histories, Agrosystemic Strategies, and Ecological Performance." *Journal of Field Archaeology* 23:141–50.

Butzer, Karl W., and Elisabeth K. Butzer. 1995. "Transfer of the Mediterranean Livestock Economy to New Spain: Adaptation and Ecological Consequences." In *Global Land Use Change: A Perspective from the Columbian Encounter*, edited by B. L. Turner II, 151–93. Consejo Superior de Investigaciones Científicas, Madrid.

Byers, Douglas S., and Richard S. MacNeish, eds. 1967–75. *The Prehistory of the Tehuacan Valley*. 5 vols. University of Texas Press, Austin.

Caballero, Margarita, Beatriz Ortega, Francisco Valadez, Sarah E. Metcalfe, José Luis Macías, and Yoko Sugiura. 2002. "Santa Cruz Atizapan: A 22-ka Lake Level Record and Climatic Implications for the Late Holocene Human Occupation in the Upper Lerma Basin, Central Mexico." *Palaeogeography, Palaeoclimatology, Palaeoecology* 186:217–35.

Caran, S. Christopher, and James A. Neely. 2006. "Hydraulic Engineering in Prehistoric Mexico." *Scientific American* 295(4):78–85.

Carballo, David M. 2014. "La Laguna: Site Mapping and Domestic Excavations in Areas D and H." In *Formative Lifeways in Central Tlaxcala*, vol. 1: *Excavations, Ceramics, and Chronology*, edited by Richard G. Lesure, 89–111. Cotsen Institute of Archaeology Press, Los Angeles.

Charlton, Thomas H. 1977. "Report on a Pre-Hispanic Canal System, Otumba, Edo. de México: Archaeological Investigations, August 10–19, 1977." Report on file at the Archivo Técnico, Instituto Nacional de Antropología e Historia, Mexico City.

Charlton, Thomas H. 1978. *Investigaciones arqueológicas en el municipio de Otumba, primera parte: Resultados preliminares de los trabajos de campo, 1978*. Instituto Nacional de Antropología e Historia, Mexico City.

Charlton, Thomas H. 1979a. "Investigaciones arqueológicas en el municipio de Otumba, segunda parte: La cerámica." Report on file at the Archivo Técnico, Instituto Nacional de Antropología e Historia, Mexico City.

Charlton, Thomas H. 1979b. "Investigaciones arqueológicas en el municipio de Otumba, quinta parte: El riego y el intercambio." Report on file at the Archivo Técnico, Instituto Nacional de Antropología e Historia, Mexico City.

Charlton, Thomas H. 1990. "Operation 12, Field 20 Irrigation System Excavations." In *Early State Formation Processes: The Aztec City-State of Otumba, Mexico*, pt. 1: *Preliminary Report on Recent Research in the Otumba City State*, edited by Thomas H. Charlton and Deborah L. Nichols. Report on file at the Department of Anthropology, University of Iowa, Iowa City.

Charlton, Thomas H., and Deborah L. Nichols. 2005. "Settlement Pattern Archaeology in the Teotihuacan Valley and the Adjacent Northeastern Basin of Mexico A.P. (After Parsons)." In *Settlement, Subsistence, and Social Complexity: Essays Honoring the Legacy of Jeffrey R. Parsons*, edited by Richard E. Blanton, 43–62. Cotsen Institute of Archaeology, Los Angeles.

Cook, Sherburne F. 1949. *Soil Erosion and Population in Central Mexico*. University of California Press, Berkeley.

Cordova, Carlos E. 1997. "Landscape Transformation in Aztec and Spanish Colonial Texcoco, Mexico." PhD dissertation, University of Texas, Austin.

Cordova, Carlos E., Ana Lillian Martín del Pozzo, and Javier López Camacho. 1994. "Paleolandforms and Volcanic Impact on the Environment of Prehistoric Cuicuilco, Southern Mexico City." *Journal of Archaeological Science* 21:585–96.

Cordova, Carlos E., and Jeffrey R. Parsons. 1997. "Geoarchaeology of an Aztec Dispersed Village on the Texcoco Piedmont of Central Mexico." *Geoarchaeology* 12:177–210.

Cyphers, Ann, Judith Zurita Noguera, and Marci Lane Rodríguez. 2013. *Retos y riesgos en la vida olmeca*. Instituto de Investigaciones Antropológicas, Mexico City.

Doolittle, William E. 1990. *Canal Irrigation in Prehistoric Mexico: The Sequence of Technological Change*. University of Texas Press, Austin.

Doolittle, William E. 2006a. "Agricultural Manipulation of Floodplains in the Southern Basin and Range Province." *Catena* 65(2):179–99.

Doolittle, William E. 2006b. "An Epilogue and Bibliographic Supplement to 'Canal Irrigation in Prehistoric Mexico: The Sequence of Technological Change.'" *Mono y conejo* 4:3–15.

Doolittle, William E., and Jonathan B. Mabry. 2006. "Environmental Mosaics, Agricultural Diversity, and the Evolutionary Adoption of Maize in the American Southwest." In *Histories of Maize: Multidisciplinary Approaches to the Prehistory, Linguistics, Biogeography, Domestication, and Evolution of Maize*, edited by John E. Staller, Robert H. Tykot, and Bruce F. Benz, 109–21. Elsevier, Amsterdam.

Evans, Susan T. 1985. "The Cerro Gordo Site: A Rural Settlement of the Aztec Period in the Basin of Mexico." *Journal of Field Archaeology* 12:1–18.

Evans, Susan T. 1988. *Excavations at Cihuatecpan, an Aztec Village in the Teotihuacan Valley*. Vanderbilt, Nashville, TN.

Evans, Susan T. 1990. "The Productivity of Maguey Terrace Agriculture in Central Mexico during the Aztec Period." *Latin American Antiquity* 1:117–32.

Evans, Susan T. 1991. "Architecture and Authority in an Aztec Village: Form and Function of the Tecpan." In *Land and Politics in the Valley of Mexico: A Two Thousand-Year Perspective*, edited by Herbert R. Harvey, 63–92. University of New Mexico Press, Albuquerque.

Evans, Susan T. 1996. "Cihuatecpan: An Aztec Period Village in the Teotihuacan Valley." In *Arqueología mesoamericana: Homenaje a William T. Sanders*, edited by Alba Guadalupe Mastache, Jeffrey R. Parsons, Robert S. Santley and Mari Carmen Serra Puche, vol. 1, 399–415. Instituto Nacional de Antropología e Historia, Mexico City.

Evans, Susan T. 2000a. "The Cerro Gordo South Slope: An Aztec Period Rural Settlement." In *The Teotihuacan Valley Project Final Report*, vol. 5: *The Aztec Period Occupation of the Valley*, pt. 2: *Excavations at T.A. 40 and Related Projects*, edited by William T. Sanders and Susan T. Evans, 687–710. Department of Anthropology, The Pennsylvania State University, University Park.

Evans, Susan T. 2000b. "Research at Cihuatecpan (T.A. 81) in 1984: A Summary." In *The Teotihuacan Valley Project Final Report*, vol. 5: *The Aztec Period Occupation of the Valley*, pt. 2: *Excavations at T.A. 40 and Related Projects*, edited by William T. Sanders and Susan T. Evans, 789–840. Department of Anthropology, The Pennsylvania State University, University Park.

Evans, Susan T. 2001. "Aztec-Period Political Organization in the Teotihuacan Valley." *Ancient Mesoamerica* 12:89–100.

Evans, Susan T. 2005. "Men, Women, and Maguey: The Household Division of Labor among Aztec Farmers." In *Settlement, Subsistence, and Social Complexity: Essays Honoring the Legacy of Jeffrey R. Parsons*, edited by Richard E. Blanton, 198–228. Cotsen Institute of Archaeology, University of California, Los Angeles.

Fargher, Lane F., Richard E. Blanton, and Verenice Y. Heredia Espinoza. 2010. "Egalitarian Ideology and Political Power in Prehispanic Central Mexico: The Case of Tlascallan." *Latin American Antiquity* 21:227–51.

Fargher, Lane F., Richard E. Blanton, Verenice Y. Heredia Espinoza, John Millhauser, Nezahualcoyotl Xiuhtecutli, and Lisa Overholtzer. 2011. "Tlaxcallan: The Archaeology of an Ancient Republic in the New World." *Antiquity* 85:172–86.

Faugère, Brigitte, ed. 2007. *Dinámicas culturales entre el occidente, el centro-norte y la Cuenca de México, del Preclásico al Epiclásico*. Colegio de Michoacán, Zamora.

Feinman, Gary M., and Linda M. Nicholas. 1989. "The Role of Risk in Formative Period Agriculture: A Reconsideration." *American Anthropologist* 91:198–203.

Flannery, Kent V. 1983. "Precolumbian Farming in the Valleys of Oaxaca, Nochixtlan, Tehuacan, and Cuicatlan: A Comparative Study." In *The Cloud People: Divergent Evolution of the Zapotec and Mixtec Civilizations*, edited by Kent V. Flannery and Joyce Marcus, 323–38. Academic Press, New York.

Flannery, Kent V. 1986. *Guilá Naquitz: Archaic Foraging and Early Agriculture in Oaxaca, Mexico*. Academic Press, New York.

Fowler, Melvin L. 1969. "A Preclassic Water Distribution System in Amalucan, Mexico." *Archaeology* 22:208–15.

Fowler, Melvin L. 1987. "Early Water Management at Amalucan, State of Puebla, Mexico." *National Geographic Research* 3:52–68.

Frederick, Charles D. 1997. "Landscape Change and Human Settlement in the Southeastern Basin of Mexico." Report on file at the University of Sheffield.

Frederick, Charles D. 2007. "Chinampa Cultivation in the Basin of Mexico: Observations on the Evolution of Form and Function." In *Seeking a Richer Harvest: The Archaeology of Subsistence Intensification, Innovation and Change*, edited by Tina L. Thurston and Christopher T. Fisher, 107–24. Springer, New York.

Frederick, Charles D., and Carlos E. Cordova. 2019. "Prehispanic and Colonial Landscape Change and Fluvial Dynamics in the Chalco Region, Mexico." *Geomorphology* 331:107–26.

Frederick, Charles D., Carlos E. Cordova, Barbara M. Winsborough, Emily McClung de Tapia, Mary G. Hodge, and Jaime Urrutia Fucugauchi. 2000. "Multi-Disciplinary Study of an Early Aztec Chinampa in the Southeast Basin of Mexico." Paper presented at the 65th Annual Meeting of the Society for American Archaeology, Philadelphia, PA.

Frederick, Charles D., Nicholas James, Luis Morett Alatorre, Virginia S. Popper, and Fernando Sánchez. 2002. "Origin and Development of Chinampa Agriculture in the Basin of Mexico." Report to National Geographic Society, Grant no. 7195-02. Report on file at the National Geographic Society, Washington, DC.

Frederick, Charles D., Luis Morett Alatorre, Virginia S. Popper, and Fernando Sánchez Martínez. ca. 2003. Report on excavations carried out by the project "Agroecosistemas de ciénaga en la Cuenca de México: Diversidad y secuencia de desarrollo." In possession of Charles D. Frederick.

Frederick, Charles D., Barbara M. Winsborough, and Virginia S. Popper. 2005. "Geoarchaeological Investigations in the Northern Basin of Mexico." In *Production and Power at Postclassic Xaltocan*, edited by Elizabeth M. Brumfiel, 71–115. University of Pittsburgh, Pittsburgh, PA.

Frederick, Charles D., Virginia S. Popper, Luis Morett Alatorre, and Fernando Sánchez Martínez. 2007. "Dynamic Agricultural Landforms in a Changing Landscape: Chinampa Agriculture in the Southern Basin of Mexico." Paper presented at the 72nd Annual Meeting of the Society for American Archaeology, Austin, TX.

Frederick, Charles D., Luis Morett Alatorre, and Fernando Sánchez Martínez. 2008. "Evolution of an Irrigation Canal in the Yautepec Valley of Morelos, Mexico." Paper presented at the 73rd Annual Meeting of the Society for American Archaeology, Vancouver, BC.

Friedman, Jonathan. 1987. "An Interview with Eric Wolf." *Current Anthropology* 28:107–18.

García Cook, Ángel. 1976. *El desarrollo cultural en el norte del valle poblano: Inferencias de una secuencia cultural, espacial y temporalmente establecida*. Instituto Nacional de Antropología e Historia, Mexico City.

García Cook, Ángel, and Raziel Mora López. 1974. "Tetepetla: Un sitio fortificado del Clásico en Tlaxcala." *Comunicaciones del Proyecto Puebla-Tlaxcala* 10:23–29.

González Crespo, Norberto, Silvia Garza Tarazona, Hortensia de Vega Nova, Pablo Mayer Guala, and Giselle Canto Aguilar. 1995. "Archaeological Investigations at Xochicalco, Morelos: 1984 and 1986." *Ancient Mesoamerica* 6:223–36.

González Jácome, Alba. 1999. "El paisaje lacustre y los procesos de desecación en Tlaxcala, México." In *Estudios sobre historia y ambiente en América*, vol. 1: *Argentina, Bolivia, México, Paraguay*, edited by Bernardo García Martínez and Alba González Jácome, 191–218. Colegio de México, Mexico City.

González Jácome, Alba. 2007. *Agua y agricultura: Ángel Palerm, la discusión con Karl Wittfogel sobre el modo asiático de producción y la construcción de un modelo para el estudio de Mesoamérica*. Universidad Iberoamericana, Mexico City.

González Jácome, Alba. 2008. *Humedales en el suroeste de Tlaxcala: Agua y agricultura en el siglo XX*. Universidad Iberoamericana, Mexico City.

González, Silvia, Alejandro Pastrana, Claus Siebe, and Geoff Duller. 2000. "Timing of the Prehistoric Eruption of Xitle Volcano and the Abandonment of Cuicuilco Pyramid, Southern Basin of Mexico." In *The Archaeology of Geological Catastrophes*, edited by William J. McGuire, Dafydd R. Griffiths, Paul L. Hancock, and Iain S. Steward, 205–24. Geological Society, London.

Grove, David C., ed. 1987. *Ancient Chalcatzingo*. University of Texas Press, Austin.

Grove, David C., ed. 2000. "The Preclassic Societies of the Central Highlands of Mesoamerica." In *The Cambridge History of the Native Peoples of the Americas*, vol. 2: *Mesoamerica*, edited by Richard E. W. Adams and Murdo J. MacLeod, pt. 1, 122–55. Cambridge University Press, New York.

Grove, David C., and Ann Cyphers Guillén. 1987. "The Excavations." In *Ancient Chalcatzingo*, edited by David C. Grove, 21–62. University of Texas Press, Austin.

Heine, Klaus. 1976. "Schneegrenzdepressionen, Klimaentwicklung, Bodenerosion und Mensch im zentralmexikanischen Hochland im jüngeren Pleistozän und Holozän." *Zeitschrift für Geomorphologie* Supplementband 24:160–76.

Heine, Klaus. 1978. "Mensch und geomorphodynamische Prozesse in Raum und Zeit im randtropischen Hochbecken von Puebla / Tlaxcala, Mexiko." *Verhandlungen des Deutschen Geographentages* 41:390–406.

Heine, Klaus. 1983. "Outline of Man's Impact on the Natural Environment in Central Mexico." *Jahrbuch für Geschichte von Staat, Wirtschaft und Gesellschaft Lateinamerikas* 20:121–31.

Heine, Klaus. 2003. "Paleopedological Evidence of Human-Induced Environmental Change in the Puebla-Tlaxcala Area (Mexico) during the Last 3,500 years." *Revista mexicana de ciencias geológicas* 20:235–44.

Hicks, Frederic. 2001. Texcotzingo (México, Mexico). In *The Archaeology of Ancient Mexico and Central America: An Encyclopedia*, edited by Susan T. Evans and David L. Webster, 745. Garland, New York.

Hirth, Kenneth G., ed. 2000a. *The Xochicalco Mapping Project.* University of Utah Press, Salt Lake City.

Hirth, Kenneth G. 2000b. *Ancient Urbanism at Xochicalco: The Evolution and Organization of a Pre-Hispanic Society.* University of Utah Press, Salt Lake City.

Hirth, Kenneth G. 2013. "Economic Consumption and Domestic Economy in Cholula's Rural Hinterland, Mexico." *Latin American Antiquity* 24:123–48.

Hirth, Kenneth G., and Ann Cyphers. 1988. *Tiempo y asentamiento en Xochicalco.* Universidad Nacional Autónoma de México, Mexico City.

Hunt, Robert C. 1988. "The Size and Structure of Authority in Canal Irrigation Systems." *Journal of Anthropological Research* 44(4):335–55.

Huster, Angela C., and Michael E. Smith. 2015. "A New Archaeological Chronology for Aztec-Period Calixtlahuaca, Mexico." *Latin American Antiquity* 26:3–25.

Kaerger, Karl. 1986. *Agricultura y colonización en México en 1900.* Universidad Autónoma Chapingo, Chapingo.

Kirch, Patrick V. 1994. *The Wet and the Dry: Irrigation and Agricultural Intensification in Polynesia.* University of Chicago Press.

Kirkby, Anne. 1973. *The Use of Land and Water Resources in the Past and Present Valley of Oaxaca, Mexico.* Memoirs of the Museum of Anthropology, no. 5. University of Michigan, Ann Arbor.

LaFevor, Matthew C. 2014. "Conservation Engineering and Agricultural Terracing in Tlaxcala, Mexico." PhD dissertation, University of Texas, Austin.

Lechuga García, María del Carmen, and Francisco Rivas Castro. 1994. "Asentamientos del Formativo Terminal: Rescate en Xico, 1989." In *Matices y alcances: Nuevas investigaciones en salvamento*, 15–38. Subdirección de Salvamento Arqueológico, Instituto Nacional de Antropología e Historia, Mexico City.

Lechuga García, María del Carmen, María Elena Vivanco Bonilla, and Lauro González Quintero. 1995. "La isla Xico: Consideraciones del asentamiento prehispánico en el lago de Chalco." In *Primer seminario internacional de investigadores de Xochimilco*, edited by Erwin Stephan-Otto, vol. 1, 64–79. Asociación Internacional de Investigadores de Xochimilco, Mexico City.

Leigh, David S., Stephen A. Kowalewski, and Genevieve Holdridge. 2013. "3400 Years of Agricultural Engineering in Mesoamerica: *Lama-bordos* of the Mixteca Alta, Oaxaca, Mexico." *Journal of Archaeological Science* 40:4107–11.

Lesure, Richard G., ed. 2008. "The Neolithic Demographic Transition in Mesoamerica? Larger Implications of the Strategy of Relative Chronology." In *The Neolithic Demographic Transition and its Consequences*, edited by Jean-Pierre Bocquet-Appel and Ofer Bar-Yosef, 107–38. Springer, New York.

Lesure, Richard G., ed. 2014a. *Formative Lifeways in Central Tlaxcala*, vol. 1: *Excavations, Ceramics, and Chronology.* Cotsen Institute of Archaeology Press, Los Angeles.

Lesure, Richard G., ed. 2014b. "Macroregional Research Topics for Formative Central Tlaxcala." In *Formative Lifeways in Central Tlaxcala*, vol. 1: *Excavations, Ceramics, and Chronology*, edited by Richard G. Lesure, 363–70. Cotsen Institute of Archaeology Press, Los Angeles.

Lesure, Richard G., Aleksander Borejsza, Jennifer Carballo, Charles Frederick, Virginia Popper, and Thomas A. Wake. 2006. "Chronology, Subsistence, and the Earliest Formative of Central Tlaxcala, Mexico." *Latin American Antiquity* 17:474–92.

Lesure, Richard G., Thomas A. Wake, Aleksander Borejsza, Jennifer Carballo, David M. Carballo, Isabel Rodríguez López, and Mauro de Ángeles Guzmán. 2013. "Swidden Agriculture, Village Longevity, and Social Relations in Formative Central Tlaxcala: Towards an Understanding of Macroregional Structure." *Journal of Anthropological Archaeology* 32:224–41.

Lesure, Richard G., Jennifer Carballo, David M. Carballo, Aleksander Borejsza, and Isabel Rodríguez López. 2014. "A Formative Chronology for Central Tlaxcala." In *Formative Lifeways in Central Tlaxcala*, vol. 1: *Excavations, Ceramics, and Chronology*, edited by Richard G. Lesure, 315–62. Cotsen Institute of Archaeology Press, Los Angeles.

Lewis, Oscar. 1951. *Life in a Mexican Village: Tepoztlan Restudied*. University of Illinois Press, Urbana.

Lewis, Oscar. 1960. *Tepoztlan*. Holt, Rinehart & Winston, New York.

Logan, Michael H., and William T. Sanders. 1976. "The Model." In *The Valley of Mexico: Studies in Pre-Hispanic Ecology and Society*, edited by Eric R. Wolf, 31–58. University of New Mexico Press, Albuquerque.

López Corral, Aurelio. 2000. "Dos mil años de tradición agrícola: Technología y organización social durante el formativo terminal en Tetimpa, Puebla." Bachelor's thesis, Universidad de las Américas, Cholula.

López Corral, Aurelio. 2006. "Productividad agrícola y explotación de recursos naturales durante el Formativo en Tetimpa, Puebla." Master's thesis, Universidad de las Américas, Cholula.

López Corral, Aurelio, Lane F. Fargher, and Ramón Santacruz Cano. 2016. "La república de Tlaxcallan." *Arqueología mexicana* 25(139):42–53.

Lozano García, Socorro, Susana Sosa Nájera, Yoko Sugiura, and Margarita Caballero. 2005. "23,000 yr of Vegetation History of the Upper Lerma, a Tropical High-Altitude Basin in Central Mexico." *Quaternary Research* 64:70–82.

Lugo Hubp, José, Moshe Inbar, Alejandro Pastrana, Antonio Flores, and Juan J. Zamorano. 2001. "Interpretation of the Geomorphic Setting of the Cuicuilco Basin, Mexico City, Affected by the Prehispanic Eruption of the Xitle Volcano." *Géomorphologie: Relief, processus, environnement* 7:223–32.

Mabry, Jonathan B. 2005. "Diversity in Early Southwestern Farming and Optimization Models of Transitions to Agriculture." In *Subsistence and Resource Use Strategies of*

Early Agricultural Communities in Southern Arizona, edited by Michael W. Diehl, 113–52. Center for Desert Archaeology, Tucson.

MacNeish, Richard S., Melvin L. Fowler, Ángel García Cook, Frederick A. Peterson, Antoinette Nelken-Terner, and James A. Neely. 1975. *The Prehistory of the Tehuacan Valley*, vol. 5: *Excavations and Reconnaissance*. University of Texas Press, Austin.

Martínez Donjuán, Guadalupe. 1986. "Teopantecuanitlán." In *Arqueología y etnohistoria del estado de Guerrero*, edited by Roberto Cervantes Delgado, 55–80. Instituto Nacional de Antropología e Historia, Mexico City.

Martínez Donjuán, Guadalupe. 1994. "Los olmecas en el estado de Guerrero." In *Los olmecas en Mesoamérica*, edited by John E. Clark, 142–63. El Equilibrista, Mexico City.

Mastache, Alba Guadalupe, Jeffrey R. Parsons, Robert S. Santley, and Mari Carmen Serra Puche, eds. 1996. *Arqueología mesoamericana: Homenaje a William T. Sanders*. 2 vols. Instituto Nacional de Antropología e Historia, Mexico City.

McClung de Tapia, Emily. 1977. "Recientes estudios paleo-etnobotánicos en Teotihuacán, México." *Anales de antropología* 14:49–61.

McClung de Tapia, Emily. 1979. *Ecología y cultura en Mesoamérica*. Universidad Nacional Autónoma de México, Mexico City.

McClung de Tapia, Emily. 2015. "Holocene Paleoenvironment and Prehispanic Landscape Evolution in the Basin of Mexico." *Ancient Mesoamerica* 26:375–89.

McClung de Tapia, Emily, and Diana Martínez Yrizar. 2005. "Paleoethnobotanical Evidence from Postclassic Xaltocan." In *Production and Power at Postclassic Xaltocan*, edited by Elizabeth M. Brumfiel, 207–32. University of Pittsburgh, Pittsburgh, PA.

McClung de Tapia, Emily, Mari Carmen Serra Puche, and Amie Ellen Limón de Dyer. 1986. "Formative Lacustrine Adaptation: Botanical Remains from Terremote-Tlaltenco." *Journal of Field Archaeology* 13:99–113.

Medina, Miguel A. 1997. *Arte y estética de El Tetzcotzinco: Arquitectura de paisaje en la época de Netzahualcóyotl*. Universidad Nacional Autónoma de México, Mexico City.

Melville, Elinor G. K. 1994. *A Plague of Sheep: Environmental Consequences of the Conquest of Mexico*. Cambridge University Press, Cambridge.

Merino Carrión, Beatriz Leonor. 1989. *La cultura Tlaxco*. Instituto Nacional de Antropología e Historia, Mexico City.

Metcalfe, Sarah E., F. Alayne Street-Perrott, R. Alan Perrott, and Douglas D. Harkness. 1991. "Palaeolimnology of the Upper Lerma Basin, Central Mexico: A Record of Climatic Change and Anthropogenic Disturbance since 11600 yr BP." *Journal of Paleolimnology* 5:197–218.

Millon, René F. 1957. "Irrigation Systems in the Valley of Teotihuacan." *American Antiquity* 23:160–66.

Morehart, Christopher T. 2010. "The Archaeology of Farmscapes: Production, Place, and the Materiality of Landscape at Xaltocan, Mexico." PhD dissertation, Northwestern University, Evanston.

Morehart, Christopher T. 2012. "Mapping Ancient Chinampa Landscapes in the Basin of Mexico: A GIS and Remote Sensing Approach." *Journal of Archaeological Science* 39:2541–51.

Morehart, Christopher T. 2014. "The Potentiality and the Consequences of Surplus: Agricultural Production and Institutional Transformation in the Northern Basin of Mexico." *Economic Anthropology* 1:154–66.

Morehart, Christopher T. 2016. "*Chinampa* Agriculture, Surplus Production, and Political Change at Xaltocan, Mexico." *Ancient Mesoamerica* 27:183–96.

Morehart, Christopher T. 2018. "The Political Ecology of Chinampa Landscapes in the Basin of Mexico." In *Water and Power in Past Societies*, edited by Emily Holt, 19–39. State University of New York Press, Albany.

Morehart, Christopher T., and Dan T. A. Eisenberg. 2010. "Prosperity, Power, and Change: Modeling Maize at Postclassic Xaltocan, Mexico." *Journal of Anthropological Archaeology* 29:94–112.

Morehart, Christopher T., and Charles D. Frederick. 2014. "The Chronology and Collapse of Pre-Aztec Raised Field (*Chinampa*) Agriculture in the Northern Basin of Mexico." *Antiquity* 88:531–48.

Morett Alatorre, Luis, Fernando Sánchez Martínez, José Luis Alvarado, and Charles Frederick. 1999. "Proyecto Arqueobotánico Ticúman: V temporada, 1999." Report on file at the Archivo Técnico, Instituto Nacional de Antropología e Historia.

Morett Alatorre, Luis, Charles D. Frederick, Fernando Sánchez Martínez, and José Luis Alvarado, eds. 2000. "Proyecto Arqueobotánico Ticúman, VI temporada, 2000." Report on file at the Archivo Técnico, Instituto Nacional de Antropología e Historia.

Neely, James A. 2001. "A Contextual Study of the 'Fossilized' Prehispanic Canal Systems of the Tehuacan Valley, Puebla, Mexico." *Antiquity* 75:505–6.

Neely, James A. 2005. "Mesoamerican Formative Period Water Management Technology: An Overview with Insights on Development and Associated Method and Theory." In *New Perspectives on Formative Mesoamerican Cultures*, edited by Terry G. Powis, 127–46. Archaeopress, Oxford.

Neely, James A. 2016. "The Beginnings of Water Management and Agricultural Intensification in Mesoamerica: The Case of the Prehistoric San Marcos Well, the Purrón Dam and the 'Fossilized' Canal Systems of the Tehuacan Valley, Puebla." In *The Origins of Food Production*, edited by Nuria Sanz, 134–47. United Nations Educational, Scientific and Cultural Organization, Mexico City.

Neely, James A. In press. "Prehistoric Water Management in Highland Mesoamerica." In *The UNESCO History of Water and Civilization*, edited by Vernon L. Scarborough and Yoshinori Yasuda. Springer, New York.

Neely, James A., and Blas Román Castellón Huerta. 2003. "Avance del estudio contextual de los sistemas de canales 'fosilizados' del Valle de Tehuacán, Puebla." *Arqueología* 29:157–60.

Neely, James A., and Blas Román Castellón Huerta. 2014. "Una síntesis del manejo prehispánico del agua en el Valle de Tehuacán, Puebla, México." *Arqueología* 47:182–98.

Neely, James A., Michael J. Aiuvalasit, and Vincent A. Clause. 2015. "New Light on the Prehistoric Purrón Dam Complex: Small Corporate Group Collaboration in the Tehuacan Valley, Puebla, Mexico." *Journal of Field Archaeology* 40:347–64.

Nelson, Ben A. 1992. "El maguey y el nopal en la economía de subsistencia de La Quemada, Zacatecas." In *Origen y desarrollo de la civilización en el occidente de México: Homenaje a Pedro Armillas y Ángel Palerm*, edited by Brigitte Boehm de Lameiras and Phil C. Weigand, 359–82. Colegio de Michoacán, Zamora.

Nichols, Deborah L. 1982. "A Middle Formative Irrigation System near Santa Clara Coatitlan in the Basin of Mexico." *American Antiquity* 47:133–43.

Nichols, Deborah L. 1987a. "Prehispanic Irrigation at Teotihuacan, New Evidence: The Tlajinga Canals." In *Teotihuacan: Nuevos datos, nuevas síntesis, nuevos problemas*, edited by Emily McClung de Tapia and Evelyn Rattray, 133–60. Universidad Nacional Autónoma de México, Mexico City.

Nichols, Deborah L. 1987b. "Risk and Agricultural Intensification during the Formative Period in the Northern Basin of Mexico." *American Antiquity* 89:596–616.

Nichols, Deborah L. 1988. "Infrared Aerial Photography and Prehispanic Irrigation at Teotihuacan: The Tlajinga Canals." *Journal of Field Archaeology* 15:17–27.

Nichols, Deborah L. 1989. "Reply to Feinman and Nicholas: There Is No Frost in the Basin of Mexico?" *American Anthropologist* 91:1023–26.

Nichols, Deborah L. 2006. "Archaeology on Foot: Jeffrey Parsons and the University of Michigan." In *Retrospectives: Works and Lives of Michigan Anthropologists*, edited by Derek Brereton, 106–35. Michigan Discussions in Anthropology. University of Michigan, Ann Arbor.

Nichols, Deborah L., and Charles D. Frederick. 1993. "Irrigation Canals and Chinampas: Recent Research in the Northern Basin of Mexico." *Research in Economic Anthropology* 7:123–50.

Nichols, Deborah L., Michael W. Spence, and Mark D. Borland. 1991. "Watering the Fields of Teotihuacan: Early Irrigation at the Ancient City." *Ancient Mesoamerica* 2:1119–29.

Nichols, Deborah L., Charles D. Frederick, Luis Morett, and Fernando Sánchez. 2006. "Water Management and Political Economy in Formative Period Central Mexico." In *Precolumbian Water Management*, edited by Lisa Lucero and Bill Fash, 31–66. University of Arizona Press, Tucson.

Niederberger, Christine. 1996. "Olmec Horizon Guerrero." In *Olmec Art of Ancient Mexico*, edited by Elizabeth P. Benson and Beatriz de la Fuente, 94–103. National Gallery of Art, Washington, DC.

Palerm, Ángel. 1952. "La civilización urbana." *Historia mexicana* 2(2):184–209.

Palerm, Ángel. 1955. "The Agricultural Basis of Urban Civilization in Mesoamerica." In *Irrigation Civilizations: A Comparative Study*, edited by Julian H. Steward, 28–42. Pan American Union, Washington, DC.

Palerm, Ángel. 1961. "Sistemas de regadío prehispánico en Teotihuacan y en el Pedregal de San Ángel." *Revista interamericana de ciencias sociales* 1:297–302.

Palerm, Ángel. 1969–70. "Una defensa del modo asiático de producción según Marx y Wittfogel." *Comunidad* 22, 23, 24, 25, 26:763–81, 31–45, 137–51, 249–60, 360–69.

Palerm, Ángel, and Eric R. Wolf. 1961. "Sistemas agrícolas y desarrollo del área clave del imperio texcocano." *Revista interamericana de ciencias sociales* 1:281–87.

Parsons, Jeffrey R. 1971. *Prehistoric Settlement Patterns in the Texcoco Region, Mexico*. University of Michigan, Ann Arbor.

Parsons, Jeffrey R. 1976. "The Role of Chinampa Agriculture in the Food Supply of Aztec Tenochtitlan." In *Cultural Change and Continuity: Essays in Honor of James Bennett Griffin*, edited by Charles E. Cleland, 233–57. Academic Press, New York.

Parsons, Jeffrey R. 2001. *The Last Saltmakers of Nexquipayac, Mexico: An Archaeological Ethnography*. Anthropological Papers, no. 92. Museum of Anthropology, University of Michigan, Ann Arbor.

Parsons, Jeffrey R. 2006. *The Last Pescadores of Chimalhuacán, Mexico: An Archaeological Ethnography*. Anthropological Papers, no. 96. Museum of Anthropology, University of Michigan, Ann Arbor.

Parsons, Jeffrey R. 2010. "The Pastoral Niche in Pre-Hispanic Mesoamerica." In *Pre-Columbian Foodways: Interdisciplinary Approaches to Food, Culture and Markets in Ancient Mesoamerica*, edited by John E. Staller and Michael D. Carrasco, 109–36. Springer, New York.

Parsons, Jeffrey R. 2015. "An Appraisal of Regional Surveys in the Basin of Mexico, 1960–1975." *Ancient Mesoamerica* 26:183–96.

Parsons, Jeffrey R., Elizabeth M. Brumfiel, Mary H. Parsons, and David J. Wilson. 1982. *Prehispanic Settlement Patterns in the Southern Valley of Mexico: The Chalco-Xochimilco Region*. Memoirs of the Museum of Anthropology, no. 14. University of Michigan, Ann Arbor.

Parsons, Jeffrey R., Mary H. Parsons, Virginia S. Popper, and Mary Taft. 1985. "Chinampa Agriculture and Aztec Urbanization in the Valley of Mexico." In *Prehistoric Intensive Agriculture in the Tropics*, edited by Ian S. Farrington, 49–96. British Archaeological Reports, Oxford.

Parsons, Jeffrey R., Elizabeth Brumfiel, and Mary Hodge. 1996. "Developmental Implications of Earlier Dates for Early Aztec in the Basin of Mexico." *Ancient Mesoamerica* 7:217–30.

Patrick, Larry L. 1977. "A Cultural Geography of the Use of Seasonally Dry, Sloping Terrain: The Metepantli Crop Terraces of Central Mexico." PhD dissertation, University of Pittsburgh, Pittsburgh, PA.

Peña Castillo, Agustín, and Carmen Rodríguez. 1976. "Excavaciones en Daini, Tula, Hgo." In *Proyecto Tula*, edited by Eduardo Matos Moctezuma, pt. 2, 85–90. Instituto Nacional de Antropología e Historia, Mexico City.

Pérez Pérez, Julia. 2006. "Agricultura en terrazas en el cerro San Lucas, Valle de Teotihuacán." Report on file at the Foundation for the Advancement of Mesoamerican Studies, Coral Gables.

Pérez Pérez, Julia. 2013. "San Lucas, un altepemaitl en el señorío del Acolhuacan." PhD dissertation, Universidad Nacional Autónoma de México, Mexico City.

Pérez Pérez, Julia, Emily McClung de Tapia, Luis Barba Pingarrón, Jorge Gama Castro, and Armando Peralta Higuera. 2012. "Remote Sensing Detection of Potential Sites in a Prehispanic Domestic Agricultural Terrace System in Cerro San Lucas, Teotihuacan, Mexico." *Boletín de la Sociedad Geológica Mexicana* 64:109–18.

Pérez Rodríguez, Verónica, and Kirk C. Anderson. 2013. "Terracing in the Mixteca Alta, Mexico: Cycles of Resilience of an Ancient Land-Use Strategy." *Human Ecology* 41:335–49.

Piperno, Dolores R., J. Enrique Moreno, José Iriarte, Irene Holst, Matthew S. Lachniet, John G. Jones, Anthony J. Ranere, and Ronald Castanzo. 2007. "Late Pleistocene and Holocene Environmental History of the Iguala Valley, Central Balsas Watershed of Mexico." *Proceedings of the National Academy of Sciences* 104:11874–81.

Plunket, Patricia, and Gabriela Uruñuela. 1998a. "Preclassic Household Patterns Preserved under Volcanic Ash at Tetimpa, Puebla." *Latin American Antiquity* 9:287–309.

Plunket, Patricia, and Gabriela Uruñuela. 1998b. "The Impact of the Popocatepetl Volcano on Preclassic Settlement in Central Mexico." *Quaternaire* 9:53–59.

Plunket, Patricia, and Gabriela Uruñuela. 2000. "The Archaeology of a Plinian Eruption of the Popocatepetl Volcano." In *The Archaeology of Geological Catastrophes*, edited by William J. McGuire, Dafydd R. Griffiths, Paul L. Hancock, and Iain S. Steward, 195–203. Geological Society, London.

Plunket, Patricia, and Gabriela Uruñuela. 2005. "Recent Research in Puebla Prehistory." *Journal of Archaeological Research* 13:89–127.

Plunket, Patricia, and Gabriela Uruñuela. 2008. "Mountain of Sustenance, Mountain of Destruction: The Prehispanic Experience with Popocatepetl Volcano." *Journal of Volcanology and Geothermal Research* 170:111–20.

Plunket, Patricia, and Gabriela Uruñuela. 2012. "Where East Meets West: The Formative in Mexico's Central Highlands." *Journal of Archaeological Research* 20:1–51.

Price, Barbara J. 1971. "Prehispanic Irrigation Agriculture in Nuclear America." *Latin American Research Review* 6:3–60.

Price, T. Jeffrey, and Michael E. Smith. 1992. "Agricultural Terraces." In *Archaeological Research at Aztec-Period Rural Sites in Morelos, Mexico*, vol. 1: *Excavations and Architecture*, edited by Michael E. Smith, 267–92. University of Pittsburgh, Pittsburgh, PA.

Prindiville, Mary, and David C. Grove. 1987. "The Settlement and Its Architecture." In *Ancient Chalcatzingo*, edited by David C. Grove, 63–81. University of Texas Press, Austin.

Pulido Méndez, Salvador. 1993. "Xico, Estado de México, en el Preclásico." In *A propósito del Formativo*, edited by María Teresa Castillo Mangas, 33–44. Subdirección de Salvamento Arqueológico, Instituto Nacional de Antropología e Historia, Mexico City.

Pulido Méndez, Salvador, and Francisco Ortuño Cos. 1994. "Algunos sitios arqueológicos del área oriental de la Cuenca de México: Problemática y perspectivas de preservación." *Arqueología* 11–12:119–22.

Rogé, Paul, and Marta Astier. 2015. "Changes in Climate, Crops, and Tradition: Cajete Maize and the Rainfed Farming Systems of Oaxaca, Mexico." *Human Ecology* 43:639–53.

Rojas Rabiela, Teresa, ed. 1991. *Pedro Armillas: Vida y obra.* 2 vols. Centro de Investigaciones y Estudios Superiores en Antropología Social, Mexico City.

Rosenswig, Robert M. 2006. "Sedentism and Food Production in Early Complex Societies of the Soconusco, Mexico." *World Archaeology* 38:330–55.

Sánchez González, José de Jesús, José Ariel Ruiz Corral, Guillermo Medina García, Gabriela Ramírez Ojeda, Lino de la Cruz Larios, James Brendan Holland, Roberto Miranda Medrano, and Giovanni Emmanuel García Romero. 2018. "Ecogeography of Teosinte." *PLOS ONE* 13:e0192676.

Sanders, William T. 1956. "The Central Mexican Symbiotic Region: A Study in Prehistoric Settlement Patterns." In *Prehistoric Settlement Patterns in the New World*, edited by Gordon R. Willey, 115–27. Viking Fund, New York.

Sanders, William T. 1965. *The Cultural Ecology of the Teotihuacan Valley*. Department of Sociology and Anthropology, The Pennsylvania State University, University Park.

Sanders, William T. 1971. "Settlement Patterns in Central Mexico." In *Handbook of Middle American Indians*, vol. 10: *Archaeology of Northern Mesoamerica*, edited by Gordon F. Ekholm and Ignacio Bernal, pt. 1, 3–44. University of Texas Press, Austin.

Sanders, William T. 1976. "The Agricultural History of the Basin of Mexico." In *The Valley of Mexico: Studies in Pre-Hispanic Ecology and Society*, edited by Eric R. Wolf, 101–59. University of New Mexico Press, Albuquerque.

Sanders, William T. 1997. "El final de la gran aventura: El ocaso de un recurso natural." *Arqueología* 17:3–20.

Sanders, William T., and Deborah L. Nichols. 1988. "Ecological Theory and Cultural Evolution in the Valley of Oaxaca." *Current Anthropology* 29:33–80.

Sanders, William T., and Barbara J. Price. 1968. *Mesoamerica: The Evolution of a Civilization*. Random House, New York.

Sanders, William T., and Robert S. Santley. 1977. "A Prehispanic Irrigation System near Santa Clara Xalostoc in the Basin of Mexico." *American Antiquity* 42:582–88.

Sanders, William T., Jeffrey R. Parsons, and Robert S. Santley. 1979. *The Basin of Mexico: Ecological Processes in the Evolution of a Civilization*. Academic Press, New York.

Seele, Enno. 1973. "Restos de milpas y poblaciones prehispánicas cerca de San Buenaventura Nealtican, Puebla." *Comunicaciones del Proyecto Puebla-Tlaxcala* 7:77–86.

Serra Puche, Mari Carmen. 1988. *Los recursos lacustres de la Cuenca de México durante el Formativo*. Instituto de Investigaciones Antropológicas, Mexico City.

Serra Puche, Mari Carmen. 1994. *Xochimilco arqueológico*. Patronato del Parque Ecológico de Xochimilco, Mexico City.

Serra Puche, Mari Carmen. 1998. *Xochitecatl*. Gobierno del Estado de Tlaxcala, Tlaxcala.

Serra Puche, Mari Carmen, and Jesús Carlos Lazcano Arce. 2008. "La vida lacustre durante el Formativo en la región de Tlaxcala." In *Ideología política y sociedad en el periodo Formativo: Ensayos en homenaje al dotor David C. Grove*, edited by Ann Cyphers and Kenneth G. Hirth, 233–48. Instituto de Investigaciones Antropológicas, Mexico City.

Serra Puche, Mari Carmen, and Jesús Carlos Lazcano Arce. 2011. *Vida cotidiana, Xochitecatl-Cacaxtla: Días, años, milenios*. Instituto de Investigaciones Antropológicas, Mexico City.

Siebe, Claus. 2000. "Age and Archaeological Implications of Xitle Volcano, Southwestern Basin of Mexico City." *Journal of Volcanology and Geothermal Research* 104:45–64.

Skopyk, Bradley. 2010. "Undercurrents of Conquest: The Shifting Terrain of Indigenous Agriculture in Colonial Tlaxcala, Mexico." PhD dissertation, York University, Toronto, ON.

Skopyk, Bradley. 2017. "Rivers of God, Rivers of Empire: Climate Extremes, Environmental Transformation and Agroecology in Colonial Mexico." *Environment and History* 23:491–522.

Smith, C. Earle. 1965. "Agriculture, Tehuacan Valley." *Fieldiana Botany* 31:53–100.

Smith, Michael E., ed. 1992. *Archaeological Research at Aztec-Period Rural Sites in Morelos, Mexico*, vol. 1: *Excavations and Architectures*. University of Pittsburgh, Pittsburgh, PA.

Smith, Michael E., and John F. Doershuk. 1991. "Late Postclassic Chronology in Western Morelos, Mexico." *Latin American Antiquity* 2:291–310.

Smith, Michael E., and T. Jeffrey Price. 1994. "Aztec-Period Agricultural Terraces in Morelos, Mexico: Evidence for Household-Level Agricultural Intensification." *Journal of Field Archaeology* 21:169–79.

Smith, Michael E., Aleksander Borejsza, Angela C. Huster, Charles D. Frederick, Isabel Rodríguez López, and Cynthia Heath-Smith. 2013. "Aztec Period Houses and Terraces at Calixtlahuaca: The Changing Morphology of a Mesoamerican Hilltop Urban Center." *Journal of Field Archaeology* 38:227–43.

Spencer, Charles S. 1979. "Irrigation, Administration, and Society in Formative Tehuacan." In *Prehistoric Social, Political, and Economic Development in the Area of the Tehuacan Valley: Some Results of the Palo Blanco Project*, edited by Robert D. Drennan,

13–75. Technical Reports, no. 11. Museum of Anthropology, University of Michigan, Ann Arbor.

Spores, Ronald. 1969. "Settlement, Farming Technology, and Environment in the Nochixtlan Valley." *Science* 166:557–69.

Steward, Julian H. 1955. *Theory of Culture Change: The Methodology of Multilinear Evolution*. University of Illinois Press, Urbana.

Sugiura Yamamoto, Yoko, ed. 2009. *La gente de la ciénega en tiempos antiguos: La historia de Santa Cruz Atizapán*. Instituto de Investigaciones Antropológicas, Mexico City.

Sugiura Yamamoto, Yoko, Mari Carmen Serra Puche, Aurelio Monroy García, and Sirenio Martínez. 1983. "Notas sobre el modo de subsistencia lacustre, la laguna de Santa Cruz Atizapán, Estado de México." *Anales de antropología* 20:9–26.

Sugiura Yamamoto, Yoko, Antonio Flores, Beatriz Ludlow, Francisco Valadez, Michèle Gold, and Jean-Michel Maillol. 1994. "El agua, la tierra, el bosque y el hombre en el Alto Lerma: Un estudio multidisciplinario: Resultados preliminares." *Arqueología* 11–12:29–45.

Sugiura Yamamoto, Yoko, José Alberto Aguirre Anaya, Magdalena Amalia García Sánchez, Edgar Carro Albarrán, and Sandra Figueroa Sosa. 1998. *La caza, la pesca y la recolección: Etnoarqueología del modo de subsistencia lacustre en las ciénegas del Alto Lerma*. Instituto de Investigaciones Antropológicas, Mexico City.

Trautmann, Wolfgang. 1973. "Los cultivos de humedad en la historia mexicana." *Boletín del Instituto Nacional de Antropología e Historia* 5:43–48.

Trautmann, Wolfgang. 1981. *Las transformaciones en el paisaje cultural de Tlaxcala durante la época colonial*. Steiner, Wiesbaden.

Trombold, Charles D., and Isabel Israde Alcántara. 2005. "Paleoenvironment and Plant Cultivation on Terraces at La Quemada, Zacatecas, Mexico: The Pollen, Phytolith and Diatom Evidence." *Journal of Archaeological Science* 32:341–53.

Urrutia Fucugauchi, Jaime. 1996. "Palaeomagnetic Study of the Xitle-Pedregal de San Ángel Lava Flow, Southern Basin of Mexico." *Physics of the Earth and Planetary Interiors* 97:177–96.

Webster, David L. 2011. "Backward Bottlenecks: Ancient Teosinte/Maize Selection." *Current Anthropology* 52:77–104.

Webster, David L., and Susan T. Evans. 2008. "*In memoriam*: 'Even Jades Are Shattered . . .': William Timothy Sanders, 1926–2008." *Ancient Mesoamerica* 19:157–63.

West, Robert C. 1970. "Population Densities and Agricultural Practices in Pre-Columbian Mexico, with Special Emphasis on Semi-Terracing." In *Verhandlungen des XXXVIII Internationalen Amerikanistenkongresses (1968)*, vol. 2, 361–69. Renner, Munich.

Whitmore, Thomas M., and B. L. Turner II. 2001. *Cultivated Landscapes of Middle America on the Eve of Conquest*. Oxford University Press, Oxford.

Wilken, Gene C. 1967. "Drained-Field Agriculture in Southwest Tlaxcala, Mexico." PhD dissertation, University of California, Berkeley.

Wilken, Gene C. 1969. "Drained-Field Agriculture: An Intensive Farming System in Tlaxcala, Mexico." *Geographical Review* 59:215–41.

Wilken, Gene C. 1987. *Good Farmers: Traditional Agriculture and Resource Management in Mexico and Central America.* University of California Press, Berkeley.

Winsborough, Barbara M., S. Christopher Caran, James A. Neely, and Salvatore Valastro Jr. 1996. "Calcified Microbial Mats Date Prehistoric Canals—Radiocarbon Assay of Organic Extracts from Travertine." *Geoarchaeology* 11:37–50.

Wittfogel, Karl A. 1957. *Oriental Despotism: A Comparative Study of Total Power.* Yale University Press, New Haven, CT.

Wittfogel, Karl A. 1972. "The Hydraulic Approach to Pre-Spanish Mesoamerica." In *The Prehistory of the Tehuacan Valley*, vol. 4: *Chronology and Irrigation*, edited by Frederick Johnson, 59–80. University of Texas Press, Austin.

Wolf, Eric R. 1959. *Sons of the Shaking Earth.* University of Chicago Press.

Wolf, Eric R., ed. 1976. *The Valley of Mexico: Studies in Pre-Hispanic Ecology and Society.* University of New Mexico Press, Albuquerque.

Wolf, Eric R., and Ángel Palerm. 1955. "Irrigation in the Old Acolhua Domain, Mexico." *Southwestern Journal of Anthropology* 11:265–81.

Woodbury, Richard B., and James A. Neely. 1972. "Water Control Systems of the Tehuacan Valley." In *The Prehistory of the Tehuacan Valley*, vol. 4: *Chronology and Irrigation*, edited by Frederick Johnson, 81–153. University of Texas Press, Austin.

11

Postclassic/Early Colonial Period *Chinampas* at El Japón, San Gregorio Atlapulco, Xochimilco

Construction and Chronology

EMILY MCCLUNG DE TAPIA AND GUILLERMO ACOSTA OCHOA

INTRODUCTION

The publication in 1979 of Sanders, Parsons, and Santley's *The Basin of Mexico: Ecological Processes in the Evolution of a Civilization* represented a landmark in the instrumentation of the cultural ecological framework developed by Sanders through the years (for example, Sanders 1957, 1962, 1972; Sanders and Price 1968). From its roots in the Teotihuacan Valley Project during the 1960s, the original methodological approach continued in numerous surveys of the remaining sectors of the Basin of Mexico carried out largely by Sanders and Jeffrey Parsons and their students through the 1980s (Blanton 1972; Parsons 1971; Parsons et al. 1982, 1983). Among several objectives of the Basin of Mexico research, two are relevant for our current study of *chinampa* agriculture: "the development of agriculture, with a special focus on irrigation and terracing"; and "the relationship between . . . settlement patterns, agricultural techniques and demography. . . ." (Sanders et al. 1979:5). Although terrace systems will not be discussed here, analysis of Postclassic terraces on the adjacent piedmont system in Milpa Alta, southeast of Xochimilco is currently underway.

https://doi.org/10.5876/9781646424078.c011

Regarding the role of irrigation in the rise of urban centers in Central Mexico, time and archaeological evidence have shown that the complexity of subregional agricultural systems in the Basin is more diverse than originally perceived. Presently, there is limited evidence suggesting large-scale state-controlled hydraulic systems prior to the Postclassic period. While the chronological terminology proposed in the 1979 volume was met with resistance and ultimately rejected by scholars, settlement pattern data remained a fundamental source of regional and subregional information, still widely used by archaeologists at different scales. The volume of site-location data–the original surveys and more recent updates to cover areas not originally accessible—and the adjustments to usable coordinate systems (e.g., Sanders and Gorenflo 2007) constitute an invaluable resource for past, present, and future research in the Basin.

HISTORICAL AND MODERN CHINAMPAS

Together with the historic center of Mexico City, the *chinampa* area of Xochimilco was declared a UNESCO World Heritage site in 1987 (Carballo 2006; Schulze and Carballo 2006), based on the exceptional universal value attributed to the extant *chinampas*, the most extensive area of this Prehispanic agroecosystem still preserved in the Basin of Mexico. The archaeological site of El Japón, focus of the research discussed here is situated in the third section of the Ejido San Gregorio Atlapulco in Xochimilco (see figure 11.1). Unfortunately, the World Heritage status of the *chinampa* system and its cultural relevance is at risk as a consequence of poor management, urban sprawl, significant land-use changes, and environmental degradation (Ruiz-Gutierrez 2012).

Chinampas represent a traditional agroecosystem of Prehispanic origin, characteristic of the southern Basin of Mexico, preserved today mainly in the administrative districts of Xochimilco, Mixquic, and Tlahuac in Mexico City. Modern *chinampas* generally consist of rectangular plots constructed from layers of aquatic vegetation (reeds and rushes, *Schoenoplectus* sp., *Typha* sp.), grasses, silt dredged from the lakebed and terrestrial sediment from the lakeshore, occasionally anchored by *ahuejotes* (*Salix* sp.) to maintain the integrity of the structures. Plots are separated by relatively narrow canals. The productivity of the *chinampas* is maintained by high organic material content together with constant humidity. The term *chinampa* derives from the Nahuatl word *chinámitl*, roughly translated to mean woven canes or branches, referring to the layers of aquatic plants employed in their construction (Molina 1970 [1571]).

Chinampas are among the most widely studied agroecosystems in the New World; popular descriptions are well-known (e.g., Coe 1964; West and Armillas 1950). However, most of the available descriptions are based on ethnohistoric or ethnographic accounts (see Rojas Rabiela 1983 for a historical compilation) and relatively few archaeological studies (Frederick 2007).

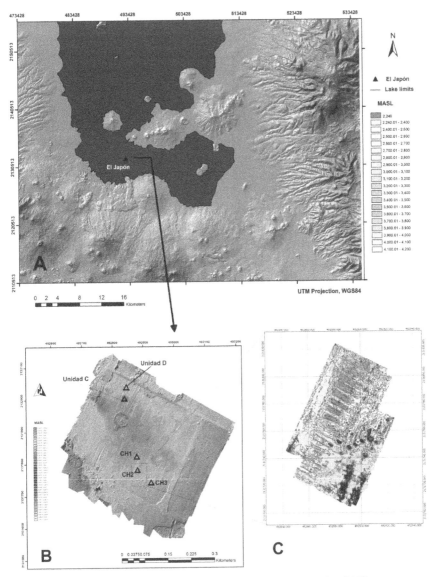

FIGURE 11.1. *(a) Location of El Japón, San Gregorio Atlapulco, Xochimilco; (b) Photogrammetric model (image from unmanned aerial vehicle, UAV) of El Japón; (c) Contour-level detail of the* chinampa *system.*

José de Acosta (2020 [1590]:367) referred to *chinampa* construction in the late sixteenth century, indirectly suggesting the concept of "floating gardens" by referring to cultivated plots as *sementeras movedizas en el agua* (movable plots in the water). Nonetheless, the first detailed information related to construction techniques was provided in the eighteenth century by Antonio de Alzate (1993:14–15), who described the *chinampa* as surrounded by four channels, plots wider from East to West and smaller from North to South, and leveled horizontally. Apenes (1943:30) was one of the first to suggest a role of *tlateles* in *chinampa* construction. These descriptions largely coincide with those in ethnographic sources (Rojas Rabiela 1983), based on the superposition of layers of silt, mud, and organic material alternating with bulrushes (*Schoenoplectus* spp.) and branches, anchored by rows of willows (ahuejote, *Salix bonplandiana* var. *ferruginata*).

Although *chinampas* represent a highly productive agroecosystem that requires almost no fallowing, other than periodic maintenance, two factors are significant: a constant water level, sufficient to allow manual irrigation but hinder inundation of the fields; and control of salinization resulting from the accumulation and evaporation of lacustrine sediment and vegetation. The latter is well recognized by both modern *chinamperos* and edaphologists (Ramos-Bello et al. 2011). Alzate (1993:19–21) also referred to the importance of continual renovation of the *chinampa* surface with new mud to control salinization.

CHINAMPA CONSTRUCTION AT EL JAPÓN, XOCHIMILCO

El Japón, in San Gregorio Atlapulco, Xochimilco (Mexico City), was a Postclassic-Early Colonial *chinampa* community, previously reported and partially surveyed by Lechuga (1977), Parsons and colleagues (1982, 1985), Ávila (1996) and González (1996). In 2013, investigators from the Instituto de Investigaciones Antropológicas of the Universidad Nacional Autónoma de México initiated a geoarchaeological, paleoethnobotanical, and chronological study of the site, which is severely threatened by encroaching urbanization and land-use changes. The Postclassic habitational platform previously described by Parsons and colleagues (1982, 1985) is largely destroyed, and a broad area of *chinampas* has been lost, regardless of the efforts to preserve it (González 1996). Ceramic evidence from surface and recent excavations of these *chinampas* indicate their initial occupation toward the end of the fifteenth century CE and abandonment after approximately two centuries. Geoarchaeological analyses and accelerator mass spectrometry dating indicate that *chinampa* construction in this area was more complex than anticipated, including the reutilization of mid-Holocene sediments from the documented preceramic occupation of the site in addition to the use of layers of diatomaceous sediments, the function of which is yet to be confirmed.

The results of this research contribute to a diagnosis of landscape / *lakescape* modification as a consequence of processes including initial settlement of the area; development of early agricultural practices; agricultural intensification in relation to sociopolitical phenomena; impact of *chinampa* cultivation on the lakescape; and impact of land-use change (agricultural to urban), particularly over the past century.

While the site is relevant to our understanding of Mid-Holocene preceramic life in the lacustrine setting of Lake Xochimilco (Acosta 2017; Acosta et al. 2020; McClung and Acosta 2015), its Postclassic-period component contributes significant information on agricultural techniques as indicators of the continuing evolution of human communities within this unique ecological habitat.

Current research concerning the development of Prehispanic *chinampa* agriculture in Xochimilco focuses on four relevant aspects of this complex agroecosystem:

- Ecological and social integration within the lacustrine surroundings—the **lakescape** (GIS/Remote sensing image interpretation, social space, urbanization, etc.).
- Excavation and subsequent laboratory procedures within a **geoarchaeological framework** in order to evaluate *chinampa* structure, including construction techniques, edaphic properties, salinity, and fertility, among others.
- Re-evaluation of the **cultigens** traditionally considered as basic components of *chinampa* agriculture and the role of *chinampas* in provisioning urban Tenochtitlan.
- **Chronology** and the difficulties of accurately dating different stages of *chinampa* development and use.

CHINAMPAS IN THE LAKESCAPE

While it is often assumed that much is known about the construction and maintenance of Prehispanic *chinampas*, Frederick (2007:107) notes that detailed archaeological studies are few in number; basically, the localities of Xaltocan (Morehart 2010, 2012, 2016; Morehart and Frederick 2014) in the northern part of Basin, and Iztapalapa (Ávila 1991), Chalco (Frederick 2007; Parsons et al. 1985) Xochimilco (Acosta 2017; Acosta et al. 2020; Armillas 1971; Ávila 1996, 1998), and Mixquic (Parsons et al. 1985) in the southern part of the Basin.

Chinampas are often considered a response to the need to intensify agricultural production, related to demographic growth in the regions in which they have been detected (Sluyter 1994). The importance of *chinampa* agriculture in the Basin of Mexico in sustaining the demographic development and territorial expansion of the Triple Alliance, prior to the arrival of the Spaniards, has been suggested by some authors (Armillas 1971; Coe 1964; Gibson 1964; Parsons et al. 1985). However, *chinampa* communities in the southern Basin apparently contributed little in the way of agricultural produce as regular tribute, although wood and charcoal from adjacent woodlands were provided for ceremonial occasions, mainly celebrations of successful conquests, deaths, and coronations of rulers (Alvarado Tezozomoc 1997 [1598]:288–89), rafts and canoes for hydraulic works, and emergency responses to floods (Durán 1967 [1581]:2:380). The *Matrícula de Tributos* (Corona 1977) suggests that manufactured goods such as cloth and military apparel were more important tribute items. Markets likely provided a viable alternative to provisioning much of the realm (Smith 1980) and the construction of *chinampas* responded to the need for lakeshore communities to increase the available surface for domestic habitation as well as subsistence and commercial farming.

The range of adaptations characteristic of the lacustrine communities of the southern Basin of Mexico extended at least as far back as 4000 BCE, including techniques similar to *chinampa* construction to increase available land surfaces within the lakescape, for example, at Terremote-Tlaltenco (Serra 1995; Tolstoy 1975). Excavations of the *chinampas* preserved at the site of El Japón, Xochimilco, demonstrate that the islet was intensively occupied during the Playa II (5500–4500 BCE) and Atlapulco (4500–3500 BCE) phases with evidence for the preparation of the islet for habitational purposes as early as the fifth century BCE (Rivera 2019). Apparently, the islet was abandoned between 3800 BCE and 1350 CE. Radiocarbon determinations and ceramic evidence suggests that it was reoccupied during the mid-fourteenth century CE, when the surface was raised with at least one meter of lacustrine sediment (Ávila 1996), probably to avoid occasional inundations of the domestic units built on the platform.

Recent excavations in one of the Postclassic habitational mounds revealed the original *chinampas* were constructed to extend the surface of the islet. Photogrammetry using unmanned aerial vehicles (UAV, drones) indicated that the agricultural *chinampas* were filled and joined together to create wider plots on which domestic units were eventually built. González (1996), in excavations at the extreme northeast of the site, recognized this technique, presumably also employed in the *chinampas* of Tenochtitlan. This working hypothesis agrees with the theoretical underpinnings of Sanders, Parsons, and Santley who stated that the extensive construction of *chinampas*, beginning with the original islets followed by the shore of Lake Xochimilco, was stimulated by the greater demand for food and by the need to expand living space for farmers under increasing demographic pressure during the Late Postclassic period (1350–1521 CE).

Quick Bird satellite images complemented the analysis by UAV coverage, indicate that the Prehispanic *chinampas* averaged a width and length of 3 and 50 meters, respectively, whereas Luna Golya's (2014) regional analysis suggests that *chinampas* pertaining to the Colonial and later periods are considerably wider. Meanwhile, infrared and thermographic images obtained from drones suggest that even in leveled areas the spectral image of canals and *chinampas* persists, permitting reconstruction of their form and extension during the Prehispanic and contact periods (see figure 11.2).

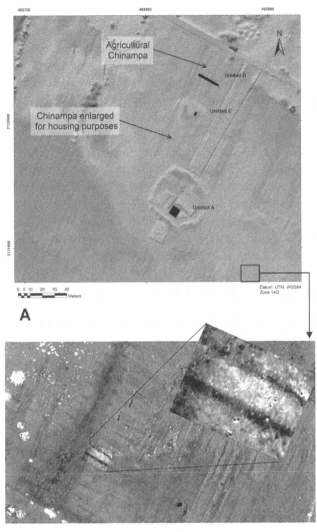

A

B

FIGURE 11.2. *(a) Detail of figure 11.1(b), showing* chinampa, *domestic unit excavation areas, and location of thermographic image; (b) Thermographic image superimposed on a near-infrared image of* chinampas *at El Japón.*

THE STRUCTURE OF PREHISPANIC
CHINAMPAS IN XOCHIMILCO

Sanders, Parsons, and Santley (1979:277) considered the development of Postclassic period *chinampa* systems in Lakes Chalco-Xochimilco as the "most impressive drainage" project undertaken in the Basin of Mexico. Sanders

(1965:44) had described modern *chinampa* construction as the formation of artificial islands, similar to Coe's (1964) description, emphasizing the high productivity and labor intensity of the system. He suggested that the expansion of the system over time incorporated most of the open waters of Lakes Chalco-Xochimilco into a network of *chinampas* that facilitated transport of products to local urban markets. Armillas's (1971) survey of the system revealed greater diversity of *chinampa* construction, depending on particular characteristics of the lakebed in different areas. He proposed that initially, in the relatively shallow lakes (1–2 m), an extensive network of drainage canals facilitated water management, allowing exposure of natural "islands," ultimately permitting their use for cultivation. He considered the excavation of canals to have been the initial step in *chinampa* construction. Furthermore, the canals provided transportation routes between islands, peninsulas, and shores within the lake system. Both authors and others (e.g., Parsons et al. 1982, 1985; Sanders et al. 1979) emphasized the fifteenth-century intensification and expansion of the system.

GEOARCHAEOLOGY AND THE STUDY OF CHINAMPAS IN LAKE XOCHIMILCO

Modern geoarchaeological approaches to evaluate the construction techniques employed in the fossil *chinampas* are few as yet (Ávila 1991; Frederick 2007; Parsons et al. 1985), but agree insofar as the edaphic sequences of the *chinampas* studied show some degree of laminations indicating successive construction stages in which organic material alternates with lacustrine sediment or sediments from other sources (see figure 11.3).

Based on archaeological evidence and Colonial-period historical sources, Frederick (2007) proposed at least three types of *chinampas* according to their construction technique. Our observations at both El Japón together with modern *chinampas* likely used at least from the Colonial period in San Gregorio, as well as other sectors of Xochimilco (Ávila 1993, 1996; Serra 1994), agree with Frederick's perception of a more complex construction process than that described in well-known sources. A notable characteristic in San Gregorio is the absence of evidence for the use of *ahuejotes* (willows) to anchor the edges of the Prehispanic *chinampa* plots. *Ahuejotes* are seemingly absent in the archaeological *chinampas* excavated in Mixquic (Parsons et al. 1985) and Ayotzingo (Frederick 2007), as well.

The stratigraphic sequence is visibly marked by the alternation of lighter strata (light brown, gray or white) with darker lacustrine sediments. Guzman and colleagues (1994) suggested that the lighter strata resulted from alternating periods of desiccation of the lake, whereas Ávila (1993) proposed layers of volcanic ash; however, no analyses were undertaken in either case to support these hypotheses.

X-ray fluorescence analysis (XRF) was employed to evaluate the elemental composition of the individual strata of a *chinampa* and adjacent canal at El Japón

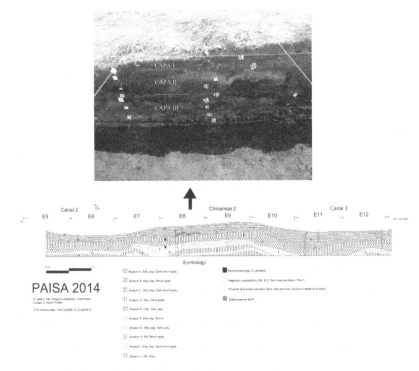

FIGURE 11.3. *Profile of Unit D, El Japón, San Gregorio Atlapulco.*

(see table 11.1), resulting in notable differences between the two components. In the *chinampa*, concentrations of phosphorous (P), silica (Si) and potassium (K) were higher from enrichment of organic material, whereas the canal showed higher concentrations of calcium (Ca) and iron (Fe), likely from the dissolution of these elements in the lake water, precipitation and reductomorphic conditions (see figure 11.4).

With respect to laminations in the *chinampa*, XRF indicates Fe, Ca, and Si as the most relevant elements to define differences between light and dark strata. Principal Components Analysis based on twenty-one elements was used to evaluate these differences, indicating a clear separation of light and dark strata (see figure 11.5a). Clear separations of these strata are also notable in representations of Fe and Si, in which Fe is predominant in the dark strata (see figure 11.5b), likely due to lacustrine sediment, whereas Si is predominant in the light strata, possibly the result of volcanic ash or diatoms. In the case of Si and Ca, the lighter tone of the strata does not result from calcium carbonate concentrations, as calcium is considerably higher in the dark strata (see figure 11.5c).

Lauro González-Quintero (personal communication, 2016) suggested that the lighter strata were intentional inclusions as part of the construction technique,

TABLE 11.1. XRF analysis of major elements by stratum, Unit D, El Japón, San Gregorio Atlapulco (net photon counts)

Stratum	Color	Al	Ca	Fe	K	Mg	Mn	Na	S	Si	Ti	P
Stratum_A	Dark	15977	138976	443707	28909	2171	8107	162	3568	449393	27162	1065
Stratum_B	Dark	16183	146083	460734	26206	1806	8609	140	3331	435483	29644	888
Stratum_C	Light	14729	71354	247299	19525	1373	6257	504	4630	555529	18722	417
Stratum_D	Dark	11701	140125	227105	18264	1400	5087	234	6543	492309	13742	764
Stratum_E	Light	11328	90666	218389	16521	1598	4471	268	4247	552666	10734	495
Stratum_F	Dark	18099	107209	413243	38958	1612	8013	99	2781	429109	23912	207
Stratum_G	Light (-)	14852	84766	279961	27716	1454	6323	165	3955	525519	16501	137
Stratum_H	Light	15315	94270	287044	29807	1357	6090	195	4468	517530	17135	190
Stratum_I	Light	10300	97569	170547	13965	1385	4031	521	4639	551450	9811	325

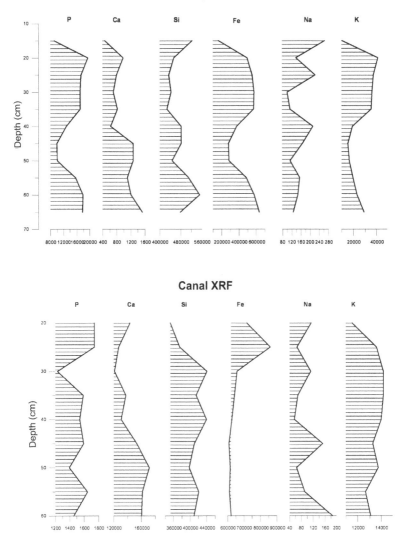

FIGURE 11.4. *Enrichment of major elements in the* chinampa *and canal, Unit D, El Japón,
San Gregorio Atlapulco.*

possibly to increase permeability. The microscopic examination of sediment
samples from the alternating light strata revealed large quantities of diatoms,
suggesting enrichment with diatomaceous sediment, although the practical utility of this procedure has yet to be confirmed. Robles and colleagues (2018) stress
the need to control access of plant roots to adequate humidity by establishing an

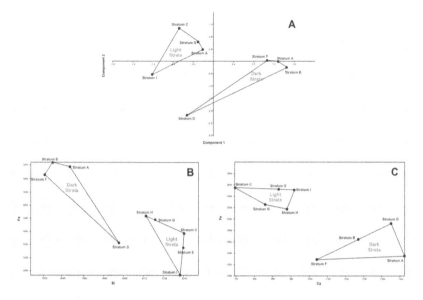

FIGURE 11.5. *(a) Principal component analysis (PC1 vs. PC2, 21 elements) showing a clear separation between light and dark strata; (b) Iron versus silica; (c) Silica versus calcium.*

appropriate balance between the water table and the height of the planting surface. Needless to say, the water table is affected by seasonal and annual changes as well as occasional catastrophic events, such as the 1455 and 1475 earthquakes that damaged several *chinampas* in Tenochtitlan and Chalco (García and Rojas 1992:13). The layers of diatomaceous soil may also have played a part in limiting root exposure to excess humidity.

EVIDENCE FOR AGRICULTURAL PRODUCTION IN *CHINAMPAS*

Several authors suggested that intensive maize production in *chinampas* represented a fundamental resource for the expansion of the Triple Alliance as well as motivation for the conquest of the *chinampa* zone in the early fifteenth century (Coe 1964; Parsons et al. 1985). However, although paleoethnobotanical remains of maize were recovered from *chinampas* in Xaltocan in the northern Basin of Mexico (Morehart and Eisenberg 2010), indicating its importance in this sector, this evidence suggests production for local consumption, as the Triple Alliance had not yet taken control of the island polity.

Evidence for maize in *chinampas* is scarce in the southern part of the Basin. Popper (1995) reported abundant, well-preserved plant resources from a highly stratified sequence of midden deposits interlaced with fill, at the site of Ch-AZ-195. A broad range of cultivated taxa, including maize, beans, squash, as

well as subaquatic taxa such as Cyperaceae, among others, were densely represented. However, although the site was presumably associated with a *chinampa*
community, no direct evidence of *chinampas* themselves was recovered. Other
chinampas in the area of Mixquic were also recorded by Parsons and colleagues
(1985), but plant remains were not recovered.

In the *chinampas* excavated in Iztapalapa, the first concerted effort to recover
plant remains, Ávila (1991) argued that amaranth (*Amaranthus* sp.) was probably
the main cultigen, given the abundance of macrobotanical remains, some of
which were identified as *Amaranthus leucocarpus* (currently classified as *A. hypo-
chondriacus, huauhtli*). Carbonized remains of maize were scarce. Also present
were cultivated or tolerated plants such as *Physalis* sp. (tomatillo), *Solanum rostra-
tum, Chenopodium* sp. (*quelite*) and *Chenopodium ambrosioides* (currently *Dysphania
ambrosioides, epazote*, wormseed).

Similar plant remains, although in significantly larger quantities, were reported
from excavations of *chinampas* and residential platforms in Xochimilco by Ávila
(1993). Maize (*Zea mays*), beans (*Phaseolus* sp.), and chiles (*Capsicum annuum*) were
largely confined to residential platforms and hearths, whereas *Chenopodium* spp.
And *Amaranthus* spp., *Physalis* sp., *Portulaca* sp. Were present in both residential
platforms as well as *chinampas*. Cyperaceae, *Typha* sp. And other subaquatic taxa
were associated with both *chinampa* and canal contexts.

At Ayotzingo, at the former edge of Lake Chalco, Frederick (2007) reported
macrobotanical remains from a *chinampa* deposit in which *Physalis* sp. Was the
most abundant, with evidence for *Chenopodium* sp. In the upper surface. Silva
(2003) undertook a detailed analysis of pollen from the Ayotzingo *chinampa*
and adjacent canal: three pollen subzones were recognized within the *chinampa*
sediments: 1 (360–230 cm); 2 (320–275 cm); and 3 (275–230 cm). The predominant
arboreal taxa represented among the taxa include *Pinus, Quercus* and *Alnus*, to a
lesser degree *Abies*, as well as *Salix*. Aquatic taxa including *Schoenoplectus, Typha*,
and *Polygonum*, and Amaranthaceae were predominant in subzone 1, with spo-
radic presence of *Zea mays* (maize), *Physalis* sp. In subzone 2, aquatic taxa such
as those previously mentioned, and other herbaceous flora associated with agricultural plots were reported. In subzone 3, the upper surface of the *chinampa*,
a single grain of maize was reported among the herbaceous taxa. Although
scarce, *Salix* was present in all three zones. The overlying sediments represented redeposited alluvial sediments from the Amecameca River (Frederick
and Cordova 2019; Silva 2003). Three subzones were also defined for the canal
sediments: 1 (402–352 cm); 2 (352–290 cm), and 3 (290–270 cm). Maize, together
with *Phaseolus, Physalis, Opuntia* (nopal), was detected in subzone 1 of the canal,
together with the aquatic taxa previously mentioned. Amaranthaceae was predominant in subzone 2, accompanied by *Physalis*, and *Zea mays*. In subzone 3, a
notable reduction in pollen is evident. Subaquatic taxa continue, but herbaceous

taxa are considerably diminished: Amaranthaceae (30), *Physalis* (4), *Zea mays* (2) and one of *Phaseolus* (1). Again, the canal is covered by alluvial sediments deposited by the Amecameca River.

Flotation samples from El Japón include families such as Portulacaceae and Amaranthaceae (*Chenopodium* spp.), Cyperaceae (*Schoenoplectus* spp.), and Solanaceae (*Datura stramonium*). Pollen from the *chinampa* in Unit D and the adjacent canal reflect local vegetation in the surrounding area, indicating temperate forest (*Pinus* sp., *Quercus* sp.), associated grassland (Poaceae), and lacustrine taxa including Cyperaceae and *Typha* sp. No macrobotanical evidence for cultivated plants (e.g., maize, squash, beans) was recovered. However, the constant presence of Amaranthaceae (*Chenopodium*-Amaranthaceae) pollen throughout the stratigraphic sequence suggests possible cultivation, although these taxa may also represent indicators of abandonment in which opportunistic plants such as Amaranthaceae, Asteraceae, and Poaceae (grasses) are among the initial colonizers. Starch grains were scarce (Fig. 11.6), but *Capsicum* sp. (chile), *Phaseolus* sp. (frijol) and *Zea mays* (maize) were identified from sediment samples of the *chinampa* (Unidad D), adjacent to the domestic units (Unidad C). Additional sampling and projected analyses based on more recent excavations are in process to broaden the picture of plant taxa associated with the *chinampas*.

To summarize, the macrobotanical and microbotanical evidence available from archaeological *chinampas* is scarce, although consistent. Subaquatic plants, herbaceous taxa (either cultivated or opportunistic edible plants), and a scarce presence of more well-known cultivated plants: maize, beans, squash are similarly represented in the contexts studied to date.

CHINAMPA CHRONOLOGY: DIRECT AND INDIRECT DATING

Dating *chinampa* construction and use is complicated, given the characteristics of the construction techniques involved. Although the technology itself was used to increase land surface within the lakeshore communities as early as the Formative period (Serra 1995; Tolstoy 1975), the construction of *chinampas per se* appears to have been introduced somewhat later. Ávila (1998) reported Middle and Late Postclassic ceramics associated with *chinampas* excavated in the area of San Luis Tlaxialtemalco. In the Parque Ecológico Xochimilco, Serra (1994) reported *chinampas* possibly associated with a nearby Epiclassic occupation. In both instances, associated archaeological materials provided indirect dates that are difficult to confirm given the dynamics associated with typical construction techniques. As Frederick (2007) emphasizes, sediments exogenous to the lacustrine area are frequently employed in the basal layers of *chinampa* construction, which is also evident at El Japón.

Direct dating of *chinampas* from Xaltocan (Morehart 2016; Morehart and Frederick 2014) and Ayotzingo (Frederick and Cordova 2019) suggests that

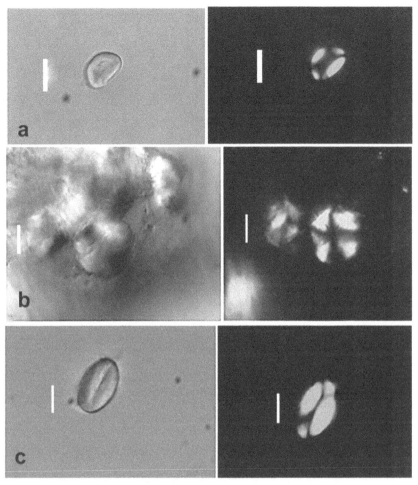

FIGURE 11.6. *Starch grains from Unit D* (chinampa), *El Japón, San Gregorio Atlapulco.* *(a)* Phaseolus *sp.* *(b)* Zea mays. *(c)* Capsicum *sp.*

colonization of the lacustrine plain and initial *chinampa* building took place during the Middle Postclassic, between the twelfth and thirteenth centuries CE. However, determinations obtained from carbonized vegetal material at Xaltocan and in the southern sector of the Basin of Mexico indicate Late Postclassic / Early Colonial construction and utilization.

Radiocarbon determinations from El Japón indicate this period as well. Five ^{14}C determinations were obtained from *chinampas* (CH01) and a nearby domestic mound constructed above an abandoned *chinampa* (Unit C) (see figure 11.2a, figure 11.7, and table 11.2).

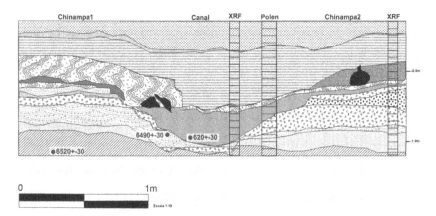

FIGURE 11.7. *Profile of* Chinampa *CH01, El Japón, San Gregorio Atlapulco. Location of radiocarbon-dated charcoal samples and XRF/pollen sampling sequence at 5 cm intervals.*

TABLE 11.2. Radiocarbon determinations from Late Postclassic *chinampas* (Unit D) and domestic area. All calibrations were undertaken in OxCal version 4.3.2 (Bronk Ramsey 2017) using the IntCal 13 atmospheric curve (Reimer et al. 2013).

Beta lab no.	Material	Conventional RCYBP	Calibrated years	Excavation Unit/layer/level
423135	Charred material	600±30	1297(95.4) 1409 cal CE	C/layer III, level 7
423134	Charred material	300±40	1489(69.6%)1604 cal CE 1611(25.8%)1654 cal CE	C/layer IV, level 8
498610	Charred material	6520±30	5547 (88.6%)5465 cal BCE 5441 (23%)5423 cal BCE 5407 (4.5%)5384 cal BCE	D/underlying canal
498612	Charred material	6490±30	5511 (95.4) 5374 cal BCE	D *chinampa*
498613	Charred material	620±30	1292 (95.4%)1401 cal CE	D canal

Radiocarbon dates on charcoal indicate that the basal sediment of the *chinampas* corresponds to material from the preceramic occupation of the original *tlatel*. Two determinations from charcoal from the base of one of the excavated *chinampas*, constructed using sediments from the *tlatel*, were congruent with the preceramic Playa-phase occupation: 6490±30 (Beta 498612) and 6520±30 (Beta

498610) RCYBP. A third, from the base of the adjacent canal: 620±30 (Beta 498613) RCYBP, calibrated to between 1292 and 1400 CE, agrees with the initial Late Postclassic occupation and ceramics (ca. 1400 CE). Two charcoal samples from a domestic platform next to the *chinampas* suggest the upper limit to *chinampa* occupation at the site: 600±30 (Beta 423135) from Level 7 of Layer III, toward the end of the Late Postclassic, and 300±30 (Beta 423134) from Level 8 of Layer IV, during the Early Colonial occupation.

CONCLUSION

The legacy of transformation of the lacustrine environment into a highly productive agroecological system persists today. An interesting example of how the lacustrine context has been impacted by *chinampa* agriculture is the "domestication" of *Salix bonplandiana* var. *fastigiata* (*ahuejote*), the willow species that reproduces exclusively by vegetative propagation rather than by seedlings and was possibly used since historic times to secure the edges of *chinampa* plots (Corona and Chimal 1994).

Although analyses of different aspects of the *chinampa* system at El Japón continues, research at San Gregorio represents a contribution to the study of this agroecological system. The characteristics of Prehispanic–Colonial *chinampas* in this sector of Xochimilco are considerably more diverse than historical and ethnographic depictions suggest, which argues for broader studies of *chinampas* and related structures in the Basin. Beyond details concerning *chinampa* construction and chronology, the geoarchaeological and ecological focus of analyses in progress contributes to an understanding of human adaptations to variable geological, geomorphological and ecological conditions, from the earliest evidence for preceramic occupation to the present, in which *chinamperos* struggle to maintain traditional cultivation in the face of modernization.

Furthermore, recent excavations at El Japón provide new data while simultaneously raising new questions that require continued research. Photogrammetric studies and systematic test excavations indicate that the original islet was amplified in both extension and elevation around the fourteenth century. From then until the end of the sixteenth century, site dimension increased within the lake through the construction of agricultural *chinampas*. Simultaneously, habitational space increased through infilling of canals between *chinampas* in some areas, above which habitational platforms such as Unit C were constructed. González (1996:87) observed this process during excavations undertaken at the western edge of the site, where *chinampas* were visible below the fill of habitational platforms. The extension of *chinampa* agriculture at the beginning of the fifteenth century likely corresponds to the demographic expansion of Tenochtitlan, and a significant investment in large-scale hydraulic works to reduce the risks of construction on the unstable lakeshore plain and to guarantee control over the water level and potential salinity of the lake system, undertaken mainly during the mid-fifteenth century at the behest of the first three Mexica rulers (Palerm 1973). Excavations at sites peripheral to Tenochtitlan would be useful to further evaluate the role of *chinampa* technology in facilitating urban growth around the Mexica capital.

While ethnohistoric research and analysis of documents concerning *chinampas* (Rojas Rabiela 1983, 1995) represent a fundamental underpinning for understanding hydraulic technology and traditional indigenous agricultural techniques in the Basin, modern geoarchaeological applications suggest greater diversity in construction techniques and adaptation to particular conditions. Apparently, not only lacustrine sediments were employed to build up agricultural surfaces, but also terrestrial sediments from the *tlateles* as well as piedmont soils, on occasion. The appearance at El Japón of diatomaceous sediments alternating with other strata is likely intentional, although its specific function has yet to be determined.

Evidence for plants cultivated on Prehispanic *chinampas* has been inconclusive at best. Analyses of flotation samples provides some evidence for possible cultigens—largely Amaranthaceae—however, poor preservation of macrobotanical remains often limits the ability to differentiate between cultivated taxa and their sympatric weeds. Incorporation of analyses of microbotanical remains (polen, phytoliths, and starch grains) on a systematic basis will contribute to resolving such questions. However, the dynamics of *chinampa* construction and periodic renovation, including constant aggregation of lacustrine and exogenous materials, potential contamination from domestic refuse, and removal of the surface to reduce the effects of salinization, confuse the interpretation of plant remains recovered from excavation.

Finally, dating the periods during which *chinampas* were in use is hindered by the construction techniques themselves. While relative dating based on diagnostic ceramic types is helpful to some extent, the use of exogenous sediments during renovations offers multiple opportunities for mixing artifacts. Direct dating of sediment organic material is impractical given the dynamics of construction and maintenance, thus requiring the recovery of charcoal in sediments deposited as the result of human activities. However, results obtained so far from El Japón and, apparently, Ayotzingo as well, indicate that the basal sediments of *chinampas* may be considerably older than the structures themselves. Thus, the importance of datable materials from the upper levels of *chinampas*, or from adjacent canals in which decapitated surfaces were undoubtedly redeposited. Needless to say, the construction techniques of the *chinampas* studied to date do not favor the preservation of optimal remains for radiocarbon dating.

As a final reflection, we leave more questions for continuing the study of archaeological *chinampas*, rather than firm conclusions. However, research continues at El Japón, as additional excavations undertaken in 2019 will benefit from the lessons learned during past seasons.

Acknowledgments. The study of *chinampas* in San Gregorio Atlapulco has received financial support from the following grants: *El desarrollo de las sociedades agrarias en la Cuenca de México* (PAPIIT/DGAPA-UNAM-IG400513, E. McClung de Tapia/G Acosta, Co-PI's); *Impacto humano en el área de Xochimilco durante los últimos 8,000 años* (PAPIIT/DGAPA-UNAM-IG400217, E. McClung de Tapia/L. Beramendi, Co-PI's); *Sedentarismo Temprano y Primeras Comunidades Agrarias en la Cuenca de México* (CONACYT-CB-253664, G. Acosta, PI). Additional financial and logistical support is provided by the Instituto de Investigaciones Antropológicas and Instituto de Geología, UNAM. Thanks to Diana Martínez and Kenya Díaz (macrobotanical analysis), Carmen Cristina Adriano (phytoliths and diatoms), Carlos Matos Llanes (starch grains), Laura Beramendi-Orosco, Galia González-Hernández (interpretation of radiocarbon determinations). A special thanks to Virginia Popper, for providing a digital version of her PhD dissertation, saving the day in an otherwise rarefied research environment and the inaccessibility of bibliographic resources in our respective laboratories.

REFERENCES

Acosta, Guillermo. 2017. "Early Agricultural Modes of Production in Mesoamerica: New Insights from Southern and Central Mexico." In *Modes of Production and Archaeology*, edited by Robert M. Rosenswig and Jerimy J. Cunningham, 73–98. University Press of Florida, Gainesville.

Acosta, Guillermo, Patricia Pérez, Joaquín Arroyo, Emily McClung, Dian Martínez, Cristina Adriano, Irán Rivera, Jorge Ezra, Emilio Ibarra, Víctor Hugo García, Diana Blancas, Jessica Hernández, and Francisco López. 2020. "Informe técnico." Tercera fase del Proyecto Poblamiento, Agricultura Inicial y Sociedades Aldeanas en la Cuenca de México (PAISA): Excavaciones en san Gregorio Atlapulco, CDMX. Informe remitido al Consejo de Arqueología del INAH. UNAM, Mexico City.

Acosta, José de. 2020 [1590]. *Historia natural y moral de las Indias*. Red Ediciones, Mexico City.

Alvarado Tezozomoc, Hernando. 1997 [1598]. *Crónica mexicana*, edited by Díaz Migoyo, Gonzalo and Germán Vázquez Chamorro, Historia 16-Información e Historia S.L. Madrid. Electronic document. https://iaa801905.us.archive.org/22/items/CronicaMexicanaEdicionDEG.DiazMigoyo/H.AlvaradoTezozomocCrnicaMexicana.pdf, accessed August 28, 2020.

Alzate, José Antonio de. 1993. "Memoria sobre Agricultura (1791)." In *Agricultura chinampera, compilación histórica*, edited by Teresa Rojas, 13–30. Universidad Autónoma Chapingo, Chapingo.

Apenes, O. 1943. "The 'Tlateles' of Lake Texcoco." *American Antiquity* 9:29–32.

Armillas, P. 1971. "Gardens on Swamps." *Science* 17:653–61.

Ávila, Raúl. 1991. *Chinampas de Iztapalapa, D. F.* Instituto Nacional de Antropología e Historia, Mexico City.

Ávila, Raúl. 1993. *La ocupación del espacio lacustre en Xochimilco.* Informe entregado la Dirección de Salvamento Arqueológico del INAH, Mexico City.

Ávila, Raúl. 1996. *Excavaciones arqueológicas en San Gregorio Atlapulco, Xochimilco.* Informe entregado la Dirección de Salvamento Arqueológico del INAH, Mexico City.

Ávila, Raúl. 1998. *Investigaciones del Proyecto Arqueologico San Luis Taxialtemalco. Primera Parte: Las chinampas arqueológicas.* Technical report submitted to INAH. Salvamento Arqueológico, Mexico City.

Blanton, Richard. 1972. *Prehispanic Settlement Patterns of the Ixtapalapa Peninsula Region, Mexico.* Occasional Papers in Anthropology, no. 6. Department of Anthropology, The Pennsylvania State University, University Park.

Bronk Ramsey, Christopher. 2017. "Methods for Summarizing Radiocarbon Datasets." *Radiocarbon* 59:1809–33.

Carballo, Ciro, ed. 2006. *Xochimilco: Un proceso de gestión participativa.* UNESCO México, Mexico City.

Coe, Michael. 1964. "The Chinampas of Mexico." *Scientific American* 260:90–96.

Corona, Eduardo. 1977. *Formas de organización política en el México Prehispánico*, INAH, Mexico City.

Corona, Víctor, and Aurora Chimal. 1994. "Algunos árboles ornamentales notables del Valle de México." *Revista Chapingo. Serie Horticultura* 1:96–99.

Durán, Fray Diego. 1967 [1581]. *Historia de las Indias de Nueva España e Islas de la Tierra Firme*, vol. 2, translated by Angel Ma. Garibay. Editorial Porrua, S.A., Mexico City.

Frederick, Charles D. 2007. "Chinampa Cultivation in the Basin of Mexico: Observations on the Evolution of Form and Function." In *Seeking a Richer Harvest: The Archaeology of Subsistence Intensification, Innovation, and Change*, edited by T. Thurston and C. T. Fisher, 107–24. Studies in Human Ecology and Adaptation. Springer US, New York.

Frederick, Charles D., and Carlos E. Cordova. 2019. "Prehispanic and Colonial Landscape Change and Fluvial Dynamics in the Chalco Region, Mexico." *Geomorphology* 331:107–26.

García, Virginia, and Teresa Rojas. 1992. "Los sismos como fenómeno social: Una visión histórica." In *Macrosismos. Aspectos físicos, sociales, económicos y políticos*, edited by Emilio Rosenblueth, 9–16. Impresiones Cuadratin, Mexico City.

Gibson, Charles. 1964. *The Aztecs under Spanish Rule.* Stanford University Press, Redwood City, CA.

González, Carlos Javier. 1996. "Investigaciones arqueológicas en 'El Japón': Sitio chinampero en Xochimilco." *Arqueología* 16:81–93.

Guzman, María Esther, Carlos Lazcano, and Guillermo Pérez. 1994. "Las Excavaciones Arqueológicas." In Mari Carmen Serra, ed. *Xochimilco arqueológico.* Patronato Parque Ecológico Xochimilco, Mexico City.

Lechuga, Martha. 1977. "Análisis de un elemento de la estructura económica azteca: La chinampa." Master's thesis in Archaeology. Escuela Nacional de Antropología e Historia, Mexico City.

Luna Golya, Robert. 2014. "Modeling the Aztec Agricultural Waterscape of Lake Xochimilco: A GIS Analysis of Lakebed Chinampas and Settlement." PhD dissertation, Department of Anthropology, The Pennsylvania State University, University Park.

McClung, Emily, and Guillermo Acosta. 2015. "Una ocupación del periodo de agricultura temprana en Xochimilco (ca. 4200–4000 a.n.e.)." *Anales de antropología* 49(2):299–315.

Molina, Alonso de. 1970 [1571]. *Vocabulario en lengua castellana y mexicana y mexicana y castellana.* Editorial Porrua, Mexico City.

Morehart, Christopher T. 2010. "The Archaeology of Farmscapes: Production, Place, and the Materiality of Landscape at Xaltocan, Mexico." PhD dissertation, Department of Anthropology, Northwestern University, Evanston, IL.

Morehart, Christopher T. 2012. "Mapping Ancient Chinampa Landscapes in the Basin of Mexico: A Remote Sensing and GIS Approach." *Journal of Archaeological Science* 39:2541–51.

Morehart, Christopher T. 2016. "Chinampa Agriculture, Surplus Production, and Political Change at Xaltocan, Mexico." *Ancient Mesoamerica* 27(1):183–96.

Morehart, Christopher T., and Dan T. A. Eisenberg. 2010. "Prosperity, Power, and Change: Modeling Maize at Postclassic Xaltocan, Mexico." *Journal of Anthropological Archaeology* 29:94–112.

Morehart, Christopher T., and Charles D. Frederick. 2014. "The Chronology and Collapse of Pre-Aztec Raised Field (Chinampa) Agriculture in the Northern Basin of Mexico." *Antiquity* 88(340):531–48.

Palerm, A. 1973. *Obras hidráulicas prehispánicas en el sistema lacustre del Valle de México.* Secretaría de Educación Pública, Instituto Nacional de Antropología e Historia, Mexico City.

Parsons, Jeffrey R. 1971. *Prehispanic Settlement Patterns in the Texcoco Region, México.* Memoirs of the Museum of Anthropology, no. 3. University of Michigan. Ann Arbor.

Parsons, Jeffrey R., Elizabeth Brumfiel, Mary H. Parsons, and David J. Wilson. 1982. *Prehispanic Settlement Patterns in the Southern Valley of México: The Chalco-Xochimilco Región.* Memoirs of the Museum of Anthropology, no. 14. University of Michigan, Ann Arbor.

Parsons, Jeffrey R., Kintigh Keith, and Susan Gregg. 1983. *Archaeological Settlement Pattern Data from the Chalco, Xochimilco, Ixtapalapa, Texcoco, and Zumpango Regions, México.* Technical Reports, no. 14. Museum of Anthropology, University of Michigan, Ann Arbor.

Parsons, Jeffrey R., Mary H. Parsons, Virginia S. Popper, and Mary Taft. 1985. "Chinampa Agriculture and Aztec Urbanization in the Valley of Mexico." *Prehistoric*

Intensive Agriculture in the Tropics, edited by I. S. Farrington, 49–96. BAR International Series, no. 232. British Archaeological Reports, Oxford.

Popper, Virginia S. 1995. "Nahua Plant Knowledge and Chinampa Farming in the Basin of Mexico: A Middle Postclassic Case Study." PhD dissertation, Department of Anthropology, University of Michigan, Ann Arbor.

Ramos-Bello, Rosalía, Norma García-Calderon, Manuel Ortega-Escobar, and Pavel Krasilnikov. 2011. "Artificial Chinampas Soils of Mexico City: Their Properties and Salinization Hazards." *Spanish Journal of Soil Science* 1:71–85.

Reimer, Paula J., Edouard Bard, Alex Bayliss, J. Warren Beck, Paul G. Blackwell, Christopher Bronk Ramsey, Caitlin Buck, Hai Cheng, R. Lawrence Edwards, Michael Friedrich, Pieter M. Grootes, Thomas P. Guilderson, Haflidi Haflidason, Irka Hajdas, Christine Hatté, Timothy J. Heaton, Dirk L. Hoffman, Alan G. Hogg, Konrad A. Hughen, K. Felix Kaiser, Bernd Kromer, Sturt W. Manning, Mu Niu, Ron W. Reimer, David A. Richards, E. Marian Scott, John R. Southon, Richard A. Staff, Christian S. M. Turney, and Johannes van der Plicht. 2013. "IntCal13 and Marine13 Radiocarbon Age Calibration Curves 0–50,000 Years cal BP." *Radiocarbon* 55:1869–87.

Rivera, Irán. 2019. "Los grupos precerámicos de las playas lacustres de la Cuenca de México: Ocupación y transformación del entorno durante el Holoceno Medio." PhD dissertation in Mesoamerican Studies, Universidad Nacional Autónoma de México, Mexico City.

Robles, Braulio, and Jorge Flores, Jose Luis Martínez, and Patricia Herrera. 2018. "The Chinampa: A Mexican Sub-Irrigation System." *Irrigation and Drainage* 68:115–22, https://doi.org/10.1002/ird.2310.

Rojas Rabiela, Teresa. 1983. *Agricultura chinampera, compilación histórica*. Universidad Autónoma Chapingo, Chapingo.

Rojas Rabiela, Teresa. 1995. *Presente, pasado y futuro de las chinampas*. CIESAS, Mexico City.

Ruiz-Gutiérrez, Ernesto. 2012. "El patrimonio cultural y ambiental de Xochimilco en riesgo." Tesis, Maestría en Políticas Públicas Comparadas. FLACSO México, Mexico City.

Sanders, William T. 1957. "Tierra y Agua (Soil and Water): A Study of the Ecological Factors in the Development of Meso-American Civilizations." PhD dissertation, Harvard University, Cambridge, MA.

Sanders, William T. 1962. "Cultural Ecology of Nuclear Mesoamerica." *American Anthropologist* 64:34–44.

Sanders, William T. 1965. *The Cultural Ecology of the Teotihuacan Valley*. University Park, Department of Sociology and Anthropology, The Pennsylvania State University.

Sanders, William T. 1972. "Population, Agricultural History and Societal Evolution in Mesoamerica." In *Population Growth: Anthropological Implications*, edited by B. Spooner, 101–53. Cambridge, MA, MIT Press.

Sanders, William T., and Barbara J. Price. 1968. *Mesoamerica: The Evolution of a Civilization*. Nueva York, Random House.

Sanders, William T., Jeffrey R. Parsons, and Robert S. Santley. 1979. *The Basin of México: Ecological Processes in the Evolution of a Civilization*. Academic Press, New York.

Sanders, William T. and Larry J. Gorenflo. 2007. *Prehispanic Settlement Patterns in the Cuautitlan Region, Mexico*. Occasional Papers in Anthropology, no. 29. Department of Anthropology, The Pennsylvania State University, University Park.

Schulze, Niklas, and Ciro Carballo. 2006. "Xochimilco: Un sistema de valores patrimoniales, atributos y amenazas." In *Xochimilco: Un proceso de gestión participativa*, edited by Ciro Caraballo, 101–12. UNESCO México, Mexico City.

Serra, Mari Carmen, ed. 1994. *Xochimilco arqueológico*. Patronato Parque Ecológico Xochimilco, Mexico City.

Serra, Mari Carmen. 1995. "Terremote-Tlaltenco una aldea lacustre de la Cuenca que no construyó Chinampas." In *Presente, pasado y futuro de las chinampas*, coordinated by Teresa Rojas, 47–52. CIESAS, Mexico City.

Silva, María Gabriela. 2003. *Análisis palinológico del perfil de una antigua chinampa en Ayotzingo, Chalco, Edo. de México*. Maestría en Biología Vegetal, Facultad de Ciencias, Universidad Nacional Autónoma de México, Mexico City.

Sluyter, Andrew. 1994. "Intensive Wetland Agriculture in Mesoamerica: Space, Time, and Form." *Annals of the Association of American Geographers* 84(4):557–84.

Smith, Michael. 1980. "The Role of the Marketing Systems in Aztec Society and Economy: Reply to Evans." *American Antiquity* 45(4):876–83.

Tolstoy, Paul. 1975. "Settlement and Population Trends in the Basin of Mexico (Ixtapaluca and Zacatenco Phases)." *Journal of Field Archaeology* 2:331–49.

West, Robert, and Pedro Armillas. 1950. "Las Chinampas de México." *Cuadernos americanos* 2:165–82.

PART V

Reexamining the Political Economy of Interaction in the Basin of Mexico and Beyond

12

Advances in the Study of Archaeological Ceramics of the Epiclassic and Early Postclassic Basin of Mexico

DESTINY L. CRIDER

INTRODUCTION

Teotihuacan maintained territorial control of the Basin of Mexico until its political demise. Due in large part to the Basin of Mexico (BOM) survey projects, this region provides a rich setting for assessing social, political, and economic responses to state collapse. Archaeological ceramics are utilized to identify regional trends that span the Epiclassic period (ca. 650–850 CE) immediately following the collapse of Teotihuacan, and then the rise of the Early Postclassic period (ca. 850–1150 CE) states of Tula and Cholula. Ceramic analysis provides evidence for assessing the degree of local participation in regional cultural complexes, as well as for the rearrangement of social and economic ties between the newly created polities following Teotihuacan's decline.

Specifically, formal and decorative traditions communicate knowledge of and membership in broader shared traditions, reflecting expression of shared sociopolitical identity among regional participants. Compositional analysis provides evidence for exchange of pottery products between neighboring regions. Thus, the combination of stylistic and compositional patterns can differentiate shared

https://doi.org/10.5876/9781646424078.c012

identity, emulation, and direct trade. Similar techniques for the BOM indicate that the extent of stylistic and compositional patterns are meaningful measures for social interaction (e.g., Hodge and Minc 1990; Nichols et al. 2002; see also Parkinson 2005 for a non-state example of boundary formations). Evidence from exchange and local production reflect alternative models of interaction between neighboring areas within the BOM and Tula to the northwest.

CHRONOLOGY OF REGIONAL CERAMIC COMPLEXES AND TYPE CONCORDANCE, AND SAMPLING

Archaeological studies have recognized co-occurrences of *ceramic types*, placed into *ceramic complexes*, and provide a framework for comparisons of ceramic assemblages among settlements that span the Epiclassic to Early Postclassic periods (see table 12.1). The Epiclassic is divided into the *Early Epiclassic* and *Coyotlatelco Epiclassic*, the Early Postclassic is divided into the *Early Postclassic Mazapan, Early Postclassic Tollan,* and *Early Postclassic Aztec I / Chalco-Cholula* pottery complexes (see table 12.1). These partitions allow exploration of relative chronological placement and facilitates synchronic and diachronic assessment of interaction.

The archaeological chronology of the BOM suffers from the common problem of multiple, but inconsistent, pottery typologies. For example, a few Epiclassic and Early Postclassic diagnostic types are easily identifiable, but regional inter-site comparison has been rare. Consequently, while sufficient for the purposes of relative chronology in the BOM surveys (e.g., Sanders et al. 1979), the importance of resolving a type concordance was recognized early in the study of Basin archaeology, where "no genuinely adequate typology of Late Classic [i.e., Epiclassic] and Early Postclassic Valley of Mexico ceramics is available, although such is an indispensable prerequisite to a satisfactory understanding of the nature of the transition between the Classic and Postclassic in this key Mesoamerica area" (Nicholson and Hicks 1961:9).

My process of constructing a concordance of Epiclassic and Early Postclassic Central Mexican pottery builds on the detailed documentation of my predecessors and colleagues, including (but not limited to) Teotihuacan (Bennyhoff 1967; Rattray 1966; Sanders 1986), Cerro Portezuelo (Hicks 2005), Tula (Cobean 1978, 1990), Xico-Chalco (Hodge 2008; O'Neill 1962; Parsons et al. 1982), and Cholula (Lind 1994; McCafferty 2001; Noguera 1954; Suárez Cruz 1995). This baseline step works toward rectifying the persistent problem of conflicting type-naming conventions used by researchers over the decades, which inhibits a macro-regional synthesis. Such a concordance is essential for assessing interaction among major settlements and to build consensus in ceramic classification and also track sub-regional variation.

BOM survey collections and related excavations provided samples for technological, stylistic, and compositional data collection (see table 12.2). However, not

TABLE 12.1. Schematic of associated pottery types by chronological periods and phases for Tula and Basin of Mexico

CE	Period	Tula		Teotihuacan		Southern Basin Complex	
		Phase	Types	Phase	Types	Phase	Types
550	Terminal Classic	La Mesa (?)	CS bowls Coyotlatelco style	Metepec		Early Epiclassic	CS bowls Tezonchichilco Zone Incised Incised and Punctate stamp simple
650							
750	Epiclassic	Prado	Guadalupe Incised Ana Maria RB Clara Luz Black Incised	Oxtoticpac	CS bowls resist stamp simple		
850		Corral	Coyotlatelco Jimenez Stamped	Xometla	stamp complex? Coyotlatelco	Coyotlatelco	Coyotlatelco stamp complex?
		Terminal Corral	Wavy Line Blanco White	Mazapan	Wavy Line (Matte)	Mazapan	Wavy Line (Burnished)
950	Early Postclassic	Early Tollan	Joroba Cream Slip Ink Stamped? Macana Proa Cream Slip Blanco Levantado Sillon incised		Joroba Cream Slip Sloppy RN Macana		Joroba Cream Slip Sloppy RN Macana
1050		Late Tollan		Atlatongo	Proa Cream Slip Blanco Levantado Orange Incised Jara Pulido Ira Stamped	Tollan / Aztec I / Early Aztec	Proa Cream Slip Blanco Levantado Orange Incised Jara Pulido Ira Stamped
1150		Fuego	Jara Pulido Ira Stamped	Aztec II		Aztec II	Aztec I Chalco-Cholula Polychrome
1250	Middle Postclassic						
1350							

TABLE 12.2. Collections used in this study by region and time period. Permissions of use for the collections were provided by various individuals and institutions.

Region and Project			Collection Strategy	Period
Northwestern Basin	Tula. Hidalgo			
		Tula Chico (Cobean)	Excavation	EPI
		Household/Workshop (Healan)	Excavation	EPC
		Tula Salvage (Gamboa, INAH)	Excavation	EPI, EPC
North Basin	Zumpango			
		Zumpango Regional Survey (Parsons)	Survey	EPI, EPC
	Xaltocan			
		ET (Early Toltec) Site (Brumfiel)	both	EPI
		Xaltocan (Brumfiel)	Excavation	EPC, AZ I
NE Basin	Teotihuacan			
		Teotihuacan Mapping Project (Cowgill)	Survey	EPI, EPC
		Vaillant Mazapan Burials (AMNH)	Excavation	EPI, EPC
		Teotihuacan Valley Rural Survey (Sanders)	Survey	EPI, EPC
Southern Basin	Cerro Portezuelo			
		UCLA Excavations	both	EPI, EPC
	Chalco			
		Chalco Regional Survey (Parsons)	Survey	EPI, EPC
		Chalco Mound 65 (Hodge)	Excavation	EPI, EPC
		Xico Chinampa (Parsons)	Excavation	EPI, EPC
		Xico Survey Collection (AMNH)	Survey	EPI, EPC
	Ixtapalapa			
		Ixtapalapa Regional Survey (Blanton)	Survey	EPI, EPC

EPI = Epiclassic; EPC = Early Postclassic; AZ I = Early Aztec; AMNH = American Museum of Natural History; UCLA = University of California Los Angeles all pottery types or styles are found in abundance throughout the Basin; effort was made to include as many samples as available. Judgment was used with the time available to select specimens exhibiting local variation of attributes. Best efforts were made to select a representative sample given practical consideration of logistics.

INCLUDING FOCUS ON THE DETAILS: WHY ATTRIBUTES MATTER

Technological Attribute Analysis

The attribute details of vessel form, design, and stylistic are the smallest quantifiable or describable levels of data collection (see table 12.3). They are used to identify patterns of variation at local and regional scales. Technological attributes identify production steps and choice in vessel formation, like shapes, paste, firing, surface treatment, and overall quality of design execution and investment in construction. They are selected to address the social and economic dimensions of past societies. Lechtman (1977, 1993) invokes "technological style" for discussing the "nonmaterial dimensions of prehistoric behavior from the identification of the rule-bound similarities empirically manifest in material culture" (Dobres and Hoffman 1994:218). I follow the methodological agenda set by Dietler and Herbich (1998:238), who argue for an integrated view of "material" style that identifies patterning in technological, formal, and decorative aspects (Dietler and Herbich 1989; Herbich 1987; Herbich and Dietler 1991) in order to view production of material culture as a series of operational choices (Dietler and Herbich 1998; Dobres 2000; Dobres and Hoffman 1994; Schiffer and Skibo 1987; Van der Leeuw 1993).

Patterned and repeated selection of particular technological, formal, and decorative practices is a material manifestation of participation in a particular worldview (Dobres and Hoffman 1994:220). The producer is an active agent in the technological and decorative choices of pottery manufacture, described as "the producer's rational responses to the context of manufacture and use" (Arnold 2007:86). In the context of craft production, style represents a unique way to understand the interplay between the skill and creativity of the producer and the prevailing aesthetics and demand for their decorative products. Producers are aware of the technological and decorative practices of neighboring groups and make choices about their own products that reflect differences with those groups (Lemonnier 1986:161). I selected metrics and qualitative attributes within pottery types to record preferences reflective of potters' choices in production attributes when also conforming to regional demand for ceramic types and forms. In some cases, I am able to discern localized practices (e.g., the use of bird effigy supports on Macana-type *molcajetes* at Cerro Portezuelo), distinctive breaks in surface finish and motif between areas (e.g., burnished or

TABLE 12.3. Types of data collected for attribute studies across all types (from Crider 2011, 2013a).

Tracking Information	Technological Analysis	Decorative Analysis
Collection/Project	General Form	Interior and Exterior Surface Treatment
Specimen Identification	Form Details	Dimensions of Painted Rim Band
Temporal Designation	Rim Shape	Decorative Technique
Pottery Complex	Rim Angle	Decorative Motif
INAA Sample Number	Vessel Measurements	Vessel Color
	Wall to Base Angle	Pail/Slip Color
	Rim Diameter	Quality of Manufacture
	Base Diameter	Quality of Decoration
	Length of Support	Quality of Paint
	Angle of Support	Motif and Design Elements
	Location of Support	Vessel Support Shape
	Wall Thickness	
	Paste Qualities	
	Carbon Core	
	Fire Clouding	

matte surface on Wavy Line), and selection of recipes in paint and paste (e.g., the use of specular hematite in Coyotlatelco).

Decoration and Stylistic Attribute Analysis

Ethnographic studies suggest that decoration is sensitive to the context of vessel use (e.g., Arnold 1985; Arnold 2000; Costin 2000; Kramer 1985). In this sense, Arnold (2007:107) reminds us that stylistic and decorative elements were chosen in anticipation of their most "decoration demanding" context (e.g., feasting, gifting, burial). Thus, to assess the range of variation in aesthetics, attributes were selected to record decorative techniques (e.g., painted, incised, and stamped), design elements and motifs, and design layout (see table 12.3). Decorative choice conveys meaning and messages in socially constructed contexts (Wobst 1977, 1999). Decorative attributes that are highly visible and are easily copied and emulated might include decorative motifs and design elements that convey messaging by *what* is depicted. Other stylistic attributes are dependent on *how* they are implemented; low-visibility or close-proximity learning can be expressed via design grammars used among local potters. (Chilton 1998:134, 1999:50). The overall patterning of these attributes indicates production choices in vessel finish that distinguish production areas from one another and that highlight choices common between producers either to distinguish their products from others' and also to conform to aesthetic conventions required by consumers. Consequently, the patterned and repeated use of design can provide some clues to the visual domain and worldview of the pottery users and can suggest long-distance interactions, as local potters emulate and incorporate regionally important icons into local pottery.

COMPOSITIONAL ANALYSIS

Sampling for chemical characterization using instrumental neutron activation analysis (INAA) at the Missouri University Research Reactor (MURR) includes comparable pottery types across several regional blocks of the BOM. Specimens from previous studies of Epiclassic pottery from the Teotihuacan projects (Crider et al. 2007) and from Cerro Portezuelo (Crider 2013a; Nichols et al. 2002; Nichols et al. 2013) are included with newly acquired specimens (Crider 2011).

Developing Compositional Groups

My first step was to define reference groups within the MURR Central Mexican Database that would utilize specimens with compositional group assignments that were available not only for the Basin of Mexico, but also for Puebla, the Gulf Coast, the Toluca Valley, and Yautepec regions. The MURR-derived reference collection would provide the statistical parameters for defining compositional groups for Central Mexico pottery (cf. Glascock 1992; Neff 2000; Neff and Glascock 1998). Regional INAA studies demonstrate that the geomorphological characteristics of Central Mexico allow differentiation within the BOM (cf. Bennyhoff and Heizer 1965; Crider et al. 2007; Garraty 2006; Hodge and Minc 1990; Rodríguez-Alegría 2002; Stoner et al. 2015). The chemical resolution for Basin clays is such that compositional groups can be distinguished along a north-south and an west-east axis, roughly corresponding to BOM-derived quadrants. Discriminant analysis (DA) using SPSS statistical software with MURR-defined compositional assignments informed the reference group definitions. Through an interactive process, specimens were examined for probability of fit to membership in a group, dropping low probability members each round in order to distill the reference groups into statistically significant sets of reference specimens. The newly defined Compositional Group Reference Set was then used in DA, and new Epiclassic and Early Postclassic specimens were assigned to groups (see Crider 2011 for more detail).

HIERARCHY IN COMPOSITIONAL GROUP MEMBERSHIP

The Central Mexican Database from MURR was at the time heavily represented by Postclassic (Aztec occupations), and compositional group naming conventions often reference Aztec site names. Sanders, Parsons, and Santley (1979) show how settlement clusters, as defined by regional surveys, shift over time. Aztec settlements were often in different locations than earlier settlements. I implement

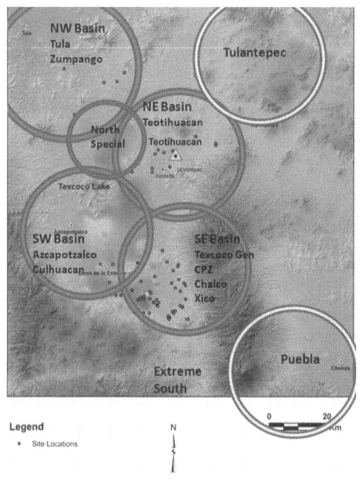

FIGURE 12.1. *Schematic of probable regions of compositional groups discussed in table 12.3.*

a scalable hierarchy of compositional group membership that favors inclusion at the highest regional level first, and then to more localized scales of group membership as statistically defensible (see table 12.4). This results in few "unassigned" designations, and when possible allows for group refinement within (1) the macro-regional quadrants of the Basin of Mexico, and (2) within-quadrant and subgroups (see Crider et al. 2018 for more refined Teotihuacan Valley subgroups). Element scatterplots were used to visually interrogate structures in the multivariate data to refine subgroup definitions. It was not always possible to connect compositional groups to specific locales on the landscape, but most specimens are placed somewhere within the hierarchy of BOM group membership. The resulting compositional groups (see figure 12.1) are discussed in

TABLE 12.4. Schematic of probable locations for compositional groups and subgroups in the Basin of Mexico. Compositional groups are organized by quadrant within the Basin of Mexico and then into smaller subgroups within relative quadrant. Counts represent amounts per type assigned to compositional groups. Results indicate multiple production locales across the region. There is some regional specialization across and within ceramic types.

	Compositional Group Hierarchy	Tulantepec (Non-Basin North)	Tula	Tula G2	Tula Outlier	Basin NW	North X BL	North X	Xaltocan ET	Xaltocan BO-2	Teotihuacan	Texcoco	CPZ	Chalco	Xico	Azcapotzalco	Culhuacan	South 3	Yautepec	Puebla	Unassigned	Grand Total
Selected Epiclassic Pottery	Tezonchichilco										2		2	22	3	2		2				33
	Zone Incised								1		1		4	18	4							28
	Composite Silhouette (CS)										11	6	43	1		2	9					72
	Incised & Punctate										6		6	3	2		6					23
	Resist										5	1	1	2	4		1					14
	Incised—Carved		1					1	15		2	1	1	1	4							26
	Monochrome stamp							2	4		10		12	1	3							32
	Misc Red-on-natural										18	2	1	1								22
	Coyotlatelco painted	7	28	8	4	1		1	3		70	2	48	14	12	12	2	1			2	215
	Grand Total Epiclassic	7	29	8	4	1		4	23		125	12	118	63	32	16	18	3			2	465
Selected Early Postclassic Pottery	Wavy Line (Burnished Variety)										1		10		9			1				21
	Wavy Line (Matte Variety)	9	30	2			2				59	10										111
	Macana		37	3	1	1					38	41	12	7		13		4	3		1	182
	Joroba Cream Slip		12	4							2	25	2	2								56
	Proa Cream Slip		26			1					3	17	2	8		2			6	5		72
	Jara Pulido Cream Slip		27	1	2						10			1		2	1					44
	Ira Stamped		2			2					2			1								7
	Grand Total Early Postclassic	9	136	11	3	5	2				115	100	26	19	9	22	1	15	9	5	1	493
Aztec/Early Postclassic — Selected Early Postclassic	Aztec I B/O Mixquic						2				1	5	2	6	5	1		1				23
	Aztec I B/O Culhuacan Var															9	9					20
	Aztec I B/O Chalco													10							3	13
	Chalco-Cholula Poly									11									3	9		28
	Grand Total AZI/CCPC						2			11	1	5	3	17	5	1	9	1	3	9	3	84

relation to ceramic complexes and notable technological and stylistic attributes discernable by production and consumption patterns. Was pottery produced in multiple locations? Does the exchange of vessels indicate pathways or barriers to interaction between communities nearby or further away?

THE EPICLASSIC IN THE BASIN OF MEXICO

Epiclassic Period BOM was fragmented into a series of city-states, each with a small regional center (Charlton and Nichols 1997:190–94; García Chávez 2004:352–54; Manzanilla 2005; Nichols et al. 2002; Parsons 2006; Rattray 1996; Sanders et al. 1979:129–37). Cross-cultural comparison of city-state systems suggests that, "because of their proximity and economic interdependence, city-states also tended to be culturally interdependent and to share religious beliefs, artistic conventions, and symbolism, especially as these related to upper-class culture" (Trigger 2003:101). This supports the pattern of having the Coyotlatelco Epiclassic ceramic complex distributed throughout the BOM and shared stylistic attributes more broadly in Central Mexico (cf. Solar Valverde 2006), despite having no large, centralized state to organize activities. Most agree that Coyotlatelco-like ceramic traditions originated northwest of the Basin (Beekman and Christensen 2003; Brambila and Crespo 2005; Braniff Cornejo 2005; Cobean 1990:174–17; Cowgill 1996:329; Hernández and Healan 2019; Hirth and Cyphers Guillén 1988:150; López Pérez and Nicolás Caretta 2005; Manzanilla 2005; Manzanilla and López 1998; Manzanilla et al. 1996: Mastache and Cobean 1989; Mastache and Cobean 2002:70–71; Paredes Gudiño 1998, 2005; Rattray 1996, 1998). Accordingly, the spread of the Coyotlatelco ceramic style into the BOM may signal the movement of northern migrants into the Basin, marking an ethnic shift and localized displacement of populations (Cowgill 2013; García Chávez et al. 2006; Rattray 1996; see also Beekman and Christenson 2003:144–45). Others are hesitant to correlate the regional adoption of Coyotlatelco pottery with widespread immigration (Blanton et al. 1993:137–38; Sanders 2006). It is likely that "proto-Coyotlatelco" pottery entered the BOM early in the Epiclassic and then developed locally by means of city-state interactions resulting in shared traditions of designs, vessel forms, and techniques of production distinctive to BOM Coyotlatelco.

For analytical purposes, my framework includes an "Early Epiclassic" component to better capture local responses in the immediate aftermath of the collapse of Teotihuacan, in which local settlements broke socioeconomically from the state and renegotiated interactions with neighbors, long-distance connections outside the Basin, and aligned with new administrative centers developing into the balkanized city-state configuration (akin to the Oxtoticpac phase in Teotihuacan Valley; Sanders 2006). Ceramics will not resolve the debate about ethnic population replacement, but local variations in ceramic complexes provide clues about relations among Epiclassic polities (cf. García Chávez 1991, 2004:351–54). The competitive political environment of the Coyotlatelco Epiclassic city-state system likely set the stage for later political confederacies and alliances (Hirth 2000:247).

Teotihuacan continued to maintain an Epiclassic occupation on the order of 10,000–20,000 people, although settlement was dispersed into concentrated areas throughout the Teotihuacan Mapping Project survey area (Crider et al. 2007; Diehl 1989). Because Teotihuacan was the state capital and center at the time of its Classic-period cataclysmic collapse, its residents may have been faced with unique challenges in reestablishing regional interactions, as compared to other Epiclassic city-states. For other parts of the Basin, the loosening of the political bonds with the Teotihuacan state opened opportunities for participation in local and regional networks. However, it is unclear to what extent Basin polities were directly interacting with the large Epiclassic centers elsewhere in the Central Highlands. Scholars outside of the BOM are active in documenting Epiclassic chronology and interaction (cf. Nelson and Crider 2005; Pomédio et al. 2013; Solar Valverde 2006); providing new leads to place the BOM in broader context.

THE EARLY POSTCLASSIC IN THE BASIN OF MEXICO

After approximately 250 years of Epiclassic city-state configuration, two compet-ing polities emerged on the periphery and expanded influence into the Basin: Tula to the northwest and Cholula to the southeast. They vied for influence and allegiance from polities within the Basin (Brumfiel 2005a; Parsons 1971:250). The thinly settled landscape between Epiclassic centers filled with settlements as people dispersed from city-state centers (Sanders et al. 1979:138). Early Postclassic population density and rural distribution is highest in the northern Basin, the area closest to Tula, within the influence of the Tula state (Charlton and Nichols 1997:196). The large Epiclassic regional centers were dramatically reduced in size and replaced by a series of smaller administrative centers; southern Basin settlement continued as hamlets and rural occupation. As Coyotlatelco pot-tery was being replaced by Mazapan pottery in the Terminal Corral phase (ca. 850–900 CE), Tula underwent an urban transformation with the increase of its population and area. Thus, its population covered an area of almost 16 km^2 that amounted to about 50,000 to 60,000 residents with another 60,000 in its immediate hinterland (Healan et al. 1989:245; Mastache and Cobean 2003:217; Sanders et al. 1979). Red-on-Buff pottery continued as an important serving and food preparation ware, while the introduction of Cream Slip bowls marks a significant new pottery tradition of the Early Postclassic, perhaps derived from Veracruz and the Gulf region to the east. Tula's urban zone was supported by workshop production of various craft goods, including pottery of many forms and styles (Cobean et al. 1999; Mastache and Cobean 2002:167).

Comparatively, the southern Basin settlements adopted a competing ceramic complex (García Chávez 2004; Hodge 2008; O'Neill 1962; Sanders et al. 1979). Aztec I Black-on-Orange pottery and the earliest of the Chalco-Cholula polychromes most commonly occurs within the southern Basin in an area extending at least from Chalco to Culhuacan, with a single outlier at the northern island settlement at Xaltocan (Brumfiel 2005a, 2005b; Parsons and Gorenflo, this volume). Cholula, to the southeast of the Basin, re-emerged as an important Early Postclassic religious and political center (McCafferty 1994). The political and economic extent of Cholula's influence in the Basin is poorly understood, but there are strong stylistic affiliations in the Early Postclassic Aztec I Chalco-Cholula pottery complex (discussed below, and in Hodge 2008; Parsons et al. 1982:appendix 1). Chemical characterization of Aztec I Black-on-Orange pottery has established multiple locales of manufacture that map onto distribution areas for stylistic variants of the ware (Brumfiel 2005b; García Chávez 2004; Hodge and Minc 1990; Minc et al. 1994). Three distinct zones of Aztec I distribution may represent separate city-states and market interaction (Minc et al. 1994). Small quantities of Tula-related pottery (Brumfiel 2005a; Hodge 2008; Parsons and Gorenflo, this volume), suggest boundaries between Tula and the southern Basin Aztec I Chalco-Cholula related city-states. There is growing consensus for significant chronological overlap between the Aztec I Chalco-Cholula and the Mazapan-Tollan complexes in the Early Postclassic period (Parsons et al. 1996). Hodge (1997:224) reports that radiocarbon dating places the Aztec I pottery complex at Mound 65 excavations of Chalco to start at 1100 CE (calibrated intercept), but at other sites such as Ch-Az-195, much earlier at 690 CE (calibrated intercept), and Xaltocan at 880 CE (calibrated intercept, Brumfiel 2005a:75; Parsons et al. 1996:225). Aztec I variants likely persisted in some areas well beyond the downfall of the Tula state. I advocate for the definition of separate pottery complexes, where possible, that are related to Aztec I (beginning within the Early Postclassic and likely extending into the Middle Postclassic) and Aztec II (correlating to Middle Postclassic and following Tula's state collapse) rather than the more general term *Early Aztec*.

DISCUSSION OF ANALYSIS OF SELECTED CERAMICS

Early Epiclassic Complex of the Southern Basin

There are three regional centers identified from the settlement survey (Sanders et al. 1979) that reveal stylistic attribute differences in production between them, while unified by common decorative traditions and pottery types. One example is the *Tezonchichilco* flaring tripod bowl with outflaring rims (so named at Cerro Portezuelo by Crider 2013a:111; Hicks 2005:5–46), which is identifiable by the use of stamping combined with red-painted geometric designs that are outlined by incising (see figure 12.2a). The rare instance of zoomorphic motif, one stamped

FIGURE 12.2. *Selection of Early Epiclassic ceramics predominant in the southern Basin of Mexico: (a) Tezonchichilco RN variant for Cerro Portezuelo, Chalco compositional group: (a) MURR ID AZC 486 (b) Incised and Punctate Light Line Variant, Cerro Portezuelo, Trench 93 Cache 13–14, MURR ID AZC 1102, Culhuacan compositional group. Half-star design element, alternating from top and then bottom of design panel. (c–d) Incised and Punctate Heavy Line Variant from Cerro Portezuelo: (c) Trench 93 Burial 4—Cache 9, specimen 204.2034, (d) Trench 93 Burial 4—Cache 9, specimen 204.2035 (e–g) Composite Silhouette bowls from Cerro Portezuelo: I upright wall form, specimen 204.2124, Trench 93, Burial 14-Cache 25. (f) flared wall form, specimen 204.2121, Trench 93, Burial 8-Cache 15. (g) flared wall form, specimen 204.2120, Trench 93, Burial 8-Cache 15. (h–j) Composite Silhouette bowl with incised decoration: (h) Oxtoticpac, Teotihuacan, MURR ID DLC 601, Cerro Portezuelo compositional group, (i) Oxtoticpac, Teotihuacan, MURR ID DLC 603, Cerro Portezuelo compositional group, (j) Oxtoticpac, Teotihuacan, MURR ID DLC 605, Cerro Portezuelo compositional group. (k–l) Zone Incised bowls (k) Cerro Portezuelo, specimen 204.19133; (l) CH-ET-28 (Xico), MURR ID DLC 397, Xico compositional group. (Photographs by author, from Crider 2011.)*

design may depict the feathered serpent, a referent to the Cult of Quetzalcoatl, which was widespread in the Epiclassic period (Ringle et al. 1998). Two-thirds of the thirty-three Tezonchichilco INAA samples (67%) are the Chalco compositional group; predominantly distributed across Cerro Portezuelo and Chalco area settlements. This ceramic is a specialized product of the Chalco compositional group in the southeastern Basin.

Another example is the *Zone Incised* pottery, which appears across the southern Basin (Crider 2013a:111). It is identified on the basis of a band of incising on the upper exterior the vessel. Patterns are geometric and include alternating crosshatching, rectilinear and curvilinear design elements (see figures 12.2k to 12.2l). These bowls have well-smoothed surfaces, either plain or with a red-painted design. The Chalco compositional group accounts for 67 percent (n=18/27) of the INAA sample and is distributed across the Cerro Portezuelo and Chalco settlement clusters in the southeastern Basin. Cerro Portezuelo and Xico Island produced local versions, each representing 15 percent of the total for this type (n=2 for each). This suggests specialized pottery production in the southeastern Basin.

Additionally, the *Incised and Punctate* is notable for the alternating zones of incised geometric designs and punctation in a wide band on bowl exteriors (Crider 2013a:113–14). At least two stylistic variants are notable based on the qualities of the incisions (see figures 12.2b to 12.2d). The first, a heavy, deep line, is also characterized by alternating zones of matte and polished surface treatment. The second is a light, incised line with a similar polish across the entire surface, with no zones of matte finish. One motif occurring across both is the half star, another symbol of the Cult of Quetzalcoatl. The distribution of the twenty-three INAA specimens are distributed across multiple compositional groups including Cerro Portezuelo (26% of total), Teotihuacan (26% of total), the southwestern Basin–Culhuacan group (17% of total). Ritual deposition of partial and complete vessels with burials at a temple structure at Cerro Portezuelo in multiple variations and compositional-group assignments suggests a hosting of neighboring city-states for feasting and dedicatory activity at this important regional center.

The *composite silhouette* grey/brown paste bowls (Crider 2013a:111; *Portezuelo Grey*) may provide a promising pathway for evaluating the migration, interaction, and spread of new ceramic traditions entering from Hidalgo and northwest areas and into the BOM early in the Epiclassic. Sanders (1986) placed this vessel in the Oxtoticpac Phase occupation in Teotihuacacn Valley's Oxtoticpac Cave just after the fall of Teotihuacan. Also recovered in excavations in the caves behind the Pyramid of the Sun (López Pérez 2003; Manzanilla et al. 1996; Nicolás Careta 2003), it is not common elsewhere in Teotihuacan. I observed that sherds of this type are scattered around collections in the BOM survey, but it is most concentrated in Cerro Portezuelo (Hicks 2005:5–25 reports over 2,600 sherds). Decoration varies and can include red-painted monochrome, plain ware, resist (large circles), and incised (an exterior band of repeated scallops); vessel walls may be outflaring or more upright (see figures 12.2e to 12.2j). Not reported for Tula Chico, Monochrome Red, upright walls and same-vessel form is reported for the hilltop settlement of La Mesa, Hidalgo (Martinez Landa 2009) and Cerro Magoni (personal observation). The quantities at Cerro Portezuelo suggest a longer duration, beyond the "Early Epiclassic." The Cerro Portezuelo (60%) and Teotihuacan (15%) group accounts most of the production from the 72-sherd sample (selected from Cerro Portezuelo, Oxtoticpac Cave, and survey collections). Locally produced and consumed in the southern Basin, the Oxtoticpac-derived collection includes three different regional compositional group assignments, with the local compositional group accounting for a smaller proportion of its total than the Cerro Portezuelo group. We are left to postulate on what activities drew people to this cave, and whether it was for short- or long-term use, and by whom.

EPICLASSIC COYOTLATELCO COMPLEX

The Coyotlatelco complex was first documented by Tozzer (1921) and then confirmed to follow the Teotihuacan Classic period (Rattray 1966). Various forms and motifs occur in Coyotlatelco pottery throughout the BOM (cf. García Chávez 1995; López-Pérez et al. 2006; Manzanilla and López 1998; Rattray 1966, 1996), the Tula region including Tula Chico (Cobean 1978, 1990; Healan and Cobean 2019:74–80), the Tula area's hilltop centers (Anderson et al. 2015; Martinez Landa 2009; Mastache and Cobean 1989), and in the Toluca Valley (Sugiura 2006). The diversity of vessel forms, the quality of production, and the wide range of decorative motifs results in an extensive catalog of variability to differentiate by locale (see figure 12.3a to 12.3g). A total of 215 Coyotlatelco INAA specimens are included in this study and document a strong pattern of local production and use at multiple locations across the BOM and Tula; notable are the high rates of local consumption within the Tula and Teotihuacan settlement clusters (Crider 2011; Crider et al. 2007; Crider et al. 2018). The Cerro Portezuelo settlement cluster has mostly local pottery, and some pottery from neighboring areas in the Basin. As an emerging Epiclassic center, the exchange may be more related to small-scale interactions due to social obligations rather than investment in BOM market exchange. The population estimate for Cerro Portezuelo at this time is about 12,000 people, second only to the Teotihuacan cluster. Comparison of compositional assignments to motifs and form attributes hints at selection of some attributes by potters according to preference in local manufacture.

EARLY POSTCLASSIC: MAZAPAN COMPLEX

The Mazapan phase of the Early Postclassic is marked by the continuity of red-painted pottery, though vessel forms, design techniques, and motifs change. The

FIGURE 12.3. *Selection of Coyotlatelco (a–g) and Mazapan Wavy Line (h–o): Coyotlatelco pottery from Xometla, Teotihuacan compositional group: (a) MURR ID TTV 037, (b) Pennsylvania State University type collection, (c) MURR ID TTV 035, (d) Pennsylvania State University type collection; (e) Pennsylvania State University type collection; Coyotlatelco pottery from Cerro Portezuelo with motifs similar to those of Zone Incised and Tezonchichilco pottery, Cerro Portezuelo compositional source group: (f) exterior decoration, painted and stamped, MURR ID AZC 443; (g) interior decoration, MURR ID AZC 432; Wavy Line, Matte Variety, interior decorated, specimens from Cerro Portezuelo, Teotihuacan composition group: (h) MURR ID AZC 214, (i) MURR ID AZC 216, (j) MURR ID AZC 234, (k) MURR ID AZC 242, (l) MURR ID AZC 243; Wavy Line, Burnished Variety, interior decoration and Cerro Portezuelo compositional group: (m) Cerro Portezuelo, MURR ID AZC 219, (n) Cerro Portezuelo, MURR ID AZC 239, (o) Cerro Portezuelo, MURR ID AZC 241. (Photographs by author, from Crider 2011.)*

most distinctive pottery of this complex is Mazapan Wavy Line (see figures 12.3h to 12.3o), once believed to originate within the Teotihuacan Valley (Cobean 1978, 1990). However, consumption was more broadly distributed in rural Tula, in the Zumpango region south to Azcapotzalco in the western Basin, and in Cerro Portezuelo in the eastern Basin (Bey 1986; García Chávez 2004; Nichols et al.

2002; Parsons 2008), and limited in the Chalco region and parts of extreme southern Basin. I confirmed Hicks's (2005) identification of two variants of Wavy Line at Cerro Portezuelo (Crider 2013a). The matte finish variant uses a specialized multi-prong brush to create upwards of eighteen parallel paint lines to design waves, rainbows, crossed panels and interlocking scrolls. This variant occurs throughout the Basin and includes Tula region, with some localized preferences in motif. Replication experiments suggest apprenticeship and shared technology was important for production across the potting industry for this variant (Crider 2017). The INAA's study of 148 specimens indicates that Tula region pottery is almost entirely local in production, with a small amount potentially of Teotihuacan origin. Although not as highly sampled as other settlement blocks, the northwestern Basin acquired Tula-produced Wavy Line in addition to locally produced vessels. This indicates the initial expansion of Tula's economic reach into the Basin. Comparatively, the Teotihuacan Valley is largely local production, as is consistent with Epiclassic patterns of production and consumption, although the production techniques are similar for multiprong painted designs, suggesting specialized knowledge shared with Tula's industry.

The burnished finish variant of Wavy, painted with a single brush and smeared at the time of polishing, is a persistent finishing technique from Coyotlatelco pottery. Design motifs are more simplified, limited mostly to parallel undulating lines. Compositional results indicate local production and distributions to the area around Cerro Portezuelo. Although Cerro Portezuelo and nearby settlements also accessed significant quantities of Teotihuacan-produced matte Wavy Line. This indicates that Cerro Portezuelo was peripheral to production of matte Wavy Line and the use of the multi-prong brush, and emulated the distinctive pottery of the northern Basin using localized production techniques, but at some point, the area became a recipient of Teotihuacan-produced goods (Crider 2013a).

The introduction of the Cream Slip, Orange Paste wares departs from the brown paste wares of the Epiclassic. Following Cobean's Tula typology (1978, 1990), Cream Slip bowls occur in several types, each likely correlating to differing archaeological phases within the Early Postclassic. Joroba Cream simple bowls of the Mazapan Phase have red-orange painted designs with simplistic elements such as the large "S" scroll or vertical sets of parallel lines (see figures 12.4e and 12.4f). The distribution extends south into the Chalco survey block, including the site of Xico. Of the fifty-six specimens included in INAA, most are locally produced within settlement blocks with minor amounts of Tula-produced items in the Teotihuacan Valley sampling. The "ruralization" of settlement and production patterns emergent in the Mazapan phase likely contributed to acquisition of new clay sources in use following the Epiclassic. Potters' workshops may have moved to more rural locations, and/or immigrant potters may have moved into the region from northern areas, utilizing a slightly different resource from the

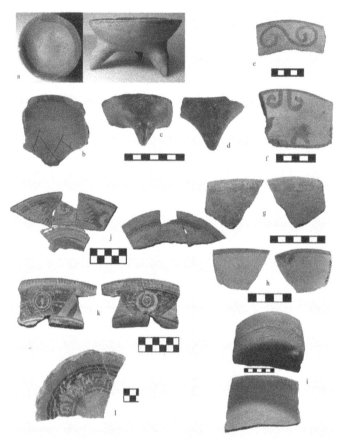

FIGURE 12.4. *Selection of Early Postclassic pottery: (a–d) Macana with hollow supports (a) diamond-incised pattern in vessel base interior, collected from Vaillant excavation at Teotihuacan in Las Palmas district (American Museum of Natural History collections, specimen 30.1/3260); (b) Cerro Portezuelo, MURR ID AZC 277, Texcoco General compositional group; (c) Cerro Portezuelo, MURR ID AZC 312, Texcoco General compositional group; (d) Cerro Portezuelo, MURR ID AZC 306, Texcoco General compositional group; (e–i) Cream Slip variIs: (e) Joroba Cream Slip pottery, Tula, MURR ID DLC 177, Tula compositional group; (f) Joroba Cream Slip pottery, Cerro Portezuelo, MURR ID AZC 268, Texcoco General compositional group; (g) Proa Cream Slip, Ch-LT-09, MURR ID DLC 324, Chalco compositional group; (h) Proa Cream Slip, Tula, MURR ID DLC 062; Tula composition group: (i) Ira Stamped / Jara Pulido Cream Slip, Tula, MURR ID DLC 181, Tula Compositional group (exterior stamp, interior slip); (j-l) Xaltocan Early Aztec/Late Postclassic: (j) Chalco-Cholula Polychrome, Xaltocan, MURR ID DLC 672 a Chalco source group, left is the vessel interior, right is the vessel exterior; (k) Chalco-Cholula Polychrome, Xaltocan, MURR ID DLC 665, Puebla source group; (l) Xaltocan Aztec I Culhuacan Black-on-Orange, MURR ID DLC 660, Xaltocan source group. (Figures by author from Crider 2011.)*

local Cerro Portezuelo source group. This assignment to the Texcoco General compositional group is persistent in all of the Cerro Portezuelo–cluster Cream Slip variants. Nevertheless, Basin=produced Joroba Cream is stylistically similar to that of Tula, indicating a more direct knowledge of the techniques and traditions at Cerro Portezuelo than is exhibited in the Wavy Line.

EARLY POSTCLASSIC: TOLLAN COMPLEX

The Tollan-phase pottery was produced at the time when Tula maintained its most extensive reach as a regional state capital. Proa Cream pottery, similar to Joroba but lacking the painted motifs, was the basic service ware in the BOM (see figures 12.4f to 12.4g). The submission of seventy-two specimens to the INAA show that Tula-produced Proa Cream was used in Tula and the Zumpango settlements. Teotihuacan Valley people continued to make and use their own Proa Cream, with only the occasional acquisition of Tula-made pots. Future investigation should focus on differing access to goods based on site function, as I would expect administrative centers to have higher access to Tula-produced products. For example, Cerro Portezuelo is comprised of the Texcoco General composition but includes the first significant amount of Tula-produced pottery. It is likely that Cerro Portezuelo was eventually incorporated into Tula's state control as an administrative center despieriodrall decline in population (Crider 2013a; Hicks 2013). No Tula imports are identified for the Chalco settlement cluster. Proton-induced x-ray emission analysis confirms differences in the Cream Slip recipes between southern Basin and Tula variants (Crider 2013b).

The Macana red-painted tripod *molcajetes* are common throughout BOM collections (see figures 12.4a to 12.4d). Multiple production locales are evident in the 182 INAA specimens. Tula supplied almost all of the Tula and Zumpango northwestern Basin settlements with Macana, signaling the continued integration of the northern Basin into Tula's economy. Local production is evident in the Teotihuacan, Cerro Portezuelo, and Chalco settlement clusters. Small amounts of Tula imports are noted for Teotihuacan and Cerro Portezuelo settlements, but no further south. In the southern Basin, the pattern suggests a subregional zone of exchange during the early part of the Tollan phase; while most pottery is locally produced, exchange is limited to this part of the Basin. This interaction zone does not appear dependent on Tula-produced pottery, but rather has more interaction with the "extreme south" toward Morelos.

Jara Cream Slip pottery is the latest variant among the Tula Cream Slip-on-Orange wares. It is similar to the Proa bowls, but with an added overcoat of orange paint. Included is Ira Stamped, which is Jara, but with a molded design on the exterior of the bowl (see figure 12.4i). Jara was the service ware in Tula in the latter part of the Tollan phase, replacing Proa in popularity at the urban center (Bey 1986; Cobean 1978, 1990). However, in the BOM I document a dramatic drop in its use beyond the Tula and Zumpango (northwestern Basin), in which I sampled nearly all of the specimens identified. Although the Cerro Portezuelo excavations provided many hundreds of Cream Slip sherds, I located only twenty-three Jara sherds (no Ira Stamped) (Crider 2013a). Nevertheless, there are small amounts of Jara and Ira Stamped in collections as far south as Chalco. A total of fifty-two specimens of Jara and Ira Stamped are included in the INAA analysis. The Tula and Zumpango settlement clusters continue to cohere, and all of the specimens are from the Tula and northwestern Basin compositional groups. Despite the small sample size (n=10), the Teotihuacan settlement cluster is split between a local Teotihuacan compositional group (n=5) and the Tula compositional group (n=4). Samples collected from Cerro Portezuelo have a small amount of Jara assigned to the Tula compositional group (n=4), and the remainder from among the southeastern Basin compositional groups. Again, given the small sample size for the Chalco survey block (n=7), a small amount of Jara is assigned to local compositional groups, the "extreme south" and the southwestern Basin compositional groups. In addition, two Ira Stamped sherds are assigned to the Tula/northwestern Basin compositional groups. The significant drop in the use of Jara and Ira Stamped vessels in the Basin as compared to the Tula core area suggests that people in southern parts of the Basin were shifting their attention from Tula and more toward areas south of the Basin.

EARLY POSTCLASSIC—AZTEC I AND CHALCO-CHOLULA POLYCHROME COMPLEX

Inclusion of the Early Postclassic variants of Aztec I and Chalco-Cholula Polychromes (CCPC) for INAA are related to developments in the southern Basin with ties to Puebla-Tlaxcala and the prominent center of Cholula. Significantly, the Aztec I Black-on-Orange pottery, in all of its style variants, is distributed throughout the southern Basin and the northern island of Xaltocan. My compositional results indicate that Xaltocan produced Aztec I Culhuacan variety vessels (Crider 2011:424–27). However, exchange with Culhuacan for Aztec I and Chalco for CCPC indicates strong interaction between the isolated island kingdom (Xaltocan surrounded by Tula-related settlements inland) and the groups of the southern Basin (see Parsons and Gorenflo, this volume). Xaltocan-produced Aztec I matched the stylistic variant produced around Culhuacan (see figure 12.4l) (Minc et al. 1994). Significantly, Xaltocan never participated in the Tula-related pottery sphere, and had direct access to Puebla-produced CCPC (very likely Cholula specifically). The Chalco-produced CCPC is at a glance stylistically equivalent to that of the Puebla-produced specimens (see figures 12.4j to 12.4k). In additional compositional distinction, Chalco-produced CCPC includes voids from cattail fluff in vessel paste, whereas Puebla-produced CCPC does not, and so some visual inspection could distinguish Basin versus non-Basin production (Crider 2011).

SUMMARY AND DISCUSSION

In summary, this research examines the regional interaction in the time period following the collapse of the Teotihuacan state and prior to the rise of the Aztec empire. Sampling of specimens was conducted from throughout the region spanning the period from about 550 to 1150 CE to include multiple pottery complexes of the Epiclassic and Early Postclassic periods for stylistic, technological, and compositional variability. This framework of analysis provides new avenues for evaluating interactions among the major settlement clusters in the study area. The ceramic complexes and their compositional and stylistic signatures provide physical evidence of these otherwise intangible aspects of this exciting period of prehistory in the Basin of Mexico.

Building on successful compositional study of the BOM, my studies have significantly expanded the sampling of Epiclassic and Early Postclassic decorated wares for the region, as well as moving toward establishing Tula region compositional assays. The establishment of Tula compositional groupings is necessary for comparison to BOM pottery at a time when Tula emerged as an influential regional state capital. While further refinements will occur in the definition of the group and subgroups, especially the geochemical relationship between the Tula and Northern Basin, contributions from areas outside of the Teotihuacan Valley provide a new baseline for multi-scalar comparison in pottery production.

With such a regional synthetic study, several new trends are suggested that warrant further research. The combination of stylistic and compositional analysis provides a powerful framework for the investigation of economic interaction, but cannot resolve questions about the flow of people in and out of the Basin. To what degree did migrants bring pottery styles, techniques, and worldview into the Basin as the Teotihuacan state withdrew oversight and control of resources (including people)? Chronological resolution to date has poorly reflected what was likely a complex negotiation of the material landscape of the Basin of Mexico after the fall of Teotihuacan and the rise of Epiclassic city-states. Further excavation is needed throughout the southern Basin (e.g., Clayton 2021; García Chávez 1991) to resolve whether there is a widespread gap in occupation between the withdrawal of the Teotihuacan state and new occupants from elsewhere, or whether the changing occupational landscape occurred concurrently as Teotihuacan declined and the southern Basin occupants regrouped to form a regionally coherent sphere of interaction and defense. A similar process in the Tula region documents the abandonment of Teotihuacan Chingu as people moved into the area and established competing hilltop settlements (Anderson et al. 2015). A distinct "Early Epiclassic" pottery complex unites the southern Basin regional centers of Cerro Portezuelo, Cerro de la Estrella, and Xico. Some pottery types, especially the composite silhouette bowls, are used at other sites outside the southern Basin cluster, but they are also stylistically and technologically related to at least some of the hilltop centers in the Tula region. Compositional studies show separate production locales and multiple potters across the Epiclassic world—but sharing designs, techniques, motifs, and vessel shapes. We must look beyond ceramics to other materials to find departures and similarities in the stuff of daily life at small and large sites.

By the close of the Epiclassic period, the Coyotlatelco pottery style united large portions of Central Mexico. Again, pottery consumption tends predominantly to draw on local production, despite shared aesthetics in the use of deep red-painted motifs, banded layouts, and repetitious geometric design elements, a common characteristic of a regional city-state culture. This service ware was flexible for local needs in vessel form, size, and service function. Localized preferences are detectible in attribute study, given large enough sampling and confirmation in production localities. Exchange of decorated pottery was limited to small quantities between neighboring communities or within settlement clusters, suggesting direct relationships between groups of people among regional city-states, rather than any development of a regional market system of ceramic product.

While Cerro Portezuelo played a significant role as an important Epiclassic administrative and ritual center, it may have been the city-state centered on Tula Chico that begins to expand influence and perhaps grow its borders in the Mazapan phase (Crider 2013a). Emerging from the Epiclassic city-state structure, Tula begins to influence the northern Basin, especially incorporating the Zumpango settlement cluster. This corresponds to a process of settlement ruralization, in which people appear to be filling in the empty countryside with small villages and farming hamlets (Sanders et al. 1979). The Teotihuacan settlement cluster shares significant stylistic and technological similarities in pottery production with the Tula area, especially Wavy Line bowls, although exchange in pottery goods was still highly limited. Based on its pottery complex, the Cerro Portezuelo settlement was initially operating relatively independently of the developments in the northern Basin and the Tula region during the Mazapan phase; but may have been gradually incorporated into Teotihuacan's market zone. By the early part of the Tollan phase in the Early Postclassic, Cerro Portezuelo was further integrated into the influence of the Tula state, likely as an important administrative center with direct access to Tula-produced products and ritual items (Crider 2013a; Hicks 2013).

The southern Basin and the Yautepec survey area further south had limited participation in the production or use of Tollan-style pottery (Smith and Montiel 2001), and by the close of the Early Postclassic, southern Basin interactions had shifted toward Morelos and Puebla. Xaltocan, allied early with southern Basin people, as expressed through direct exchange of Aztec I and CCPC pottery in the Early Postclassic, notably exhibited unique access to Puebla-produced polychromes. Tula's state regional influence was likely on the wane as Xaltocan and southern Basin polities gave rise to the new Black-on-Orange ceramic traditions that persisted into Postclassic and Aztec specialization of ceramics and true market exchange among producers throughout the BOM (see Garraty 2006; Parsons and Gorenflo, this volume).

CONCLUSION

This study aligns with literature invoking processes of secondary state formation, and as such refers to the concept of "regeneration," which is defined as "the reappearance of societal complexity (states, cities, etc.) after periods of decentralization, not the reappearance of specific complex societies" (Anderson et al. 2015; Schwartz and Nichols 2006:7). There is an opportunity to identify the local impacts of shifting regional patterns of sociopolitical and economic organization in post-collapse periods. By discerning temporal sub-phases associated with diagnostic ceramic types and pottery complexes and comparing stylistic and compositional variants across the Basin of Mexico, it has been possible to define directions of interaction and shifts in group boundaries. Processes employed in regeneration might emphasize the importance of trade, shifting interaction networks, social mobility, and participation in sociopolitical ideologies.

REFERENCES

Anderson, J. Heath, Dan Healan, and Robert H. Cobean. 2015. "Collapse, Regeneration, and the Origins of Tula and the Toltec State." In *Beyond Collapse: Archaeological Perspectives on Resilience, Revitalization, and Transformation in Complex Societies*, edited by Ronald K. Faulseit, 431–58. Southern Illinois University Press, Carbondale.

Arnold, Dean E. 1985. *Ceramic Theory and Cultural Process*. Cambridge University Press, Cambridge.

Arnold, Philip J., III. 2000. "Does the Standardization of Ceramic Pastes Really Mean Specialization?" *Journal of Archaeological Method and Theory* 7(4):333–75.

Arnold, Philip J., III. 2007. "Ceramic Production at la Joya, Veracruz: Early Formative Techno Logistics and Error Loads." In *Pottery Economics in Mesoamerica*, edited by Christopher A. Pool and George J. Bey III, 86–113. The University of Arizona Press, Tucson.

Beekman, Christopher S., and Alexander F. Christensen. 2003. "Controlling for Doubt and Uncertainty through Multiple Lines of Evidence: A New Look at the Mesoamerican Nahua Migrations." *Journal of Archaeological Method and Theory* 10(2):111–64.

Bennyhoff, James A. 1967. "Chronology and Periodization: Continuity and Change in the Teotihuacán Ceramic Tradition." *Teotihuacán, Onceava Mesa Redonda*, 19–29. Sociedad Mexicana de Antropología, Mexico City.

Bennyhoff, James A., and Robert Fleming Heizer. 1965. "Neutron Activation Analysis of Some Cuicuilco and Teotihuacan Pottery: Archaeological Interpretation of Results." *American Antiquity* 30(3):348–49.

Bey, George J., III. 1986. "A Regional Analysis of Toltec Ceramics, Tula, Hidalgo, Mexico." PhD dissertation, Tulane University, New Orleans, LA.

Blanton, Richard E., Stephen A. Kowalewski, Gary M. Feinman, and Laura M. Finsten. 1993. *Ancient Mesoamerica: A Comparison of Change in Three Regions*. Cambridge University Press, Cambridge.

Brambila Paz, Rosa, and Ana María Crespo. 2005. "Desplazamientos de poblaciones y creación de territorios en el Bajío." In *Reacomodos demográficos del Clásico al Posclásico en el centro de México*, edited by Linda Manzanilla, 155–74. Universidad Nacional Autónoma de México, Instituto de Investigaciones Antropológicas, Mexico City.

Braniff Cornejo, Beatriz. 2005. "Los chichimecas a la caída de Teotihuacan y durante la conformación de la Tula de Hidalgo." In *Reacomodos demográficos del Clásico al Posclásico en el centro de México*, edited by Linda Manzanilla, 45–56. Universidad Nacional Autónoma de México, Instituto de Investigaciones Antropológicas, Mexico City.

Brumfiel, Elizabeth M. 2005a. "Opting In and Opting Out: Tula, Cholula and Xaltocan." In *Settlement, Subsistence, and Social Complexity: Essays Honoring the Legacy of Jeffrey R. Parsons*, edited by Richard E. Blanton, 63–88. Cotsen Institute of Archaeology, University of California, Los Angeles.

Brumfiel, Elizabeth M. 2005b. *Production and Power at Postclassic Xaltocan*. Department of Anthropology, University of Pittsburgh and the Instituto Nacional de Antropología e Historia, Pittsburgh and Mexico City.

Charlton, Thomas H., and Deborah L. Nichols. 1997. "Diachronic Studies of City-States: Permutations on a Theme—Central Mexico from 1700 BC to AD 1600." In *The Archaeology of City-States: Cross Cultural Approaches*, edited by Deborah L. Nichols and Thomas H. Charlton, 169–208. Smithsonian Institution Press, Washington, DC.

Chilton, Elizabeth S. 1998. "The Cultural Origins of Technical Choice: Unraveling Algonquian and Iroquoian Ceramic Traditions in the Northeast." In *The Archaeology of Social Boundaries*, edited by Miriam T. Stark, 132–60. Smithsonian Institution Press, Washington, DC.

Chilton, Elizabeth S. 1999. "One Size Fits All: Typology and Alternatives for Ceramic Research." In *Material Meanings: Critical Approaches to the Interpretation of Material Culture*, edited by Elizabeth S. Chilton, 44–60. University of Utah Press, Salt Lake City.

Clayton, Sarah. 2021. "Coalescence at Chicoloapan, Mexico." In *Mobility and Migration in Ancient Mesoamerican Cities*, edited by M. Charlotte Arnauld, Christopher Beekman, and Grégory Pereira, 189–207. University Press of Colorado, Louisville.

Cobean, Robert H. 1978. "The Pre-Aztec Ceramics of Tula, Hidalgo, Mexico." PhD dissertation, Harvard University, Cambridge, MA.

Cobean, Robert H. 1990. *La cerámica de Tula, Hidalgo*. Instituto Nacional de Antropología e Historia, Mexico City.

Cobean, Robert H., Alba Guadalupe Mastache, and María Elena Suárez. 1999. "Un taller de alfareros en la Antigua ciudad de Tula." *Arqueología* 22:69–87.

Costin, Cathy Lynne. 2000. "The Use of Ethnoarchaeology for the Archaeological Study of Ceramic Production." *Journal of Archaeological Method and Theory* 7:377–403.

Cowgill, George L. 1996. "A Reconsideration of the Postclassic Chronology of Central Mexico." *Ancient Mesoamerica* 7:325–31.

Cowgill, George L. 2013. "Possible Migrations and Shifting Identities in the Central Mexican Epiclassic." *Ancient Mesoamerica* 21:131–49.

Crider, Destiny L. 2011. "Epiclassic and early Postclassic Interaction in Central Mexico as Evidenced by Decorated Pottery." PhD dissertation, Anthropology, Arizona State University, Tempe. Proquest UMI Number 3453647.

Crider, Destiny L. 2013a. "Shifting Alliances: Epiclassic and Early Postclassic Interactions at Cerro Portezuelo." *Ancient Mesoamerica* 24:107–30.

Crider, Destiny L. 2013b. "Assessing Mexican Pottery Paint Recipes Using Particle-Induced X-Ray Emission." *Open Journal of Archaeometry* 1:e5:20–25.

Crider, Destiny L. 2017. "Complementary Approaches for Understanding Mazapan Pottery." In *Innovative Approaches and Explorations in Ceramic Studies*, edited by Sandra L. López Varela, 89–106. Archaeopress Archaeology, Oxford.

Crider, Destiny L., Deborah L. Nichols, Hector Neff, Michael D. Glascock. 2007. "In the Aftermath of Teotihuacan: Epiclassic Pottery Production and Distribution in the Teotihuacan Valley, Mexico." *Latin American Antiquity* 18(2):123–43.

Crider, Destiny L., Deborah L. Nichols, and Christopher Garraty. 2018. "Ceramic Production in the Teotihuacan Valley: Toward a Microregional Understanding." In *City, Craft, and Residence in Mesoamerica: Research Papers Presented in Honor of Dan M. Healan*, edited by Ronald K. Faulseit, Nezahualcoyotl Xiohtecutli, and Haley Holt Mehta, 85–112. Publication no. 72. Middle American Research Institute, Tulane University, New Orleans, LA.

Diehl, Richard. 1989. "A Shadow of Its Former Self: Teotihuacan during the Coyotlatelco Period." In *Mesoamerica after the Decline of Teotihuacan, A.D. 700–900*, edited by Richard A. Diehl and Janet C. Berlo, 9–18. Dumbarton Oaks, Washington, DC.

Dietler, Michael, and Ingrid Herbich. 1989. "*Tick Matek*: The Technology of Luo Pottery Production and the Definition of Ceramic Style." *World Archaeology* 21:148–64.

Dietler, Michael, and Ingrid Herbich. 1998. "*Habitus*, Techniques, Style: An Integrated Approach to the Social Understanding of Material Culture and Boundaries." In *The Archaeology of Social Boundaries*, edited by Miriam T. Stark, 232–63. Smithsonian Institution Press, Washington, DC.

Dobres, Marcia-Anne. 2000. *Technology and Social Agency: Outlining a Practice Framework for Archaeology*. Blackwell, Oxford.

Dobres, Marcia-Anne, and Christopher R. Hoffman. 1994. "Social Agency and the Dynamics of Prehistoric Technology." *Journal of Archaeological Method and Theory* 1(3):211–58.

García Chávez, Raúl E. 1991. "Desarrollo cultural en Azcapotzalco ye el area surocci-dental de la Cuenca de México, desde el Preclasico Medio hasta el Epiclásico." Tesis de Licenciado. Escuela Nacional de Antropología e Historia, Mexico City.

García Chávez, Raúl E. 1995. "Variabilidad cerámica en la Cuenca de México durante el Epícalssico." Tesis de Maestría, Escuela Nacional de Antropología e Historia, Mexico City.

García Chávez, Raúl E. 2004. "De Tula a Azcapotzalco: Characterization arqueológica de los altepetl de la Cuenca de México del Posclásico Temprano y Medio, a través del estudio cerámico regional." Tesis doctoral, Facultad de Filosofía y Letras, Universi-dad Nacional Autónoma de México, Mexico City.

García Chávez, Raúl, Luis Manuel Gamboa, Nadi Vélez Saldaña, and Natalia Moragas Segura. 2006. "Clasificación y análisis ¿Para qué? La cerámica de fase coyotlatelco de la Cuenca de México, como indicador del proceso de descentralización política." In *El fenómeno coyotlatelco en el centro de México: Tiempo, espacio y significado*, edited by Laura Solar Valverde, 83–111. Nacional de Antropología e Historia, Mexico, Mexico City.

Garraty, Christopher P. 2006. "The Politics of Commerce: Ceramic Production and Exchange in the Basin of Mexico, A.D. 1200–1650." PhD dissertation, School of Human Evolution and Social Change, Arizona State University, Tempe.

Glascock, Michael D. 1992. "Characterization of Archaeological Ceramics at MURR by Neutron Activation Analysis and Multivariate Statistics." In *Chemical Characterization of Ceramic Pastes in Archaeology*, edited by Hector Neff, 11–26. Monographs in World Archaeology, no. 7. Prehistory Press, Madison, WI.

Healan, Dan M., and Robert H. Cobean. 2019. "Three Migration Case Studies from the Tula Region." In *Migrations in Late Mesoamerica*, edited by Christopher S. Beekman, 66–87. University Press of Florida, Gainesville.

Healan, Dan M., Robert H. Cobean, and Richard Diehl. 1989. "Synthesis and Conclu-sions." In *Tula of the Toltecs: Excavations and Survey*, edited by Dan M. Healan, 239–52. University of Iowa Press, Iowa City.

Herbich, Ingrid. 1987. "Learning Patterns, Potter Interaction and Ceramic Style among the Luo of Kenya." *African Archaeological Review* 5:193–204.

Herbich, Ingrid, and Michael Dietler. 1991. "Aspects of the Ceramic System of the Luo of Kenya." In *Töpferei- und Keramikforschung*, vol. 2, edited by H. Lüdtke and R. Vos-sen, 105–35. Habelt, Bonn.

Hernández, Christine, and Dan M. Healan. 2019. "Migration and the Coyotlatelco Ceramic Tradition, Evidence from El Bajío." In *Migrations in Late Mesoamerica*, edited by Christopher S. Beekman, 88–108. University Press of Florida, Gainesville.

Hicks, Frederic. 2005. "Excavations at Cerro Portezuelo, Basin of Mexico." Third Partial and Incomplete Draft. January. Unpublished. UCLA Anthropology.

Hicks, Frederic. 2013. "The Architectural Features of Cerro Portezuelo." *Ancient Meso-america* 24:72–85.

Hirth, Kenneth G., ed. 2000. *The Xochicalco Mapping Project: Archaeological Research at Xochicalco.* 2 vols. University of Utah Press, Salt Lake City.

Hirth, Kenneth G., and Ann Cyphers Guillén. 1988. *Tiempo y asentamiento en Xochicalco.* Universidad Nacional Autónoma de México, Mexico City.

Hodge, Mary G. 1997. "When Is a City-State? Archaeological Measures of Aztec City-States and Aztec City-State Systems." In *The Archaeology of City-States: Cross Cultural Approaches,* edited by Deborah L. Nichols and Thomas H. Charlton, 209–28. Smithsonian Institution Press, Washington, DC.

Hodge, Mary G. 2008. *Place of Jade: Society and Economy in Ancient Chalco.* University of Pittsburgh Department of Anthropology and Instituto Nacional de Antropología e Historia, Pittsburgh and México, Mexico City.

Hodge, Mary G., and Leah D. Minc. 1990. "The Spatial Patterning of Aztec Ceramics: Implications for Prehispanic Exchange Systems in the Valley of Mexico." *Journal of Field Archaeology* 17:415–37.

Kramer, Carol. 1985. "Ceramic Ethnoarchaeology." *Annual Review of Anthropology* 14:77–102.

Lechtman, Heather. 1977. "Style in Technology: Some Early Thoughts." In *Material Culture: Style, Organization, and Dynamics of Technology,* edited by Heather Lechtman and Robert S. Merrill, 3–20. West Publishing Co., Saint Paul, MN.

Lechtman, Heather. 1993. "Technologies of Power: The Andean Case." In *Configurations of Power: Holistic Anthropology in Theory and Practice,* edited by John S. Henderson and Patricia J. Netherly, 244–80. Cornell University Press, Ithaca, NY.

Lemonnier, Pierre. 1986. "The Study of Material Culture Today: Towards an Anthropology of Technical Systems." *Journal of Anthropological Archaeology* 5:147–86.

Lind, Michael. 1994. "Cholula and Mixteca Polychromes: Two Mixteca-Puebla Regional Sub-Styles." In *Mixteca-Puebla: Discoveries and Research in Mesoamerican Art and Archaeology,* edited by H. B. Nicholson and Eloise Quiñones Keber, 79–100. Labyrinthos Press, Culver City, CA.

López Pérez, Claudia M. 2003. "Análisis cerámico de las areas de actividad el la 'Cueva de las Varillas,' Teotihuacan." Tesis de Licenciada en Arqueología, Escuela Nacional de Antropología e Historia. México, Mexico City.

López Pérez, Claudia M., and Claudia Nicolás Careta. 2005. "La cerámica de tradición norteña en el valle de Teotihuacan durante el Epiclásico y el Posclásico temprano." In *Reacomodos demográficos del Clásico al Posclásico en el centro de México,* edited by Linda Manzanilla, 275–86. Universidad Nacional Autónoma de México, Instituto de Investigaciones Antropológicas, México, Mexico City.

López Pérez, Claudia M., Claudia Nicolás Careta, and Linda Manzanilla. 2006. "Atributos morfológicos y estilísticos de la cerámica coyotlatelco en el centro ceremonial de Teotihuacan." In *El fenómeno coyotlatelco en el centro de México: Tiempo, espacio y significado,* edited by Laura Solar Valverde, 201–16. Instituto Nacional de Antropología e Historia, México, Mexico City.

Manzanilla, Linda. 2005. "Migrantes epiclásicos en Teotihuacan: Propuesta metodológica para análisis de migraciones del Clásico al Posclásico." In *Reacomodos demográficos del Clásico al Posclásico en el centro de México*, edited by Linda Manzanilla, 261–74. Universidad Nacional Autónoma de México, Instituto de Investigaciones Antropológicas, México, Mexico City.

Manzanilla, Linda, and López, Claudia. 1998. "Ocupación coyotlatelco de túneles al este de la Pirámide del Sol en Teotihuacan." In *Antropología e historia del occidente de México: XXIV Mesa Redonda*, vol. 3, 1611–27. Sociedad Mexicana de Antropología, México, Mexico City.

Manzanilla, Linda, Claudia López, and AnnCorrine Freter. 1996. "Dating Results from Excavations in the Quarry Tunnels behind the Pyramid of the Sun at Teotihuacan." *Ancient Mesoamerica* 7:245–66.

Martinez Landa, Blanca Estela. 2009. "La cerámica arqueológica de La Mesa, Hidalgo." Liecenciatura thesis, Escuela Nacional de Antropología e Historia, Mexico City.

Mastache, Alba Guadalupe, and Robert H. Cobean. 1989. "The Coyotlatelco Culture and the Origins of the Toltec State." In *Mesoamerica after the Decline of Teotihuacan*, edited by Richard A. Diehl and Janet C. Berlo, 49–68. Dumbarton Oaks Research Library and Collections, Washington, DC.

Mastache, Alba Guadalupe, and Robert H. Cobean. 2002. *Ancient Tollan: Tula and the Toltec Heartland*. University Press of Colorado, Boulder.

Mastache, Alba Guadalupe, and Robert H. Cobean. 2003. "Urbanism at Tula." In *Urbanism in Mesoamerica*, edited by Alba Guadalupe Mastache, Robert H. Cobean, Ángel García Cool, and Kenneth G. Hirth, vol. 1, 217–56. Pennsylvania State University, State College, PA.

McCafferty, Geoffrey G. 1994. "The Mixteca-Puebla Stylistic Tradition at Early Post-classic Cholula." In *Mixteca-Puebla, Discoveries and Research in Mesoamerican Art and Archaeology*, edited by Henry B. Nicholson and Eloise Quiñones Keber, 53–78. Labyrinthos, Culver City, CA.

McCafferty, Geoffrey G. 2001. *Ceramics of Postclassic Cholula, Mexico: Typology and Seriation of Pottery from the UA-1 Domestic Compound*. Monograph no. 54. Cotsen Institute of Archaeology, University of California, Los Angeles.

Minc, Leah, Mary G. Hodge, and M. James Blackman. 1994. "Stylistic and Spatial Variability in Early Aztec Ceramics: Insights into Pre-Imperial Exchange Systems." In *Economies and Polities in the Aztec Realm*, edited by Mary Hodge and Michael E. Smith, 330173. Institute for Mesoamerican Studies, State University of New York, Albany.

Neff, Hector. 2000. "Neutron Activation Analysis for Provenance Determination in Archaeology." In *Modern Analytical Methods in Art and Archaeology*, edited by E. Ciliberto and G. Spoto, 81–134. John Wiley and Sons, New York.

Neff, Hector, and Michael D. Glascock. 1998. "Variation in Ceramic Raw Materials from the Basin of Mexico and Adjacent Regions." Ms. on file, Missouri University Research Reactor, University of Missouri, Columbia.

Nelson, Ben A., and Destiny Crider. 2005. "Posibles pasajes migratorios en el norte de México y el suroeste de los Estados Unidos durante el Epiclásico y el Postclásico." In *Reacomodos demográficos del Clásico al Posclásico en el centro de México*, edited by Linda Manzanilla, 75–102. Instituto de Investigaciones Antropológicas, Universidad Nacional Autónoma de México, México, City.

Nichols, Deborah L., Elizabeth Brumfiel, Hector Neff, Mary Hodge, Thomas H. Charlton, and Michael D. Glascock. 2002. "Neutrons, Markets, Cities, and Empires: A 1000-Year Perspective on Ceramic Production and Distribution in the Postclassic Basin of Mexico." *Journal of Anthropological Archaeology* 21:25–82.

Nichols, Deborah L., Hector Neff, and George L. Cowgill. 2013. "Cerro Portezuelo: States and Hinterlands in the Prehispanic Basin of Mexico." 24:47–71.

Nicholson, Henry B., and Frederic Hicks. 1961. "A Brief Progress Report on the Excavations at Cerro Portezuelo, Valley of Mexico." *American Antiquity* 27:106–8.

Nicolás Careta, Claudia. 2003. "Análisis cerámico del la Cueva del Pirul: Transición entre el complejo Coyotlatelco y el complejo Mazapa en Teotihuacan." Tesis de Licenciada en Arqueología, Escuela Nacional de Antropología e Historia, México, Mexico City.

Noguera, Eduardo. 1954. *La cerámica arqueológica de Cholula*. Editorial Guaranía, México, Mexico City.

O'Neill, George. 1962. "Postclassic Stratigraphy at Chalco in the Valley of Mexico." PhD dissertation, Department of Anthropology, Columbia University, New York.

Paredes Gudiño, Blanca. 1998. "Evidencias de ocupación del periodo Coyotlatelco en la Zona Arqueolólogica de Tula Hidalgo." In *Antropología e historia del occidente de México*, vol. 3: *XXIV Mesa 57 Redonda*, 1628–44. Sociedad Mexicana de Antropología, Universidad Nacional Autónoma de México, México D.F.

Paredes Gudiño, Blanca. 2005. "Análisis de flujos migratorios y composición multiétnica de la población de Tula, Hgo." In *Reacomodos demográficos del Clásico al Posclásico en el centro de Méxoco*, edited by Linda Manzanilla, 203–26, Universidad Nacional Autónoma de México, Instituto de Investigaciones Antropológicas, Mexico City.

Parkinson, William A. 2005. "Tribal Boundaries: Stylistic Variability and Social Boundary Maintenance during the Transition to the Copper Age on the Great Hungarian Plain." *Journal of Anthropological Archaeology* 25:33–58.

Parsons, Jeffrey R. 1971. *Prehistoric Settlement Patterns in the Texcoco Region, Mexico*. Memoirs of the Museum of Anthropology, no. 3. University of Michigan, Ann Arbor.

Parsons, Jeffrey R. 2006. "A Regional Perspective on Coyotlatelco in the Basin of Mexico: Some New Thoughts about Old Data." In *El fenómeno coyotlatelco en el centro de México: Tiempo, espacio y significado*, edited by Laura Solar Valverde, 69–82. Instituto Nacional de Antropología e Historia, México, Mexico City.

Parsons, Jeffrey R. 2008. *Prehispanic Settlement Patterns in the Northwestern Valley of Mexico: The Zumpango Region.* Memoirs of the Museum of Anthropology, no. 45. University of Michigan, Ann Arbor.

Parsons, Jeffrey R., Elizabeth Brumfiel, Mary H. Parsons, and David J. Wilson. 1982. *Prehispanic Settlement Patterns in the Southern Valley of Mexico: The Chalco-Xochimilco Region.* Memoirs of the Museum of Anthropology, no. 14. University of Michigan, Ann Arbor.

Parsons, Jeffrey R., Elizabeth Brumfiel, and Mary Hodge. 1996. "Developmental Implications of Earlier Dates for Early Aztec in the Basin of Mexico." *Ancient Mesoamerica* 7(2):217–30.

Pomédio, Chloé, Grégory Pereira, Eugenia Fernández-Villanueva, eds. 2013. *Tradiciones cerámicas del Epiclásico en el Bajío y regions aledañas: Cronología e interacción.* BAR International Series, no. 2519. Paris Monographs in American Archaeology, no. 31. Archaeopress, Oxford.

Rattray, Evelyn C. 1966. "An Archaeological and Stylistic Study of Coyotlatelco Pottery." *Mesoamerican Notes* 7–8:87–211.

Rattray, Evelyn C. 1996. "A Regional Perspective on the Epiclassic Period in Central Mexico." In *Arqueología mesoamericana: Homenaje a William T. Sanders*, edited by Alba Guadalupe Mastache, Jeffrey R. Parsons, Robert S. Santley, and Mari Carmen Serra Puche, 213–31. Instituto Nacional de Antropología e Historia, México, Mexico City.

Rattray, Evelyn C. 1998. "El período Epiclásico en México central: Una perspectiva regional." In *Antropología del Occidente de México, XXIV Mesa Redonda de la SMA*, vol. 3, 1645–1670, Mexico City.

Ringle, William M., Tomas Gallaneta Negron, and George J. Bey III. 1998. "The Return of Quetzalcoatl: Evidence for the Spread of a World Religion during the Epiclassic Period." *Ancient Mesoamerica* 9:183–232.

Rodríguez-Alegría, Enrique. 2002. "Food, Eating and Objects of Power: Class Stratification and Ceramic Production and Consumption in Colonial Mexico." PhD dissertation, Department of Anthropology, The University of Chicago.

Sanders, William T. 1986. "Ceramic Chronology." In *The Teotihuacan Valley Project Final Report*, vol. 4: *The Toltec Period Occupation*, edited by William T. Sanders, 367–73. Occasional Papers in Anthropology, no. 13. Department of Anthropology, The Pennsylvania State University, University Park.

Sanders, William T. 2006. "Late Xolalpan-Metepec/Oxotitpac-Coyotlatelco; Ethnic Succession or Changing Patterns of Political Economy: A Reevaluation." In *El fenómeno coyotlatelco en el centro de México: Tiempo, espacio y significado; Memoria del Primer Seminario-Taller sobre Problemáticas Regionales*, edited by Laura Solar Valverde, 169–86. INAH, México, Mexico City.

Sanders, William T., Jeffrey Parsons, and Robert S. Santley. 1979. *The Basin of Mexico: Ecological Processes in the Evolution of a Civilization.* Academic Press, New York.

Schiffer, Michael B., and James M. Skibo. 1987. "Theory and Experiment in the Study of Technological Change." *Current Anthropology* 28:595–622.

Schwartz, Glenn M., and John J. Nichols, eds. 2006. *After Collapse: The Regeneration of Complex Societies.* University of Arizona Press, Tucson.

Smith, Michael E., and Lisa Montiel. 2001. "The Archaeological Study of Empires and Imperialism in Pre-Hispanic Central Mexico." *Journal of Anthropological Archaeology* 20:245–84.

Solar Valverde, Laura, ed. 2006. *El fenómeno coyotlatelco en el centro de México: Tiempo, espacio y significado; Memoria del Primer Seminario-Taller sobre Problemáticas Regionales.* INAH.

Stoner, Wesley D., Deborah L. Nichols, Bridget A. Alex, Destiny L. Crider. 2015. "The Emergence of Early-Middle Formative Exchange Patterns in Mesoamerica: A View from Altica in the Teotihuacan Valley." *Journal of Anthropological Archaeology* 39:19–35.

Suárez Cruz, Sergio. 1995. "La cerámica lisa cholulteca." *Arqueología* 13–14:109–20.

Sugiura Yamamoto, Yoko. 2006. "¿Cambio gradual o discontinuidad en la cerámica?: Discusión acerca del paso del Clásico al Epiclásico, visto desde el Valle de Toluca." In *El fenómeno coyotlatelco en el centro de México: Tiempo, espacio y significado.* Memoria del Primer Seminario-Taller sobre Problemáticas Regionales, edited by Laura Solar Valverde, 113–48. INAH, México, Mexico City.

Tozzer, Alfred M. 1921. *Excavations at a Site at Santiago Ahuitzotla, D.F., Mexico.* Smithsonian Institution. Bureau of American Ethnology, Bulletin 74. Washington, DC.

Trigger, Bruce G. 2003. *Understanding Early Civilizations: A Comparative Study.* Cambridge University Press, Cambridge.

Van der Leeuw, Sander E. 1993. "Giving the Pottery a Choice: Conceptual Aspects of Pottery Techniques." In *Technological Choices: Transformation in Material Cultures since the Neolithic,* edited by P. Lemonnier, 238–88. Routlege, London.

Wobst, H. Martin. 1977. "Stylistic Behavior and Information Exchange." In *For the Director: Research Essays in Honor of James B. Griffin,* edited by C. E. Cleland, 317–42. Anthropological Papers, no. 61. Museum of Anthropology, University of Michigan, Ann Arbor.

Wobst, H. Martin. 1999. "Style in Archaeology or Archaeologists in Style." In *Material Meanings: Critical Approaches to the Interpretation of Material Culture,* edited by Elizabeth S. Chilton, 118–32. University of Utah Press, Salt Lake City.

13

Pax Tolteca?

Collapse, Conflict, and the Formation of the Tula State

CHRISTOPHER MOREHART, ANGELA HUSTER,
ABIGAIL MEZA-PEÑALOZA, AND SOFÍA PACHECO-FORÉS

INTRODUCTION

In complex societies, the relative stability of the political landscape shapes the nature of war, conflict, violence, and coercion. Geopolitical and sociological views of conflict indicate that an inverse relationship exists between political stability and violence (e.g., Aron 1966; Kalyvas 2006; Tilly 1990). The idea that regional violence and conflict are widespread characteristics of fragmented, decentralized political landscapes also has archaeological support (e.g., Arkush and Allen 2006). Arkush and Tung (2013), for example, examined Andean settlement patterns and osteological data and argued that levels of violence were highest during periods of low regional centralization, which likely reflected conflict between competing groups. Such conflict and such instability are the product of competition between actors in a political landscape where regional mechanisms for integration and, hence, stability do not or no longer exist. The sociopolitical landscapes that exist in the wake of state collapse are not a simple return to previously existing organizational conditions (Feinman 1998:111–12). But regional decentralization is nonetheless common

https://doi.org/10.5876/9781646424078.c013

and observable, and such balkanization is a potential challenge to any efforts at subsequent regional integration.

Ending, undermining, or rechanneling the conflict that stems from competition is requisite for any incipient or extant regime that requires an expansive political economy. Regional stability partly requires a degree of popular legitimacy, at least publicly, and both economic and ideological mechanisms, including legal systems, develop to facilitate it (see Earle 1997; Mann 1986; Sinopoli and Morrison 1995; Smith 2003:108–9; Tilly 1990; Trigger 2003; Weber 1947:78–80). In the absence of legitimacy, however, violence and coercion are necessary to overcome the discontent that emanates from competitively oppositional behavior, including fluctuating competition between relatively equal actors in a decentralized (i.e., heterarchical) system or between unequal actors in a hierarchical or expanding hierarchical system. Indeed, the dynamic interaction between legitimacy and violence constitute fundamental political relations in the establishment of inter-polity sovereignty and intra-polity subjection (Aron 1966:738; Smith 2011:416). The virtual universality of armies, military institutions, and warriors in state societies (see Trigger 2003) attests not to the need for violent imperial expansion per se but rather to the limits of legitimacy and the fragility of political centralization.

Conflict that stems from regional instability in the political landscape is, frankly, bad for business. The establishment of geopolitical stability, a "regional peace," is not an altruistic characteristic of states and empires: it is a strategic necessity for centralization, consolidation, control, and expansion. Such an imposed regional peace has characterized a number of diverse political systems throughout history, including the Roman Empire's *Pax Romana*, the British *Pax Britannica*, and Incan efforts to undercut the independence of local rulers and warlords, or the *Pax Inca* (e.g., Aron 1966; Costin and Earle 1989; Earle 1997; Parchami 2009; Smith et al. 2012). In all these cases, any stability in relations or even an improvement in standards of living were, in a sense, epiphenomenal byproducts of the consolidation of power by a ruling regime dependent on the imposition of a hegemonic social order, one ultimately backed up by force.

In this chapter, we focus on the potential archaeological evidence of violence and conflict after the collapse of the Classic-period state of Teotihuacan and prior to the development of the Early Postclassic state of Tula. Although these states had expansive geographies of influence (cf. Smith and Montiel 2001), we center specifically on the archaeological record in the northern Basin of Mexico and the southern Mezquital Valley, a region where several political centers emerged after Teotihuacan's collapse, and whose development was an important historical prerequisite for the subsequent formation of the Early Postclassic state centered at the city of Tula Grande (see figures 13.1 and 13.2). In other words, this area demonstrates a degree of geopolitical decentralization that archaeologists

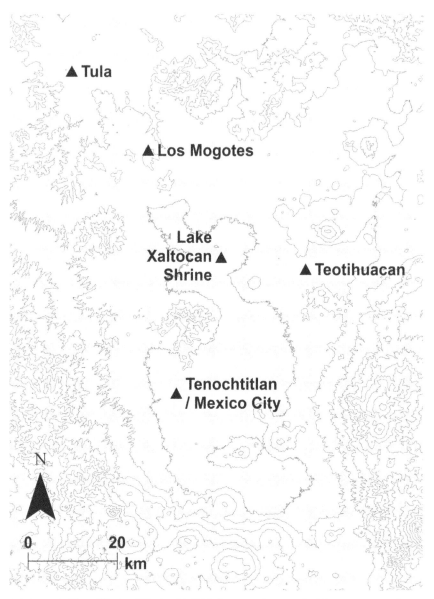

FIGURE 13.1. *Map of Basin of Mexico, highlighting area of case study. Map was generated using 30 m Shuttle Radar Topography Mission data (SHRTM) with lines originally at 100 m contours modified to extenuate landscape. Locations of a selection of well-studied sites relevant to the chapter are shown.*

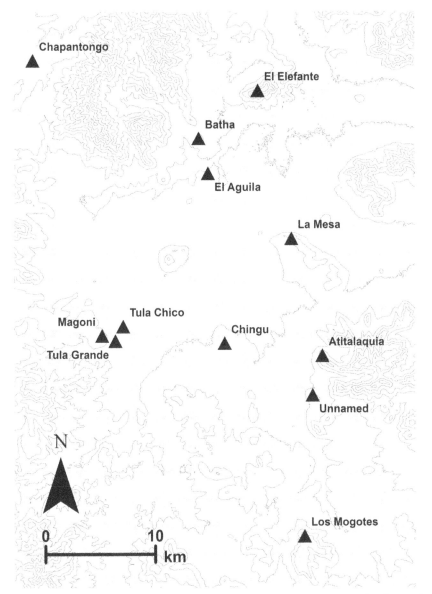

FIGURE 13.2. *Topographic map of northern Basin of Mexico/southern Mezquital Valley, with focus on Tula region and surrounding areas, generated from a 15 m DEM available from the Instituto Nacional de Estadistica y Geografia (https://www.inegi.org.mx). Lines generated at 100 m contours. Locations of sites discussed in text are shown.*

predict might result in the regional instability that leads to conflict and violence, structural characteristics of the political landscape that must be considered if we are to understand the formation of any subsequent centralized state system, such as that centered at Tula Grande.

The goal of this chapter is exploratory. We first offer a somewhat broad and coarse introduction to this period of regional political instability in the archaeological literature (see also Crider; Parsons and Gorenflo, this volume). We then review some of the archaeological evidence for violence, first considering iconographic representations and then bioarchaeological data. Next, we examine evidence of regional instability and possibly conflict in the archaeological record of this region's settlement history. Although we do not find any simple smoking guns that "prove" this region was subject to endemic warfare after Teotihuacan's collapse, we do observe several potential indicators of political competition and probably conflict. We conclude by exploring how this structural characteristic of the political landscape may have conditioned the subsequent formation of the Early Postclassic state of Tula.

THE EPICLASSIC PERIOD

The collapse of Teotihuacan in the early to mid-seventh century CE created a fundamental rupture in the fabric of society in Central Mexico and beyond (see figure 13.1). The subsequent period, referred to as Epiclassic, Early Toltec, or sometimes Late Classic (ca. 650–900 CE), is considered a time of social, cultural, political, and economic transformation and reorganization (see figure 13.3). Scholars argue that the landscape was marked by population movement and cultural change (Beekman and Christensen 2003; Berlo 1989; Clayton 2013, 2016; Cowgill 2013; Crider 2013; Crider et al. 2007; Gaxiola González 2010; Healan 2012; Healan and Cobean 2019; Hirth 2000; Mastache and Cobean 1989, 1990; Nichols et al. 2013; Rattray 1996; Serra Puche and Lazcano Arce 2005; Solar Valverde 2006; Sugiura 2006). It was a time of economic reorganization: earlier regional production and distribution systems of key goods, like obsidian, collapsed and new distribution networks emerged (Cobean 2002). Pottery styles suggest extensive and even distant cultural ties but with production and exchange tied to local polities or communities (Clayton 2016; Crider 2011; Crider, this volume; Crider et al. 2007). Out of this complex, decentralized landscape, the Tula state would emerge by the tenth to eleventh century CE (Anderson et al. 2015; Healan 2012). Hence, the Epiclassic period in Central Mexico offers a critical opportunity to understand historical transformation in both local and regional terms.

Teotihuacan's decline may have created a political vacuum that fostered competitive geopolitics (Blanton 1975; Charlton and Nichols 1997; Clayton 2013; Crider 2011; Diehl and Berlo 1989; Fournier et al. 2006; Fournier and Martínez Lemus 2010; García Chávez 2004; Gaxiola González 2010; Nichols et al. 2013;

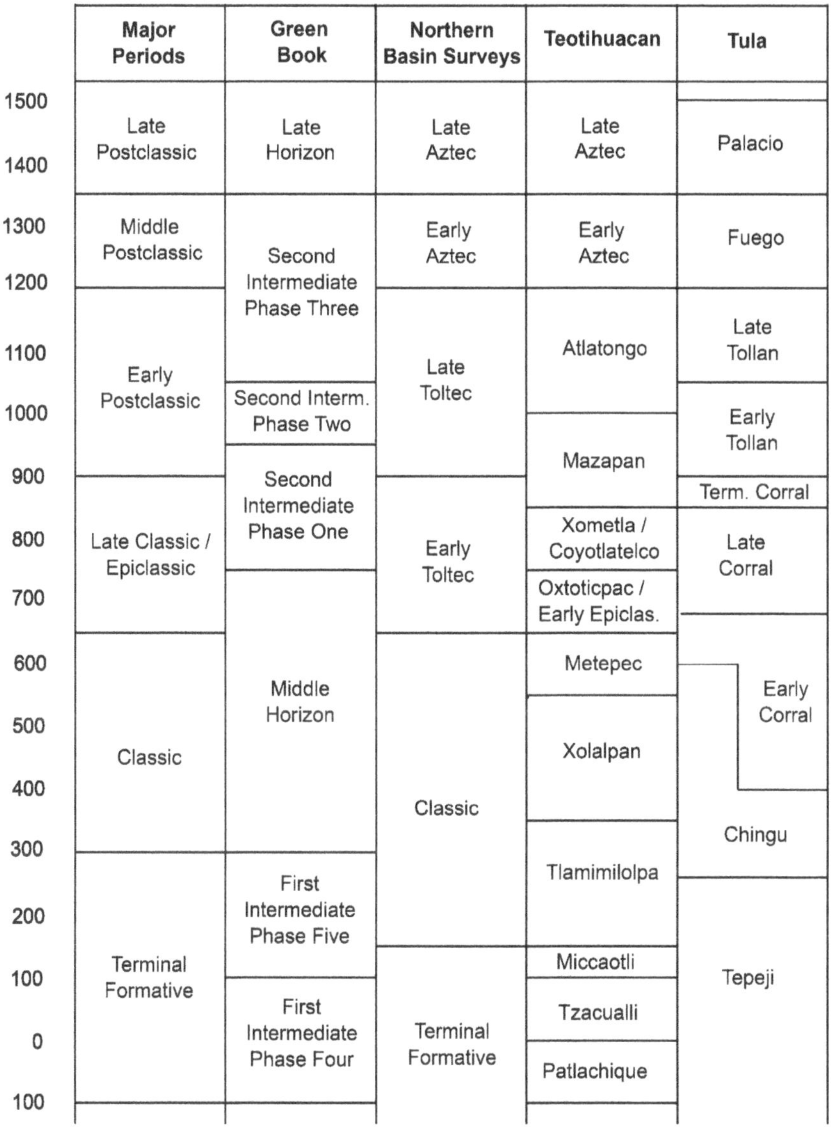

Years	Major Periods	Green Book	Northern Basin Surveys	Teotihuacan	Tula
1500 / 1400	Late Postclassic	Late Horizon	Late Aztec	Late Aztec	Palacio
1300 / 1200	Middle Postclassic	Second Intermediate Phase Three	Early Aztec	Early Aztec	Fuego
1100	Early Postclassic		Late Toltec	Atlatongo	Late Tollan
1000		Second Interm. Phase Two		Mazapan	Early Tollan
900		Second Intermediate Phase One			Term. Corral
800	Late Classic / Epiclassic		Early Toltec	Xometla / Coyotlatelco	Late Corral
700				Oxtoticpac / Early Epiclas.	
600	Classic	Middle Horizon	Classic	Metepec	Early Corral
500				Xolalpan	
400					Chingu
300		First Intermediate Phase Five		Tlamimilolpa	
200	Terminal Formative				Tepeji
100				Miccaotli	
0		First Intermediate Phase Four	Terminal Formative	Tzacualli	
100				Patlachique	

FIGURE 13.3. *Major time periods from the Terminal Formative to the Late Postclassic periods in the northern Basin of Mexico and the southern Mezquital Valley. Regional chronological phases compiled and synthesized from Cowgill 2015; Rattray 2001; Sanders 1986:4 for Teotihuacan; Cobean 1990; Healan 2012 for Tula; Parsons 2008 for the northern Basin survey; Sanders et al. 1979 for the Green Book's full Basin synthesis.*

Parsons 1971, 2006). The resulting political landscape of Central Mexico was quite variable, ranging from large regional states to constellations of city-states (Anderson et al. 2015; Charlton and Nichols 1997). The nature of governance across the region also most certainly differed, with variable organizational pathways. In the Basin of Mexico and surrounding areas, scholars have suggested a regionalization of political economic spheres with interrelated provinces centered in the north, east, west, and south (e.g., Crider 2011; Charlton and Nichols 1997:190; Diehl 1989; García Chávez and Martinez Yrízar 2006; Parsons 1971:203; Rattray 1996; Sanders et al. 1979:129–37). Blanton (1975:230) argued that competitive relationships explain the characteristics of the settlement system: "the Early Toltec period was a time of 'Balkanization' in the Valley of Mexico, following the decline of Teotihuacan, when there was a series of discrete sociopolitical units, each in competition with each other, and each surrounded by a 'shatter-zone' of abandoned, contested land." Parsons (1971:207, 242) suggested that areas of the Basin of Mexico with particularly low populations were buffer zones between two polities that became increasingly powerful by the Early Postclassic period, Tula to the north and Cholula to the southeast.

During the Epiclassic period, the northern Basin of Mexico and the southern Mezquital witnessed the formation of several small political centers, many on hilltops (Mastache 1996; Mastache et al. 2002) (see figure 13.2). One of these centers, Tula Chico, located on a lower hill in the west-central part of Tula valley, has long been thought as the most important center and the progenitor of the Early Postclassic city of Tula Grande (see, e.g., Anderson et al. 2015; Cobean 1982:40–41; Diehl 1983; Healan 2012; Mastache and Cobean 1989; Mastache et al. 2002). Tula Chico is an early to late Epiclassic period settlement, occupied during what archaeologists once referred to as the Prado and the Corral phases (Cobean 1990) and now as the Early and Late Corral phase (Healan et al. 2021). The identification of other Epiclassic period hilltop centers, however, complicated the view of Tula Chico's preeminence. Archaeologists proposed that the hilltop centers predated Tula Chico, during what was called the Mesa phase (Anderson et al. 2015; Healan 2012; Mastache and Cobean 1989, 1990). The Mesa-phase settlements were thought to be settled by immigrants into a valley still occupied by settlements with ties to the declining Teotihuacan state, but they were abandoned when Tula Chico emerged as a regional power. Although the interpretation of these sites' chronological overlap with Teotihuacan-related settlements is likely correct (see below), recent research demonstrates that they were largely contemporaries of Tula Chico (Cobean et al. 2021; Healan et al. 2021). Indeed, the Epiclassic occupation underlying what would become Tula Grande might also be underestimated (Paredes Gudiño 1998; Sterpone 2000). Consequently, the northern Basin of Mexico and the southern Mezquital Valley well illustrate the regional fragmentation considered a characteristic of the Epiclassic period.

However, the connection between potential balkanization and instability, including possible conflict, warfare, and violence, is not well understood. Even more, the Tula state's Early Postclassic development requires rethinking now that we know it emerged out of a constellation of political centers.

ICONOGRAPHIC EVIDENCE OF CONFLICT AND VIOLENCE DURING THE EPICLASSIC TO THE EARLY POSTCLASSIC PERIOD

For some, the nature of politics during the Epiclassic period integrated conflict and violence and connected with new ideological systems that expanded in the absence of the cultural hegemony of Teotihuacan (López Austin and López Luján 2000). Militaristic themes are widespread in the iconography at political centers dating to this time (Baird 1989; Bey and Ringle 2011; Hers 2010; Hirth 1989; Koontz 2009; Mastache and Cobean 1989; Miller 1999; Ringle et al. 1998; Taube 1994). Ringle and colleagues (1998) suggested the emergence of a macro-regional system that integrated polities throughout much of Mesoamerica in a militaristic Quetzalcoatl cult that celebrated warfare, human sacrifice, and decapitation.

Iconographic evidence of warfare and militarism is clear in the iconography of Tula Grande during its Early Postclassic (Tollan phase) heyday. Although later in time, many of these representational themes appear to reflect the culmination of an ideology with antecedents in the Epiclassic period, if not earlier (Anderson et al. 2015:449; Cobean et al. 2021; Healan et al. 2021; Jordan 2016; Mastache and Cobean 1989; Mastache et al. 2002). The Atlantean (or caryatid) sculptures currently on the summit of Pyramid B, one of the city's principal ceremonial structures, represent probable warriors (Acosta 1943; Jiménez García 1998). Equally well known are the reclining chacmools, likely associated with sacrifice (Healan 2012:64). The pillars found on Pyramid B also exhibit depictions of warriors, with headdresses, name glyphs, and weapons, such as knives and atlatls (Acosta 1941:242; Kristan-Graham 1989; Mastache et al. 2009). Jiménez García (2021) suggests they represent real individuals, possibly rulers (see also Acosta 1941:243). Relief friezes in the central complex of Tula Grande, such as Vestibule 1 and Building 4, contain an array of individuals in processions, ranging from possible merchants (Kristan-Graham 1993) to possible armed rulers, who share similarities with the individuals on the pillars on Pyramid B (Mastache et al. 2009:303). The reclining figures on the frieze panels that once adorned the Palacio Quemado might depict ancestors of kings and warriors (Jiménez García 1998; Mastache et al. 2009). Processions of individuals in other rooms of the Palacio Quemado are interpreted as elite lords and as warriors (Mastache et al. 2009:309, 2002:116–27).

Depictions of defleshed individuals, skeletons, skulls, and likely sacrifices also occur at Tula Grande (see Jordan 2013). A structure has been identified as a *tzompantli*, or skull rack, in the central plaza, just east of Ballcourt 2, based on the presence of cranial fragments and human teeth in upper excavation levels and a stone knife in an offering box (Matos Moctezuma 1972:115). The structure at Tula Grande shares a number of similarities with the *tzompantli* identified at Chichén Itza in Yucatan. Nevertheless, relatively little additional data exist to verify its interpretation as a skull rack (Healan 2012:63). However, crania sculptures like those found at Chichén Itza's *tzompantli* have been recovered, such as those at an altar at the Canal complex north of the city center (Healan 1989:126–27). An unprovenanced panel from Tula Grande depicts a seated individual, probably a warrior, carrying a shield with a skull in the center (Jiménez García 1998:311–13; Mastache et al. 2002:139–41). Figures depicted on the friezes of the Corral pyramid at Tula Chico north of the city center depict fleshless crania and crossed bones (De la Fuente et al. 1988:132–33; Jiménez García 1998:260–61). The friezes of the Coatepantli, on the north face of Pyramid B, portray skeletal figures emerging from serpents (Jiménez García 1998:288; Jordan 2013).

BIOARCHAEOLOGICAL EVIDENCE OF CONFLICT AND VIOLENCE DURING THE EPICLASSIC TO THE EARLY POSTCLASSIC PERIOD

One of the clearest examples of the connections between violence and ritual during the Epiclassic period was documented at a small site in the former lakebed of Lake Xaltocan in the northern Basin of Mexico (Morehart 2015; Morehart et al. 2012) (see figure 13.1). Constructed and first used perhaps as early as the mid-sixth century CE, the site was the focus of ritual activities, including human sacrifice. Excavations uncovered the remains of at least three hundred individuals represented either by complete crania or cranial fragments. Almost all of the crania exhibit features that allow them to be identified as biological males. Virtually no sub-cranial bones were present, although some crania have finger bones in the orbital sockets and most have associated cervical vertebrae that suggest adequate flesh was present at interment to maintain the articulation of head to neck. Extensive cut marks on the remains are indicative of defleshing and decapitation. Radiocarbon dates and key pottery types fall mainly in the Epiclassic period and both earlier and later Epiclassic (to transitional Early Postclassic) types were found (Morehart et al. 2012; Pacheco-Forés et al. 2021). Analyses on the human remains continue, but current information indicates that the human sacrifices differ biologically from earlier and contemporaneous populations in Central Mexico (Meza-Peñaloza et al. 2019; Meza-Peñaloza et al., this volume). Isotopic analysis suggests that the majority were born outside the Basin of Mexico, though most relocated to the region before their deaths, which Pacheco-Forés and colleagues (2021) suggest is indicative of identity-based violence.

Similar deposits are not common but have been found at other Epiclassic sites in the broader Tula region. For example, Fournier and Vargas Sanders

(2002:49–50), describe Epiclassic period sacrifices at Chapantongo, northwest of Tula (see figure 13.2). The west-facing crania of twelve individuals were recovered from an altar at the site (see also Fournier and Bolaños 2011). Like the materials from Lake Xaltocan, the skulls were associated with cervical vertebra and finger bones (as well as foot bones).

Additional bioarchaeological evidence of sacrifice dating to the Epiclassic period was observed at the Epiclassic hilltop site Los Mogotes. Los Mogotes is south of Tula but likely part of the decentralized political system of the Tula region during the Epiclassic period (Healan 2012:76–77; Mastache 1996:45; Parsons 2008:174) (see figures 13.2, 13.4; see also below). The site has two major groups of monumental architecture, a range of households and terraces. The community is also surrounded by a wall fortification, which we discuss more below. Two burials associated with monumental architecture at one of the principal groups suggest that they were sacrifices. One burial (Burial 1), located to the east of the largest pyramid (Structure 1) consists of a juvenile in a tightly flexed position with the hands behind the back, suggesting the individual was a sacrificed captive (García Velsaco et al. 2017). Another burial (Burial 5), located on the southern side of a large courtyard compounds adjacent to the same monumental group as Structure 1, contained three flexed male adults in a line following the building's orientation (García Velascco and Meza-Peñaloza 2018; Morehart et al. 2018). One of the individuals had the tip of an obsidian in the right femoral region, which, given its location, could easily have damaged the femoral artery and caused death. Not unlike the sacrificial deposits at Xaltocan, biodistance analysis suggests that they were not related to individuals interred in household burials (Meza-Peñaloza et al. 2021), reinforcing the notion that ethnic differences may have been factors in the selection of sacrificial victims (Pacheco-Forés et al. 2021).

Evidence of human sacrifice in this region appears more common during the Early Postclassic period, and the practice of cranial burials continued. Gamboa Cabezas and Healan (2021:58–59) describe a similar deposit as found at Chapantongo on the outskirts of Tula Grande. They recovered twelve west-facing crania in architectural terrace construction fill, which they suggest might be connected to the display of skulls as a dedication ritual. Most excavated ceramic materials date to the Early Postclassic Tollan phase, and some of the crania were found in Tollan-phase vessels. Elson and Mowbray (2005) describe similar interments at a site on the outskirts of Teotihuacan. Here, crania were found in both Mazapan and Toltec Red-on-Buff pottery types. Although these types are frequently used to identify Early Postclassic sites or deposits, they are transitional types between the Epiclassic and the Early Postclassic (Cobean 1990; Crider 2011; Crider, this volume; Healan et al. 2021).

Evidence of child sacrifice, such as found at Los Mogotes, is not well documented during the Epiclassic period but appears during the apogee of the Early

Postclassic Tula state. Gómez Serafín and colleagues (1994:87–91, 100) reported the presence of child crania with associated cervical vertebrae from Tollan-phase burials at Tula Grande, which they interpret as decapitated sacrifices that were subsequently burned and placed within vessels. Furthermore, excavations just outside of Tula Grande uncovered a mass burial that contained forty-nine individuals (Medrano Enríquez 2021). Almost all are children with considerable evidence of cut marks indicative of defleshing and likely sacrifice. The practice of child sacrifice at Tula Grande might be similar to state-sponsored, child sacrifices under the Late Postclassic–period Aztec empire (Medrano Enríquez 2021:92).

Attempting to piece together temporal patterns in the regional practice of human sacrifice might shed some light on the nature of conflict or violence during this time. Although mass human sacrifice in public, monumental buildings is documented during the Classic period at Teotihuacan (e.g., Castro et al. 1991; Sugiyama 1989; Sujiyama and Lopez Luján 2007), little evidence exists that such activities were widespread outside of the urban center. Given the spatial and the temporal distribution of these, admittedly, select examples, the regionalization in the practice of ritual decapitation might emerge after Teotihuacan's collapse, at least in the northern Basin of Mexico to the Mezquital Valley (Morehart et al. 2012). These practices occurred during the Epiclassic period but may have either continued or have become more common later in this period or in the earlier and later facets of the Early Postclassic period. The possibility exists that the regionalization of sacrifice reflected political balkanization during the Epiclassic period, a ritual practice that was centralized as the Early Postclassic state at Tula Grande expanded influence and cultural hegemony.

The offering of crania suggests some degree of violence, possibly related to conflict or war, but the significance of these burials is not necessarily clear. For the Postclassic Aztecs, the head was the source of a powerful force called *tonalli* (López Austin 1988). Victors in battle sought to harness the power of a fierce combatant by taking the head of a vanquished warrior (Durán 1971). Hence, some of these deposits might represent the ritual offering of trophy heads taken in battle. Yet additional possibilities also exist that are either independent of any acts of violence or integrated with them, not unlike the complex, layered symbolism seen in iconographic representations of skeletal material. The offering of crania in Lake Xaltocan was likely connected to rituals undertaken to deities or spiritual forces associated with water (Morehart et al. 2012). At Chapantongo, the cranial offerings might reflect the ritualization of a cosmology that emphasized the cycles of the moon or other astronomical patterns (Fournier and Bolaños 2011; Fournier and Vargas Sanders 2002). At Tula, the skull burials and other cranial material found from the same site might have some connection to the *tzompantli* in the city center (Healan et al. 2021). The evidence of child sacrifice might reflect earlier versions of state-sponsored rituals better known among the Aztecs (Medrano Enríquez 2021).

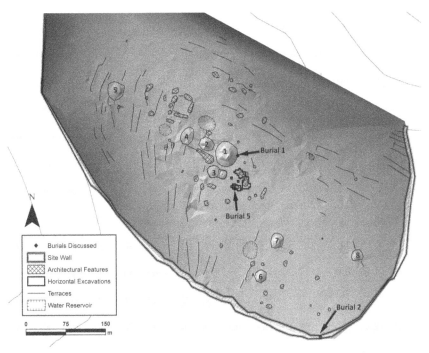

FIGURE 13.4. *DEM of Los Mogotes generated in ArcGIS using field total-station data. Major structures, agricultural terraces, probable water reservoirs, and fortifications are shown. One horizontal excavation area is displayed. The locations of Burials 1, 2, and 5 are indicated.*

However, it is also possible that some of these remains are not sacrifices at all, at least not as commonly conceived and framed above. Instead, they could reflect burial practices that resist simple comprehension. Although no sub-cranial materials were associated with the crania recovered in vessels near Teotihuacan, Charlton (1998, cited in Elson and Mowbray 2005:209) uncovered a burial in the Teotihuacan Valley that contained an individual identified as female with a complete Mazapan vessel placed where the head should have been. In some cases, individual crania (especially those not in vessels) associated with complete skeletons might also reflect the depositional disturbances of a repeatedly re-used burial location (e.g., Gómez Serafín et al. 1994:82). Others might be secondary burials rather than primary interments of human sacrifices.

Sacrifices are ritualized acts with localized representations in the archaeological record. Bioarchaeological evidence of injuries would be a better index for the intensity of conflict and violence. However, such information, particularly the premortem pathologies that result from combat, have been inadequately documented. Many of the cut marks on the crania from Xaltocan and on the child burials from Tula Grande likely resulted from the ritual process of sacrifice rather than from combat. Gómez Serafín and colleagues (1994:76) report an individual from an Epiclassic period burial near Tula Grande with a perforated right scapula possibly due to injury from violence, but nothing similar for later interments. At Los Mogotes, excavations in the wall that surrounds the site uncovered a single burial of a tightly flexed, male adult (Burial 2, figure 13.4). This individual was interred with two, large gray obsidian bifaces. These might be offerings, and burials with obsidian bifaces have been documented at Los Mogotes (Cesaretti et al. 2018; Morehart et al. 2018), at other hilltop sites in the region, such as La Mesa (Mastache and Cobean 1989:60; Mastache et al. 2002:66), and from Epiclassic period burials near Tula Grande (Gómez Serafín et al. 1994:70, 73). In the Los Mogotes case, however, the points may have been associated with the cause of death. One point was recovered within the thoracic cavity and the other was found within the pelvic bones, which exhibit perimortem lesions consistent with wounds from a projectile point (García Velsaco et al. 2017:126).

A SETTLEMENT OF CONFLICT?

In the northern Basin of Mexico and the southern Mezquital Valley, the population changed dramatically after the collapse of Teotihuacan. Our regional understandings of demographic changes relate to the chronological reconstructions of archaeological sites. In the Tula region, the Classic period occupation seems to have been its highest during the Early to Middle Classic period, associated with the Tlamimilolpa phase at Teotihuacan, when the area may have been occupied by local residents (possibly Hñähñu), groups with relationships to Teotihuacan, and groups with strong Oaxacan affiliations (Fournier and Vargas Sanders 2002:40; Healan and Cobean 2019:75; Holt Mehta 2018; Mastache et al. 2002:59; Sandoval 2017). The population apparently declined later in the Classic period, during Teotihuacan's Xolalpan and Metepec phases. Our assessment of this trajectory in the adjacent northern Basin of Mexico is limited by the chronological resolution of the survey data, where Classic period sites were not subdivided into phases (Gorenflo and Sanders 2007; Parsons 2008). Greater chronological refinement exists for the data from the Teotihuacan Valley, which document a rural population decline in the early Xolalpan phase similar to the Tula region data (Sanders and Kolb 1996:676–77). Farther away in the southern Basin of Mexico, Teotihuacan's influence also appears to have greatly diminished by the sixth century CE (Clayton 2016). A population decline during the Xolalpan phase might suggest the retraction of Teotihuacan's regional influence before the collapse of its political system (Healan 2012:76; Manzanilla 2003; Rattray 1996).

Nevertheless, archaeologists working in both regions have documented a considerable decline in population after the fall of Teotihuacan. In the northern Basin (Zumpango) survey area, for example, Parsons (2008:86) documented an almost 40 percent population decline. A similar trend seems to have occurred in the Tula region (Fournier and Martínez Lemus 2010:188; Healan 2012:76; Mastache and Cobean 1989:55; Mastache et al. 2002:59–60). Some small settlements existed in the valley bottomlands, but, as we discussed earlier, most of the regional population during the Epiclassic period was nucleated on hilltops (see figure 13.2). The majority of these settlements have not been mapped or excavated, and some of them are not named. They exhibit diversity in architectural organization but typically have central ceremonial precincts, plazas, a variety of households, and systems of terraces; some have ballcourts (see Anderson 2018; Anderson et al. 2015; Bonfil Olivera 2005; Fournier and Martínez Lemus 2010:190; Fournier and Vargas Sanders 2002; Healan 2012; Healan and Cobean 2019; Mastache and Cobean 1989, 1990; Mastache et al. 2002; Morehart 2016; Parsons 2008).

Settlement on hilltops might suggest the need for protection and defense, given that they overlook wide swaths of fertile alluvial bottomlands (Anderson et al. 2015:441; Mastache and Cobean 1989:55). These centers have expansive views of the region and are more difficult to reach. Building settlements in defensible positions would make sense if settled by relatively recent migrants who began moving into a still occupied, possibly even hostile, area. In the Basin of Mexico, the classification of survey sites according to broad phases, such as Classic versus Early Toltec, makes it difficult to assess overlap between the chronological markers of either period of time. However, overlap is likely. As Parsons (2008:371) notes for settlements outside of centers in the northern Basin, Zumpango survey region, "most Early Toltec sites in the Zumpango Region also have Classic occupations, and at such multicomponent sites it has often proved difficult to disentangle the two periods ceramically." Indeed, Parsons (2006, 2008:371) notes that the most common ceramic marker for the Epiclassic period, Coyotlatelco Red-on-Buff, is found in hilltop centers but not at hinterland sites. The chronological overlap between materials associated with both periods is much clearer in the Tula region, where transitional sites in non-hilltop locations have been documented (Mastache 1996:36; Mastache et al. 2002:60–61) and where hilltop sites lack any evidence of Teotihuacan-related occupation (Healan and Cobean 2019:75; Mastache and Cobean 1989:56).

In other words, the collapse of Teotihuacan may have had a gradual impact on its surrounding settlement system, concomitant with the regional demographic decline during the Xolalpan phase. In the wake of Teotihuacan's retracting and then collapsing political system, not only new migrants but autonomous political actors possibly entered the area who may have found themselves in competition with the preexisting population. Mastache and Cobean (1989:56) interpret this overlap and the differences between the hilltop centers and the sites in the bottomlands: "This difference makes us believe that the earliest Coyotlatelco groups settled only high, easily defended hilltops because the better quality lands at lower elevations having a potential for irrigation were still occupied by Teotihuacan-related populations." Although it's speculative, such competition may have resulted in hostility, conflict, and violence (see also Yadeun 1975:33–34).

Hilltop locations have a number of strategic advantages. First, these hilltop sites were likely relatively easier to defend from attacking forces. To our knowledge, most of the Tula region hilltop centers lack evidence of fortifications. As we introduced previously, one exception is the site Los Mogotes (see figure 13.4). Los Mogotes was surrounded by a large wall feature that encloses the community's southern, eastern, and western borders from the rest of the uninhabited (though terraced) mesa (Morehart 2016). The northern side of the site, which faces the Tula valley, is unfortified though marked by cliffs and precipitous slopes. Excavations of the wall produced Coyotlatelco Red-on-Buff and other Epiclassic types (Huster 2018), exposed a basal width of approximately 6 meters, and, as we described, a burial of an individual who exhibits evidence of injuries (Cesaretti et al. 2017; García Velasco et al. 2017).

Another strategic advantage of a hilltop position is communicative. The hilltop locations may have served as an effective means of communication between allied centers during episodes of conflict, possibly through the use of fire or smoke signals. If this was the case, the hilltop sites should exhibit a high degree of intervisibility. To assess this possibility, an exploratory visibility analysis was undertaken of a series of centers identified in the greater Tula region (see figure 13.2, table 13.1). Settlement locations were compiled using GPS data for Los Mogotes. For the Tula area sites, site locations were determined by comparing published regional and site maps with high-resolution satellite data. Named centers in the Tula area maps were used, though one site south of Atitalaquia was listed as unknown, since its name is not included in regional site maps. Another site, Chapantongo, was included, given its location on a hill and its material relations with and general proximity to Epiclassic Tula area sites, though Chapantongo is somewhat farther away from the valley (see Fournier and Vargas Sanders 2002). El Elefante is typically not listed as one of the Epiclassic hilltop sites, though it possibly was one given the presence of Epiclassic period artifacts (Castillo Bernal 2019; Martínez Magaña 1994).

Once site locations were determined, the site data were exported into ArcMap 10.7. A 15-meter digital elevation model (DEM) of the region from the Instituto Nacional de Estadística y Geografía was used for the elevation data needed to assess visibility. Except for Los Mogotes and La Mesa, most of the hilltop sites are inadequately reported. Hence, accurate polygon boundaries for each site cannot be produced to generate a series of observation points. Consequently, buffer polygons were created with 500-meter radii around each point, which approximates the area of the larger sites. Separate viewsheds were calculated for each site in ArcMap 10.7, which produced a binary raster with pixels assigned a

TABLE 13.1. Visibility matrix of hilltop sites (1= visible, 0= not visible)

	Tula Chico	Magoni	La Mesa	Los Mogotes	Atitalaquia	El Aguila	Batha	Unknown	El Elefante	Chapantongo
Tula Chico		1	1	0	1	0	1	1	1	0
Magoni	1		1	1	1	0	1	1	1	0
La Mesa	1	1		1	1	1	1	1	1	0
Los Mogotes	0	1	1		1	1	1	1	1	0
Atitalaquia	1	1	1	1		1	1	1	1	0
El Aguila	0	0	1	1	1		1	1	1	0
Batha	1	1	1	1	1	1		1	1	0
Unnamed	1	1	1	1	1	1	1		1	0
El Elefante	1	1	1	1	1	1	1	1		0
Chapantongo	0	0	0	0	0	0	0	0	0	
Totals	6	7	8	7	8	6	8	8	8	0

value of 0 (not visible) or 1 (visible). The raster viewsheds were converted into polygons to compare against the polygon buffers for each site. Sites were identified as visible if their buffer polygons overlapped with the viewshed polygons.

Although exploratory, this analysis suggests a high degree of intervisibility among all the sites (see table 13.1). Magoni, La Mesa, Atitalaquia, the Unnamed Center, El Elefante, Batha, and Los Mogotes have the highest number of sites in their respective viewsheds, particularly La Mesa, Atitalaquia, El Elefante, the Unnamed Center, and Batha. Tula Chico's viewshed, despite its possible significance for the eventual founding of Tula Grande, contains fewer sites, the same number as El Aguila, located farther to the north. Both El Aguila and Tula Chico are on hills, though much lower in relief and elevation. Chapantongo is the only site with zero visibility to the other sites. This is not surprising since its location is separated from the Tula Valley by a range of low mountains.

Another strategic advantage of hilltops is their regional surveillance function. They should have better views of the landscape than other settlement locations. To assess this possibility, an additional visibility analysis was conducted to compare the visibility from hilltop sites against the visibility from other observer locations. Ideally, this process would involve the construction of a cumulative viewshed of the study area using all the area's sites (see Conolly and Lake 2006:225–33; Wheatley 1995). Then the visibility of groups of specific observer locations (i.e., hilltop sites from non-hilltop sites) could be compared against the cumulative viewshed. Given that the coordinates of most survey sites are not available in the Tula region, a total viewshed of the area was instead estimated

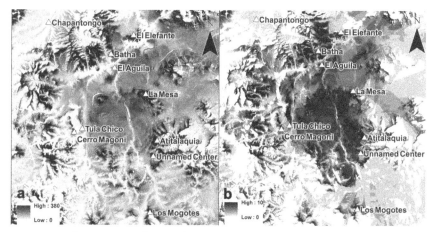

FIGURE 13.5. *Raster images of two exploratory viewshed analyses generated in ArcGIS from a 15 m DEM, available from the Instituto Nacional de Estadística y Geografía (https://www .inegi.org.mx). (a) A total viewshed data product generated from 1,000 random points as observer locations. Pixel values represent the number of points from which a pixel is visible. (b) A cumulative viewshed data product generated from the hilltop site locations as observer locations. Pixel values represent the number of hilltop sites from which a pixel is visible.*

based on a random pool of 1000 points. This produces a raster image in which cell values are the number of observers visible from a locus (see figure 13.5a). Once produced, a new sample of five hundred random points was generated across a somewhat smaller area (to accommodate possible edge effects) and treated as potential site locations / observer points within the total viewshed to compare with hilltop sites. Raster data values in the total viewshed were then appended to the 500-random-point attribute table. To append the raster values to the hilltop buffer polygons, the Extract by Mask tool was used to create new rasters for each polygon boundary, and the mean value of each raster was tabulated for each site. A non-parametric, two sample Kolmogorov-Smirnov test of the cumulative distributions of the raster values of both samples allows us to reject the null hypothesis that the samples are from the same distribution ($D=0.626$, p= <0.0001, $\alpha=0.01$).

Lastly, the total viewshed raster from 1,000 random points was compared with a cumulative viewshed produced only using the hilltop polygons (see figure 13.5b). The values of all 14,310,769 pixels in each raster were converted to column vectors in R, and a non-parametric Wilcoxon Rank Sum test was performed. This test allows us to reject the null hypothesis that the two distributions are identical with a locational shift between their medians equal to zero (W = $9.6459e+13$, p-value < $2.2e$-16), though some caution should be exercised given the extremely small size of the p-value. Nevertheless, when combined with the previous analyses, this finding reinforces the identified difference between hilltop site visibility and the overall visibility of observer loci in the study region.

Given that the visibility analyses are exploratory, no additional topographic (i.e., slope, aspect, etc.) or other settlement characteristics (soil quality, etc.) were taken into consideration (see Wright et al. 2014). Moreover, we did not specify the height of target locations, only observers (1.5 m). Any feature that increases the height of a target location might increase its visibility. Plumes of smoke from fires, in other words, might be visible to observer loci that otherwise cannot see their locations. We also did not specify a radial distance of view due to uncertainty in determining an appropriate value to use, as well as the variable impact of terrain, elevation, and target mass on light and other atmospheric conditions, though we note that visibility from some of these hilltops (i.e., Cerro Ahumada) surpasses 20 kilometers, particularly for prominent natural or anthropogenic features. Reducing the radial distance certainly would reduce pixel visibility as well as hilltop site intervisibility and, hence, this analysis should be viewed as exploratory and preliminary.

A PAX TOLTECA?

By the Early Postclassic period (Tollan phase), the northern Basin of Mexico and much of the Mezquital Valley were integrated into the Tula state. As mentioned above, one perspective proposes that this process of expansion began at Tula Chico during the Epiclassic period prior to the establishment of Tula Grande (Anderson et al. 2015:447). In this view, Tula Chico served as a conquest state that began to integrate the area, leading to the abandonment of competing hilltop centers and a consolidation of power that later shifted to Tula Grande (Mastache et al. 2002:75). The revision of the chronology of Tula Chico and the hilltop centers complicates this interpretation (Healan et al. 2021; see above). Tula Chico and the hilltop centers were contemporaneous settlements. While speculative, it is possible that any alliances that may have connected local centers during the Epiclassic period were fragile and prone to conflict. As regional settlements with previous ties to Teotihuacan continued to decline, these centers could have become increasingly competitive with one another, their hilltop locations continuing to serve strategically important defensive roles.

At least two hilltop centers, Magoni and Los Mogotes, have evidence of occupation contemporaneous with the emergence of the regional Tula state (Anderson 2018; Morehart 2019). Eliminating the independent power of these sites would have been essential for expansion. These hilltop settlements were largely abandoned during the Early Postclassic period, but this occurred after, not prior to, Tula's establishment. At Los Mogotes, for example, we have recovered Late Corral and Early Tollan–phase pottery that date to Tula's development, especially from our excavations at the site's central, public spaces (Huster 2017,

2018). It is possible that the appearance of Toltec pottery in the site center reflects efforts to incorporate or control publicly important spaces of previously independent polities, a process that eventually led to their abandonment.

It is also possible that the trajectory that led to the abandonment of hilltop centers involved violent conquest. Some of the archaeological and bioarchaeological evidence of violence and conflict presented earlier may have been related to the regional instability that led to the dominance of Tula Grande. Although some of the symbolic depictions related to warfare or violence had antecedents during the Epiclassic period, the iconographic corpus of Early Postclassic Tula suggests that a pervasive ideology of militarism was institutionalized by the state. Previous suggestions that Tula Chico was violently destroyed and burned prior to the formation of Tula Grande have been called into question based on recent stratigraphic analysis (Cobean et al. 2021). At Los Mogotes, however, vitrified daub is virtually ubiquitous from all excavations (Morehart 2019). The use of pottery kilns could cause vitrification, but this interpretation seems likely given the wide distribution of vitrified adobe in several household and non-household contexts across the site. Although not certain, the abundance of vitrified daub might suggest conflagrations due to conquest.

The change in the settlement system during the Early Postclassic period is perhaps one of the most significant lines of evidence that document Tula's influence. Around Tula, population increased, and previously unoccupied areas were settled, a process that Mastache and colleagues (2002:179) referred to as "the Toltec colonization of the area," which is observable throughout the Mezquital Valley (Fournier et al. 2006; Fournier and Martínez Lemus 2010). In the northern Basin of Mexico just south of the Mezquital, Parsons (2008:88) recorded both regional population growth and a filling-in of areas uninhabited during the Epiclassic period. This trend also occurred in the Teotihuacan Valley (Charlton 1987:566). In addition, the settlement system moved away from the prevalence of population nucleation at local centers, including on hilltops, and sites classified as villages and hamlets increased (Castillo Peña and Guevara Chumacero 2009; Mastache et al. 2002:209; Parsons 2008; Sanders et al. 1979). Across the Basin of Mexico as a whole, for example, only 30 percent of the population resided in centers, as compared to 75 percent during the Epiclassic period (Sanders et al. 1979:139). This process has been referred to as a prevalent "ruralization" of the settlement system (Sanders et al. 1979:138).

The term ruralization, however, can lead us to overlook the impact of politics on the settlement system. Although the demographic change from the Epiclassic period is well demonstrated, the survey data demonstrate a hierarchical settlement system. In the northern Basin of Mexico, for example, Parsons (2008:89) documented a three-tier settlement hierarchy based on site area across the entire survey zone but also the existence of local centers operating in site clusters comprised of a hierarchy of smaller sites (see also Castillo Peña and Guevara Chumacero 2009). Including the site of Tula Grande would minimally create a four-part hierarchy. Settlement data in the Tula region also document the appearance of site hierarchies not seen previously (Mastache et al. 2002:192). Tula Grande likely functioned as the largest, primary center that integrated the regional political economy via hierarchical ties to several secondary centers that, in turn, served as local political nodes over variously sized constituent communities.

This dramatic change in the landscape might suggest the appearance of what might be called a Pax Tolteca. As we discussed at the beginning of this chapter, competition and conflict is a threat to the legitimacy of a political system across a landscape and is bad for business. The abandonment of previously independent polities and the wide distribution of settlements indicates less instability than during the Epiclassic. The emergence of a regional site hierarchy points toward greater centralized control over the area. Although speculative, the iconographic and bioarchaeological data might indicate that violence and warmaking became centralized and institutionalized as the legitimate prerogative of the Tula State. A Pax Tolteca would have also provided the kind of political stability necessary for demographic and economic growth, a more stable population from which to extract surplus products and labor to finance the political economy. As with other states and empires, such a regional peace does not mean less militarism or even war but, rather, internal stability within the political economy of a developing and/or expanding state.

As the settlement system changed, we might also expect the economy to change, possibly with more centers of production distributed across the landscape. Epiclassic communities in the broader Tula region appear to have been largely consumers (rather than producers) of already crafted obsidian tools (Anderson 2018:120; Blumenfeld 2021), possibly dependent on unstable and scarce supplies (Cobean 2002). In contrast, Early Postclassic workshops were involved in the full range of core and blade reduction (Healan et al. 1983:143). Early Postclassic sites near Tula intensified the production and distribution of tools made from Pachuca obsidian from the Sierra de las Navajas and from Otumba in the eastern Basin of Mexico, both dominant sources during the Classic period (Cobean 2002; Healan 1993, 2012; Healan et al. 1983). These sources are closer than the primary obsidian sources used during the Epiclassic period, much of which came from the Ucareo source in present-day Michoacan (Cobean 2002).

The change in the obsidian economy suggests the development of more stable economic institutions needed to expand the production and distribution of these sources. Regional data to examine this possible process are scarce. However, Parsons (2008:208) recorded Early Postclassic (Late Toltec) sites with substantial flaked stone debris, possibly suggesting local workshops. Even with the political expansion of the Tula state, this change does not mean that economic production was state controlled. Although obsidian products were likely paid as tribute or taxes to the state, little evidence suggests direct state control (Healan 1993). Rather, economic transformations during this time might indicate a configuration of mutually influencing processes that simultaneously reflect regional political integration, the development of new local institutions, the economic (i.e., tributary) needs of state institutions, the economic needs of an expanding population, changing climatic conditions, and so on.

CONCLUSION

Recognition that conflict was a transformational process in the history of the Tula state is certainly not new. Quasi-mythical, historical records, such as those found in the Anales de Cuauhtitlan or the works of Alva Ixtlilxochitl and Bernardino Sahagún describe competition and conflict between nobles, which led to either the death or the exile of a powerful warrior-prince, Cē Ācatl Topiltzin Quetzalcoatl, who fled to the east (see Feldman 1974; Léon Portilla 1983). To the extent that this event has any factual basis, it has been used to explain both the collapse of Tula in the late twelfth to early thirteenth century as well as its formation. In the latter case, Cē Ācatl Topiltzin Quetzalcoatl might be viewed as an Epiclassic period ruler who was deposed, and the victors established the center of the later state. Diehl (1983:45) offers a fascinating speculation on the possible competition between factions described in these sources: "Conflicts between them could have resulted in the expulsion of the Tula Chico faction, perhaps including a leader named Quetzalcoatl. The winners consolidated their position and enlarged Tula Grande. They destroyed Tula Chico and left it unoccupied as a visual warning to other potential dissidents."

Although this chapter cannot add much to these historical sources, we have examined a range of archaeological data to explore the possibility that conflict, warfare, and violence characterized the decentralized political landscape of the Epiclassic period in the northern Basin of Mexico and Mezquital Valley. We suggested that conflict and regional instability marked a trajectory that would eventually lead to the abandonment of competing polities, the consolidation of regional power at Tula Grande, and the formation of the Tula state. We suggested that this transformation culminated in the imposition of a regional peace, or Pax Tolteca. We stress, however, that this peace was not due to any intrinsic altruism on the part of state governing regimes. Rather, we emphasize that the Pax Tolteca was a strategy of state control. The elimination of political rivals, we argued, was necessary to establish the legitimacy of state institutions, and regional integration and stability was a result. Such stability fostered an increase in population and its spread into areas that had been unoccupied. We examined the distribution of settlements that demonstrate that this "ruralization" was also articulated to the development of a hierarchical settlement system indicative of a regionally integrated state. We also briefly explored the possibility that, in conjunction with increasing population, the Pax Tolteca may have fostered the growth of economic institutions that stimulated the diversification of systems of production, distribution, and exchange at the regional scale.

Although we review and present archaeological evidence in support of these ideas, they need to be operationalized as both comparative and specific research questions and evaluated via additional data. Although much of the data can be obtained and synthesized via both the published literature and the gray literature (i.e., reports), many of these issues require new fieldwork projects. However, our ability to continue such research is threatened by development, intensive agriculture, mining, and looting (Gorenflo, this volume; Morehart and Millhauser 2016). Many of the Epiclassic hilltop centers around Tula are being destroyed. The southwest side of Cerro Ahumada, where Los Mogotes is located, is being converted to the massive condominium complexes that are being built all over Central Mexico. Mining in this area is also a threat, as is expansion of petroleum refineries. Researchers today can do what we can to continue to study these landscapes, but the record that previous generations of archaeologists, such as Jeff Parsons, produced might remain one of the only records we have of the history of this region.

REFERENCES

Acosta, Jorge R. 1941. "Los últimos descubrimientos arqueológicos en Tula, Hidalgo." *Revista mexicana de estudios antropológicos* 5:239–48.

Acosta, Jorge R. 1943. "Los colosos de Tula." *Cuadernos americanos* 2(7):138.

Anderson, J. Heath. 2018. "Obsidian Consumption in the Tula Region after Teotihuacan's Decline: A View from Cerro Magoni." In *City, Craft, and Residence in Mesoamerica: Research Papers Presented in Honor of Dan M. Healan*, edited by Ronald Faulseit, Nezahualcoyotl Xiuhtecutli, and Haley Holt Mehta, 113–24. Middle American Research Institute Publication, No. 72. Middle American Research Institute, Tulane University, New Orleans, LA.

Anderson, J. Heath, Dan M. Healan, and Robert H. Cobean. 2015. "Collapse, Regeneration, and the Origins of Tula and the Toltec State." In *Beyond Collapse: Archaeological Perspectives on Resilience, Revitalization, and Transformation in Complex Societies*, edited by Ronald Faulseit, 431–58. Center for Archaeological Investigation, Southern Illinois University, Carbondale, IL.

Arkush, Elizabeth N., and Mark W. Allen. 2006. *The Archaeology of Warfare: Prehistories of Raiding and Conquest*. University Press of Florida, Gainesville.

Arkush, Elizabeth, and Tiffiny A. Tung. 2013. "Patterns of War in the Andes from the Archaic to the Late Horizon: Insights from Settlement Patterns and Cranial Trauma." *Journal of Archaeological Research* 21(4):307–69.

Aron, Raymond. 1966. *Peace and War: A Theory of International Relations.* Praeger, New York.

Baird, Ellen T. 1989. "Star and Wars at Cacaxtla." In *Mesoamerica after the Decline of Teotihuacan, A.D. 700–900*, edited by Richard A. Diehl and Janet C. Berlo, 105–22. Dumbarton Oaks, Washington, DC.

Beekman, Christopher S., and Alexander F. Christensen. 2003. "Controlling for Doubt and Uncertainty through Multiple Lines of Evidence: A New Look at the Mesoamerican Nahua Migrations." *Journal of Archaeological Method and Theory* 19:111–64.

Berlo, Janet C. 1989. "The Concept of the Epiclassic: A Critique." In *Mesoamerica after the Decline of Teotihuacan, A.D. 700–900*, edited by Richard A. Diehl and Janet C. Berlo, 209–10. Dumbarton Oaks, Washington, DC.

Bey, George J., and William M. Ringle. 2011. "From the Bottom Up." In *Twin Tollans: Chichén Itza, Tula, and the Epiclassic to Early Postclassic Mesoamerican World*, edited by Jeff K. Kowalski and Cynthia Kristan-Graham, 299–342. Dumbarton Oaks, Washington, DC.

Blanton, Richard E. 1975. Texcoco Region Archaeology. *American Antiquity* 40(2):227–30.

Blumenfeld, Dean. 2021. "Economic Reorganization after State Decline: The Acquisition and Distribution of Flaked-Stone at Epiclassic Period (ca. 600–900 CE) Los Mogotes, Mexico." Master's thesis, Arizona State University, Tempe.

Bonfíl Olivera, Alicia. 2005. "Cultura y contexto: El comportamiento de un sitio del Epiclásico en la región de Tula." In *Reacomodos demograficos del Clasico al Posclasico en el centro de Mexico*, edited by Linda Manzanilla, 227–59. Universidad Nacional Autónoma de México, Mexico City.

Castillo Bernal, Stephen. 2019. "El 'Cópil' del cerro del Elefante, Hidalgo: Dilucidaciones sobre el personaje." *Arqueología* 58:63–83.

Castillo Peña, Patricia, and Miguel Guevara Chumacero. 2009. "Auge y colapso de los centros provinciales toltecas." *Arqueología* 42:234–51.

Castro, Rubén, Saburo Sugiyama, and George L. Cowgill. 1991. "The Templo de Quetzalcoatl Project at Teotihuacan: A Preliminary Report." *Ancient Mesoamerica* 2(1):77–92.

Cesaretti, Rudolf, Nathan Parrot, Peter Vesely, Maria Garcia Velasco, Sofía I. Pacheco-Forés, and Christopher T. Morehart. 2017. "Operación 1: Excavación de trinchera en el muro perimetral." In *Proyecto de ecología histórica del norte de la Cuenca de México: Informe de la temporada de campo 2016*, edited by Christopher T. Morehart, 9–25. Report on File, Instituto Nacional de Antropología e Historia, Mexico City.

Cesaretti, Rudolf, Dean Blumenfeld, and Christopher T. Morehart. 2018. "La investigación de la operación 6." In *Proyecto de ecología histórica del norte de la Cuenca de México: Informe de la temporada de campo 2017*, edited by Christopher Morehart, 36–56. Report on File, Instituto Nacional de Antropología e Historia, Mexico City.

Charlton, Thomas H. 1987. "Surface Survey of the Upper Valley." In *The Teotihuacan Valley Project*, Volume 4: *The Toltec Period Occupation of the Valley, Part 2—Surface*

Survey and Special Studies, edited by William T. Sanders, 539–76. Occasional Papers in Anthropology, No. 16. Department of Anthropology, The Pennsylvania State University, University Park, PA.

Charlton, Thomas H., and Deborah L. Nichols. 1997. "Diachronic Studies of City-States: Permutations on a Theme: Central Mexico from 1700 BC to AD 1600." In *The Archaeology of City-States: Cross-Cultural Approaches*, edited by Deborah L. Nichols and Thomas H. Charlton, 169–208. Smithsonian Institution Press, Washington, DC.

Clayton, Sarah C. 2013. "Measuring the Long Arm of the State: Teotihuacan's Relations in the Basin of Mexico." *Ancient Mesoamerica* 24(1):87–105.

Clayton, Sarah C. 2016. "After Teotihuacan: A View of Collapse and Reorganization from the Southern Basin of Mexico." *American Anthropologist* 118(1):104–20.

Cobean, Robert H. 1982. "Investigaciones Recientes en Tula Chico, Hidalgo." In *Estudios sobre la antigua ciudad de Tula*, edited by Alba Guadalupe Mastache, Robert H. Barlow, Ana Maria Crespo, and Dan M. Healan, 37–122. Coleccion Cientifica, no. 121. Instituto Nacional de Antropología e Historia, Mexico City.

Cobean, Robert H. 1990. *La cerámica de Tula, Hidalgo*. Instituto Nacional de Antropología e Historia, Mexico City.

Cobean, Robert H. 2002. *Un mundo de obsidiana: Minería y comercio de un vidrio volcánico en el México Antiguo*. Arqueología de México. Instituto Nacional de Antropología e Historia, Mexico City.

Cobean, Robert H., Dan M. Healan, and María Elena Suárez. 2021. "Recent Investigations at Tula Chico, Tula, Hidalgo." *Ancient Mesoamerica* 32(1):41–55.

Conolly, James, and Mark Lake. 2006. *Geographical Information Systems in Archaeology*. Cambridge University Press, Cambridge.

Costin, Cathy Lynne, and Timothy Earle. 1989. "Status Distinction and Legitimation of Power as Reflected in Changing Patterns of Consumption in Late Prehispanic Peru." *American Antiquity* 54(4):691–714.

Cowgill, George L. 2013. "Possible Migrations and Shifting Identities in the Central Mexican Epiclassic." *Ancient Mesoamerica* 24(1):131–49.

Cowgill, George L. 2015. *Ancient Teotihuacan: Early Urbanism in Central Mexico*. Cambridge University Press, New York.

Crider, Destiny L. 2011. "Epiclassic and Early Postclassic Interaction in Central Mexico as Evidenced by Decorated Pottery." PhD dissertation, Arizona State University, Tempe, Arizona.

Crider, Destiny L. 2013. "Shifting Alliances: Epiclassic and Early Postclassic Interactions at Cerro Portezuelo." *Ancient Mesoamerica* 24(1):107–30.

Crider, Destiny, Deborah H. Nichols, Hector Neff, and Michael D. Glascock. 2007. "In the Aftermath of Teotihuacan: Epiclassic Pottery Production and Distribution in the Teotihuacan Valley, Mexico." *Latin American Antiquity* 18:123–43.

De la Fuente, Beatriz, Silvia Trejo, and Nelly Gutiérrez Solana. 1988. *Escultura en Piedra de Tula*. Instituto de Investigaciones Esteticas, Universidad Nacional Autonoma de Mexico, Mexico City.

Diehl, Richard A. 1983. *Tula: The Toltec Capital of Ancient Mexico*. Thames and Hudson, London.

Diehl, Richard A. 1989. "A Shadow of Its Former Self: Teotihuacan during the Coyotlatelco Period." In *Mesoamerica after the Decline of Teotihuacan, A.D. 700–900*, edited by Richard A. Diehl and Janet C. Berlo, 9–18. Dumbarton Oaks, Washington, DC.

Diehl, Richard A., and Janet C. Berlo, eds. 1989. *Mesoamerica after the Decline of Teotihuacan, A.D. 700–900*. Dumbarton Oaks, Washington, DC.

Durán, Fray Diego. 1971. *Book of the Gods and Rites and the Ancient Calendar*. Translated by Fernando Horcasitas and Doris Heyden. University of Oklahoma Press, Norman.

Earle, Timothy. 1997. *How Chiefs Come to Power: The Political Economy in Prehistory*. Stanford University Press, Redwood City, CA.

Elson, Christina M., and Kenneth Mowbray. 2005. "Burial Practices at Teotihuacan in the Early Postclassic Period: The Vaillant and Linné Excavations (1931–1932)." *Ancient Mesoamerica* 16(2):195–211.

Feinman, Gary M. 1998. "Scale and Social Organization: Perspectives on the Archaic State." In *Archaic States*, edited by Gary M. Feinman and Joyce Marcus, 95–133. School for Advanced Research, Santa Fe, NM.

Feldman, Lawrence H. 1974. "Tollan in Hidalgo: Native Accounts of the Central Mexican Tolteca." In *Studies of Ancient Tollan: A Report of the University of Missouri Tula Archaeological Project*, edited by Richard A. Diehl, 130–49. University of Missouri Monographs in Anthropology, No. 1. Department of Anthropology, University of Missouri, Columbia.

Fournier, Patricia, and Maira Martínez Lemus. 2010. "El modo de vida precolombino de los otomíes de la región de Tula." In *Estudios de antropología e historia: Arqueología y patrimonio del Estado de Hidalgo*, edited by Natalia Moragas Segura and Manuel Alberto Morales Damián, 175–225. Universidad Autónoma del Estado de Hidalgo, Mexico City.

Fournier, Patricia, and Rocio Vargas-Sanders. 2002. "En busca de los 'dueños del silencio': Cosmovisión y ADN antiguo de las poblaciones otomíes epiclásicas de la región de Tula." *Revista de estudios otopames* 3:37–75.

Fournier, Patricia, and Victor H. Balaños. 2011. "The Epiclassic Period in the Tula Region beyond Tula Chico." In *Twin Tollans: Chichén Itza, Tula, and the Epiclassic to Early Postclassic Mesoamerican World*, edited by Jeff K. Kowalski and Cynthia Kristan-Graham, 387–428. Dumbarton Oaks, Washington, DC.

Fournier, Patricia, Juan Rosaldo Cervantes, and M. James Blackman. 2006. "Mito y realidad del estilo Epiclasico coyotlatleco." In *El fenómeno coyotlatelco en el centro de México:*

Tiempo, espacio y significado, edited by Laura Solar Valverde, 55–82. Instituto Nacional de Anthropología e Historia, Mexico City.

Gamboa Cabezas, Luís, and Dan M. Healan. 2021. "Salvage and Rescue Archaeology inside Ancient Tula: Recent Discoveries and Revelations." *Ancient Mesoamerica* 32(1):56–83.

García Chávez, Raúl. 2004. "De Tula a Azcapotzalco: Caracterización arqueológica de los Altepetl de la Cuenca de México del posclásico temprano y medio, a través del estudio cerámico regional." PhD dissertation, Universidad Nacional e Autónoma de México, México, D.F.

García Chávez, Raúl, and Diana Martínez Yrizar. 2006. "Proceso de desarrollo del estado tolteca durante las fases Coyotlatleco y Mazapa-Azteca I." In *La Produccion alfarera en el Mexico Antiguo III*, edited by Beatriz Merino Carrion and Angel Garcia Cook, 221–56. Instituto Nacional de Antropología e Historia/UNAM, Mexico City.

García Velasco, Maria, and Abigail Meza-Peñaloza. 2018. "Informe antropofísico de los restos óseos humanos halladas en las operaciones 5 y 6." In *Proyecto de ecología histórica del norte de la Cuenca de México: Informe de la temporada de campo 2017*, edited by Christopher T. Morehart, 107–24. Report on File, Instituto Nacional de Antropología e Historia, Mexico City.

García Velasco, Maria, Abigail Meza-Peñaloza, and Alejandro Cool Argüelles. 2017. "Informe antropofísico de los restos óseos humanos." In *Proyecto de ecología histórica del norte de la Cuenca de México: Informe de la temporada de campo 2016*, edited by Christopher T. Morehart, 125–44. Report on File, Instituto Nacional de Antropología e Historia, Mexico City.

Gaxiola González, Margarita. 2010. "Huapalcalco, un santuario-mercado del Epiclásico en la región de Tulancingo." In *Mercados y caminos de México*, edited by Janet L. Towell and Amalia Attolini Lecón, 185–219. Instituto Nacional de Antropología e Historia/UNAM, Mexico City.

Gómez Serafín, Susana. 1994. *Enterramientos humanos de la época Prehispánica en Tula, Hidalgo*. Instituto Nacional de Antropología e Historia, Mexico City.

Gorenflo, Larry J., and William Sanders. 2007. *Archaeological Settlement Pattern Data from the Cuautitlan, Temascalapa, and Teotihuacan Regions, Mexico*. Occasional Papers in Anthropology, no. 30. Department of Anthropology, The Pennsylvania State University, University Park.

Healan, Dan M. 1989. "The Central Group and West Group." In *Tula of the Toltecs: Excavation and Survey*, edited by Dan M. Healan, 97–148. University of Iowa Press, Iowa City.

Healan, Dan M. 1993. "Local versus Non-Local Obsidian Exchange at Tula and Its Implications for Post-Formative Mesoamerica." *World Archaeology* 24: 449–66.

Healan, Dan M. 2012. "The Archaeology of Tula, Hidalgo, Mexico." *Journal of Archaeological Research* 20(1):53–115.

Healan, Dan M., and Robert H. Cobean. 2019. "Three Migration Case Studies from the Tula Region." In *Migrations in Late Mesoamerica*, edited by Christopher S. Beekman, 66–87. University Press of Florida, Gainesville.

Healan, Dan M., Janet M. Kerley, and George J. Bey. 1983. "Excavation and Preliminary Analysis of an Obsidian Workshop in Tula, Hidalgo, Mexico." *Journal of Field Archaeology* 10(2):127–45.

Healan, Dan M., Robert H. Cobean, and Robert T. Bowsher. 2021. "Revised Chronology and Settlement History of Tula and the Tula Region." *Ancient Mesoamerica* 32(1):165–86.

Hers, Marie-Areti. 2010. "El sacrificio humano entre los Tolteca-Chichimecas: Los antecedentes norteños de las prácticas toltecas y mexicas." In *El sacrificio humano en la tradición religiosa mesoamericana*, edited by Leonardo López Luján and Guilhem Olivier 227–46. Instituto Nacional de Anthropología e Historia / UNAM, Mexico City.

Hirth, Kenneth G. 1989. "Militarism and Social Organization at Xochicalco, Morelos." In *Mesoamerica after the Decline of Teotihuacan, A.D. 700-900*, edited by Richard A. Diehl and Janet C. Berlo, 69–82. Dumbarton Oaks, Washingtion, DC.

Hirth, Kenneth. 2000. *Archaeological Research at Xochicalco*. University of Utah Press, Salt Lake City.

Holt Mehta, Haley. 2018. "More Than an Enclave? Ethnic Identity and Cultural Affiliations at El Tesoro, a Classic Period Zapotec Site in the Tula Area." In *City, Craft, and Residence in Mesoamerica: Research Papers Presented in Honor of Dan M. Healan*, edited by Ronald K. Faulseit, Nezahualcoyotl Xiuhtecutli, and Haley Holt Mehta, 125–35. Middle American Research Institute, Tulane University, New Orleans, LA.

Huster, Angela. 2017. "Análisis de cerámica." In *Proyecto de ecología histórica del norte de la Cuenca de México: Informe de la temporada de campo 2016*, edited by Christopher T. Morehart, 92–105. Report on File, Instituto Nacional de Antropología e Historia, Mexico City.

Huster, Angela. 2018. "Análisis de cerámica: Datos y resultados preliminares." In *proyecto de ecología histórica del norte de la Cuenca de México: Informe de la temporada de campo 2017*, edited by Christopher T. Morehart, 135–77. Report on File, Instituto Nacional de Antropología e Historia, Mexico City.

Jiménez García, Elizabeth. 1998. *Iconografía de Tula: El caso de la escultura*. Colección Científica, No. 364. Instituto Nacional de Antropología e Historia, México, D.F.

Jiménez García, Elizabeth. 2021. "Warriors, Kings, and Teohuaque at Tula: A Reconsideration of the So-Called 'Warrior Pillars' atop Pyramid B." *Ancient Mesoamerica* 32(1):146–64.

Jordan, Keith. 2013. "Serpents, Skeletons, and Ancestors? The Tula Coatepantli Revisited." *Ancient Mesoamerica* 24(2):243–74.

Jordan, Keith. 2016. "From Tula Chico to Chichén Itzá: Implications of the Epiclassic Sculpture of Tula for the Nature and Timing of Tula-Chichén Contact." *Latin American Antiquity* 27(4):462–78.

Kalyvas, Stathis N. 2006. *The Logic of Violence in Civil War*. Cambridge University Press, Cambridge.

Koontz, Rex. 2009. *Lightning Gods and Feathered Serpents: The Public Sculpture of El Tajín*. University of Texas Press, Austin.

Kristan-Graham, Cynthia Beth. 1989. "Art, Rulership and the Mesoamerican Body Politic at Tula and Chichén Itza." PhD dissertation, University of California, Los Angeles.

Kristan-Graham, Cynthia. 1993. "The Business of Narrative at Tula: An Analysis of the Vestibule Frieze, Trade, and Ritual." *Latin American Antiquity* 4(1):3–21.

León Portilla, Miguel. 1983. *De Teotihuacán a los Aztecas: Antología de fuentes e interpretaciones históricas*. Universidad Nacional Autonoma de México, Mexico City.

López Austin, Alfredo. 1988. *The Human Body and Ideology: Concepts of the Ancient Nahuas*. University of Utah Press, Salt Lake City.

López Austin, Alfredo, and Leonardo López Luján. 2000. "The Myth and Reality of Zuyuá: The Feathered Serpent and Mesoamerican Transformations from the Classic to the Postclassic." In *Mesoamerican Classic Heritage: From Teotihuacan to the Aztecs*, edited by Davíd Carrasco, Lyndsay Jones, and Scott Sessions, 21–84. University Press of Colorado, Boulder.

Mann, Michael. 1986. *The Sources of Social Power*, vol. 1: *A History of Power from the Beginning to AD 1760*. Cambridge University Press, Cambridge.

Manzanilla, Linda. 2003. "The Abandonment of Teotihuacan." In *The Archaeology of Settlement Abandonment in Middle America*, edited by Takeshi Inomata and Ronald Webb, 91–101. University of Utah Press, Salt Lake City.

Martínez Magaña, R. 1994. "Un rescate en el Cerro del Elefante, Tunititlán, Hidalgo." In *Simposium sobre arqueologia en el Estado de Hidalgo: Trabajos recientes*, edited by Francisco Javier Sansores and Enrique Fernandez Davila, 143–49. Instituto Nacional de Anthropología e Historia, Mexico City.

Mastache, Alba Guadalupe. 1996. "El estado tolteca: Una investigación sobre su proceso de desarrollo y estructura social y política." PhD dissertation, Universidad Nacional Autónoma de México, Mexico City.

Mastache, Alba Guadalupe, and Robert H. Cobean. 1989. "The Coyotlatelco Culture and the Origins of the Toltec State." In *Mesoamerica after the Decline of Teotihuacan, A.D. 700–900*, edited by Richard A. Diehl and Janet C. Berlo, 49–68. Dumbarton Oaks, Washington, DC.

Mastache, Alba Guadalupe, and Robert H. Cobean. 1990. "La cultura Coyotlatelco en el área de Tula." In *Las industrias líticas coyotlatelco en el área de Tula*, edited by Alba Guadalupe Mastache, Robert H. Cobean, Charles Rees, and Donald Jackson, 9–22. Instituto Nacional de Antropología e Historia, Mexico City.

Mastache, Alba Guadalupe, Robert H. Cobean, and Dan M. Healan. 2002. *Ancient Tollan: Tula and the Toltec Heartland*. University Press of Colorado, Boulder.

Mastache, Alba Guadalupe, Robert H. Cobean, and Dan M. Healan. 2009. "Four Hundred Years of Settlement and Cultural Continuity in Epiclassic and Early Postclassic Tula." In *The Art of Urbanism: How Mesoamerican Kingdoms Represented Themselves in Architecture and Imagery*, edited by William L. Fash and Leonardo Lopez Lujan, 290–328. University Press of Colorado, Boulder.

Matos Moctezuma, Eduardo. 1972. "El Tzompantli en Mesoamérica." In *Religion en Mesoamerica: XII Mesa Redonda*, edited by Jaime Litvak King and Naomi Castillo Tejero, 109–16. Sociedad Mexicana de Antropologia, Mexico City.

Medrano Enríquez, Angélica María. 2021. "Child Sacrifice in Tula: A Bioarchaeological Study." *Ancient Mesoamerica* 32(1):84–99.

Meza-Peñaloza, A., F. Zertuche, M. García-Velasco, and C. Morehart. 2019. "A Non-Metric Traits Study of Skulls from Epiclassic Xaltocan in Relation to Other Mesoamerican Cultures." *Journal of Archaeological Science: Reports* 23:559–66.

Meza-Peñaloza, Abigail, Federico Zertuche, and Christopher Morehart. 2021. "Population Level Comparisons in Central Mexico Using Cranial Nonmetric Traits." *American Journal of Physical Anthropology* 1–21.

Miller, Virginia E. 1999. "The Skull Rack in Mesoamerica." In *Mesoamerican Architecture as a Cultural Symbol*, edited by Jeff K. Kowalski, 339–60. Oxford University Press, Oxford.

Morehart, Christopher T. 2015. "Excavaciones en No-Cuadrícula 4." In *Proyecto de ecología histórica del norte de la Cuenca de México: Informe de la temporada de campo junio-agosto 2012*, edited by Christopher T. Morehart, 6–35. Report on File, Instituto Nacional de Antropología e Historia, Mexico City.

Morehart, Christopher T. 2016. "Características principales de la arquitectura de Los Mogotes." In *Proyecto de ecología histórica del norte de la Cuenca de México: Informe de la temporada de campo 2015*, edited by Christopher T. Morehart, 48–69. Report on File, Instituto Nacional de Antropología e Historia, Mexico City.

Morehart, Christopher T., ed. 2019. *Proyecto de ecología histórica del norte de la Cuenca de México: Informe de la temporada de campo 2018*. Report on File, Instituto Nacional de Antropología e Historia, Mexico City.

Morehart, Christopher, and John Millhauser. 2016. "Monitoring Cultural Landscapes from Space: Evaluating Archaeological Sites in the Basin of Mexico Using Very High Resolution Satellite Imagery." *Journal of Archaeological Science: Reports* 10:363–76.

Morehart, Christopher T., Abigail Meza-Peñaloza, Carlos Serrano Sánchez, Emily McClung de Tapia, and Emilio Ibarra Morales. 2012. "Human Sacrifice during the Epiclassic Period in the Northern Basin of Mexico." *Latin American Antiquity* 23(4):426–48.

Morehart, Christopher, Rudolf Cesaretti, Dean Blumenfeld, Christopher T. Morehart, Edgar Alarcon, and Megan Parker. 2018. "La continuación de las investigaciones en la operación 5." In *Proyecto de ecología histórica del norte de la Cuenca de México: Informe de la temporada de campo 2017*, edited by Christopher T. Morehart, 10–35. Report on File, Instituto Nacional de Antropología e Historia, Mexico City.

Nichols, Deborah L., Hector Neff, and George L. Cowgill. 2013. "Cerro Portezuelo: States and Hinterlands in the Pre-Hispanic Basin of Mexico." *Ancient Mesoamerica* 24:47–71.

Pacheco-Forés, Sofía I., Christopher T. Morehart, Jane E. Buikstra, Gwyneth W. Gordon, and Kelly J. Knudson. 2021. "Migration, Violence, and the 'Other': A Biogeochemical Approach to Identity-Based Violence in the Epiclassic Basin of Mexico." *Journal of Anthropological Archaeology* 61:101263.

Parchami, Ali. 2009. *Hegemonic Peace and Empire: The Pax Romana, Britannica, and Americana*. Routledge, London.

Paredes Gudiño, Blanca. 1998. "Evidencias de ocupación del periodo Coyotlatelco en la Zona Arqueológica de Tula, Hidalgo." In *Antropología e historia del occidente de México*, Vol. 3: *1629–1644*. Universidad Nacional Autónoma de México, Mexico City.

Parsons, Jeffrey R. 1971. *Prehistoric Settlement Patterns in the Texcoco Region, Mexico*. Memoirs of the Museum of Anthropology, no. 3. University of Michigan, Ann Arbor.

Parsons, Jeffrey R. 2006. "A Regional Perspective on Coyotlatelco in the Basin of Mexico: Some New Thoughts about Old Data." In *El fenómeno coyotlatelco en el centro de México: Tiempo, espacio y significado*, edited by Laura Solar Valverde, 83–96. Instituto Nacional de Antropología e Historia, Mexico City.

Parsons, Jeffrey R. 2008. *Prehispanic Settlement Patterns in the Northwestern Valley of Mexico: The Zumpango Region*. Memoirs of the Museum of Anthropology, no. 45. University of Michigan, Ann Arbor.

Rattray, Evelyn C. 1996. "A Regional Perspective on the Epiclassic Period in Central America." In *Arqueología mesoamericana: Homenaje a William T. Sanders*, edited by Alba G. Mastache, Jeffrey R. Parsons, Robert S. Santley, and Mari C. Serra Puche, 213–31. Instituto Nacional de Antropología e Historia, Mexico City.

Rattray, Evelyn C. 2001. *Teotihuacan: Ceramics, Chronology and Cultural Trends*. Memoirs in Latin American Archaeology, No. 13. University of Pittsburgh, Pittsburgh, PA.

Ringle, William M., Tomás Gallareta Negrón, and George J. Bey. 1998. "The Return of Quetzalcoatl: Evidence for the Spread of a World Religion during the Epiclassic Period." *Ancient Mesoamerica* 9(2):183–232.

Sanders, William T. 1986. "Preface." In *The Toltec Occupation of the Valley, Part 1; Excavations and Ceramics*, edited by William T. Sanders, 3–6. Occasional Papers in Anthropology, no. 13. Department of Anthropology, The Pennsylvania State University, College Park.

Sanders, William T., and Charles Kolb. 1996. "Urban and Rural Settlement in the Teotihuacan Valley: A Reconstruction." In *The Teotihuacan Valley Project Final Report*, vol. 3. *The Teotihuacan Period Occupation of the Valley, Part 3, The Surface Survey*, edited by William T. Sanders, 655–78. Occasional Papers in Anthropology, no. 21. Matson Museum of Anthropology, The Pennsylvania State University, University Park, PA.

Sanders, William T., Jeffrey R. Parsons, and Robert S. Santley. 1979. *The Basin of Mexico: Ecological Processes in the Evolution of a Civilization*. Academic Press, New York.

Sandoval, Gustavo. 2017. "La Presencia Teotihuacana en San Antonio-Acoculco." *Arqueología* 52:76–97.

Serra Puche, M. C., M. C., and J. C. Lazcano Arce. 2005. "El Epiclásico en el valle de Puebla-Tlaxcala y los sitios de Cacaxtla-Xochitécatl-Nativias." In *Reacomodos demográficos del Clásico al Posclásico en el centro de México*, edited by Linda Manzanilla, 298–302. Universidad Nacional Autónoma de México, Mexico City.

Sinopoli, Carla M., and Kathleen D. Morrison. 1995. "Dimensions of Imperial Control the Vijayanagara Capital." *American Anthropologist* 97(1):83–96.

Smith, Adam T. 2003. *The Political Landscape: Constellations of Authority in Early Complex Polities*. University of California Press, Berkeley.

Smith, Adam T. 2011. "Archaeologies of Sovereignty." *Annual Review of Anthropology* 40(1):415–32.

Smith, Michael E., and Lisa Montiel. 2001. "Archaeological Study of Empires and Imperialism in Pre-Hispanic Central Mexico." *Journal of Anthropological Archaeology* 20(3):245–84.

Smith, Michael E., Gary M. Feinman, Robert D. Drennan, Timothy Earle, and Ian Morris. 2012. "Archaeology as a Social Science." *Proceedings of the National Academy of Sciences* 109(20):7617–21.

Solar Valverde, Laura, ed. 2006. *El fenómeno coyotlatelco en el centro de México: Tiempo, espacio y significado*. Memoria del Primer Seminario-Taller sobre Problemáticas Regionales. Instituto Nacional de Antropología e Historia, Mexico City.

Sterpone, Osvaldo. 2000. "La Quimera de Tula." *Boletín de antropología americana* 37:141–204.

Sugiura, Yoko. 2006. "¿Continuidad o discontinuidad en la cerámica?: Discusión acerca del paso del Clásico al Epiclásico, visto desde el Valle de Toluca." In *El fenómeno coyotlatelco en el centro de México: Tiempo, espacio y significado*, edited by Laura Solar Valverde, 127–62. Instituto Nacional de Antropología e Historia, Mexico City.

Sugiyama, Saburo. 1989. "Burials Dedicated to the Old Temple of Quetzalcoatl at Teotihuacan, Mexico." *American Antiquity* 54(1):85–106.

Sugiyama, Saburo, and Leonardo López Luján. 2007. "Dedicatorial Burial/Offering Complexes at the Moon Pyramid, Teotihuacan: A Preliminary Report of the 1998–2004 Explorations." *Ancient Mesoamerica* 18:127–46.

Taube, Karl. 1994. "The Iconography of Toltec Period Chichén Itza." In *Hidden in the Hills: Maya Archaeology of the Northwestern Yucatan Peninsula*, edited by Hanns J. Prem, 212–46. Acta Mesoamericana 7, Verlag von Flemming, Möckmühl, Germany.

Tilly, Charles. 1990. *Coercion, Capital, and European States, AD 990–1990*. Blackwell, Cambridge, MA.

Trigger, Bruce, G. 2003. *Understanding Early Civilization*. Cambridge University Press, Cambridge.

Weber, Max. 1947. "Politics as Vocation." In *From Max Weber: Essays in Sociology*, translated and edited by H. H. Gerth and C. Wright Mills, 77–156. Oxford University Press, Oxford.

Wheatley, David. 1995. "Cumulative Viewshed Analysis: A GIS-Based Method for Investigating Intervisibility, and its Archaeological Application." In *Archaeology and Geographical Information Systems: A European Perspective*, edited by Gary R. Lock and Zoran Stančič, 171–86. Routledge, London.

Wright, David K., Scott MacEachern, and Jaeyong Lee. 2014. "Analysis of Feature Intervisibility and Cumulative Visibility Using GIS, Bayesian and Spatial Statistics: A Study from the Mandara Mountains, Northern Cameroon." *PLOS ONE* 9(11):e112191.

Yadeun Angulo, Juan. 1975. *El estado y la ciudad: El caso de Tula, Hgo (Proyecto Tula)*. Colección Científica, no. 25. Instituto Nacional de Antropología e Historia, Mexico City.

14

Slow Violence and Vulnerability in the Basin of Mexico

JOHN K. MILLHAUSER

INTRODUCTION

Writing over forty years ago, Sanders, Parsons, and Santley ended the culminating work of their decades of intensive survey with the warning that time was running out for large-scale, systematic archaeological research in the Basin of Mexico (1979). Ideally, they called for continued and intensified research with its own institutional structure and guiding principles. That vision was never realized. Archaeological, ethnohistoric, and paleoenvironmental research have continued apace, but neither at the scale nor with the unity of vision of the Basin of Mexico project. Nevertheless, the artifact collections and published data remain rich sources of information and inspiration for subsequent large-scale studies (see, for example, Gorenflo 2006; Hodge and Minc 1990; Minc et al. 1994). This paper continues that tradition by showing how the Basin of Mexico project data can be used in unanticipated ways.

Although the Conquest was an unprecedented event, its aftermath was shaped by long-term processes with deep historical roots. This paper reexamines the value of project data to understand the post-Conquest world in light of

https://doi.org/10.5876/9781646424078.c014

those processes. I use the evidence collected with one set of ecological premises (largely adaptationist) and reconsider them in light of new theories, specifically those derived from political ecology and especially those presented by Rob Nixon (2011) in his idea of "slow violence." Political ecology directs attention to how human-environmental interactions are always mediated by culture, and especially by the uneven distribution of power in a (Zimmerer and Basset 2003; see also Morehart et al. 2018). Political ecologists tend to focus on localized human actions and consequences, like pollution, erosion, and other forms of land degradation (Blaikie and Brookfield 1987). Slow violence expands the frame of political ecology to broader and more drawn-out processes, such as climate change, and how the harmful consequences of these processes are dispropor- tionately experienced by socially and economically marginalized people. To do so, it draws on theories of structural violence, which explain how inequality is embedded a society's structures and institutions (Farmer 2004; Galtung 1969). The notions of slow violence and political ecology are quite compatible. Indeed, Taylor (2015:296) observed that "political ecological research on disasters demon- strates that vulnerability and its related disasters are socially produced, but they are not produced overnight . . . they are processes occurring over decades, cen- turies, or perhaps longer, only clearly manifesting in acute catastrophic events."

Slow violence subsumes the uneven nature of growth in societies, especially the tendency for well-positioned individuals and groups to secure greater ben- efits from growth than outsiders and people at the margins (Bentley 2003; Bodley 1999). A more adaptationist perspective on social evolution and growth might predict that all members of a society benefit from growth (Service 1975); but as Bodley (1999) finds, it seems unavoidable that poverty is an outcome of growth (see also Harvey 2000). In the Basin of Mexico, Brumfiel (1980) challenged the adaptationist and managerial model that Sanders and Price (1968) had espoused to explain the emergence of the Aztec state. Brumfiel argued instead that politi- cal competition for administrative control were driving forces in the growth of the state. If Brumfiel's model is expanded to include the ideas of political ecology, structural violence, and slow violence, it becomes apparent how the choices people made about where to settle in the Basin of Mexico could have had unforeseen long-term consequences. In this paper, I ask whether the overall growth of populations and expansion of settlements in the Late Postclassic left some populations at a disadvantage after the Conquest. If disparities are evident, I also ask to what extent environmental factors, such as the choices of where to live in the Late Postclassic, exacerbated these disparities.

I frame these disparities in terms of precarity and vulnerability, terms that are often used in the study of crisis and disaster as well as circumstances of pro- tracted inequality (Butler 2004; Oliver-Smith and Hoffman 1999; Redman 1999; Taylor 2015; Wisner et al. 2004). Butler (2004) distinguishes precariousness, the shared human condition of uncertainty and vulnerability, from precarity, the unequally distributed experience of economic and ecological insecurity, violence, and defenselessness experienced by disenfranchised people (see also Kasmir 2018). A good portion of the population of the Basin of Mexico may have lived in a state of precarity at the time of the Conquest. Vulnerability denotes the susceptibility to harm; in this case, the many harms of the post-Conquest era. It is often couched in terms of vulnerability to harm, hazard, risk, disaster or in terms of economic vulnerability or environmental vulnerability. While precarity is difficult to measure or identify archaeologically, vulnerability can be effectively measured and compared if the result of being vulnerable is the dissolution or relocation of a community, or what archaeologists might refer to as site abandonment. If some settlements were more vulnerable to the many disruptions, upheavals, and disasters of the post-Conquest period, the data from the Basin of Mexico project may be of a scale large enough to make these patterns apparent.

SLOW VIOLENCE AND VULNERABILITY IN THE BASIN OF MEXICO

There have been considerable efforts to understand how migrants to the New World (Europeans, Africans, Asians) changed societies, environments, and the relationships among them (Gibson 1964; Lockhart 1992; Melville 1994; Sluyter 2002, 2003). Archaeologists working in the Basin of Mexico have tended to focus on the influence of European and Colonial products, trade, politics, and religion on Indigenous (Nahua) society in cities and in the countryside. One school of thought holds that the everyday influence of outsiders (primarily Europeans) was quite limited in rural areas because of the absence of non-Indigenous material culture (aside from churches) in early colonial rural sites in the Teotihuacan Valley (Charlton 1972; Charlton and Fournier-García 2011; Charlton et al. 2005; see also Hassig 1985). Another school of thought holds that interactions between Indians and non-Indians were widespread (if uneven) and regular based on the presence of non-Indigenous material culture in rural sites in the Northern Basin of Mexico (Millhauser and Morehart 2018; Millhauser et al. 2011; Overholtzer 2012; Rodríguez-Alegría 2010, 2016; Rodríguez-Alegría and Stoner 2016; Rodríguez-Alegría et al. 2013). In both perspectives, long-term continuity of Indigenous ideas, traditions, and practices is evident, but typically it has not been questioned in terms of the effects of settlement patterns and how the consequences of earlier choices about where to settle continued to ramify into the Colonial period.

As a case in point, the Basin of Mexico data allowed Sanders and colleagues to characterize settlement patterns and demographic trends over thousands of years—up until the conquest of the Aztec empire by the Conquistadors and their Indigenous allies. They noted a population boom in the period from 1000 to 1500, and especially in the final 150 years of that period, in which population rose into the hundreds of thousands and population density increased from sixty-five to two hundred people per square kilometer (Sanders et al. 1979:217–19). They speculated that this population had reached the upper limit of the Basin's carrying capacity at the time. The human impacts of the Late Aztec would have been substantial across the Basin of Mexico in ways previously never seen before. Furthermore, as settlement expanded, new communities would have had to form in areas of increasingly marginal agricultural productivity, or areas that required considerable labor to make production—from the terraced slopes of the upper piedmont, to the *chinampas* of the freshwater lakes, to the more arid farmlands of the Northern Basin, to the shorelines of the saline lakes.

By the Late Aztec period, Sanders, Parsons, and Santley (1979:251) "estimate that virtually all the areas defined as the lower, middle, and upper piedmont of the survey area, were covered with . . . terraces." Parsons (2005, 2008) has argued that the number and density of settlements around the lakes increased because of how important lake products (fish and waterfowl, among others) were for subsistence in urban centers. Gorenflo and Garraty (2017:84) proposed that Late Aztec settlement expansion into the more arid northern Basin may have been a result of competition for space. In contrast, Williams (1989:730), drawing primarily on contact period documents, suggested that the intensification of agriculture in the marginal upper piedmont, colonized at the end of the Late Postclassic, may have been a state-sponsored effort to deal with rural overpopulation rather than, or in addition to, efforts to provide food for urban populations.

The interrelationship of pre-Conquest and post-Conquest human-environmental interactions was readily apparent to Sanders and colleagues. For example, they noted that Late Aztec terracing along the piedmont may have helped to curtail erosion caused by tree cutting at higher elevations during the Late Postclassic. Subsequently, the massive sheet erosion and sedimentation of the Early Colonial period was as much a function of the deforestation and overgrazing as it was of the degradation of the terraces following population decline (Sanders et al. 1979:409). Fournier and Otis-Charlton (2017:647) point out changes that included population decline and resettlement, soil degradation from deforestation, lakes degradation from sedimentation, and the decline of the terraces (see also Gibson 1964). Drawing on documentary evidence of land use and recalculations of population estimates, Williams (1989; see also Offner 1980) questioned the validity of Sanders, Parsons, and Santley's (1979:177) statement that, at contact, the Late Aztec population of the Basin of Mexico was able to meet its own subsistence needs. The documentary evidence she examined suggest that carrying capacity had been exceeded for poor and average families in the piedmont. The precarity of these communities prior to the Spanish Conquest may have made them even more vulnerable to the hazards of the century that followed. Given inconsistencies between the available documentary and archaeological evidence, the findings of the Basin of Mexico survey provide considerable insight of human and environmental interconnections across the period of contact.

In the sections that follow, I explain my process for organizing and working with the data from the Basin of Mexico project to show its possibilities and limits for the Colonial period. I then present analyses of the correlations among demography, chronology, and environment on the one hand, and the continuity or lack of continuity of settlements after the Conquest on the other. I work from an assumption that, at the time of the Conquest, some settlements were more vulnerable than others to the calamities that would follow, from disease to forced resettlement. I interpret evidence that a community did not persist into the post-Conquest period as indicative of that vulnerability. The long-term perspective that I apply leads me to expect that the pattern of which settlements were more vulnerable was not random, but was in some ways shaped by centuries of choices and actions about where to settle and how to use the land.

ASSEMBLING THE EVIDENCE OF LATE AZTEC SETTLEMENT HISTORIES

For the remainder of this paper, I refer to the entire set of Basin of Mexico project data as the "dataset" and the subset of data that I use for this analysis as the Late Aztec sample. I treat the term *Late Aztec* as synonymous with the Late Postclassic period (1350–1521 CE), which covers the period of political consolidation and expansion in the Basin of Mexico by the Acolhua and Tepanec polities until 1430 CE and the Triple Alliance (Aztec empire) of the Mexica, Acolhua, and Tepanec polities until 1521 CE. The terms *Late Toltec* and *Early Aztec*, used in the Basin of Mexico project, roughly correspond to the Early Postclassic (900–1100 CE) and Middle Postclassic (1100–1350 CE), but for the purposes of this paper I refer to both of these periods as *pre-Imperial* to flag settlements that were established during these periods and were likely to have persisted without interruption into the Late Postclassic. Finally, I use the term *post-Conquest* to refer to the period following the Spanish Conquest of the Aztec empire, also referred to as the *Early Colonial* period, to flag settlements for which there is documentary or material evidence for persistence through the sixteenth century.

The dataset is a combination of two Microsoft Excel spreadsheets that are archived separately. One is available through The Digital Archaeology Record (tdar .org) and the University of Michigan. It covers the Chalco, Ixtapalapa, Xochimilco, Texcoco, and Zumpango surveys run by Jeff Parsons. The other, which covers the Teotihuacan, Temascalapa, and Cuauhtitlan surveys conducted by Bill Sanders, is made available through Pennsylvania State University. Once combined, the dataset has records for 3,828 sites spanning the Early Formative to the Late Postclassic.

The Late Aztec sample consists of 1,524 sites that have evidence of Late Postclassic domestic or craft-production activities. In order to select the sites for the Late Aztec sample, I began by crosschecking the information on the 1,604 Aztec sites in the dataset against the Aztec period site descriptions in the survey reports (Blanton 1972; Evans and Sanders 2000; Gorenflo and Sanders 2007; Parsons 1971; Parsons et al. 1982, 2008; Sanders and Evans 2000; Sanders and Gorenflo 2007). Where there were discrepancies, I followed the descriptions in the reports. For example, thirty-three sites in the dataset classified as "questionable" in terms of site type had more specific information in the reports that allowed me to reclassify them as four ceremonial centers, one fortification, two villages, twenty-two hamlets, three salt stations, and one saltmaking settlement. The saltmaking settlement is a new site type that I designated based on my findings that some sites recorded in the survey as "salt stations" had substantial residential components (Millhauser 2012). I used descriptions that mentioned high frequencies of saltmaking pottery at settlements and high frequencies of domestic pottery at salt stations to reclassify eighteen hamlets, nine villages, and twenty-four salt stations as saltmaking settlements.

Once the reclassification was complete, I added and removed sites to arrive at the most representative sample for this investigation. I removed sixty-six ceremonial centers and one fortification because they lacked evidence of long-term domestic activities. I excluded twelve sites classified as Aztec that had only Early Aztec pottery. I also removed fifty-five sites documented during the general survey or only noted on maps from the Teotihuacan survey and twenty sites documented only by means of ethnohistoric sources because none of these sites have archaeological data by which I can assess earlier or later occupations. I added seventy-four sites to the Late Aztec sample based on site descriptions of Late Toltec sites in the survey reports that mentioned the presence of Late Aztec pottery, but for which no Late Aztec site number was assigned. These came from the survey reports for Chalco (27), Teotihuacan (8), Xochimilco (4), and Zumpango (35). With the sample selected, the next step was to identify which sites had pre-Imperial roots, which sites were first settled in the Late Postclassic, and which sites did and did not persist into post-Conquest times.

Evidence of Pre-Imperial Roots and Post-Conquest Continuity

Within the Late Aztec sample, 746 sites have evidence of Middle or Early Postclassic origins. I arrived at this number by drawing together complementary evidence from the dataset and survey reports. The dataset includes variables (OccEA and OccLT) that record the presence of Early Aztec or Late Toltec materials in the same location as each Late Aztec site. 542 sites with Early Aztec or Late Toltec components are identified in the dataset based on the OccEA and OccLT variables. An additional 130 Late Aztec sites in the survey reports have evidence of Late Toltec or Early Aztec components (site numbers or trace amounts of pottery). Finally, I included seventy-four Late Toltec sites in the survey reports that are associated with trace amounts of Aztec pottery and for which no contiguous Late Aztec site is identified.

For the purposes of this research, I combined Early Aztec and Late Toltec sites into a single "pre-Imperial" category. I did so despite the possibility of a significant timespan between Late Toltec and Late Aztec settlements throughout the Basin of Mexico. Parsons (2008) makes this point frequently in the site descriptions for the Zumpango survey, where many sites have Late Toltec and Late Aztec but only a handful have Late Toltec, Early Aztec, and Late Aztec components. Alternatively, the preponderance of Late Toltec (Mazapan wares), especially in the Northern Basin of Mexico survey regions (Cuauhtitlan, Temascalapa, Teotihuacan, and Zumpango), may reflect a difference in regional cultural, political, and economic networks that influenced the circulation of pottery. Brumfiel (2005:63) notes that Mazapan and Aztec I Black-on-Orange pottery rarely occur at the same sites, the former associated with the northern portion of the Basin and the latter with the southern. This pattern is evident in the survey data. Late Toltec pottery is evident at 42 percent of northern sites in the Late Aztec sample and 18 percent of southern sites, with Texcoco falling in the middle. The reverse is true of Early Aztec pottery, which is reported for 35 percent of southern sites in the Late Aztec sample and 10 percent of northern sites. I have thus opted for a more liberal interpretation of the data in the interest of maximizing coverage.

Within the Late Aztec sample, there are 418 sites with evidence of continued occupation after the conquest. I use three kinds of evidence from the survey reports to document later post-Conquest settlement continuity: colonial pottery, ethnohistoric connections, and modern communities with Nahuatl names. The dataset lacks direct references to post-Conquest settlement. Examples of colonial pottery mentioned in the reports include Aztec IV Black-on-Orange pottery, glazed pottery, or "colonial" pottery. References to ethnohistoric sources in the site descriptions demonstrate continuity into late sixteenth century. They are most common in the Teotihuacan survey volumes, which are the only volumes to include an "ethnohistoric information" subheading for site descriptions. Finally, I made the connection between modern communities with Nahuatl names and post-Conquest continuity based on my observation that communities founded in the nineteenth and twentieth centuries tend to lack Nahuatl names. I used the Teotihuacan survey as a test case for the correlation between a present-day Nahuatl name and sixteenth-century occupation. Of the forty-one sites associated with modern Nahuatl communities in the Teotihuacan survey reports, thirty-eight also included references to ethnohistoric information about a sixteenth-century settlement. On this basis, I deemed the presence of a modern community with a Nahuatl name as a valid basis for assigning post-Conquest settlement continuity to sites documented in the other survey regions. I opted to combine all three lines of evidence into a single category because each one had a degree of unevenness among the survey regions. For example, no colonial pottery is mentioned in the Cuauhtitlan report and no ethnohistoric links are made in the Temascalapa report. Among the sites with evidence of post-Conquest continuity there is, therefore, considerable variability in terms of which lines of evidence apply: pottery only (72 sites), ethnohistoric links only (39 sites), modern communities only (220 sites), pottery and ethnohistoric links (10 sites), pottery and modern communities (8 sites), ethnohistoric links and modern communities (61 sites), and all three combined (4 sites).

To test of the validity my pre-Imperial and post-Conquest classification scheme, I split the sites in the Late Aztec sample into four groups based on maximum span of time and compared them based on surface area measured in hectares. I made this comparison based on the assumption that sites occupied for longer periods of time tend to cover greater surface areas. Because site size distributions were non-normal (there were many small sites and a few enormous sites), I used medians and interquartile ranges as the basis for comparison (see table 14.1). The settlements with the shortest duration (~200 years, Late Postclassic occupation only) were the smallest (median of 0.9 hectares). Settlements of the next longest duration (~350 years, Late Postclassic through post-Conquest) had a median area of 1.8 hectares. The next group (~600 years, pre-Imperial through Late Postclassic) had a median area of 2.8 hectares. The final group (~750 years, pre-Imperial through post-Conquest) were the largest, with a median of 14.5 hectares. The trend is that sites that I believe to have been occupied for longer durations tend to be larger than those occupied for shorter durations.

To test the statistical significance of this pattern, I conducted a Kruskal-Wallis test, which is the alternative to an ANOVA when working with non-normal distributions. The Kruskal-Wallis test provided strong evidence of a difference (chi-square = 340.001, d.f. = 3, p < 0.001) between the median ranks of at least one pair of groups in terms of size. A post-hoc analysis by Dunn's pairwise tests, using sites only occupied during the Late Postclassic as a control for the three pairs of groups, provided strong evidence (p < 0.001, adjusted using Bonferroni correction) of a difference between the median areas of settlements for each time period compared to the control. Kruskal-Wallis tests on subsets of the data separated by site type yielded the same statistically significant positive correlation between presumed duration and site size for all site types, with the exception of centers (see table 14.1). On this basis, the categories of pre-Imperial and post-Conquest occupation are valid and can be used to study the effects of long-term settlement on post-Conquest vulnerability to hazards and calamities.

TABLE 14.1. Comparison of site area (hectares) by timespan and site type

	Late Postclassic ~200 years (603 sites)		Late Postclassic to Post-Conquest ~350 years (180 sites)	
	Median	IQR	Median	IQR
Center	103.0	n/a – n/a	80.0	13.8 – 125.7
Village	11.3	6.7 – 21.0	10.0	7.0 – 29.0
Hamlet	0.8	0.3 – 1.8	1.0	0.7 – 2.5
Saltmaking settlement	0.6	0.4 – 4.0	1.7	0.8 – 4.8
All sites	0.9	0.2 – 2.3	1.8	0.8 – 5.2

	Pre-Imperial to Late Postclassic ~600 years (502 sites)		Pre-Imperial to Post-Conquest ~750 years (239 sites)	
	Median	IQR	Median	IQR
Center	115.3	n/a – n/a	119.3	86.3 – 239.6
Village	18.0	10.0 – 35.0	24.0	13.5 – 50.0
Hamlet	1.6	0.7 – 3.9	2.0	0.9 – 5.0
Saltmaking settlement	4.3	1.1 – 9.5	10.6	1.7 – 27.0
All sites	2.8	0.9 – 7.8	14.5	3.1 – 39.8

WHAT EFFECTS DID SETTLEMENT HISTORY HAVE ON POST-CONQUEST VULNERABILITY?

The results support the idea that the earlier a settlement was established, the more likely it was to persist into the post-Conquest period (see table 14.2). Of the 746 sites with pre-Imperial roots, 32 percent have evidence of post-Conquest continuity. In contrast, of the 778 sites established during the Late Postclassic, only 23 percent exhibit evidence of post-Conquest continuity. A Pearson Chi Square test (chi-square = 16.198, d.f. = 1, p < 0.0001) leads me to reject the null hypothesis that the probability of a site having evidence of post-Conquest occupation was independent of duration of settlement prior to the Conquest. In other words, the settlements with the deepest roots were the most capable of weathering the hazards of the post-Conquest period and the settlements that were established last were the most vulnerable.

This pattern of change leads me to two related explanations for why the settlements founded during the population boom of the Late Postclassic may have among the most precarious in the tumultuous century after the Conquest. First, older settlements may have been less vulnerable because they were built on lands more favorable to agriculture. If early settlers selected the best land for agriculture, then later settlers may have been forced into areas of marginal agricultural productivity (saline lakeshores, steep piedmont slopes, etc.). Second, older settlements may have been less vulnerable because they had more time to establish themselves and build resilient social networks. Furthermore, the challenges of the sixteenth century, such as decimating plagues and forced resettlement, would have had a more profound effect on small communities than on larger communities. In both scenarios, I would expect a strong correlation between settlement duration and vulnerability, but I would only expect a correlation with ecological factors if only the first scenario was at play.

As noted above, there is good reason to suspect a positive correlation between settlement size and duration of occupation. Based on the categorical variable of settlement type, there is evidence of post-Conquest continuity for 93 percent of centers, 50 percent of villages, and 19 percent of hamlets (see table 14.3). This trend is consistent regardless of whether settlements had evidence of pre-Imperial settlement or not (see table 14.2), and it is consistent regardless of ecological zone. While this disparity is not surprising, given what we know about the period from historical sources (and by no means would I suggest that life in the cities was easy), it is a relief to find that the archaeological evidence collected during the surveys conforms to these expectations.

To assess the relationship between vulnerability and the ecology of the Basin of Mexico, I draw on several lines of evidence recorded in the dataset that reflect climate, hydrology, soil depth, and slope. The most promising is the variable of ecological zone, which combines terrain, elevation, and rainfall as well as

TABLE 14.2. Effects of pre-Imperial roots on post-Conquest continuity

	Sites in the Late Aztec Sample (LAS)	Pre-Imperial evidence			No pre-Imperial evidence		
		Count	% without post-Conquest evidence	% with post-Conquest evidence	Count	% without post-Conquest evidence	% with post-Conquest evidence
Survey region							
Teotihuacan	163	133	38%	62%	30	57%	43%
Zumpango	331	152	76%	24%	179	84%	16%
Temascalapa	162	56	70%	30%	106	78%	22%
Cuautitlan	320	121	56%	44%	199	62%	38%
Texcoco	99	73	71%	29%	26	92%	8%
Ixtapalapa	66	35	74%	26%	31	87%	13%
Xochimilco	87	28	75%	25%	59	75%	25%
Chalco	296	148	89%	11%	148	91%	9%
Ecological zone							
Alluvium	164	74	50%	50%	90	62%	38%
Lakebed	178	47	79%	21%	131	84%	16%
Lakeshore plain	148	84	58%	42%	64	28%	9%
Piedmont—lower	898	467	70%	30%	431	78%	22%
Piedmont—upper	109	62	66%	34%	47	89%	11%
Site type							
Center	30	26	4%	96%	4	25%	75%
Village	321	244	48%	52%	77	53%	47%
Hamlet	1,094	453	82%	18%	641	81%	19%
Saltmaking settlement	49	21	57%	43%	28	75%	25%
Salt station	30	2	50%	50%	28	71%	29%
All sites in survey	1,524	746	68%	32%	778	77%	23%

plant communities and hydrology into a single category. To simply this analysis, I excluded twenty-seven sites classified as "Amecameca sub-basin" and reduced the remaining values to five: Island/Lakebed, Lakeshore plain, Alluvium, Lower Piedmont, and Upper Piedmont. The pattern of pre-Imperial settlements with respect to these zones suggests that early settlers avoided the lakebeds (see table 14.3). A Pearson Chi Square test (chi-square = 46.867, d.f. = 4, $p < 0.001$) leads

TABLE 14.3. Evidence of earlier and later settlement at Late Aztec habitation sites

	Sites in the Late Aztec Sample (LAS)	Sites with pre-Imperial evidence		Sites with post-Conquest evidence	
		Count	% of LAS	Count	% of LAS
Survey region					
Teotihuacan	163	133	82%	96	59%
Zumpango	331	152	46%	65	20%
Temascalapa	162	56	35%	40	25%
Cuautitlan	320	121	38%	129	40%
Texcoco	99	73	74%	23	23%
Ixtapalapa	66	35	53%	13	20%
Xochimilco	87	28	32%	22	25%
Chalco	296	148	50%	30	10%
Ecological zone					
Alluvium	164	74	45%	71	43%
Lakebed	178	47	26%	31	17%
Lakeshore plain	148	84	57%	53	36%
Piedmont—lower	898	467	52%	233	26%
Piedmont—upper	109	62	57%	26	24%
Amecameca sub-basin	27	12	44%	4	15%
Site type					
Center	30	26	87%	28	93%
Village	321	244	76%	162	50%
Hamlet	1,094	453	41%	203	19%
Saltmaking settlement	49	21	43%	16	33%
Salt station	30	2	7%	9	30%
All sites in survey	1,524	746	49%	418	27%

me to reject the null hypothesis that the probability of a site having evidence of pre-Imperial settlement was independent of ecological zone. Lakebed settlements are the driver of this pattern—only 26 percent had pre-Imperial roots as compared to 44 percent to 55 percent of sites in the other ecological zones. When lakebed settlements are removed, the null hypothesis holds (chi = 5.487, d.f. = 3, p > 0.10). Among the lakebed sites that were first settled in the Late

Postclassic, the majority were identified in the Cuautitlan (19%), Chalco (31%), and Xochimilco (44%) survey regions and reflect the expansion and intensification of saltmaking (Cuauhtitlan) and *chinampa* farming (Chalco and Xochimilco) during this period. If Mexico city had not covered the southwestern portion of Lake Texcoco at the time of the surveys, I expect a similar pattern would be evident there, too.

Ecological zone also appears to have been a factor in the vulnerability of settlements to the dangers of the post-Conquest period. In terms of overall patterns of post-Conquest continuity without reference to pre-Imperial roots, a Pearson Chi Square test (chi-square = 36.391, d.f. = 4, $p < 0.001$) leads me to reject the null hypothesis that the probability of a site continuing into the post-Conquest period was independent of ecological zone. Although lakebed sites were also the most likely to have ended without evidence of post-Conquest occupation (only 17% continued), in this case, removing them from the analysis does not change the conclusion. In fact, no single ecological zone is the driver of post-Conquest continuity—the picture is more complicated. For example, in all ecological zones, sites with pre-Imperial roots were more likely to persist after the conquest than those founded in the Late Postclassic (see table 14.2). However, for sites with pre-Imperial components, lakebed sites were the most vulnerable, whereas for sites without pre-Imperial components, sites on the lakeshore plain and in the upper piedmont were the most vulnerable. These patterns suggest that settlements in and around the lakes and in the upper piedmont were the most vulnerable to post-Conquest disruptions. This vulnerability may have been the result of pre-Conquest precarity, especially in the Upper Piedmont, if farmers were pushing the limits of the productive capacity of their land (Williams 1989). Alternatively, sites in these ecological zones may have been the most vulnerable to ecological disruptions such as the erosion of soils in the upper piedmont, and sedimentation and flooding in the lakebed and lakeshore plain, which became prevalent in the aftermath of the conquest.

It is worth noting that other ecological factors do not present simple relationships with the vulnerability of settlements. Annual amounts of rainfall do not demonstrate a consistent pattern in terms of vulnerability. Sites that that lacked post-Conquest continuity averaged 686 ± 118.3 mm of rainfall as compared to sites that continued, which averaged 645 ± 83.5 mm. Similarly, sites with pre-Imperial roots averaged 671 ± 110.4 mm as compared to sites established in the Late Postclassic, which averaged 669 ± 111.7 mm. I suspect that the lack of correspondence in terms of rainfall reflects micro-regional adaptations that made agricultural viable in the wetter southern Basin and the drier northern Basin. The same lack of correlation is evident for elevation. I do note that sites in the upper piedmont with pre-Imperial roots tend to be lower in elevation (average of 2555 meters above sea level) as compared to those founded during the Late

Postclassic (average of 2590 meters above sea level), which conforms to the pattern of expansion in the upper piedmont that Williams (1989) observed.

As a final observation that patterns identified at a large scale are still subject to variation under local conditions, I turn to the case of saltmaking settlements. Given that saltmaking expanded considerably as a livelihood and reason for settlement around the saline lakes in the Late Postclassic (Millhauser 2012; Parsons 2001), it is reasonable to ask whether these settlements were disproportionately vulnerable to the post-Conquest adversity. Saltmaking settlements were unlikely to have pre-Imperial roots; they were located in areas of marginal agricultural productivity in the lakebed and along the lakeshores of the saline lakes; they were at risk of flooding; and they were among the many communities devastated by the hydrological projects of the early Colonial government (Candiani 2014; Millhauser and Morehart 2018). And yet, among sites in the lakebed and lakeshore plains, 33 percent of saltmaking settlements persisted after the Conquest as compared to 19 percent of hamlets (chi square = 4.209, d.f. = 1, p = 0.040), a pattern that holds regardless of whether or not the sites had pre-Imperial roots. Even if the lands that saltmakers occupied were challenging to survive on from an agricultural perspective, they seem to have provided some benefit that allowed for greater flexibility or resilience than expected, compared to other settlements in the survey.

CONCLUSIONS

I began by testing the hypothesis that communities that were settled earlier in the Postclassic enjoyed an advantage relative to those that were settled later when they experienced the hardships of the sixteenth-century Spanish Colonial regime. My premise was that later settlers would have had to occupy increasingly marginal lands—marginal in terms of the productivity of the soil, access to water or other resources, or exposure to risks, such as flooding, erosion, frosts, drought, and the like. Using the entire set of survey data, evidence of early occupation was positively correlated with evidence of post-Conquest continuity. In other words, it seems likely that many of the people who settled previously unoccupied or sparsely populated regions of the Basin in the Late Aztec period (upper piedmont, saline lakeshores, etc.) may have been doubly marginalized in the post-Conquest era. Smaller communities were more likely to have been settled on marginal land and more vulnerable to the many challenges of the sixteenth century. Seen from a long-term perspective, the data support both of my initial goals in attempting this project. First, they support the notion that survey data can be used to look beyond the Conquest to begin to understand what happened across the Basin of Mexico in the sixteenth century and beyond. Second, in expanding the frame of analysis, they make it possible to ask how choices and habits made in the Early and Middle Postclassic influenced the outcomes of the post-Conquest period.

Drawing together ideas of structural violence, slow violence, and the political ecology of disasters, I have attempted to consider the social, natural, and political factors that shaped the environment and settlement patterns of the Basin of Mexico into what they were at the time of the Conquest, and which shaped outcomes in the centuries that followed. The results of this study demonstrate that there is still more to learn from the Basin of Mexico survey data. I have drawn out information on earlier and later settlements that has only become available with the publication of full survey reports to test hypotheses about how what happened before the Conquest affected what happened after. Without a doubt, the Conquest was a calamitous event for people living across the Basin of Mexico. As with other disasters, my findings are consistent with similar long-term studies that draw together archaeological and historical evidence in a political ecology framework to "highlight the truly long temporal framework within which disasters emerge and people respond" (Taylor 2015:305). Based on ideas from political ecology, and especially notions of environmental inequality and "slow violence," I have been able to consider how the aftermath of the conquest unfolded in a world shaped by the choices and actions of people who had populated the regions for thousands of years.

REFERENCES

Bentley, R. Alexander. 2003. "Scale-Free Network Growth and Social Inequality." In *Complex Systems and Archaeology*, edited by R. A. Bentley and H. D. G. Maschner, 27–45. University of Utah Press, Salt Lake City.

Blaikie, Piers M., and H. C. Brookfield. 1987. *Land Degradation and Society*. Methuen, London.

Blanton, Richard E. 1972. *Prehispanic Settlement Patterns of the Ixtapalapa Peninsula Region, Mexico*. Vol. 6. The Pennsylvania State University Department of Anthropology, University Park.

Bodley, John H. 1999. "Socioeconomic Growth, Culture Scale, and Household Well-Being: A Test of the Power-Elite Hypothesis." *Current Anthropology* 40(5):595–620.

Brumfiel, Elizabeth M. 1980. "Specialization, Market Exchange, and the Aztec State: A View from Huexotla." *Current Anthropology* 21:459–78.

Brumfiel, Elizabeth M. 2005. "Ceramic Chronology at Xaltocan." In *Production and Power at Postclassic Xaltocan*, edited by E. M. Brumfiel, 117–52. University of Pittsburgh and Instituto Nacional de Antropología e Historia, Pittsburgh, PA and Mexico City.

Butler, Judith. 2004. *Precarious Life: The Powers of Mourning and Violence*. Verso, London.

Candiani, Vera S. 2014. *Dreaming of Dry Land: Environmental Transformation in Colonial Mexico City*. Stanford University Press, Redwood City, CA.

Charlton, Thomas H. 1972. *Post-Conquest Developments in the Teotihuacán Valley, Mexico*: Part 1, *Excavations*. Office of the State Archaeologist of Iowa, Iowa City.

Charlton, Thomas H., and Patricia Fournier-García. 2011. "Pots and Plots: The Multiple Roles of Early Colonial Red Wares in the Basin of Mexico (Identity, Resistance, Negotiation, Accommodation, Aesthetic Creativity, or Just Plain Economics?)." In *Enduring Conquests: Rethinking the Archaeology of Resistance to Spanish Colonialism in the Americas*, edited by M. Liebmann and M. S. Murphy, 127–48. School for Advanced Research Press, Santa Fe, NM.

Charlton, Thomas H., Cynthia L. Otis Charlton, and Patricia Fournier-García. 2005. "The Basin of Mexico A.D. 1450–1620: Archaeological Dimensions." In *The Postclassic to Spanish-era Transition in Mesoamerica: Archaeological Perspectives*, edited by S. Kepecs and R. T. Alexander, 49–64. University of New Mexico Press, Albuquerque.

Evans, Susan T., and William T. Sanders, eds. 2000. *The Teotihuacan Valley Project Final Report*, vol. 5: *The Aztec Period Occupation of the Valley*, pt. 1: *Natural Environment, Twentieth-Century Occupation, Survey Methodology, and Site Descriptions*. The Pennsylvania State University, University Park.

Farmer, Paul. 2004. "An Anthropology of Structural Violence." *Current Anthropology* 45(3):305–25.

Fournier G., Patricia, and Cynthia L. Otis Charlton. 2017. "Post-Conquest Rural Aztec Archaeology." In *The Oxford Handbook of the Aztecs*, edited by D. L. Nichols and E. Rodríguez Alegría, 643–60. Oxford University Press, Oxford.

Galtung, Johan. 1969. "Violence, Peace, and Peace Research." *Journal of Peace Research* 6(3):167–91.

Gibson, Charles. 1964. *The Aztecs under Spanish Rule: A History of the Indians of the Valley of Mexico, 1519–1810*. Stanford University Press, Redwood City, CA.

Gorenflo, L. J. 2006. "The Evolution of Regional Demography and Settlement in the Prehispanic Basin of Mexico." In *Urbanism in the Preindustrial World: Cross-Cultural Approaches*, edited by G. R. Storey, 295–316. University of Alabama Press, Tuscaloosa.

Gorenflo, L. J., and Christopher P. Garraty. 2017. "Aztec Settlement History." In *The Oxford Handbook of the Aztecs*, edited by D. L. Nichols and E. Rodríguez Alegría, 73–92. Oxford University Press, Oxford.

Gorenflo, L. J., and William T. Sanders. 2007. *Archaeological Settlement Pattern Data from the Cuautitlan, Temascalapa, and Teotihuacan Regions, Mexico*. Vol. 30. Department of Anthropology Pennsylvania State University, University Park.

Harvey, David. 2000. *Spaces of Hope*. University of California Press, Berkeley.

Hassig, Ross. 1985. *Trade, Tribute, and Transportation: The Sixteenth-Century Political Economy of the Valley of Mexico*. University of Oklahoma Press, Norman.

Hodge, Mary G., and Leah D. Minc. 1990. "The Spatial Patterning of Aztec Ceramics: Implications for Prehispanic Exchange Systems in the Valley of Mexico." *Journal of Field Archaeology* 17(4):415–37.

Kasmir, Sharryn. 2018. "Precarity." In *The Cambridge Encyclopedia of Anthropology*, edited by F. Stein, S. Lazar, M. Candea, H. Diemberger, J. Robbins, A. Sanchez, and R. Stasch. Cambridge University Press, Cambridge.

Lockhart, James. 1992. *The Nahuas after the Conquest: A Social and Cultural History of the Indians of Central Mexico, Sixteenth through Eighteenth Centuries*. Stanford University Press, Redwood City, CA.

Melville, Elinor G. K. 1994. *A Plague of Sheep: Environmental Consequences of the Conquest of Mexico*. Cambridge University Press, Cambridge.

Millhauser, John K. 2012. "Saltmaking, Craft, and Community at Late Postclassic and Early Colonial San Bartolome Salinas, Mexico." PhD dissertation, Northwestern University, Evanston, IL.

Millhauser, John K., and Christopher T. Morehart. 2018. "Sustainability as a Relative Process: A Long-Term Perspective on Sustainability in the Northern Basin of Mexico." *Archaeological Papers of the American Anthropological Association* 29(1):134–56.

Millhauser, John K., Enrique Rodríguez-Alegría, and Michael D. Glascock. 2011. "Testing the Accuracy of Portable X-Ray Fluorescence to Study Aztec and Colonial Obsidian Supply at Xaltocan, Mexico." *Journal of Archaeological Science* 38:3141–52.

Minc, Leah D., Mary G. Hodge, and M. James Blackman. 1994. "Stylistic and Spatial Variability in Early Aztec Ceramics: Insights into Pre-Imperials Exchange Systems." In *Economies and Polities in the Aztec Realm*, edited by M. G. Hodge and M. E. Smith, 133–74. Institute for Mesoamerican Studies, Albany, NY.

Morehart, Christopher T., John K. Millhauser, and Santiago Juarez. 2018. "Archaeologies of Political Ecology—Genealogies, Problems, and Orientations." *Archeological Papers of the American Anthropological Association* 29(1):5–29.

Nixon, Rob. 2011. *Slow Violence and the Environmentalism of the Poor*. Harvard University Press, Cambridge, MA.

Offner, Jerome. 1980. "Archival Reports of Poor Crop Yields in the Early Postconquest Texcocan Heartland and Their Implications for Studies of Aztec Period Population." *American Antiquity* 45(4):848–56.

Oliver-Smith, Anthony, and Susannah M. Hoffman. 1999. *The Angry Earth: Disaster in Anthropological Perspective*. Routledge, New York.

Overholtzer, Lisa. 2012. "Empires and Everyday Material Practices: A Household Archaeology of Aztec and Spanish Imperialism at Xaltocan, Mexico." PhD dissertation, Northwestern University, Evanston, IL.

Parsons, Jeffrey R. 1971. *Prehistoric Settlement Patterns in the Texcoco Region, Mexico*. Memoirs of the Museum of Anthropology, no. 3. University of Michigan, Ann Arbor.

Parsons, Jeffrey R. 2001. *The Last Saltmakers of Nexquipayac, Mexico: An Archaeological Ethnography*. Anthropological Papers, no. 92. Museum of Anthropology, University of Michigan, Ann Arbor.

Parsons, Jeffrey R. 2005. "The Aquatic Component of Aztec Subsistence: Hunters, Fishers, and Collectors in an Urbanized Society." *Michigan Discussions in Anthropology* 15:49–89.

Parsons, Jeffrey R. 2008. "Beyond Santley and Rose (1979): The Role of Aquatic Resources in the Prehispanic Economy of the Basin of Mexico." *Journal of Archaeological Research* 64(3):351–66.

Parsons, Jeffrey R., Elizabeth Brumfiel, Mary H. Parsons, and David J. Wilson. 1982. *Prehispanic Settlement Patterns in the Southern Valley of Mexico: The Chalco-Xochimilco Region.* Memoirs of the Museum of Anthropology, no. 14. University of Michigan, Ann Arbor.

Parsons, Jeffrey R., L. J. Gorenflo, Mary H. Parsons, and David J. Wilson. 2008. *Prehispanic Settlement Patterns in the Northwestern Valley of Mexico: The Zumpango Region.* Memoirs of the Museum of Anthropology, no. 45. University of Michigan, Ann Arbor.

Redman, Charles L. 1999. *Human Impact on Ancient Environments.* University of Arizona Press, Tucson.

Rodríguez-Alegría, Enrique. 2010. "Incumbents and Challengers: Indigenous Politics and the Adoption of Spanish Material Culture in Colonial Xaltocan, Mexico." *Historical Archaeology* 44(2):51–71.

Rodríguez-Alegría, Enrique. 2016. *The Archaeology and History of Colonial Mexico: Mixing Epistemologies.* Cambridge University Press, New York.

Rodríguez-Alegría, Enrique, and Wesley D. Stoner. 2016. "The Trade in Cooking Pots under the Aztec and Spanish Empires." *Ancient Mesoamerica* 27(1):197–207.

Rodríguez-Alegría, Enrique, John K. Millhauser, and Wesley D. Stoner. 2013. "Trade, Tribute, and Neutron Activation: The Colonial Political Economy of Xaltocan, Mexico." *Journal of Anthropological Archaeology* 32(4):397–414.

Sanders, William T., and Susan T. Evans, eds. 2000. *The Teotihuacan Valley Project Final Report* Volume 5: *The Aztec Period Occupation of the Valley,* Part 2, *Excavations at T.A. 40 and Related Projects.* Pennsylvania State University, University Park.

Sanders, William T., and Lawrence Gorenflo. 2007. *Prehispanic Settlement Patterns in the Cuautitlan Region, Mexico.* Occasional Papers in Anthropology, no. 29. Department of Anthropology, Pennsylvania State University, University Park.

Sanders, William T., and Barbara J. Price. 1968. *Mesoamerica: The Evolution of a Civilization.* Random House, New York.

Sanders, William T., Jeffrey R. Parsons, and Robert S. Santley. 1979. *The Basin of Mexico: Ecological Processes in the Evolution of a Civilization.* Academic Press, New York.

Service, Elman R. 1975. *Origins of the State and Civilization: The Process of Cultural Evolution.* Norton, New York.

Sluyter, Andrew. 2002. *Colonialism and Landscape: Postcolonial Theory and Applications.* Rowman & Littlefield, Lanham, MD.

Sluyter, Andrew. 2003. "Material-Conceptual Landscape Transformation and the Emergence of the Pristine Myth in Early Colonial Mexico." In *Political Ecology: An*

Integrative Approach to Geography and Environment-Development Studies, edited by K. S. Zimmerer and T. J. Bassett, 221–39. Guildford Press, New York.

Taylor, Sarah. 2015. "The Construction of Vulnerability along the Zarumilla River Valley in Prehistory." *Human Organization* 74(4):296–307.

Williams, Barbara J. 1989. "Contact Period Rural Overpopulation in the Basin of Mexico: Carrying-Capacity Models Tested with Documentary Data." *American Antiquity* 54(4):715–32.

Wisner, Ben, Piers Blaikie, Terry Cannon, and Ian Davis. 2004. *At Risk: Natural Hazards, Peoples' Vulnerability, and Disasters*. Routledge, New York.

Zimmerer, Karl S., and Thomas J. Bassett, eds. 2003. *Political Ecology: An Integrative Approach to Geography and Environment-Development Studies*. Guildford Press, New York.

Index

finger bones, in Epiclassic sacrificial burials, 324
flooding, in wetland agriculture, 200–201
flotation samples, from El Japón, 272
Fluvisols, 176, 78
Formative Period, 35, 219, 237; agricultural terraces, 223–24, 225–26; Ch-MF-5, 139–40; irrigation systems, 230–31; paleosol cover, 177, 178
Frente 3 (Teotihuacan), 120
fresh water, controlling, 206

Gamio, Manuel, 3, 29; *La población prehispánica*, 75
Gándara, Manuel, 37
gap areas, 134; artifact scatters and, 136–37; buried sites, 146–47
geoarchaeology, 15, 16, 262, 263; of *chinampas*, 266–70; lacustrine sites, 200–202, 202f; swidden agriculture and, 219–21
geochemistry, Black San Pablo Paleosol, 182
Geographic Information Systems (GIS), 145
geomorphology, 135, 136, 203, 291
geophysics, 43
geopolitics: competitive, 320–21; decentralization, 317–18
GI Bill of Rights, 31
GIS database, 38
Glaeser, Edward, 28
Golya, Luna, 37
GPS technology, 37
Gran Tunal, 238
Granular ware, 68
Great Compound (Teotihuacan), 73
Griffin, James, 34
Guadalupe, Sierra de, 35, 204
Guanajuato, Bajío, 201
Guerrero, 238
Guzmán, Eulalia, 3

Handbook of South American Indians, 63
Heyden, Doris, 3
Hidalgo, Central Mexican Symbiotic Region, 31
hilltop sites/centers, 223, 306, 324; Epiclassic, 299, 322, 325, 329–30, 337; and Tula, 333–34; viewsheds/intervisibility, 330–33
Historia Antigua de México (Clavijero), 197
Hodge, Mary, 38
house mounds, 1960s, 156
Huatepec Hill, 199, 201, 202f, 203, 204
human-environment relations, 42, 177, 349
hydraulic technology, 276
hydraulic theory, 37

iconography: Early Postclassic Tula, 334, 335; warfare, 323–24
illuvial processes, 182
INAH. *See* Instituto Nacional de Antropología e Historia
Incised and Punctate ceramics, 298
inequality: protracted, 349–50
Institute of Andean Research, 63
Instituto de Investigaciones Antropológicas, 262
Instituto Nacional de Antropología e Historia (INAH), 12, 30, 63
Instituto Nacional de Estadística y Geografía, 330
instrumental neutron activation analysis (INAA), ceramic compositional analyses, 291, 298
Ira Stamped, 304
irrigation systems, 11, 12, 37, 38, 217, 218, 236, 238, 239, 259, 260, 262; canals, 227–31; and soil characteristics, 184, 185
Ixtapalapa. *See* Iztapalapa
Iztapalapa, 207, 234t; *chinampas*, 263, 271
Iztapalapa Peninsula, 204
Iztapalapa (Ixtapalapa) region, 34, 98, 152, 194; ceramics, 100, 106, 288t

Jara Cream Slip, 303, 304
Jara Pulio Cream Slip, 302f
Joroba Cream slip ware, 301, 302f, 303

King, Jaime Litvak, 200
kitchen gardens, terracing and, 223
Kolb, Charles, 34, 71, 79
Kroeber, Alfred, 63

labor, agricultural, 217
La Concepción, swidden agriculture, 221t
lacustrine environments, 8, 37, 196, 200, 275; and settlements, 202–3; Texcoco region, 198–99, 203–6; Xochimilco, 142–43
laguna, vs. lago, 197
lakebeds, 135; survey of, 16, 194; *tlateles* on, 195–96; Xochimilco, 142–45
lakes, 204; Conquest/Colonial period, 196–98
lakescapes, *chinampas* in, 263–65
lake shores: Lake Texcoco, 194, 195; uses of, 203–4
Lake Texcoco Ecological Park, 206
La Ladera, swidden agriculture, 221t
La Laguna, agriculture, 220t, 225t, 225–26
La Mesa (Hidalgo), 299, 328, 330, 331
landscape archaeology, 31, 37

Contributors

GUILLERMO ACOSTA OCHOA: Instituto de Investigaciones Antropológicas, Universidad Nacional Autónoma de México, Mexico City, Mexico

ALEKSANDER BOREJSZA: Independent archaeologist based in Mexico

CARLOS E. CORDOVA (editor): Department of Geography, Oklahoma State University, USA

DESTINY L. CRIDER: Luther College, USA

SUSAN T. EVANS (author of book's dedication): Department of Anthropology, The Pennsylvania State University, USA

CHARLES FREDERICK: Research fellow, Department of Geography, University of Texas at Austin and consulting geoarchaeologist, Dublin, Texas, USA

RAÚL GARCÍA CHÁVEZ: Centro INAH Estado de México, Instituto Nacional de Antropología e Historia, Mexico City, Mexico

L. J. GORENFLO: Department of Landscape Architecture, The Pennsylvania State University, USA

ANGELA HUSTER: School of Human Evolution and Social Change, Arizona State University, USA

GEORGINA IBARRA-ARZAVE: Instituto de investigaciones en Ecosistemas y Sustentabilidad, Universidad Nacional Autónoma de Mexico, Morelia, Mexico

CHARLES C. KOLB: National Endowment for the Humanities (retired), USA

FRANK LEHMKUHL: Department of Geography, Rheinisch-Westfälische Technische Hochschule, Aachen University, Germany

EMILY MCCLUNG DE TAPIA: Instituto de Investigaciones Antropológicas, Universidad Nacional Autónoma de México, Mexico City, Mexico

ABIGAIL MEZA-PEÑALOZA: Instituto de Investigaciones Antropológicas, Universidad Nacional Autónoma de México, Mexico City, Mexico

JOHN K. MILLHAUSER: Department of Sociology and Anthropology, North Carolina State University, USA

CHRISTOPHER T. MOREHART (editor): School of Human Evolution and Social Change, Arizona State University, USA

DEBORAH L. NICHOLS: Department of Anthropology, Dartmouth College, USA

SOFÍA PACHECO-FORÉS: Department of Anthropology, Hamline University, USA

JEFFREY R. PARSONS: Museum of Anthropology, University of Michigan, USA (deceased)

SERAFÍN SÁNCHEZ-PÉREZ: Escuela Nacional de Antropología e Historia, Mexico City

PHILIPP SCHULTE: Department of Geography, Rheinisch-Westfälische Technische Hochschule, Aachen University, Germany

SERGEY SEDOV: Instituto de Geología, Universidad Nacional Autónoma de México, Mexico City, Mexico

ELIZABETH SOLLEIRO-REBOLLEDO: Instituto de Geología, Universidad Nacional Autónoma de México, Mexico City, Mexico

DAISY VALERA-FERNANDEZ: Instituto de Geofísica, Universidad Nacional Autónoma de México, Mexico City, Mexico

FEDERICO ZERTUCHE: Instituto de Matemáticas, Universidad Nacional Autónoma de México, Cuernavaca, Mexico